Slavery, Freedom and Gender

The Dynamics of Caribbean Society

Edited by

Brian L. Moore

B.W. Higman

Carl Campbell *and*

Patrick Bryan

UNIVERSITY OF THE WEST INDIES PRESS

Barbados • Jamaica • Trinidad and Tobago

University of the West Indies Press
1A Aqueduct Flats   Mona
Kingston 7   Jamaica

© 2001, 2003 by the Department of History,
University of the West Indies
All rights reserved. Published 2001
Paperback edition 2003

07 06 05 04 03   5 4 3 2 1

CATALOGUING IN PUBLICATION DATA

Slavery, freedom and gender: the dynamics of Caribbean society /
edited by Brian L. Moore . . . [et al.]

p. cm.

Elsa Goveia Memorial Lectures delivered between 1987 and 1998.
Individual lectures previously published: Kingston:
University of the West Indies, Department of History.

Includes bibliographical references.

ISBN: 976-640-111-X (casebound)
ISBN: 976-640-137-3 (paperback)

1. Slavery – West Indies – History. 2. Slaves – Emancipation –
West Indies. 3. Freedmen – West Indies. 4. Women slaves –
West Indies – History. 5. Women – West Indies – History.
6. Goveia, Elsa. I. Moore, Brian L. II. Goveia, Elsa.
III. Elsa Goveia Memorial Lectures.

HT1071.S543 2003   309.1'729

Set in Plantin Light 10/14 x 24

Book and cover design by Robert Harris
roberth@cwjamaica.com

Cover illustration: Gloria Escoffery, *Women at Wharf* (1965).
Collection of the University of the West Indies.

Printed in the United States of America

To the memory of

Elsa Vesta Goveia

Historian and scholar par excellence,
who for thirty years, 1950–1980,
gave outstanding and selfless service
to the University of the West Indies
and the Caribbean region

Contents

Introduction

BRIAN L. MOORE

My first acquaintance with the name Elsa Goveia was second hand, through the vision and words of my high school history teacher who had graduated from the University of the West Indies at Mona where he had studied under her. As we prepared for the Ordinary Level examination in West Indian history, he made constant reference to her brilliant lectures. One immediately sensed that this was an extraordinary person whom he regarded almost with reverence and awe. It was another three years before I met the great lady in person and sat in the very classes that he had been privileged to take. It was then that I fully understood and shared his admiration. As I listened to her lectures, history took on new meaning. It was not just the study of long past events (and dates), no longer an esoteric exercise. This was *our* history, *our* past – a past that we were not simply spectators to but the principal participants in, a past that our ancestors actively shaped. *We* were at the centre of our own history. In the 1960s this was an entirely new view of West Indian history. No wonder her lectures were overcrowded. To get a seat in the lecture room one had to turn up at least fifteen minutes early. Without disrespect to the other lecturers, hers were by far the best received of any I attended during my undergraduate years.

I was further privileged when she was selected to be one of my postgraduate research supervisors. Then I saw her at work close up. She was very demanding of high standards of performance, yet kind and encouraging. In our one-on-one sessions, she was always probing and urging me to greater effort, to extract the utmost from the sources and data, and to challenge other interpretations. Her critiques of the draft chapters of my thesis were incisive and candid, yet not harsh or cutting. And above all, she was patient and very thorough. On completion I was confident that the work could withstand any criticism or examination.

This collection is a tribute to a remarkable individual and an outstanding scholar. The essays reflect the two principal aspects of the persona and life of Elsa Goveia – as a woman overcoming the inherent social obstacles against her gender, and as a scholar of West Indian society during and after slavery. As a "coloured" woman (part black, part Portuguese), she embodied in her person the creole fusion of different ethnicities and cultures that make up the Caribbean. Born in Guyana (then British Guiana) in 1925, she grew up and was educated there up to the secondary level and won the prestigious Guiana Scholarship. This was no mean distinction, for there were only two available for the whole country. Elsa was one of the first women to win one of these scholarships.

She read history at the University of London, winning the Pollard Prize along the way to her BA honours degree in 1948, and then began her doctoral research. In 1950 while still a PhD candidate, she was appointed a lecturer at the University College of the West Indies, and two years later completed her doctoral thesis. In 1958 she was promoted to senior lecturer and three years later she became the first female professor at the University of the West Indies with a personal chair in West Indian History.

Elsa Goveia was one of the pioneers of the study of Caribbean history not only in the university but also in the high schools throughout the region. Along with colleagues such as Douglas Hall, Sir Roy Augier and that generation of West Indian historians, she put Caribbean history squarely at the centre of the academic curriculum. They set out to rewrite that history, bringing to it a new vision and perspective from the inside. This represented a major break from the past, because in so far as the history of the region was taken seriously, it was treated as a mere appendage of European imperial history.

Elsa Vesta Goveia still remains an icon among historians of slavery world-wide and among scholars of Caribbean history. She was considered the premier social historian of the Caribbean and she contributed to the vigorous debates that raged during the 1960s over the nature and form of West Indian societies, whether integrated/unified or plural. Her seminal work entitled *Slave Society in the British Leeward Islands at the End of the Eighteenth Century*[1] remains a masterpiece of historical scholarship on slavery. The hallmark of her thesis in that work was to demonstrate that there was an inherent unity underlying the seemingly antagonistic segments or sections of West Indian slave society, a unity that was in part maintained by force and legislation and was in part consensual.

Elsa Goveia also made an outstanding contribution to the intellectual history of the Caribbean through her remarkable book *A Study on the Historiography of the British West Indies.*[2] Although confined to published works on the British West Indies, its scope was extensive, covering the seventeenth through the nineteenth centuries; she clearly demonstrated how the state of society, whether slave or free, influenced the ideas and views of the writers of history during that time frame. In addition she wrote several shorter essays which were no less outstanding for their insight and analytical perception. The best known of these was "The West Indian Slave Laws of the Eighteenth Century", in the Chapters in West Indian History series published by the University of the West Indies Departments of History.[3] This extended the scope of her scholarship to encompass the non-anglophone Caribbean, and there remains no better example of comparative history than this. Elsa Goveia's scholarship was both rigorous in its methodology and documentation, and brilliant in its analysis and vision. She always stressed the importance of sound empirical data as the foundation of good historical research.

Her death in 1980 came as a shock to the academic world, and more particularly to university communities in the Caribbean. She was still a relatively young person for whom many more years of active scholarship were anticipated. Even in death, her commitment to higher learning in the region was vividly demonstrated in her bequest of all her worldly possessions to the University of the West Indies. Her legacy has been large and enduring.

In 1986 the Department of History, Mona, where she spent all of her working life, decided to commemorate and honour her by inaugurating an annual series of lectures. These have become a red-letter event in the academic calendar of the department and the campus, and are now fully funded by the vice chancellor's and campus principals' offices. These lectures are so highly regarded by academics the world over that it has not been difficult to attract scholars of great distinction and international repute to deliver them. A remarkable coincidence worth noting is that all but three of the Elsa Goveia lecturers featured in this collection either worked with her as colleagues or were her students. Of the distinguished lecturers who have graced this series with their scholarship, eight were male and five female. One of these, Professor Emeritus Douglas Hall, a close friend and colleague of Elsa Goveia, died in 1999.

The collection consists of thirteen lectures delivered between 1987 and 1998.While each lecturer chose the subject of the particular lecture, together they form the two broad subject areas into which this volume has been divided, and which also reflect the life and scholarship of Elsa Goveia. The collection of essays, therefore, is not structured by the chronological order in which the lectures were delivered, but rather according to theme. Section 1, entitled In Slavery and Freedom, features essays by seven of the leading scholars who have worked on slavery and post-emancipation society. Joseph E. Inikori (1993) revisited the relationship between capitalism and slavery that Eric Williams examined in the 1930s and 1940s. Notwithstanding the controversy that Williams' thesis generated, Inikori provided a broad body of data to substantiate his view that Williams was correct, and that British capitalism was built on the backs of African slaves. Colin A. Palmer (1996) argued that these same African slaves played a major role in defining the texture of Caribbean societies. He examined the life patterns and cultures, and argued that while there was undoubtedly syncretism in the contact situation, the retention of African core beliefs and customs –what he called Africa's cultural soul –was just as critical to laying the cultural foundations of Caribbean society.

In his lecture, Barry Higman (1998) embarked on an intriguing voyage of discovery for the origin of the concept of "slave society" which Elsa Goveia employed in her famous book. After a searching examination of the historical literature, he located its roots in the United States in pro-slavery thought, almost a century before Goveia first used it. In his examination of the impact that slavery had on shaping early Cuban society, Franklin W. Knight (1988) argued that it was no accident that "slave societies" developed in the Caribbean; they were carefully and consciously constructed. Using Cuba to illustrate this point, he showed that although there were black slaves in that island from the sixteenth century, Cuba was not a "slave society" until the eighteenth century when sugar plantations came to dominate the economy. Thereafter sharp distinctions were made according to race and colour, and menial labour was equated with blacks/slaves. Douglas Hall's 1987 lecture focused on the horticultural interests of eighteenth-century Jamaican planters, farmers and gardeners, and showed that the principals in slave society were not exclusively confined to the production of staples for export. As he put it, "Life in our slave society of the eighteenth century went beyond master-driver-and-whip, and sugar-rum-and-molasses."

Two lectures treated aspects of post-emancipation life. Woodville K. Marshall (1990) revisited the debate over free labour after emancipation. This centres on the issue of whether the former slaves deserted the plantations after slavery, especially in territories where unused land was available. Historiographical in focus, this lecture explored the historical literature in detail and pointed to the shortcomings among historians in explaining the post-emancipation labour situation. Marshall found that the best approach comes not from historians, but from anthropologist Michel-Rolph Trouillot. Monica Schuler (1991) examined the activities of liberated Africans in Guyana after emancipation. She argued that while organizing themselves as separate self-regulating ethnic communities, they shared similar interests with the creoles, in particular, in relation to other immigrants. They survived by combining wage labour with small farming, and their presence reinforced African cultural traits in Guyana.

Section 2 of the collection groups together the lectures on gender issues, although some could easily have been treated in the first section. In a highly thought-provoking lecture, Blanca Silvestrini (1989) challenged the traditional approach of professional historians in relation to women's experiences. She asserted that Caribbean women have been invisible in the historical records, and their experiences kept outside the realms of history. To correct that she advocated a greater use of oral sources, to allow the women, especially unlettered working women, to speak for themselves. But she went further to challenge traditional historical methodology which aims at "objectivity". For her, the quest for objectivity excludes from historical analysis feelings, emotions and subjective experience. Historians, therefore, should interact with the experiences of the subjects they are studying. "History would become, thus, a dialogue in which both historians and historical subjects would participate, creating a new paradigm for history – a paradigm that recognizes that we as historians are part of the history we reconstruct."

A research student of Elsa Goveia, Lucille Mathurin Mair is the pioneer women's historian in the Caribbean. She observed that new research has successfully brought women out of the shadows of the historical records, and her 1986 lecture clearly showed that slave women were the mainstay of the economy in Jamaica by the late eighteenth century.

Hilary Beckles contested the view of the invisibility of women in the historical records; he claimed that there has been a reluctance among Caribbean historians, including females, to adopt gender as an instrument of historical investigation and analysis. His 1997 lecture, therefore, sought to address this by treating the representations of gender in slavery, its ideological relations and effects, as well as its social construction and reconstructions. Far from agreeing that black women in slavery were invisible, he argued that it was the enslaved men who were largely invisible in the historical records. Black male slaves, in being "kept" and "kept down" by the white male hegemony, were in effect "feminized" and emasculated. On the other hand, black women were visible as slave mothers and slave lovers of white men. "The general intimacy of slave women with the empowered agents of the colonial world . . . placed them at the top of the documentary queue", even as they were exploited, discriminated against and rendered disprivileged within the gendered hierarchy of West Indian slave society.

Adhering to the conventional view that women have left far fewer traces of their experiences in the historical records than men, Bridget Brereton paid tribute to recent efforts of Caribbean historians to "rescue women of the past from their invisibility". She supported Silvestrini's call for historians to make greater use of oral and written testimonies of women to achieve this, and she pointed to literary works as useful sources, as well as autobiographical writings and memoirs, diaries and journals, and private letters. Her lecture examined the writings of Caribbean women to illustrate her argument that, together with oral testimony and the mainstream historical records generated by men, these other sources can facilitate the "engendering" of Caribbean history.

Further evidence of this was provided by Elizabeth Fox-Genovese's 1992 lecture which employed Toni Morrison's novel *Beloved* [4] as a source of the voices of African American women in slavery. Fox-Genovese stated that this novel served as a very useful supplement to the fragmentary traditional sources in her reconstruction of the experiences of slave women. Her analysis demonstrated clearly how the historian can employ literature to understand, in this case, the emotions of women, an issue raised by Blanca Silvistrini.

Rex Nettleford's 1995 lecture on society's debt to history, and to Elsa Goveia in particular, serves as an excellent epilogue to this collection of essays. Now vice chancellor of the University of the West Indies, he was a student of Goveia, and pointed out that she was part of a tradition of intellectuals who challenged the idea that the Caribbean had no history. For him, history properly conceptualized and written is essential to society's development. History serves to teach present-day society of the errors of the past with a view to avoiding them in the future. History, he argued, teaches mankind that we are less than the angels; it teaches humility; it teaches that mankind is not omniscient. Elsa Goveia was an excellent exemplar of this view of history.

Notes

1. Elsa Goveia, *Slave Society in the British Leeward Islands at the End of the Eighteenth Century* (New Haven: Yale University Press, 1965).
2. Elsa Goveia, *A Study of the Historiography of the British West Indies* (Mexico City: Instituto Panamericano de Geografia e Historia, 1956).
3. Elsa Goveia, *The West Indian Slave Laws of the Eighteenth Century,* Chapters in West Indian History (Barbados: Caribbean Universities Press, 1970).
4. Toni Morrison, *Beloved* (New York: Plume, 1987).

SECTION I

In Slavery and Freedom

Slavery and the Rise of Capitalism

JOSEPH E. INIKORI

Over half a century ago, the late Eric Williams of Trinidad and Tobago wrote a brilliant doctoral thesis for Oxford University, subsequently published in 1944 under the title *Capitalism and Slavery*. The declaration of intent in the preface shows both broad and specific objectives that Williams sought to accomplish. The broad objective is his attempt to "place in historical perspective the relationship between early capitalism as exemplified by Great Britain, and the Negro slave trade, Negro slavery and the general colonial trade of the seventeenth and eighteenth centuries". Stating the specific objective, Williams says the book is "strictly an economic study of the role of Negro slavery and the slave trade in providing the capital which financed the Industrial Revolution in England and of mature industrial capitalism in destroying the slave system".[1] Throughout, Williams seems to have kept the broader goal in view, but his arguments are explicitly related to the narrower one, especially the second part of it as reflected in the title of the book, *Capitalism and Slavery*. For this and other reasons we need not go into, the politics of abolition has dominated the voluminous literature generated by reactions to Williams.[2] Beyond the politics of abolition, virtually all the reactions have been limited to considerations of private profits and their role: private profits from the slave trade and from the employment of African slave labour to produce commodities in the Americas.³ This narrowing of the subject has also tended to contract the geographical focus of the analysis. Thus, studies of the contribution of slavery to British economic development typically focus exclusively on British colonial America, even though it is clear enough that the connection between slavery and the British economy extended to all the Americas and Europe. In this way, the study by Eric Williams and the reactions to it moved farther and farther away from the broad issue of how slavery served as midwife to the birth of capitalism. That is the story of this chapter. For this reason I stand Eric Williams on his head in my title, "Slavery and the Rise of Capitalism".

This analytical and discursive story requires that we place the rise of capitalism in time and place and join issue with the general literature on the rise of capitalism, which in various ways has tended to minimize or totally ignore the central role of slavery. I will argue that the first capitalist economy in the world emerged in Britain and that capitalism did not become the dominant system of production in that country until well into the first half of the nineteenth century. I will argue further that the debate on the transition from feudalism to capitalism was misdirected; that in fact there was no such transition. I argue that the collapse of feudalism was followed by several centuries of petty commodity production (that is, family-based commercial agriculture) by self-employed cultivators freed from extra-economic coercion. Similarly, I argue that the chronological separation of the development of agrarian and industrial capitalism, in which the former is given the role of the prime mover, is factually wrong. It will be shown that industrial and agrarian capitalism developed simultaneously in England and that it was the expansion of proto-industrial production that made possible the full development of the constituent elements of capitalism in British agriculture. Finally, the crux of my argument is that the expansion of proto-industrial production in Britain during the two hundred years from 1650 to 1850 was primarily a function of the institutional and production response of the British economy and society to the pressures and opportunities emanating from the growth of the slave-based Atlantic economic system.

I

No scientific proof of the several hypotheses advanced can be offered without a clear, precise and measurable definition of our central term, capitalism. It is ironic that this term, which is applied by everyone to describe Western societies of today and to which there is so much emotional and ideological commitment by conservative scholars and students in Western universities, was invented not by Adam Smith, nor David Ricardo, nor Alfred Marshall, but by a scholar no less radical than Karl Marx himself. And for many decades, as Rodney Hilton assures us, all scholars interested in the history of capitalism, both Marxists and non-Marxists, followed Marx in their specification of the constituent elements that define the social phenomenon to which the term applies: "the division of classes between propertyless wage-earners and entre-preneurs who own capital".[4]

More recently, however, there has been some implicit attempt by several scholars to redefine capitalism with emphasis on elements such as attitudes, commercial relations and large-scale organization of production.[5] While these rather limited recent conceptions tend to confuse rather than clarify issues, on closer examination one finds that they all still derive ultimately from two traditions that were established much earlier – Marx and Weber. This implicit attempt to redefine thus appears to be a rereading of Marx and Weber. This implied reinterpretation has generated an open debate only among scholars of the Marxian tradition. No such controversy surrounds the apparent reread-ing of Weber's conception of capitalism. A brief discussion of both sides of the subject is pertinent to the definition of capitalism that informs our treatment of the main subject of the chapter.

The recent debate among the Marxists centres on Gunder Frank's use of the term and the support given by Immanuel Wallerstein. The bone of contention is whether elements in the sphere of exchange or those in the sphere of production more unambiguously distinguish capitalism from all other social forms. Frank argues for elements in the sphere of exchange, classifying economies as capitalist or non-capitalist in accordance with whether or not they are connected to extensive markets. Wallerstein concurs. By this concep-tion, Frank and Wallerstein are able to regard the slave-based plantation and mining economies and *encomienda* systems of the Americas as capitalist from the sixteenth century.[6]

Most Marxist scholars, however, insist that elements in the sphere of production are central. Ernesto Laclau's critique of Frank leads the way. Laclau stresses that "the fundamental economic relation of capitalism is constituted by the free labourer's sale of his labour-power, whose necessary precondition is the loss by the direct producer of ownership of the means of

production".[7] The defining elements of capitalism are similarly specified by
Maurice Dobb, who equates capitalist relations of production with relations
of wage labour to capital.[8] For R.S. Neale, the specification of the defining
characteristics of capitalism as a social form starts, as it were, with first
principles, that is, the meaning of the term capital, from which Karl Marx
derived capitalism. Neale points out that both Marx and the classical economists defined capital in terms of "things used to produce more things". But
for Marx, unlike the classical economists, things used to produce more things
become capital *only* when these things are used under certain socioeconomic
relations. The socioeconomic relations in question are specified by Marx as
those between free wage labour separated from the instruments of production
and the entrepreneur owning these instruments.[9] By this conception, tools
owned and used by self-employed producers, whether in agriculture, manufacturing or commerce are not capital. If the things used by self-employed
workers are not capital, it follows that economic systems in which their form
of the labour process predominates are not capitalist.[10] Again, this is the
conception adopted by Ellen Wood in her recent stimulating critique of the
currently fashionable argument that the problems of the British economy in
the more recent past derive from its much earlier incomplete development of
capitalism. Specifying free wage labour and capital-owning entrepreneurs,
with market-dominated production, as the defining properties of capitalism,
she is able to argue persuasively that the British economy developed capitalism
to a much greater extent than subsequent capitalist economies, in which
non-capitalist elements, especially state intervention, tend to loom large.[11]
Finally, placing the issue in the context of a historical process, Robert Brenner
states that the historical problem of the origins of capitalist economic development in relation to precapitalist socioeconomic formations is reducible to
that of the origin of the "property/surplus extraction system (class system) of
free wage labour".[12]

R.H. Tawney, a towering figure in British economic historiography who
was far from being a Marxist, also defined capitalism in terms of free wage
labour. As though in anticipation of some of the recent conceptions, he held
that capitalism defined in terms of profits from commerce, buccaneering, war
or large-scale organization of production would be indistinguishable from
socioeconomic systems that have existed throughout history. So defined, there
would be no problem of the "rise of capitalism", since it would always have
existed, virtually everywhere. As he put the point,

Capitalism, in the sense of great individual undertakings, involving the control of large financial resources, and yielding riches to their masters as a result of speculation, money-lending, commercial enterprise, buccaneering and war, is as old as history. Capitalism, as an economic system, resting on the organization of legally free wage-earners, for the purpose of pecuniary profit, by the owner of capital or his agents, and setting its stamp on every aspect of society, is a modern phenomenon.[13]

Tawney's point about capitalism as an economic system that structures every aspect of society needs to be stressed. Max Weber's earlier conception of capitalism contains similar elements. Weber drew a clear distinction between what he called "modern capitalism", which he argued developed only in the West from the sixteenth century, and other social forms that have existed in all "civilized countries" throughout history. Thus he declared at the very beginning of his *Protestant Ethic,*

The impulse to acquisition, pursuit of gain, of money, of the greatest possible amount of money, has in itself nothing to do with capitalism. This impulse exists and has existed among waiters, physicians, coachmen, artists, prostitutes, dishonest officials, soldiers, nobles, crusaders, gamblers and beggars. One may say that it has been common to all sorts and conditions of men at all times and in all countries of the earth, wherever the objective possibility of it is or has been given. It should be taught in the kindergarten of cultural history that this naive idea of capitalism must be given up once and for all.[14]

Weber even argued that rational calculation as a characteristic of capitalism, though important, does not distinguish it unmistakably from other forms of socioeconomic organization that can be found in different places throughout history.

We will define a capitalistic economic action as one which rests on the expectation of profit by the utilization of opportunities for exchange that is on (formally) peaceful chances of profit. . . . Where capitalistic acquisition is rationally pursued, the corresponding action is adjusted to calculations in terms of capital. . . . Everything is done in terms of balances: at the beginning of the enterprise an initial balance, before every individual decision a calculation to ascertain its probable profitableness, and at the end a final balance to ascertain how much profit has been made. . . . Now in this sense capitalism and capitalistic enterprises, even with a considerable rationalization of capitalistic calculation, have existed in all civilized countries of the earth, so far as economic documents permit us to judge.[15]

Weber believed that the employment of free wage labour as the dominant form of the labour process is what distinguishes the capitalism that developed only in the West in modern times from all other social forms. As he expressed it,

> [I]n modern times the Occident has developed, in addition to this, a very different form of capitalism which has appeared nowhere else: the rational capitalistic organization of (formally) free labour. . . . The modern rational organization of the capitalistic enterprise would not have been possible without two other important factors in its development: the separation of business from the household, which completely dominates modern economic life, and closely connected with it, rational book-keeping. . . . However, all these peculiarities of Western capitalism have derived their significance in the last analysis only from their association with the capitalistic organization of labour. Even what is generally called commercialization, the development of negotiable securities and the rationalization of speculation, the exchanges, etc., is connected with it. For without the rational capitalistic organization of labour, all this, so far as it was possible at all, would have nothing like the same significance, above all for the social structure and all the specific problems of the modern Occident connected with it. Exact calculation – the basis of everything else – is only possible on the basis of free labour.[16]

Weber's emphasis on free wage labour as the defining characteristic of Western capitalism is brought out even more clearly in his *Economy and Society*. Here his characterization of capitalism as a socioeconomic system is completely identical with that of Marx. The separation of workers from the means of production is seen as the main driving force in the economic, social and political processes in a capitalist economy and society.

> The relative independence of the artisan, the producer under the putting-out system, the free seigneurial peasant, the travelling associate in a *commenda* relationship, the knight and vassal rested on their ownership of tools, supplies, finances and weapons with which they fulfilled their economic, political and military functions and maintained themselves. In contrast, the hierarchical dependence of the wage worker, the administrative and technical employee, the assistant in the academic institute *as well as* that of the civil servant and the soldier is due to the fact that in their case the means indispensable for the enterprise and for making a living are in the hands of the entrepreneur or the political ruler. . . . This all-important economic fact: the 'separation' of the worker from the material means of production, destruction, administration, academic research, and finance in general is the common basis of the modern state, in its political, cultural and military sphere, and of the private capitalist economy.[17]

For the historian interested in studying the historical origin of capitalism as a socioeconomic system, Weber instructed that the problem to resolve is not the development of capitalistic economic activity *per se,* but the origin of the social relations of production between the capital-owning entrepreneur and the free wage worker separated from the means of production. As he put it, "in a universal history of culture the central problem for us is not, in the last analysis, even from a purely economic view-point, the development of capitalistic activity as such, differing in different cultures only in form. . . . It is rather the origin of this sober bourgeois capitalism with its rational organization of free labour."[18]

Viewed against the foregoing exposition of Weber's conception of capitalism, one must conclude that recent conceptions based on attitudes, market relations or large-scale organization of production, which implicitly claim Weber as their parent, are a clear misreading of those texts. Alan Macfarlane (1978 and 1987) may be taken as a fair illustration.[19] In Macfarlane's view,

> Ultimately the uniqueness of capitalism lies in its attitudes towards such things as money, time, effort, accumulation and so on. Weber believed that what happened under capitalism was that accumulation, saving, and profit-seeking had become ethically and emotionally attractive, whereas before they had been unacceptable. The ethic of endless accumulation, as an end and not as a means, is the central peculiarity of capitalism.[20]

Certainly, Weber considered the element identified by Macfarlane, and by some others, as important. But he did not see it as the defining element that distinguishes capitalism unambiguously from other socioeconomic systems to be found in various places throughout history. Weber, like Marx, was primarily concerned with an effort to understand the economic, social and political forces which capitalism brought into Western societies. Through this understanding both Marx and Weber attempted to predict the future direction of the history of Western capitalist societies. Emphasis on attitudes would be inadequate for this purpose. Although radically differing in their predictions,[21] both Marx and Weber saw the division of society into free wage-earners separated from the means of production and entrepreneurs owning those means as the element that was central to the forces that propelled Western capitalist societies of their day.

It is clear enough from the literature on capitalism that the vast majority of scholars, Marxists and non-Marxists, specify propertyless but legally free wage workers and entrepreneurs owning capital but dependent on the labour power of the free wage labourers as the constituent elements that distinguish capitalism unmistakably from all other forms of social organization. The issue, however, is not just a question of majority view, which happens to correspond with that of Marx and Weber. The point simply is that this conception of capitalism captures the dynamics of the capitalist system far more precisely and accurately than all others. It captures the forces that compel the system to produce mainly for market exchange rather than for the immediate consumption of the direct producer; it encapsulates the inner logic of the system that motivates the entrepreneurs to pursue endless increases in labour productivity through innovations in technology and organization; it incorporates the source of class interests and conflict; in a word, it captures the central dynamic elements of the system in the economic, social and political arenas. Brenner puts it succinctly:

> Only under conditions of free wage labour will the individual producing units (combining labour power and the means of production) be forced to sell in order to buy, to buy in order to survive and reproduce, and ultimately to expand and innovate in order to maintain [its] position in relationship to other competing productive units. Only under such a system, where both capital and labour power are thus commodities . . . is there the necessity of producing at the 'socially necessary' labour time in order to survive, and to surpass this level of productivity to ensure continued survival.[22]

As demonstrated by John Taylor, all of this is due to the fact that the separation of the direct producer from the means of production in the capitalist system provides a specifically economic mechanism for surplus extraction within the production process itself, as opposed to the extra-economic mechanisms of all other systems.[23] The form of combination of labour power and capital, which is compelled by the employment of free wage labour, facilitates the appropriation of surplus value by the owner of capital through the payment of wages that are less than the value produced by labour. This form of appropriation is subtle, relative to all other forms; it takes place without the glaring view and consciousness of the labourer and it does not entail the use of non-market and non-economic force. But because both wage labour and capital move freely on the market, there is a strict minimum level beyond which labour wage cannot fall. In consequence, the owner of capital is compelled to engage in an eternal effort to raise labour productivity, on which alone the magnitude of his appropriated surplus and survival depend in the long run. These are the central dynamics of capitalism that distinguish it unambiguously from all other systems of production. And they are fully and precisely captured only by the conception of capitalism centred on free wage labour.

From the foregoing, I can now state my operational definition of capitalism. By this term I mean a system of production for market exchange, in which the direct producers – separated from the means of production – voluntarily sell their labour power to the owners of capital, whose motivation is profit and the reproduction of capital on an expanded scale.

II

The question now is where and when this system of production first emerged in the world. Conceptions of capitalism centred on attitudes or on production for market exchange *per se* have encouraged the extension of the history of capitalism to almost all historical periods and to several geographical areas. Based on evidence showing a phenomenal expansion of commerce and industrial production for international trade in the Mediterranean region from the late thirteenth century, referred to by some as a "commercial revolution", several writers trace the rise of capitalism to medieval Europe, particularly the Italian city-states.[24] Cox states specifically that capitalism was invented in Venice "between the period of the fall of the Roman Empire in the west and . . . the signing of Magna Carta in England".[25] In the opinion of Cox, other Italian city-states developed capitalism in succession until the capitalist system of production was further elaborated in Holland in the seventeenth century.[26]

To be sure, the economies of the Italian city-states from the thirteenth to the sixteenth century, and the Dutch economy in the sixteenth and seventeenth centuries, contained some capitalist elements, though embryonic in nature. These were commercialized economies in which some of the most important commercial institutions of the capitalist system, such as bills of exchange, insurance and banking, were first elaborately developed. They had large industrial sectors that were heavily dependent on export markets and agricultural sectors producing largely for market exchange and free from feudal constraints. Yet these economies remained dominated by self-employed producers owning their means of production. There was free wage labour, but it was not the dominant form of labour in these economies, especially in agriculture where petty commodity production remained overwhelmingly dominant. Even in manufacturing in the Italian city-states, where free wage labour was concentrated, the evidence indicates that much of the labour was not yet wage labour in the proper sense. As one of the authorities tells us,

> In Venice slaves formed part of the labour force for certain operations such as the beating of cotton and were inscribed in the appropriate guild alongside free artisans. The workers carried out their tasks either in the house of the entrepreneur

or in their own homes and, depending upon their specialty, were paid either by the piece or by a daily wage. The implements of work were in some cases owned by the artisan, but more often were provided by the employer.[27]

By definition, therefore, the Italian and Dutch economies, though containing some individual units of capitalist production, were as a whole not capitalist. In fact, they are treated in recent times as economies that failed in their transition to industrial capitalism.[28]

Judging from the familiar historical literature, one turns now to Britain as the next candidate for consideration. While some may be inclined to push the history of capitalism to the Middle Ages, and so to Renaissance Italy, it is fair to say that most students of the subject agree that the first truly capitalist economy in the world emerged in Britain some time between 1450 and 1850.[29] But there is much confusion on when precisely capitalism became the dominant system of production in the British economy. Part of the confusion arises from the tendency to separate in time the development of agrarian and industrial capitalism. Several writers are guilty of this view, but the case is more explicitly stated by Wallerstein. As he puts it,

> I think finally that there are two historical transitions. One is the basic transition from feudalism to capitalism. In my mind that occurred in Europe between 1450 and 1550, and since then we have been living in a capitalist world-economy, which then expanded to the whole world. The second transition is industrialization or industrialism, that is, the point where capitalism became primarily geared to industry rather than agriculture. . . . That . . . occurred between 1760 and 1830.[30]

This view, which has general support in the literature, raises a problem of timing as well as causation. It derives partly from the original scheme articulated by Marx, in which economies were expected to move progressively from one mode of production to another as the productive forces developed over time. Capitalism was expected to follow feudalism. From theoretical expectation, historians moved on to the uncritical acceptance that capitalism did in fact follow feudalism. What was disputed came to be the nature and causes of the transition from feudalism to capitalism.[31] What is more, it is argued implicitly by some and explicitly by others that, of all precapitalist forms of socioeconomic organization, feudalism is the most structurally suited to the development of capitalism. While Eric Hobsbawm queries "whether we can speak of a *universal* tendency of feudalism to develop into capitalism", he nevertheless accepts that in western Europe and part of the Mediterranean capitalism did emerge from feudalism.[32] But was the British economy which emerged from the collapse of feudalism in the fifteenth-century capitalist? Even if we take Wallerstein's more limited hypothesis mentioned earlier, was the British agriculture of the mid-sixteenth-century capitalist?

With due allowance for the acknowledged weaknesses in the quantitative evidence, our measurable definition of capitalism allows precise answers to these questions. Based on Henry VIII's tax subsidy of 1525, David Levine estimates that there was a total of 600,000 free wage workers and their dependents in England out of a total population of roughly 2.4 million at this time.[33] On the basis of the same source, the number of peasants, taken to mean "people who worked the land as family farmers", is computed to be 1.65 million, being 70 per cent of the total population.[34] It is not possible to say what proportion of the wage labourers were in agriculture, but it is clear enough from this evidence that self-employed producers overwhelmingly dominated English agriculture in the first half of the sixteenth century. Clapham's analysis of the social statistics by Gregory King shows that even by the late seventeenth century – that is, almost one and a half centuries later – wage-earning families did not greatly outnumber self-employed families in British agriculture, being 573,000 and 330,000 respectively.[35] The correction of King's figures by Peter Lindert, and by Lindert and Williamson, further reduces the difference considerably.[36] According to Lindert and Williamson, there were in England in 1688, 227,440 self-employed families in agriculture and 284,997 wage-earning families in all sectors. The figures for 1759 are 379,008 and 240,000, respectively. As G.E. Mingay has argued, the transformation of copyholders and freeholders into wage labourers occurred largely after 1660, due mainly to more than a hundred years of low and fluctuating agricultural prices which hit the small cultivators disproportionately hard.[37] This would mean that at the beginning of the seventeenth-century self-employed producers still outnumbered wage labourers in British agriculture. In all probability, wage labour did not dominate the agrarian labour process until well into the eighteenth century. In fact, according to Levine, the family farmers were superseded as the dominant productive force in English agriculture in the middle of the eighteenth century, their place taken by tenant farmers employing wage labour.[38]

The evidence indicates that self-employed producers dominated manufacturing even more and far longer. The literature on the British Industrial Revolution has undergone considerable revision since the 1970s, especially as relates to the pace of change in output, organization and technology.[39] The

current view holds, among other things, that the first phase of British industrialization, which covered the years 1700–1850, was characterized by the
expansion of the old domestic system, with the merchant entrepreneur
operating as a semi-employer. The unit of production was the family, which
included wives and children from a very tender age. It is now fashionable to
call this stage of industrialization, proto-industrialization. Family labour was
central to its expansion in Britain in the eighteenth and nineteenth centuries;
and the proto-industrial family generally supplied its own tools. It has been
estimated that as late as the 1840s, these family units produced over three-
quarters of industrial output.[40] It was only after 1850, during the second phase
of British industrialization, that factory and wage employment progressively
became dominant in industrial production. It follows, therefore, that industrial
capitalism emerged in Britain after the middle of the nineteenth century.
Hence, the British economy as a whole could not have become capitalist before
the nineteenth century.

Thus, for over three hundred years after the demise of feudalism in the
mid-fifteenth century, there was no capitalist economy in Britain. Hence there
could not have been a transition from feudalism to capitalism in that country.
The economy that emerged from the ashes of feudalism was dominated by
production for market exchange by family units unfettered by the extra-
economic coercion of feudalism. This socioeconomic organization did not
need the prior development of feudalism for its emergence, although the
continued existence of feudalism would have held it back in Britain. In fact,
similar socioeconomic formations existed in parts of the United States from
the colonial period and in much of twentieth-century tropical Africa without
the prior existence of feudalism.

What facilitated the development of capitalism in Britain was not the prior
development of feudalism, but the deep and extensive penetration of the
economy by market exchange at an early stage. This commercialization of
economy and society was a long drawn out process, led by the international
trade in raw wool and woollen cloth, and also by population growth from the
second half of the fifteenth century to the seventeenth century.[41] It influenced
the process of class formation and, in conjunction with the insular location of
Britain in relation to continental European events, helped to determine the
outlook of British politics generally in the decades between the collapse of
feudalism and the civil war. It will be argued subsequently that the commercialization of economy and society, especially the commercialization of

agriculture and the class structure and politics associated with it, made the British economy highly responsive to the pressures and opportunities that arose in the seventeenth and eighteenth centuries, but did not guarantee the development of capitalism. It is often not realized that the basic institutions of a capitalist economy – insurance, banking and stock exchange – developed relatively recently in the British economy. Apart from the Bank of England which was established in 1694, there were no banks in England in the proper sense before the eighteenth century. There is some indication that the banking habit was not firmly established in eighteenth-century England, even among the very wealthy. Almost at the end of the second quarter of the eighteenth century, a member of a wealthy family wrote to his friend, a merchant in the African trade,

> I wrote you last post the account of the loss of my Poor Dear Father, whose will we have since open'd, and according to my expectations he hath given his whole Fortune to my Brother, except a few legacies to the value of about £500 to me and others. He died richer than I imagined. We found this evening in one corner £6,600 and upwards in money that hath lain there many a year untouched . . . .[42]

Expressed in today's value, this is a huge sum of money to keep in the house for years untouched. Again, it will be argued in the sections that follow that the development of financial institutions in the eighteenth century was a major factor in the development of British capitalism, and that these institutions developed in response to the expansion of market demand for credit, a demand largely associated with the slave-based Atlantic economy.

III

We must first, however, confront the more important opposing explanations offered by scholars for the transformation, between 1650 and 1850, of a British economy that was dominated by family producers from the fifteenth century to the early nineteenth into one dominated by free wage labour. The controversy appropriately centres on industrial development, usually referred to as the Industrial Revolution. It must be noted that many of the writers are not concerned with the history of capitalism and often do not even mention the term. However, emphasis on free wage labour as the defining element of capitalism and the argument that industrialization was the key factor in the growth of wage labour to a position of dominance in the British economy make all contributions to the subject of British industrialization relevant.

Basically, the bone of contention is whether demand or supply was the prime mover in the process of British industrial development. The argument for supply points to technological development as the source of British industrial growth. Within the latter argument itself there are opposing views: was technological progress the work of practical men wholly innocent of scientific principles or did it depend on the growth of scientific knowledge? The literature contains several contributions on both sides of the question.[43] Writers who stress the role of demand are even more divided. Some emphasize the role of domestic demand arising from agricultural development and population growth.[44] Others emphasize export demand.[45] Again, among the latter, there are two opposing positions, exports to Europe versus extra-European exports.[46]

Probably the most current and representative statement of the supply argument is by Joel Mokyr.[47] After rejecting demand as the primary source of change, he argues that "[c]ost-reducing and factor-increasing changes occupy the center of the stage: supply rules supreme. Technological change, capital accumulation, improvements in organization and attitudes all made it possible to produce food, clothing, pots, and toys cheaper and better."[48] He stresses that these changes in technology, organization and attitudes were independent of demand and not a response to it in any way. He concludes,

> The old schoolboy view of the Industrial Revolution as a "wave of gadgets" may not be far off the mark after all, provided we allow for "more" as well as for "better" gadgets, and we include abstract improvements such as organizational change, changes in workers' attitudes, and so forth, as "gadgets" in a wider sense.[49]

How do these supply arguments stand in the face of the evidence produced by recent research? The consensus emerging from recent research may be summarized as follows. The first phase of British industrialization, 1700–1850, was characterized by a much slower rate of growth than was previously thought, and was dominated by the old domestic system, with the merchant capitalist in control of the process. The merchant entrepreneurs expanded output by spreading production to more and more family producers in rural England. These family producers usually employed their own tools, for which reason the merchant entrepreneur had no need to invest considerable sums in fixed capital expenditures. What was needed in large amounts was circulating capital for the purchase of raw materials, payments to the family producers, and the cost of distributing the finished product, especially the extension of credit to exporters.[50] Thus, as one summary of the evidence concludes, the industrialization process in England from 1700 to 1850 was "characterized by handicraft manufacturing, powered by human energy and requiring little in the way of fixed capital assets".[51]

The evidence from recent research therefore shows that British industrialization from 1700 to 1850 was led not by "gadgets", as Mokyr and others have argued, but by market demand, and that the process was appropriately controlled by merchant entrepreneurs. The main source of Mokyr's error, it would appear, was his rejection of the idea that in the years 1700–1850, British industrialization proceeded under conditions of large-scale underutilization of resources.[52] Certainly British natural resources, such as coal, iron, copper and others, were grossly underutilized before the growth of industrial production from 1700 to 1850. It has also been shown that a major element in the industrial expansion of the period was the large-scale employment of women and children in peasant households, a development which contributed significantly to increases in the incomes of rural families.[53] This can be seen as a vent-for-surplus in the economy of the peasant household. On the other hand, the adoption of homeostatic demographic behaviour by peasant families from the middle decades of the seventeenth century indicates that rural England had some population to spare before the growth of industry in the eighteenth century began. Hence, the reduction of the number of small farmers during the period of more than one hundred years before 1750, due to the combined effects of declining agricultural prices and growing employment opportunities in industry and commerce,[54] amounts to the employment of previously underutilized labour. What is more, this reduction in the number of small farmers allowed a more rational organization of British agriculture to be effected through the enlargement of farms and enclosure.

Further evidence on the critical role of market demand comes from English demographic history. As already stated, the growth of industrial output between 1700 and 1850 was due largely to a massive input of human labour. The combined evidence from the detailed demographic research of Wrigley and Schofield on the one hand, and that of Levine on the other, now shows that British industry largely created its own labour through the demographic response of peasant and proletarian families to the demand for industrial labour. The mechanism was a decline in the age at first marriage and a reduction in the number of women remaining unmarried for life. Earlier, peasant families had adopted a homeostatic demographic practice to maintain the equilibrium between family size and the family land through delayed marriage.[55] As David Levine has shown, the number of proletarians in England (that is, wage labourers and semi-wage labourers) grew from 600,000 in 1525 to 2.5 million in 1700, 14 million in 1850, and 16.5 million in 1871.[56] Levine demonstrates that the contribution of expropriated peasants to these increases in the number of proletarians was less than 50 per cent of the total, and that the main source was population growth among peasant families and the proletarian families themselves, as they both responded to employment opportunities in the expanding non-agricultural sectors, especially industrial employment.[57] In this way, the industrialization process created, as it were, additional factors of production through the mechanism of demand.

If it is clear from the evidence we have marshalled that demand was the prime mover in the first 150 years of British industrialization, the next problem is the relative importance of domestic and overseas demand. From the early 1960s, the literature on this subject was very much influenced by the *a priori* argument of Deane and Cole.[58] The authors presented some of the most solid quantitative evidence that shows the leading role of overseas markets. However, they argued that because the growth of overseas demand during the period came largely from British America, whose demand for British goods, they assumed, was derived from British consumption of colonial produce, British domestic demand was the source of that growth in the first instance. Deane and Cole explain the growth of British domestic demand in terms of agricultural improvement and population growth.

This argument has been heavily criticized over the years.[59] The main point is that, taken together, over half of the colonial produce imported into Britain, by value, was not consumed in Britain but re-exported. This was particularly the case for British North American tobacco. In addition, the British American colonies had extensive trade with the rest of the Americas and also with southern Europe, all of which, together with the growth of population in these colonies, provided sources of income growth independent of British consumer demand. These colonial incomes growing from several sources ended up being spent on British manufactures. What is more, a large amount of British export of manufactures during the period went to Portugal and Spain, paid for with incomes generated by Portuguese and Spanish American colonies. Finally, the evidence presented on British demographic history during the period makes clear the weakness of Deane and Cole's population argument. Since population growth depended on the growth of demand for labour in industry and commerce, population increase cannot be treated as an independent variable in the process.

Once the logical implication of the evidence is freed from Deane and Cole's *a priori* argument, it becomes easy to demonstrate the leading role of overseas demand in all its complexity. In this we must differentiate between the factors at play at the starting point and those that carried the process forward subsequently. As I have argued elsewhere, British industrialization followed a process of import substitution, with a long interval.[60] It started with woollen cloth in the fourteenth century. Not until the late seventeenth and early eighteenth century did several industries, such as cotton, linen, silk and some metal-using industries, develop on the basis of import substitution. The significance of this point is that industrial growth in the late seventeenth and early eighteenth century was not due to growing overall British domestic incomes at the time; it was based on pre-existing domestic demand built up over centuries of British external and internal trade. That the purchasing power of domestic consumers of manufactures in Britain at this time was not particularly high, and that it was growing rather slowly, is indicated by the short space of time within which output in these import substitution industries reached the limit of pre-existing home demand, and manufacturers began frantically to search for export markets.[61] Recent research now shows that British agriculture provided a much smaller market for British manufactures than was previously thought.[62] In terms of what carried the process forward, estimates by Crafts show that in the last two decades of the eighteenth century (treated as the early phase of the Industrial Revolution), about 60 per cent of additional industrial output was exported.[63] When the multiplier effects on the domestic market are added, especially through population growth as has been shown, the leading role of exports in British industrialization becomes unmistakably clear.

But this still leaves the problem of determining whether internal forces in Europe or those emanating from the growth of the slave-based Atlantic economy provided the dynamics for the growth of British exports during the period under consideration. One of the most forceful arguments for internal forces within Europe was developed by O'Brien.[64] In his opinion, "the commerce between Western Europe and regions at the periphery of the international economy forms an insignificant part of the explanation for the accelerated rate of economic growth experienced by the core after 1750".[65] He quotes Braudel to stress that agricultural productivity and population size were the real factors, and concludes: "Such factors, to which I would add improvements to agriculture and technical progress in industry, continued to determine the destiny of Europe throughout the mercantile era. As long as oceanic trade remained as a tiny proportion of total economic activity it could not propel Europe towards an industrial society."[66]

But as William Darity, Jr, states, a recent publication by O'Brien and Engerman indicates that O'Brien has given up this argument.[67] O'Brien and Engerman argue that exports played a leading role in British industrialization and economic growth from 1688 to 1802, and that about 85 per cent of the increment to exports sold overseas from 1697 to 1802 went to markets outside Europe.[68] Consistent with the recent research referred to earlier, they conclude, "What is reasonably clear, however, is that the demand for industrial goods that emanated from productivity growth in agriculture accounted for a far lower proportion of the increment to the sales of industrial output from 1700 to 1800 than exports – particularly when connections between exports on the one hand and domestic consumption and investment (including investment in agriculture) on the other are taken into account."[69]

The evidence shows that the contribution of the non-European Atlantic economies to the growth of British export of manufactures during the period was greater still than O'Brien and Engerman have stated. This is because a large amount of British domestic exports to Europe at this time depended on the economies of the Americas. In particular, British domestic exports to Spain and Portugal depended heavily on incomes generated by Spanish and Portuguese America.[70] In the case of Portugal, the dependence of imports from England on the Brazilian economy is reflected by the parallel movement of gold production in Brazil and English exports to Portugal in the eighteenth century.[71] It should also be noted that the substantial re-export trade in the products of British America generated incomes that were spent by British consumers on partly British manufactures and partly on the import of raw materials from Europe.

For our critical comments to reflect the current literature adequately, something must be said about recent Marxian explanations represented by Robert Brenner's writings. The difficulty here is where to locate these arguments. It is clear enough that Brenner does not believe that the emergence and growth of the slave-based Atlantic system was the main source of British industrial development in the late seventeenth and eighteenth centuries. But he does not support a supply argument as such; he does not see the autonomous development of technology as the main source of British industrialization during the period in question. A careful reading of his arguments would suggest that he sees demand arising from the growth of trade as a critical factor, but not the prime mover. For Brenner, the prime mover was "class struggle". Insofar as demand was important, it came largely from agriculture; British industrialization had its origin in British agriculture. This was possible, in the first instance, because of the early development of agrarian capitalism in England, which was due, in turn, to a unique history of class struggle in rural England, Brenner argues.[72]

This argument by Brenner has three fundamental weaknesses. First, as was demonstrated earlier, there was no capitalist agriculture in Britain in the seventeenth century. British agriculture was still dominated by family producers at this time. Second, the demand aspect of the argument derives entirely from the earlier argument of Deane and Cole.[73] This comes out clearly in a 1974 seminar exchange between Brenner and Smit. Responding to the latter's argument that exports to the Americas were the main factor which explains the differing experiences of Britain and Holland in eighteenth-century industrialization,[74] Brenner said,

> the success of England was fundamentally based on the transformation of agriculture and on major increases in agricultural productivity. As Professor Smit commented yesterday, 18th century economic growth in England was heavily dependent on colonial markets. But it may also be argued that these, in turn, depended quite strongly on the ability of the English home market to absorb the colonies' exports.[75]

As we have already shown, the Deane and Cole argument has collapsed under the weight of historical evidence. Finally, Brenner's class struggle argument has no explanatory power. He fails to show the historical process which gave rise to the formation of the classes, the factors which affected the relative strengths and weaknesses of the classes over time, and the available opportunities which determined the way the class members perceived what was in their self-interest and so influenced the choices made. Failing to do all this, Brenner presents class struggle as a *deus ex machina,* a god without history whose mysterious presence helps to explain the development of agrarian capitalism in England and the subsequent Industrial Revolution derived from the latter. Had Brenner seriously investigated the history of class formation in England from the medieval era to the mid-nineteenth century, he would have found enough evidence to be convinced that the evolution of the classes, changes in their relative strengths and weaknesses, and the conditions that determined the choices which the class members made all depended heavily on market developments over the centuries.[76]

IV

So far I have refuted supply arguments based on science and technology as autonomous variables in early British industrialization. Similarly, the weaknesses of arguments seeking to show the primacy of growing domestic demand derived from agricultural productivity and population growth have been demonstrated. I have therefore been able to stress the leading role of overseas demand and to emphasize that the growth of production and trade across the Atlantic was the key factor in the expansion of overseas demand for British manufactures during the period under consideration. The problem now is to determine the extent to which the growth of production and trade across the Atlantic depended on the slave trade from Africa and African slavery in the Americas. The assessment has to be based on the empirically verifiable premise that by 1500 actual purchasing power in all regions of the Atlantic area – western Europe, Africa and the Americas – was far below the potential level, defined as the exchangeable surplus that Atlantic societies could produce with the use of existing resources and technology. In other words, the level of effective demand and production for market exchange in these societies at the time did not depend on their ability to produce a marketable surplus, but on market opportunities. Market opportunities were strictly limited due to the low level of development of division of labour within and between Atlantic subregions. Given this situation, the expansion of commerce across the Atlantic was capable of moving purchasing power towards its potential level through a vent-for-surplus mechanism, for as long as there were new products whose consumption was seen by consumers to be worth the effort to procure the wherewithal.

For the rest of the chapter, I argue that the growth of market opportunities in the Atlantic area from the seventeenth century on arose from a *forced* division of labour at a time when land-labour ratios generally encouraged subsistence production in the Americas and Africa, and inland transportation problems and the multiplicity of restrictive tariffs limited market opportunities in Europe.[77] For this reason, the forced specialization of African slaves in the production of commodities for Atlantic commerce from the seventeenth century on operated as the main engine that propelled trade and the development of voluntary division of labour to greater heights across the Atlantic.

Before the seventeenth century, the use of coerced labour to exploit the resources of the Americas was largely in the gold and silver mines of Spanish America. Reliable demographic evidence for these early years is wanting, but the available information suggests that African slave labour was already important in the sixteenth century mines of Spanish America.[78] Spanish American bullion of the sixteenth century was the source of considerable trade between Spain and the rest of western Europe. It stimulated the growth of market production in the region. But it did not provide a significant basis for large-scale exchange of goods and services in the Atlantic area outside Europe. This came later with the development of large-scale agricultural production for Atlantic commerce in the seventeenth century.

The pioneer here was Brazil and the dominant product was sugar. Brazil remained a major producer of export commodities from the seventeenth century to the nineteenth, widening the range of products over time to include gold, coffee, tobacco and cotton. Apart from the use of Indian slaves in the early part of the sixteenth century, Brazilian production of commodities for Atlantic trade was almost entirely by African slaves. This is reflected by the ethnic composition of the populations of the export-producing regions, such as Pernambuco, Bahia, Minas Gerais, Goias and Mato Grosso. In the later colonial period, people of African origin were 68.2 per cent, 78.6 per cent, 74.6 per cent, 82.4 per cent, and 80.4 per cent of the populations of these regions, respectively.[79] The viceroy of Brazil was saying the obvious when he told the king of Portugal in 1739 that without African slaves no commodities for Atlantic trade could be produced. Worried about events in Dahomey, he wrote:

> Be it known to Your Majesty what is taking place on the Mina Coast and what has happened to our director at Ajuda, Joao Basilio, who has been detained by the King of Dahomey. . . . This matter is of the greatest importance, because of the detrimental consequences that could result for the Mina Coast trade which supports the principal interest of the state of Brazil, because without Negroes there can be neither gold, nor sugar, nor tobacco.[80]

As late as 1872, after the massive European migration to Brazil associated with the gold rush and the coffee boom of the eighteenth and nineteenth centuries respectively, people of African origin still made up about 60 per cent of the total Brazilian population of about 10 million.[81]

From Brazil large-scale production of agricultural commodities for Atlantic commerce moved to the Caribbean in the middle decades of the seventeenth century. This, again, was entirely dependent on African slave labour. Before the middle decades of the seventeenth century, the production of subsistence crops had dominated the islands' economies and export production was marginal. From the second half of the seventeenth century, the massive import of Africans made it possible for commodity production for Atlantic trade to grow rapidly, while the production of subsistence crops was drastically reduced. This is reflected by the transformation of the ethnic composition of the Caribbean population. In 1660 the combined population of Barbados, Jamaica and the Leeward Islands was made up of 33,000 whites and 22,500 African slaves; but in 1713 the whites numbered 32,000 and African slaves were 130,000.[82] And in 1772–73 there were in the British West Indies as a whole 62,034 whites and 431,984 Africans.[83] Similarly, in the French West Indies, the combined population of Martinique and St Domingue in 1678–81 comprised 6,786 whites and 7,397 African slaves,[84] but by 1780 of the total population of 514,849 in all the French West Indies, only 63,682 were whites and 451,167 were Africans.[85]

In the Spanish Caribbean, where the population of Africans remained small until the nineteenth century, subsistence production remained dominant and production for Atlantic trade was marginal until the nineteenth century. A contemporary European observer wrote in 1807 that in 1788 Cuba had 170,000 whites and 30,000 Africans. He then stated:

> Cuba is very fertile, and the lands are universally considered as being equal to the best parts of St. Domingo, nevertheless although it is 700 miles in Length and 70 miles in Breadth its produce in 1788 was little more than that of Barbados which is only 24 miles long & 14 broad. The population of Barbados at that period was 17,000 whites & 62,000 negroes . . . and to the small number of negroes & the imperfection of their negro code must the scanty produce of that fine Island be attributed.[86]

Later in the nineteenth century, when African slaves were imported massively into Cuba, its production of commodities for Atlantic trade outstripped that of the rest of the Caribbean put together.

In the United States, from the colonial period to the Civil War, African slaves also dominated the production of commodities for Atlantic trade. The main products involved were rice, tobacco and cotton. These were produced in the colonies to the south, and later in the southern states of the United States.

Between 1768 and 1772 the rice and tobacco plantations of the southern colonies exported produce worth £1,078,000 (sterling) annually, on the average.[87] In the nineteenth century, the export of raw cotton constituted the backbone of the US economy. This, again, was in the south. Cotton production in the southern states increased from 2,000,000 lb in 1790 to 1.9 billion lb in 1860, the bulk of which was exported.[88] Again, southern cotton plantations producing for Atlantic trade depended on African slaves. The regional distribution of African slaves in the United States reflected the dominance of production for Atlantic trade by African Americans before the Civil War. Of the 697,000 African slaves in the United States in 1790, 642,000 were in the south and in 1850 there were 3,117,000 African slaves in the old and new south, working mostly on the cotton plantations.[89]

In the Americas, this large-scale forced specialization of African slaves in the production of commodities for Atlantic commerce provided large markets for a wide range of products and services. The imposition of colonial law enabled producers in Europe to capture much of the markets. But several New World regions, whose natural resource endowments did not favour massive use of slaves for the production of export commodities, still managed to obtain a significant share, legally or illegally. Thus family farmers in the middle colonies of British North America took advantage of the lucrative food markets in the Caribbean slave plantations to move increasingly from subsistence farming to commercial production of foodstuffs for export to the West Indies, British and non-British. The northeastern continental colonies, on the other hand, found in the Caribbean specialization lucrative markets for their natural resource endowments in deep natural harbours and forests full of trees suitable for the building of sailing ships. This encouraged New England to specialize from the colonial period in maritime commerce, shipping and shipbuilding.[90] The Dutch island of Curaçao, with a large concentration of Jewish merchants and unsuitable for large-scale plantation agriculture, also developed a major entrepot trade linking several New World territories. Among other things, it was a distribution centre for North American foodstuffs going to several Caribbean islands.[91]

Growing trade among the American territories and between them and Europe raised incomes and purchasing power in Europe and the Americas over time, and fuelled the further growth of Atlantic commerce. Measuring the annual value of this trade in the two hundred years leading to the emergence of a capitalist economy in Britain in the mid-nineteenth century is a neglected subject. The evidence in some cases is as yet inadequate. But an attempt I made recently to provide a tentative estimate produced the following figures: £20 million per annum in the middle decades of the seventeenth century, £40 million for the middle decades of the eighteenth century, and £110 million per annum for the last decades of the eighteenth century.[92] Using the demographic evidence mentioned earlier in this section of the chapter and the trade statistics, I have also tried to provide a rough measurement of the proportionate contribution of African slaves to the production of the American commodities that formed the basis of Atlantic commerce during the period. The result of the exercise is approximately 75 per cent for the seventeenth and eighteenth centuries.[93]

A major factor explaining the development of capitalism in Britain is the disproportionate share of this volume of Atlantic commerce captured by Britain. In this, the early commercialization of economy and society in England was important. However the importance of this factor can easily be exaggerated. Economies and societies in Holland and Italy were also highly commercialized in the sixteenth and seventeenth centuries. In fact, Jan de Vries holds that "England's agricultural progress in the seventeenth century served mainly to bring her up to the standard already achieved in the Netherlands and Northern Italy, and not to leave them behind in a trail of smoke. Moreover the rural class structure in these areas appears to have been equally favourable to capitalistic farming, if not identical to the English."[94]

It is generally believed that if efficiency in the production of goods and services were all that mattered, Holland rather than Britain would have dominated Atlantic trade in the seventeenth and eighteenth centuries.[95] The truly critical factor was Britain's military superiority. This ensured her domination of the Atlantic and its territories. Added to this was the strategic role of British America in the economic life of the Americas. Through this role incomes in the New World gravitated to consumers in British America, particularly the continental colonies. And the concentrated purchasing power was spent on British manufactures, as colonial laws dictated. The slave trade that supplied the Americas their main labour force was also dominated by Britain in the eighteenth century.[96] Britain exported goods to Spain and Portugal, partly for consumption in those countries and partly for re-export to their American colonies, but all depended largely on incomes generated in the latter. In all sorts of ways, Britain also exported manufactures directly to

Portuguese and Spanish America in the eighteenth century, and still more so in the nineteenth.

While this domination of Atlantic commerce was important for all sectors of the British economy, it was even more important for sectors that were central to the industrialization process: textiles, metallurgy and financial institutions. As was mentioned earlier, the surge of industrial production in England from the late seventeenth and early eighteenth centuries was the product of import substitution, which gave rise to a host of new industries.[97] The most important of these were linens, cottons, silk and several metal-using industries. The expansion of these new industries was responsible for the growth of manufacturing employment in England from 1700 to 1850. They also spearheaded the growth of the factory system and industrial technology.

Atlantic commerce was central to the process leading to the establishment of these industries and to their subsequent development. The domestic market for their products developed in association with the growth of English overseas trade from 1660 to 1700, during which period these products were imported from European countries, mainly Holland and Germany, and from Asia. Bullion from the Americas paid for the Asian imports, while the re-export of produce from British America largely paid for the imports from Europe.[98] Ralph Davis is right in his statement that the growth of English overseas trade in the seventeenth century stimulated a rapid growth of capital investment in commerce not matched by industrial investment.[99] But it was during this period that British merchants trading overseas helped to create, on the basis of commodity production in the Americas, the incomes and markets that gave rise to the import replacement industries of the late seventeenth and early eighteenth centuries. The initial narrowness of the English domestic market made overseas purchases crucial to the sustained development of these industries very early in their history. As Davis wrote in the late 1960s,

> The expansion of the American market for iron- and brass-ware was on so great a scale that it must have contributed very significantly to the eighteenth-century development of those industries in England, and so to the process of rationalization, of division of labour, of search for new machines and new methods which helped so much towards the Industrial Revolution.[100]

As for textiles, West Africa was the main overseas market before the last two decades of the eighteenth century. Payment for slaves purchased by British traders absorbed between 30 per cent and 58 per cent of the total export of English cotton textiles from 1750 to 1776.[101] I have shown elsewhere that competition with East Indian cotton textiles on the West African coast was a major factor explaining early technological innovation in the English cotton textile industry.[102] In the linen trade, the Caribbean islands were the main export markets in the late eighteenth century. To illustrate, the total value of English linen textiles exported to all parts of the world in the five-year period 1783–87, was approximately £2.7 million (£2,693,688), out of which approximately £1.7 million (£1,666,905), went to the British Caribbean, being 62 per cent of the total.[103] The trade figures for 1700–70 show that the British Caribbean and continental colonies absorbed 81.6 per cent of all English linen textiles sold overseas during that period.[104] And linen textiles were the fourth largest industry in England by 1770, falling behind only woollen textiles, leather and building.[105] The evidence thus suggests that colonial laws made the American colonies captive markets for British import substitution industries from their early establishment.

Even a summary account of the contribution of Atlantic commerce to the expansion of industrial employment in England during the period under consideration, such as we have attempted, cannot fail to mention the shipbuilding industry that was strongly linked to the shipping of slaves and slave-produced commodities. The building of new ships, repairing old ones, and the fitting of both for each ocean voyage were a major business in England in the eighteenth century. In the twenty-one years from 1787 to 1807, a total of 12,147 new vessels, measuring altogether about 1.4 million tons (1,394,938 tons) were built in England.[106] If we take the median cost of £12 per ton of new ships in the late eighteenth and early nineteenth centuries,[107] we get £16.7 million (£16,739,256) as the total value of the new ships built in England in these twenty-one years. Adding the high cost of fitting and repairs, particularly high for ships sailing and anchoring in tropical waters for months, it is reasonable to say that the shipyards in England contributed a large proportion of the value added in the building industry at this time, estimated at £9.3 million in 1801.[108]

Finally, as already hinted, Atlantic commerce was a capital-intensive business, by the standard of the time. The purchase of slaves in Africa, shipping them to the Americas, the production of tropical and semitropical commodities in the Americas, the cost of distributing them all over the Atlantic and Europe, and the costly wars through which Britain wrested the bulk of Atlantic commerce from other nations, all these regularly called for extensive capital outlays that were several times greater than British trade at home and with Europe ever required. I have tried elsewhere to show the details of this all-important aspect of capitalist development in Britain.[109] For the present purpose, suffice it to say that the growing market for credit instruments, to which the development in question gave rise, produced pressures and opportunities that provided the impetus for the evolution of financial institutions, without which there could be no capitalism in Britain.

V

To conclude, let me stress once again that Britain's disproportionate share of Atlantic commerce between 1660 and 1850 is the main factor which explains why the first capitalist economy in the world emerged in that country in the nineteenth century. The social structures that evolved in Britain from the late medieval period to the seventeenth century made important contributions, but on their own they could not ensure the development of capitalism, as the history of Italy and Holland in the seventeenth and eighteenth centuries makes clear. The emergence of a capitalist economy, as here defined, from the precapitalist socioeconomic formations that existed across the globe before the nineteenth century required an extensive trading area within which intensive exchange of goods and services would take place on a regular basis. The initial high cost of inland transportation ruled out extensive land areas as candidates for the development of such an intensive trading zone. The rise of nation-states in western Europe from the fifteenth century, and the rivalry and balance of power that developed, limited further the possibility of such an intensive trading area ever developing within western Europe unaided by economic forces outside the region. Choked by economic nationalism, expressed in a multiplicity of restrictive tariffs, the economies of western Europe found the needed opportunity in the growth of Atlantic commerce founded upon African slave labour from the sixteenth century. But as Wallerstein has argued, the production and trading opportunities offered by the Atlantic system were not great enough to permit the development of more than one capitalist economy during the period in question; hence the cut-throat military struggle among western European nations over the opportunities.[110] In the end Britain won, cornered a lion's share of the opportunities, and developed its industries and financial institutions to launch the first capitalist economy in the world, thanks to African slaves whose forced specialization in the production of commodities for Atlantic commerce was the foundation of the Atlantic system.

Acknowledgements

The chapter benefited from helpful comments by Karen E. Fields. Stanley L. Engerman also read the first draft. To these wonderful colleagues I express my gratitude. Of course, whatever errors of fact and analysis there may be are entirely mine. I also thank Lela Sims-Gissendanner and Charlette W. Henry of the Frederick Douglass Institute for the typing.

Notes

1. Eric Williams, *Capitalism and Slavery* (Chapel Hill: University of North Carolina Press, 1944), v.
2. The best-known critics of Williams on the politics of abolition are Roger T. Anstey, *The Atlantic Slave Trade and British Abolition 1760–1810* (London: Macmillan, 1975), and Seymour Drescher, *Econocide: British Slavery in the Era of Abolition* (Pittsburgh: Pittsburgh University Press, 1977).
3. For some recent contributions to the subject see Ronald W. Bailey, "Africa, the Slave Trade, and the Rise of Industrial Capitalism in Europe and the United States: A Historiographic Review", *American History: A Bibliographic Review* II (1986): 1–91. See also J.E. Inikori, "Market Structure and the Profits of the British African Trade in the Late Eighteenth Century", *Journal of Economic History* XLI, no. 4 (1981): 745–76.
4. See the sources discussed by Rodney Hilton, "Capitalism: What's in a Name?", in *The Transition from Feudalism to Capitalism,* ed. R. Hilton (London: Verso, 1978), 145.
5. Maurice Dobb, *Studies in the Development of Capitalism* (London: Routledge and Kegan Paul, 1946), 1–32; Hilton, "Capitalism", 145–58; Andre Gunder Frank, *Capitalism and Underdevelopment in Latin America* (New York: Monthly Review Press, 1967); Immanuel Wallerstein, *The Modern World System,* vol. 1, *Capitalist Agriculture and the Origins of the European World Economy in the Sixteenth Century* (New York: Academic Press, 1974); Alan Macfarlane, *The Origins of English Individualism* (Oxford: Basil Blackwell, 1978); and Alan Macfarlane, *The Culture of Capitalism* (Oxford: Basil Blackwell, 1987).
6. See Frank, *Capitalism and Underdevelopment*; Wallerstein, *Modern World System,* 1: 126–27; and Immanuel Wallerstein, *Historical Capitalism* (London: Verso, 1983), 13–43, esp. 19.

7. Ernesto Laclau, "Feudalism and Capitalism in Latin America", *New Left Review* 67 (May–June 1971): 25.

8. Maurice Dobb, *Capitalism: Yesterday and Today* (London: Lawrence and Wishart, 1958), 20.

9. R.S. Neale, "Property, Law, and the Transition from Feudalism to Capitalism", in *Feudalism, Capitalism and Beyond*, ed. E. Kamenka and R.S. Neale (London: Edward Arnold, 1975), 18; Karl Marx, *Wage Labour and Capital* (Moscow: Progress Publishers, 1952), 27–30.

10. Neale, "Property, Law", 19.

11. Ellen Meiksins Wood, *The Pristine Culture of Capitalism: A Historical Essay on Old Regimes and Modern States* (London: Verso, 1991).

12. Robert Brenner, "The Origins of Capitalist Development: A Critique of Neo-Smithian Marxism", *New Left Review* 104 (July–August 1977): 33.

13. R.H. Tawney, Foreword to *The Protestant Ethic and the Spirit of Capitalism*, by Max Weber (New York: Charles Scribner's Sons, 1958), 1(b)–1(c).

14. Weber, *Protestant Ethic*, 17.

15. Ibid., 17–19.

16. Ibid., 21–22.

17. Max Weber, *Economy and Society: An Outline of Interpretive Sociology*, ed. G. Roth and C. Wittich, vol. 2 (Berkeley: University of California Press, 1978), 1394.

18. Weber, *Protestant Ethic*, 23–24.

19. See Macfarlane, *Origins of English Individualism* and Macfarlane, *Culture of Capitalism*.

20. Macfarlane, *Culture of Capitalism*, 226.

21. See various papers in Robert J. Antonio and Ronald M. Glassman, eds., *A Weber-Marx Dialogue* (Lawrence: University Press of Kansas, 1985).

22. Brenner, "Origins of Capitalist Development", 32.

23. John G. Taylor, *From Modernization to Modes of Production: A Critique of the Sociologies of Development and Underdevelopment* (London: Macmillan, 1979), 105–13.

24. See the sources discussed by Hilton, "Capitalism", 146–48.

25. Oliver C. Cox, *The Foundations of Capitalism* (New York: Philosophical Library, 1959), 29.

26. Ibid., 241–44.

27. Maureen F. Mazzaoui, "The Cotton Industry of Northern Italy in the late Middle Ages: 1150–1450", *Journal of Economic History* 32 (1972): 278.

28. See the various papers in Frederick Krantz and Paul M. Hohenberg, eds., *Failed Transitions to Modern Industrial Society: Renaissance Italy and Seventeenth Century Holland* (Montreal: Interuniversity Centre for European Studies, 1975).

29. This is the basis for the recent controversy on the historical origin of the contemporary problems of the British economy, centred on the nature of its development of capitalism. Some argue that, being the first capitalist economy, its development of capitalism was incomplete, and the remnants of precapitalist elements are responsible for its poor performance in contemporary times relative to economies that developed capitalism later. The opposite is also argued, that because Britain was the first capitalist nation, it developed capitalism to an extreme level relative to later capitalist nations, thereby weakening the non-capitalist elements (such as long-term focused government intervention) which enable the later comers to more effectively control the exclusively short-term considerations that characterize pure capitalism. See the stimulating discussion of these issues by Wood, *Pristine Culture.*

30. Immanuel Wallerstein, "Failed Transitions or Inevitable Decline of the Leader? The Workings of the Capitalist World-Economy: General Comments", in *Failed Transitions to Modern Industrial Society: Renaissance Italy and Seventeenth Century Holland,* ed. F. Krantz and P.M. Hohenberg (Montreal: Interuniversity Centre for European Studies, 1975), 79–80.

31. See the debate provoked by Maurice Dobb's *Studies in the Development of Capitalism* (London: Routledge and Kegan Paul, 1946) in Hilton, *Transition from Feudalism to Capitalism.*

32. Eric J. Hobsbawm, "From Feudalism to Capitalism", in *The Transition from Feudalism to Capitalism,* ed. R. Hilton (London: Verso, 1978), 160.

33. Levine believes that this is a generous estimate, because "it is unlikely that all or even the majority of those adult males assessed on wages were lifelong proletarians". See David Levine, "Production, Reproduction, and the Proletarian Family in England, 1500–1851", in *Proletarianization and Family History,* ed. D. Levine (Orlando: Academic Press, 1984), 88.

34. Levine, "Production", 112.

35. J.H. Clapham, "The Growth of an Agrarian Proletariat, 1688–1832: A Statistical Note", *Cambridge Historical Journal* I (1923): 95.

36. Peter H. Lindert, "English Occupations, 1670–1811", *Journal of Economic History* 40 (1980): 685–712; Peter H. Lindert and J.G. Williamson, "Revising England's Social Tables, 1688–1812", *Explorations in Economic History* 19 (1982): 385–408.

37. G.E. Mingay, *Enclosure and the Small Farmer in the Age of the Industrial Revolution* (London: Macmillan, 1968), 29.

38. As late as 1831 there were still numerous self-employed producers in British agriculture. The census of that year shows that out of a total of 961,100 families employed in agriculture, 275,100 were self-employed and 686,000 were wage-earning families. See Clapham, "Growth of an Agrarian Proletariat", 93; also Levine, "Production", 112.

39. Some of the most recent include: N.F.R. Crafts, *British Economic Growth during the Industrial Revolution* (Oxford: Clarendon Press, 1985); the various papers in Joel Mokyr, ed., *The Economics of the Industrial Revolution* (Totowa, NJ: Rowman and Allanhead, 1985); and François Crouzet, *The First Industrialists: The Problem of Origins* (Cambridge: Cambridge University Press, 1985). See also the literature summarized by David Levine in "Industrialization and the Proletarian Family in England", *Past and Present,* no. 107 (May 1985): 171–81.

40. Levine, "Industrialization", 177; C.K. Harley, "British Industrialization Before 1841: Evidence of Slower Growth During the Industrial Revolution", *Journal of Economic History* XLII (1982): 268.

41. See Inikori, "Slavery and the Development of Industrial Capitalism in England", *Journal of Interdisciplinary History* XVII, no. 4 (1987): 771–93.

42. Public Record Office (PRO), London, Chancery Masters Exhibits, C.103/132, Robert Hewer to Thomas Hall, Plymouth, 3 June 1743.

43. See A.E. Musson and E. Robinson, *Science and Technology in the Industrial Revolution* (Manchester: Manchester University Press, 1969); A.E. Musson, ed., *Science, Technology and Economic Growth in the Eighteenth Century* (London: Methuen, 1972); A. Rupert Hall, "What Did the Industrial Revolution in Britain Owe to Science?", in *Historical Perspectives: Studies in English Thought and Society in Honour of J.H. Plumb,* ed. N. McKendrick (London: Europa, 1974), 129–51.

44. Phyllis Deane and W.A. Cole, *British Economic Growth, 1688–1959: Trends and Structure* (Cambridge: Cambridge University Press, 1962), 40–97; A.H. John, "Agricultural Productivity and Economic Growth in England", in *Agriculture and Economic Growth in England 1650–1815,* ed. E.L. Jones (London: Methuen, 1967), 172–93; D.E.C. Eversley, "The Home Market and Economic Growth in England, 1750–1780", in *Land, Labour and Population in the Industrial Revolution,* ed. E.L. Jones and G.E. Mingay (London: Edward Arnold, 1967), 206–59; E.L. Jones, "Agricultural Origins of Industry", *Past and Present,* no. 40 (July 1968): 58–71.

45. Ralph Davis, "English Foreign Trade, 1700–1774", in *The Growth of English Overseas Trade in the Seventeenth and Eighteenth Centuries,* ed. W.E. Minchinton (London: Methuen, 1969), 99–120; Donald Whitehead, "History to Scale? The British Economy in the Eighteenth Century", *Business Archives and History* IV, no. 1 (1964): 72–83; Eric J. Hobsbawm, "The General Crisis of the European Economy in the Seventeenth Century", parts 1 and 2, *Past and Present,* no. 5 (1954): 33–53; no. 6 (1954): 44–65; Eric Hobsbawm, *Industry and Empire* (London: Pelican, 1969).

46. Patrick K. O'Brien, "European Economic Development: The Contribution of the Periphery", *Economic History Review,* 2d ser., XXXV, no. 1 (1982): 1–18;

Wallerstein, *The Modern World System,* vol. 1, and *The Modern World System,* vol. 2, *Mercantilism and the Consolidation of the European World-Economy, 1600–1750* (New York: Academic Press, 1980), and *The Modern World System,* vol. 3, *The Second Era of Great Expansion of the Capitalist World-Economy, 1734–1840s* (New York: Academic Press, 1989); Bailey, "Africa"; Inikori, "Slavery and the Development of Industrial Capitalism"; Joseph Inikori, "Slavery and the Revolution in Cotton Textile Production in England", *Social Science History* 13, no. 4 (1989): 343–79, and "The Credit Needs of the African Trade and the Development of the Credit Economy in England", *Explorations in Economic History* 27 (1990): 197–231; Ronald Findlay, "The 'Triangular Trade' and the Atlantic Economy of the Eighteenth Century: A Simple General Equilibrium Model", *Essays in International Finance,* no. 177 (Princeton: Department of Economics, Princeton University, 1990); William Darity, Jr, "British Industry and the West Indies Plantations", *Social Science History* 14, no. 1 (1990): 117–49; Patrick K. O'Brien and Stanley L. Engerman, "Exports and the Growth of the British Economy from the Glorious Revolution to the Peace of Amiens", in *Slavery and the Rise of the Atlantic System,* ed. B.L. Solow (Cambridge: Cambridge University Press, 1991), 177–209.

47. Joel Mokyr, "Demand vs. Supply in the Industrial Revolution", in *The Economics of the Industrial Revolution,* ed. J. Mokyr (Totowa, NJ: Rowman and Allanhead, 1985), 97–118.

48. Ibid., 101.

49. Ibid., 109.

50. D.S. Chapman, "Financial Restraints on the Growth of Firms in the Cotton Industry, 1790–1850", *Economic History Review,* 2d ser., 32 (1979): 50–69; Harley, "British Industrialization", 267–89; N.F.R. Crafts, "British Economic Growth, 1700–1831: A Review of the Evidence", *Economic History Review,* 2d ser., 36, no. 2 (1983), 177–99; Crafts, *British Economic Growth.*

51. Levine, "Industrialization", 172.

52. Mokyr, "Demand vs. Supply", 107–9.

53. Levine, "Industrialization", 175–76.

54. Mingay, *Enclosure and the Small Farmer,* 27–29.

55. David Levine, *Family Formation in an Age of Nascent Capitalism* (New York: Academic Press, 1977); E.A. Wrigley and R.S. Schofield, *The Population History of England, 1541–1871: A Reconstruction* (Cambridge: Harvard University Press, 1981); E.A. Wrigley, "The Growth of Population in Eighteenth-Century England: A Conundrum Resolved", *Past and Present,* no. 98 (1983): 121–50; Levine, "Production", 87–127; Levine, "Industrialization", 168–203.

56. Levine, "Production", 109 and 114; Levine, "Industrialization", 170 and 171.

57. Levine, "Production", 104–15.

58. Deane and Cole, *British Economic Growth,* 40–97.

59. Whitehead, "History to Scale?", 72–83; Joseph Inikori, "International Trade and the Eighteenth-Century Industrialization Process in England: An Essay in Criticism" (paper presented at the Institute of Historical Research seminar, University of London, 7 February 1975); T.J. Hatton, John S. Lyons and S.E. Satchell, "Eighteenth-Century British Trade: Homespun or Empire Made?", *Explorations in Economic History* 20 (1983): 163–82.

60. Inikori, "Slavery and the Development of Industrial Capitalism", 176–77, and "Slavery and the Revolution", 343–79. Also see David Ormrod, "Dutch Commercial and Industrial Decline and British Growth in the Late Seventeenth and Early Eighteenth Centuries", in *Failed Transitions to Modern Industrial Society: Renaissance Italy and Seventeenth Century Holland,* ed. F. Krantz and P.M. Hohenberg (Montreal: Interuniversity Centre for European Studies, 1975), 40–43.

61. This process has been studied in detail only for the cotton textile industry. For this, see Joseph E. Inikori, "Slavery and the Revolution", 343–79.

62. Crafts, *British Economic Growth,* 138–39.

63. Crafts, "British Economic Growth, 1700–1831", 199.

64. O'Brien, "European Economic Development", 1–18.

65. Ibid., 3.

66. Ibid., 18.

67. William Darity, Jr, "A Model of 'Original Sin': Rise of the West and Lag of the Rest", *American Economic Review* 82, no. 2 (May 1992): 162–67; O'Brien and Engerman, 177–209.

68. O'Brien and Engerman, "Exports and the Growth of the British Economy", 193.

69. Ibid., 208.

70. Inikori, "Slavery and the Development of Industrial Capitalism", 788–89.

71. James Lockhart and Stuart B. Schwartz, *Early Latin America: A History of Colonial Spanish America and Brazil* (Cambridge: Cambridge University Press, 1983), 376; H.E.S. Fisher, *The Portugal Trade: A Study of Anglo-Portuguese Commerce, 1700–1770* (London: Methuen, 1971), 142–43.

72. Robert Brenner, "Agrarian Class Structure and Economic Development in Pre-Industrial Europe", *Past and Present,* no. 70 (1976): 31–75; Robert Brenner, "The Agrarian Roots of European Capitalism", *Past and Present,* no. 97 (1982): 16–113; and Brenner, "Origins of Capitalist Development", 25–92.

73. Deane and Cole, *British Economic Growth,* 40–97.

74. J.W. Smit, "Holland: Commentary", in *Failed Transitions to Modern Industrial Society: Renaissance Italy and Seventeenth Century Holland,* ed. F. Krantz and P.M. Hohenberg (Montreal: Interuniversity Centre for European Studies, 1975), 61–63.

75. Robert Brenner, "England, Eastern Europe, and France: Socio-Historical Versus 'Economic' Interpretation", in *Failed Transitions to Modern Industrial Society: Renaissance Italy and Seventeenth Century Holland,* ed. F. Krantz and P.M. Hohenberg (Montreal: Interuniversity Centre for European Studies, 1975), 68–70.

76. On the subject of class formation and class struggle as a factor in the long-term process of economic development, Douglass North's theoretical formulation of the issues, based on an imaginative combination of neoclassical and Marxian reasoning, provides very useful insights. North does not talk about classes or class struggle, but rather socioeconomic groups and intergroup competition in the process of making and enforcing the rules and regulations under which an economy functions. His use of relative prices and relative price change over time as the central element in his theory makes his formulation amenable to historical analysis and verification. See Douglass C. North, *Institutions, Institutional Change and Economic Performance* (Cambridge: Cambridge University Press, 1990).

77. The restrictions imposed on trade by national and municipal governments in Europe in the sixteenth and seventeenth centuries are extensively examined by Charles Wilson, "Trade, Society and the State", in *Cambridge Economic History of Europe,* vol. 4, *The Economy of Expanding Europe in the Sixteenth and Seventeenth Centuries,* ed. E.E. Rich and C.H. Wilson (Cambridge: Cambridge University Press, 1967), 487–575. See also Ralph Davis, "The Rise of Protection in England, 1689–1789", *Economic History Review* XIX, no. 2 (August 1966): 306–17.

78. Enriqueta Vilar Vila, "The Large-Scale Introduction of Africans into Veracruz and Cartagena", in *Comparative Perspectives on Slavery in New World Plantation Societies,* ed. V. Rubin and A. Tuden (New York: New York Academy of Sciences, 1977), 267–80; Louisa Schell Hoberman, *Mexico's Merchant Elite, 1590–1660* (Durham: Duke University Press, 1991), 6–32.

79. Joseph Inikori, "Slavery and Atlantic Commerce, 1650–1800", *American Economic Review* 82, no. 2 (1992): 154.

80. Pierre Verger, *Trade Relations between the Bight of Benin and Bahia from the Seventeenth to Nineteenth Century* (Ibadan: Ibadan University Press, 1976), 141.

81. Thomas W. Merrick and Douglass H. Graham, *Population and Economic Development in Brazil* (London: Macmillan, 1979), 29.

82. Computed from Richard S. Dunn, *Sugar and Slaves: The Rise of the Planter Class in the English West Indies, 1624–1713* (Chapel Hill: University of North Carolina Press, 1972), 312.

83. PRO, London, Colonial Office (CO) 318/2, folio 19.

84. Richard Sheridan, *The Development of the Plantations to 1750: An Era of West Indian Prosperity 1750–1775* (Bridgetown, Barbados: Caribbean Universities Press, 1970), 35, 49.

85. Eric Williams, *From Columbus to Castro: The History of the Caribbean, 1492–1969* (London: André Deutsch, 1970), 153.

86. PRO, London, CO 318/2, folios 290–91, J. Dobson to Mr J. Stevens, 7 February 1807.

87. James F. Shepherd and Gary M. Walton, "Estimates of 'Invisible' Earnings in the Balance of Payments in the British North American Colonies, 1768–1772", *Journal of Economic History* XXIX, no. 2 (1969): 258.

88. Harold U. Faulkner, *American Economic History*, 8th ed. (New York: Harper and Brothers, 1960), 201–2.

89. J. Potter, "The Growth of Population in America, 1700–1800", in *Population in History: Essays in Historical Demography*, ed. D.V. Glass and D.E.C. Eversley (London: Edward Arnold, 1965), 641, 680.

90. Douglass North, *The Economic Growth of the United States, 1790–1860* (Englewood Cliffs: Prentice Hall, 1961); James F. Shepherd and Gary M. Walton, *Shipping, Maritime Trade, and the Economic Development of Colonial North America* (Cambridge: Cambridge University Press, 1972); Bailey, "Africa", 1–91.

91. Some account of this trade is given in the Colonial Office Papers, CO 388/12 Part II/K.66, Memorial from Mr Holt relating to the illegal trade carried on between Curaçao, St Thomas, and the British Plantations, Received 15 December 1709, Read 11 January 1710.

92. Inikori, "Slavery and Atlantic Commerce", 152.

93. Ibid., 152–55.

94. Jan de Vries, "Holland: Commentary", in *Failed Transitions to Modern Industrial Society: Renaissance Italy and Seventeenth Century Holland*, ed. F. Krantz and P.M. Hohenberg (Montreal: Interuniversity Centre for European Studies, 1975), 82.

95. For a stimulating comparative discussion of the subject, see the papers and comments in Krantz and Hohenberg. For a more recent detailed study see Jonathan I. Israel, *Dutch Primacy in World Trade, 1585–1740* (Oxford: Clarendon Press, 1989).

96. Joseph Inikori, "The Volume of the British Slave Trade, 1655–1807", *Cahiers D'Etudes Africaines* XXXII, no. 4 (1992): 643–88.

97. The sources are consistently clear on the timing of this import-replacing industrialization. Some illustration will do. In 1799 Thomas Williams, a member of the British House of Commons and a manufacturer of brass products, informed Parliament that copper ore was first discovered in Britain in the latter end of the seventeenth century, and the first brasswork in England

was erected near Bristol in 1702. He noted that in the first three decades of
the eighteenth century, most copper and brass products used in England were
imported from Germany and Holland, and stressed: "even brass pans for the
purposes of the dairies of our country could not be procured but of the
German make. So late as 1745, 1746, and 1750, copper tea kettles, saucepans,
and pots of all sizes, were imported here in large quantities from Hamburgh
and Holland; but through the persevering industry, capitals, and enterprising
spirit of our miners and manufacturers, those imports became totally
unnecessary, being all made here, and far better than any other country could
produce" (British Library, *House of Commons Reports* X [1785–1801], Report
on Copper Mines and Copper Trade, 7 May 1799, 666).

Earlier, in 1751, Samuel Touchet, a manufacturer of linen textiles in
Manchester, told a House of Commons committee that "forty years ago the
Dutch supplied our home consumption (of linen textiles), and none of the
English manufacture was exported till about 25 years since" (British Library,
House of Commons Reports II [1738–1765], Report from the Committee
Relating to Cheques and Striped Linens, 26 April 1751, Evidence of Samuel
Touchet, Merchant, 290). The cotton textile industry and several other
metal-using industries were either established or began to expand and develop
at about the same time, because the British government imposed rising tariffs
on imported European manufactures to encourage their domestic production
(Davis, "The Rise of Protection").

98. Ralph Davis, "English Foreign Trade, 1660–1700", in *The Growth of English
      Overseas Trade in the Seventeenth and Eighteenth Centuries*, ed. W.E.
      Minchinton (London: Methuen, 1969), 78–98.
99. Ibid., 93–94.
100. Ralph Davis, *A Commercial Revolution, English Overseas Trade in the
      Seventeenth and Eighteenth Centuries* (London: The Historical Association,
      1967), 20.
101. Inikori, "Slavery and the Revolution", 371–72. It should be noted that Crafts
      wrongly assigned to British America cotton textile exports to West Africa in
      1699–1701 and 1772–74 (Crafts, *British Economic Growth*, 145). The error is
      due to Crafts's misreading of Davis's table in which "North America, British
      and foreign West Indies and Spanish America, West Africa" are grouped
      together under "America". (See Davis, "English Foreign Trade", 117–18,
      120.) Crafts incorrectly grouped West Africa with "Near East, Asia, Australia,
      Latin America" and by so doing assigned to British America cotton exports to
      West Africa in the two periods, 1699–1701 and 1772–74.
102. Inikori, "Slavery and the Revolution", 358–66.
103. Exports to all parts are computed from Elizabeth Boody Schumpeter, *English
      Overseas Trade Statistics, 1697–1808* (Oxford: Clarendon Press, 1960), 32.

Exports to the British West Indies are from House of Lords Record Office, *Parliamentary Papers, Volume 84 of the General Collection, Accounts and Papers,* vol. XXVI, no. 646a, part IV (1789): Account of the quantity and value of British Manufactures exported to the British West Indies, 1783, 1784, 1785, 1786 and 1787.

104. Computed from Schumpeter, *English Overseas Trade Statistics,* 66.

105. Crafts, *British Economic Growth,* 22.

106. Joseph Inikori, "English Trade to Guinea: A Study in the Impact of Foreign Trade on the English Economy, 1750–1807" (PhD thesis, University of Ibadan, 1973), 270.

107. R. Craig, "Capital Formation in Shipping", in *Aspects of Capital Investment in Great Britain 1750–1850: A Preliminary Survey,* ed. J.P.P. Higgins and S. Pollard (London: Methuen, 1971), 143.

108. Crafts, *British Economic Growth,* 22.

109. Inikori, "Credit Needs of the African Trade", 197–231.

110. Wallerstein, "Failed Transitions or Inevitable Decline", 75–80.

CHAPTER 2

Africa in the Making of the Caribbean
The Formative Years

COLIN A. PALMER

This chapter addresses the ways in which the peoples of Africa and their progeny shaped the cultural trajectory of the Caribbean during the sixteenth and seventeenth centuries. It suggests that Africans played a central role in defining the texture of the societies in which they served primarily as slaves. Until recent times, the study of Africa did not form a part of the educational curriculum at any level in the Caribbean. In fact, even those who taught the history of the Caribbean at the University of the West Indies seldom mentioned Africa at all. These courses usually began with accounts of the arrival of Europeans, and the indigenous peoples of the hemisphere were also largely absent from the story. Any discussion of the African peoples started with their arrival in the Caribbean; we saw them as peoples without a past and as hardly anything else.

Much of this, to be sure, has changed. African history is now receiving some attention and the image of that continent and of its children has been altered, at least to some extent. This development has been the consequence of the accentuation of a racial consciousness in the diaspora and of changes on the African continent as well. So today we can recognize Africa's defining role in the history of the Caribbean and not look over our shoulders as we do so.

Still, it needs to be said that many contemporary scholars who seek to interpret the history of blacks in the Americas are embarrassingly ignorant of African history and of the peoples and cultures of the societies that comprise the continent. The conceptual paradigms that are used are often borrowed from Western societies and distort much more than they reveal about African realities. It is unthinkable that a scholar who wants to write a history of the Spaniards in sixteenth-century Mexico or Hispaniola would begin such a study without a thorough grounding in the history and culture of the Iberian peoples. The majority of scholars of the black past in the Americas, on the other hand, are distinguished by their ignorance of Africa and its history. This tells us a great deal about the lens through which we view African peoples, as much as it reflects our own cultural assumptions.

I focus on the formative period of the African presence in the Caribbean, roughly from 1502 to1700, because I think that these early years have been neglected by historians. The eighteenth and nineteenth centuries have attracted more scholarly attention, and much of what we think we know about the black past under slavery is based upon the records of the last one hundred years of the institution's existence in much of the Caribbean. The picture that is presented is often one of cultural stasis. There are good reasons for this emphasis on the latter years, to be sure. The documentation is richer and more accessible and less characterized by the silences of the earlier period.

There is some disagreement among scholars over the date when African peoples first arrived in this hemisphere. A few persons have suggested that they preceded the Europeans but the documentation is not entirely persuasive.[1] We can maintain more confidently that Africans first arrived in 1502 as unfree persons to contribute their sweat, genes and culture to the construction of the Caribbean. These persons were coerced into making the journey as the human property of the Spaniards. It is not entirely clear whether they had been born in Africa or in Spain. African slavery had existed in Spain for many years before Columbus made his momentous voyages to this part of the world.

The ever-expanding trade in African slaves to the Americas did not end until the mid-nineteenth century, although several countries terminated it much earlier. The plantation, mining and pastoral economies of the region fed the demand for African workers, and a developing racist ideology legitimized their enslavement. The broad contours of this traffic in African slaves to the Caribbean are well known. Of the roughly twelve million Africans who disembarked in this hemisphere between 1502 and 1870, about 3 per cent arrived before 1600 and 15 per cent between 1601 and 1700. Taken together, the Caribbean societies received between 450,000 and 500,000 African slaves in the two hundred years following the introduction of black slavery in Hispaniola. These figures are estimates and should be used with caution. The Spanish Caribbean societies received about 50,000 Africans during those years, the French possessions about 130,000, and the British territories about 270,000. Barbados, for example, imported about 123,000 Africans between 1640 and 1697, Jamaica about 88,000 between 1655 and 1702, and St Domingue 204,000 between 1681 and 1738.[2]

These human cargoes hailed from a variety of ethnic groups in West and West Central Africa. West Africa was the principal source in the sixteenth century but by the seventeenth century, West Central Africa (Angola and the Congo) became increasingly important. From West Africa came the Wolof, Serer, Akan, Bram, Fon and Biafada, among other peoples. West Central Africa provided the Bakongo, the Teke and the Ambundu peoples.

We do not know a great deal about the interior lives of these Africans. The records of the European traders on which we are compelled to rely are largely silent on such matters, and the few surviving descriptions are filtered through a Eurocentric lens. The English traders, particularly those who were in the employ of the Royal African Company and the South Sea Company, have left us the most detailed comments on the cultures of the Africans with whom they came in contact. These observations, frequently ill informed, helped shape the image of blacks in Europe and the Americas. Writing in 1697, a trader in the employ of the Royal African Company reported that "Africans are a people so treacherous and barbarous that no treaties of peace will oblige them and they watch all opportunities to kill and steal."[3] Another trader observed in 1708 that Africans "are illiterate people and have not (nor are govern'd by) any religion, lawes or courts of justice, or any civiliz'd rules of discipline".[4] Two years later, Sir Dalby Thomas, the company's chief agent in Africa, told his superiors that

> The natives here have neither religion nor law binding them to humanity, good behaviour or honesty. They frequently for their grandeur sacrifice an innocent man, that is, a person they have no crime to charge with; and to train their children up to cruelty they give them knives to cut and slash the person that is to be killed,

neither have they any knowledge of liberty and property. . . . Besides the blacks are naturally such rogues and bred up with such roguish principles that what they can get by force or deceit and can defend themselves from those they robb, they reckon it as honestly their own, as if they paid for it.[5]

Dalby Thomas's assessment was shared by Dr James Houstoun who was the company's physician on the West African coast. In 1725 Dr Houstoun concluded that "[the African's] natural temper is barbarously cruel, selfish, and deceitful, and their government equally barbarous and uncivil, and consequently, the men of greatest eminency amongst them, are those that are most capable of being the greatest rogues; vice being left without any check on it, becomes a virtue. As for their customs, they exactly resemble their fellow creatures and natives, the monkeys."[6]

Similar assessments of the "character" of the Africans also came from the lower-level employees of the Royal African Company. Agent John Snow believed that blacks "are not so nice. . . . [A] black man forgetts all obligations but the present." John Freeman who was stationed at York Island was convinced that "blacks are not to be trusted", and agent Hereford reported from Cabinda that the natives there were "a barbarous people". John Clarke at Sierra Leone referred contemptuously to the kings and leading traders as "the beasts of Africa". And James Phipps and Robert Bleau expressed the opinion that mendacity was inherently an African trait.[7]

Such characterizations of Africa and Africans by Europeans were neither new nor exceptional. Recent studies have shown that the European imagination constructed a variety of images of Africa from antiquity, but not all of them were negative. It is clear, however, that the positive images were gradually replaced over time by comments that were overwhelmingly pejorative. Scholars still debate when the negative images of Africa became dominant in Europe and, more importantly, the reasons for it.[8]

Historians of the Caribbean must, of course, view these representations of Africa and Africans critically, being careful to avoid the Eurocentric biases of the sources. These scholars must also be deeply immersed in the cultural moorings of the diverse African peoples in order to provide a sensitive reconstruction of their past on their own terms. These European-constructed images often reveal a great deal about the psychic, commercial and political needs of the Europeans at particular moments. When the slave trade was under assault in England during the late eighteenth century, for example, its defenders depicted African societies as governed by the rule of law and possessing very sophisticated political and cultural arrangements. These supporters of the trade contested the arguments that it had morally and socially corrosive effects on the African peoples. It was in their interest to demonstrate that the Africans were equal partners in the human commerce and were not being mistreated by the Europeans. These comments were in stark contrast to the earliest ones that justified the trade on the grounds that Africans were a barbaric people.

The purchasers of slaves in the Caribbean also formed their own images of Africa and Africans, and they were not qualitatively different from those held by the traders in Africa. Pejorative comments aside, these buyers wanted "lusty" young men or those who were called "men boys". Barbadian planters preferred boys of fourteen, fifteen and sixteen years of age and women who were "young and full breasted".[9] In 1701 the Royal African Company informed its agents at Cape Coast Castle that "We are advised from the islands that boys and girls under twelve years old sell very well. . . . Rather than buy any negroes above the age of 30, supply them with healthy boys and girls."[10] Some time later, the Company reported that a cargo of slaves that had arrived in Barbados was unsatisfactory because "a great many of the men and women . . . were old and the women had boarn 3 or 4 children".[11] In time the planters also developed preferences for slaves from particular ethnic groups, using perceptions of docility and industry as the primary criteria.

The slave trade should not be viewed solely as a movement of peoples. Africa, in all of its cultural richness and diversity, came to the Caribbean as well. These forced immigrants brought their languages, cosmology, kinship systems, culinary practices, music, dance and art to help shape and leave an indelible imprint on the host societies. Africans, however, appear in the early records of the Europeans in the Caribbean primarily as problems of public order, and as persons who posed threats to the survival of the societies that held them in thrall. Not until the seventeenth century do the recorded observations by the Europeans, primarily the English and the French, become more frequent. These comments provide glimpses into the worlds of these Africans as they began to help lay the foundations of the modern Caribbean.

Africans were not culturally homogeneous although they shared broad core understandings. Nor did the cultures they brought with them to the Caribbean and elsewhere in the Americas remain unchanged and unaffected by the new environments in which they found themselves. But much remained essentially the same, at least for a while. African belief systems and practices were nothing if not tenacious. Creoles, or locally born slaves, were not only exposed to the cultural influences of the various ethnic groups but to those of the European colonizers as well. Their culture, as it evolved, represented the contributions of different peoples but syncretism did not always occur. Certain core beliefs associated with particular ethnic groups did not blend at all, and remained remarkably resilient. On the other hand, some ethnic differences became blurred over time, producing cultures that both defined and reflected the circumstances of each society. Understandably, the pace at which this occurred varied and depended upon many variables. Those black societies that developed a significant creole population, as Barbados did in the early nineteenth century, seemed to have experienced a much faster tempering of ethnic distinctions than those islands such as St Domingue that failed to experience an annual rate of natural increase over a much more sustained period of time.

The black populations everywhere were predominantly African born before the nineteenth century. Africans may have comprised more than 80 per cent of the population in the formative years, a function of gender imbalance, low reproductive rates, and high infant mortality in the Caribbean. The resulting dependence on African societies to meet the labour needs of the developing plantation economies meant that the African-derived cultures of the Caribbean would be constantly nourished and rejuvenated.

As one of their first priorities, the African captives faced the difficult challenge of recreating their kin groups everywhere in the Caribbean. Kinship, in the words of two recent scholars, constituted "both the idiom and the metaphor for social and political relations" among the African ethnic groups.[12] Individuals existed as integral parts of a kin group and to be kinless was to be socially dead. Uprooted from their kin groups and transported to the Caribbean, the Africans lost their sense of place within their own group; they were now on their own in strange lands and denied the ritual protection and comfort that only membership in a kin group could provide.

Slaves developed enduring bonds with those persons who crossed the Atlantic with them. But these bonds among shipmates, as emotionally sustaining as they undoubtedly were, were qualitatively different from those that derived from membership in a kin group. The ties forged among shipmates were symbolic, those that flowed from the kin group were at the core of a people's identity and their sense of belonging.

There is some evidence to suggest that the Africans had some success recreating kin groups in the societies of the Caribbean, as they did elsewhere in the Americas. Methodologically, we must be very careful about the ways in which we interpret these developments. In the first place, Africans in general did not create nuclear families in the fashion of the European Christians. Many if not most societies practised polygyny. Consequently we cannot and should not apply Western and Christian conceptualizations to Africans whose family arrangements and *Zeitgeist* were fundamentally different from those who kept them as property. Africans who were Christianized and their progeny would, of course, adopt family patterns similar to those of the whites, but this was not always the case. It is likely that where demographic circumstances permitted, the African-born peoples celebrated their unions and constructed their families according to their own customs.

Given the powerful ethnic pulls in African societies, it is hardly surprising that the slaves sought partners from their own ethnic groups. This pattern has been established for Africans in Mexico during the sixteenth and seventeenth centuries. The same pattern existed in the French possessions in the Caribbean and most likely in the other societies as well.[13] Census data and plantation records from Guadeloupe and French Guiana during the latter part of the seventeenth century show that most slaves lived in what we would call family units, and these may have been constituted along familiar ethnic patterns. Data from the French islands and from Suriname in the seventeenth century indicate that even in the face of unbalanced sex ratios and high infant mortality rates, a creole population slowly emerged.[14] In general, however, slave populations found it difficult to reproduce themselves, further complicating the process of developing and nurturing kinship ties.

The most obvious and seemingly exotic manifestations of the Africans' cultural presence, namely their music, dance and religious practices are captured in the fragmentary descriptions left to us by the European writers. Hailing from societies where music and dance constituted integral parts of their sacred world, it is not surprising that the African peoples recreated such practices in their new environments and were sustained by them. The French monk Jean-Baptiste Du Tertre was struck in the 1640s and 1650s by the musical instruments of the Africans as well as by their dances. He observed drums constructed from the hollow trunks of trees and covered with the skins of animals. Du Tertre also saw Africans playing the calabash. The Frenchman did not understand the deeper cultural meanings of the dances, their rhythm and movements. But he was astonished by the physical energy of the dancers, and their seeming tirelessness.[15]

The most extended description of the music and dance of these Africans in the early years was left by Richard Ligon, an Englishman who wrote in 1653:

> On Sunday they rest, and have the whole day at their pleasure. . . . In the afternoons on Sundayes, they have their musick, which is of kettle-drums, and those of severall sises; upon the smallest the best musitian playes, and the others come in as Chorasses: the drum all men know, has but one tone; and therefore varietiy of tunes have little to doe in this musick; and yet so strangely they varie their time, as 'tis a pleasure to the most curious ears, and it was to me one of the strangest noises that ever I heard made of one tone; and if they had the varietiy of tune, which gives the greater scope in Musick, as they have of time, they would do wonders in that Art. . . .
>
> On Sundayes in the afternoon, their Musick playes, and to dancing they go, the men by themselves, and the women by themselves, no mixt dancing . . . their hands having more of motion than their feet, and their heads more than their hands. They may dance a whole day, and ne'r heat themselves; yet, now and then, one of the activest amongst them will leap bolt upright, and fall in his place again, but without cutting a capre. When they have danc'd an hour or two, the men fall to wrestle, (the Musick playing all the while) . . . the women leave off their dancing, and come to be spectators of the sport.[16]

Two years later Sir Hans Sloane reported that in Jamaica:

> The Negroes . . . will at nights, or on Feast days Dance and Sing. . . . They have several sorts of Instruments in imitation of Lutes, made of small Gourds fitted with Necks, strung with Horse hairs, or the peeled stalks of climbing Plants or Withs. These Instruments are sometimes made of hollow'd Timber covered with Parchment or other Skin wetted, having a Bow for its Neck, the Strings ty'd longer or shorter, as they would alter their Sounds. . . . They have likewise in their Dances Rattles ty'd to their Hands, with which they make a noise, keeping time with one who makes a sound answering it on the mouth of an empty Gourd or Jar with his Hand. Their Dances consist in great activity and strength of Body, and keeping time, if it can be . . .[17]

It is noteworthy that these dances occurred on Sundays, the day when the slaves, at least the field labourers, were relieved of their burdens. Not only was this leisure time, but the Africans were worshipping their gods through dance, just as their Christian owners did in their own fashion. European observers failed to understand the religious meanings of African dance, music and song.

This is not to suggest, of course, that these cultural experiences were devoid of an entertainment or recreational dimension. Rather, students of African cultures emphasize the integrated nature of the cultural moorings and practices of those societies and the impossibility of making distinctions between the religious and the secular. Sterling Stuckey has observed that for African slaves in North America, dance was a form "of spiritual recreation".[18] He also suggests that "The physical act of dance, at times so sacred, perpetuates form, cultural meaning, and one's resolve to endure."[19] Dance, to put it simply, was "a form of worship".[20]

There is one tantalizing observation from an English clergyman who went to Virginia in 1665 that suggests that some Europeans may have understood the religious significance of the dances, even if they deemed them to be "idolatrous". The Reverend Morgan Godwyn, an Englishman, concluded that

> Nothing is more barbarous, and contrary to Christianity, than their . . . Idolatrous Dances, and Revel; in which they usually spend the Sunday. . . .
>
> And here, that I may not be thought too rashly to impute Idolatry to their Dances, my conjecture is raised upon this ground . . . for that they use their Dances as a means to procure Rain: Some of them having been known to beg this Liberty upon the Week Days . . .[21]

Unable, in the main, to understand the deeper cultural meanings of the Africans' musical or praise instruments, the colonial authorities attempted, predictably, to make their use illegal. The drum was perhaps the most feared of these instruments. There seems to have been the general belief in the Americas that drums could be used to foment rebellions and that they were a crucial part of the psychology and practice of warfare in African societies. Sir Hans Sloane reported that in the 1680s African slaves in Jamaica "were allowd the use of Trumpets after their Fashion, and Drums. . . . But making use of these in the wars at home in Africa, it was thought too much inciting them to Rebellion, and so they were prohibited by the customs of the Island."[22] A law passed in St Kitts in 1711 and repeated in 1722 made it illegal for slaves to communicate "at a distance by beating drums or blowing horns".[23] A similar act was passed in Jamaica in 1717. The Barbadian Assembly attempted to punish slave owners for permitting their human property to celebrate their culture. An act of 1699 proclaimed that "Whatsoever Master, &c, shall suffer his Negro or Slave at any time to beat Drums, blow Horns, or use any other loud instruments, or shall not cause his Negro-Houses once a Week to be search'd and if any such things be there found, to be burn't . . . he shall forfeit 40 s. sterling."[24]

These restrictions, to be sure, were not always enforced and they failed of their purpose throughout the Caribbean and in the Americas as a whole. In fact the colonial authorities and the African peoples embraced different understandings of the instruments, the dances and other rituals associated with them. To the Europeans these were instruments and practices that were alien, mysterious and subversive of the social order. For the Africans they were crucial parts of their culture, their epistemology and world views. These beliefs and practices could not be easily exorcized because they went to the core of the Africans' identities and their sense of being. Their survival was more a reflection of the tenacity of these beliefs and less a failure of the effectiveness of the police regulations.

The holistic nature of the African cultures made it impossible to isolate parts of them for destruction. In other words, as Nathan Huggins has characterized it, the culture of each ethnic group constituted a "seamless web", or an organic whole.[25] Its component parts could not be disentangled because each was inextricably bound to the others, the existence of one was dependent on the existence of the others and vice versa. Under the circumstances, it is hardly surprising that African cultures withstood the assaults on them, although they were never static in their content or in their expression.

The religious ideas and practices of the Africans constituted another important arena of contestation in the Caribbean and the Americas as a whole. It is, of course, somewhat erroneous to speak of religious ideas as a distinct category in this context since this betrays a Western conceptual bias. The Africans did not divide their worlds into the religious and the secular as Westerners did. The organic unity of the cultures precluded this kind of artificial distinction. Consequently, any discussion of the religious beliefs and traditions of the Africans as if they existed apart from other ideas represents a distortion. Each society, however, possessed individuals whose responsibility it was to interpret the spirit world, serve as mediators between that world and the people, divine the future and so on. These specialists have been frequently characterized as "priests" in the Western literature, with the attendant Christian connotation. This appellation, however, is very culture bound and does not capture the essence of the functions of these people; it should be used with caution.

The African peoples who came to the Caribbean brought their complex belief systems with them. This did not mean that they all shared in the same cosmological constructs, although there were points at which similar understandings prevailed. Most ethnic groups believed in the existence of a supreme being and lesser gods, embraced the concept of ancestor worship, saw death as the continuation of life in another form, and thought that the disposition of the gods could be influenced by a variety of rituals. Some of the forced African immigrants, particularly those from the kingdom of the Kongo, would have been exposed to Catholicism. The king of the Kongo and his court had been converted to Christianity in the 1490s and the new religion continued to win converts throughout the sixteenth century and later. In addition, a number of the human captives were most likely Muslims, since Islam had begun to win adherents in Africa from the eighth century. We cannot, of course, determine the degree to which each slave cargo consisted of individuals with competing religious visions. Much depended on the sources of these cargoes and the religious configuration of the areas from which they came. It is probably safe to assume, however, that only a small minority were Christians or Muslims and that the greatest number subscribed broadly to the beliefs that characterized traditional Africa.

Africans who survived the Atlantic passage faced the difficult task of re-establishing their cultural and spiritual worlds. Much depended on whether a critical mass of persons was present from the same ethnic group to facilitate the recreation and survival of common beliefs and practices. The African-derived rituals and practices could only be celebrated in a communal context, at special times and places, and initiated by a religious specialist. Such optimum conditions seldom existed in the Caribbean in the early years except on plantations with large African populations. Bereft of the balm of community-centred rituals and observances, many Africans must have suffered a spiritual death, at least until such time as the demographic situation improved or they created new cultural mechanisms to meet their needs.

During the sixteenth century the Spanish Catholics provided their African slaves with religious instruction and baptized them in the Christian faith. We cannot say with any degree of certainty that the Spanish priests executed their functions with energy and enthusiasm. Nor is it possible to determine the degree to which the African peoples embraced the content of the Catholic version of Christianity. It is doubtful, however, that the Catholics achieved much success among the Africans, if by success one means the destruction of

African cosmologies and their replacement by Christianity. John M. Mbiti, an African scholar, has emphasized that conversion to Christianity meant a fundamental change in the African's interior being, his "thought patterns, fears, social relationships, attitudes and philosophical disposition".[26] In effect, conversion represented a shift from one cosmological universe to another. Few Africans probably wanted to change, or succeeded in effecting this transfiguration.

There is scattered evidence to suggest that even those Africans who accepted Christianity did not abandon their other beliefs. In Mexico, for example, the Holy Office of the Inquisition actively persecuted Africans who clung tenaciously to their cultural traditions.[27] Misunderstanding the nature of these beliefs and viewing them through Christian and European lenses, the Inquisitors characterized the Africans as witches and sorcerers. In 1678 a French Jesuit who went to St Kitts claimed to have identified twenty-six "sorcerers" among the African slaves. The Jesuit, Jean Mongin, possibly failed to understand the deeper cultural meanings of the Africans' practices.[28]

In general, however, the European Christians did not demonstrate much interest in the souls of the Africans during the formative years. This, in retrospect, was probably welcomed by the Africans since it allowed them the freedom to worship their gods in their own fashion. Some historians of the black experience in the Caribbean and the Americas as a whole have chastized the Europeans for ignoring the spiritual life of these Africans. This position needs to be revisited. It is based in part on the assumption that what Christianity offered was superior to that which the Africans possessed. This position may well be defensible in theological terms, but it betrays a Western and Christian condescension to the belief systems of the African peoples. The Africans' complex belief systems had served them well, and most of these people probably preferred to be left alone to worship their gods in their traditional manner and in their own seasons. The point that I am emphasizing is that if we write the history of these Africans from their own standpoint and view their realities through their own lens, we must conclude that attempts to alter their world views and cosmologies exacted a psychic price that none of us can even begin to comprehend. Not surprisingly, the Africans clung to their beliefs because they were central to their cultural assumptions and self-definitions. The evidence is not conclusive, but it appears that Christianity won most of its converts among the creoles, that is to say the persons who were born in the Caribbean. These persons, as the children and grandchildren of the Africans, were products of new cultural environments and were, by the nineteenth century, increasingly exposed to Christian proselytizers.

The tenacity of African beliefs is reflected, for example, in burial practices. Funerals were important because the individual's spirit was being sent off to join the ancestors and to connect the living with the dead. They were occasions for celebration, highlighted by sacred music, dance and the offering of gifts to the ancestors. Understandably, Europeans were baffled by these celebrations and by the absence of grief. One Englishman in Barbados thought that the joyful behaviour of the Africans at the funerals meant that they were happy that one of their number had escaped the burdens of slavery. We must grant the possibility that he was partially correct. "These poor beings," he wrote, ". . . have a hell on earth. It appears that they are sensible of this, if one may judge their behavior at their funerals. Instead of weeping and wailing, they dance and sing and appear to be the happiest mortals on earth."[29]

Charles Leslie observed similar behaviour in Jamaica. Writing in 1740, he noted that "When one is carried to his Grave, he is attended with a vast Multitude, who . . . sing all the way. . . . When they come to the Grave . . . the Negroes sacrifice a Hog . . . all the while they are covering it [the body] with Earth, the Attendants scream out in a terrible manner, which is not the Effect of Grief, but of Joy; they beat on their wooden Drums, and the Women with their Rattles make a hideous noise . . .".[30] Richard Ligon also saw slaves "clapping and wringing their hands" at the grave "and making a dolefull sound with their voyces".[31] We are not certain what "dolefull" means in this context, judging by the cultural gulf that separated the Englishman from the Africans. It is conceivable, however, that death elicited ritualized expressions of grief as well as joy.

Scholars of the belief systems of the slaves usually conclude that their cosmological worlds consisted of a syncretic combination of African traditional beliefs and Christian tenets. We have argued in this chapter that most slaves, particularly those who laboured in the islands controlled by Protestants, remained untouched by Christianity until the late eighteenth and the nineteenth centuries. There is also an abundance of evidence to suggest that those who accepted Christianity tended to retain their core African beliefs as well. In other words, a variety of African-derived beliefs existed alongside others that could be considered Christian. Consequently, there were competing religious visions in all of the Caribbean societies and in the Americas as a whole.

At one level, the Christianized Africans incorporated Christian theology into their belief systems, reinterpreting it and transforming it in the process. At another level, however, these persons also embraced beliefs that were African in their genesis and content. These were parallel beliefs, seemingly contradictory at times, but to the believer and the practitioner they formed a coherent system. Thus I should like to suggest that two (or more) belief systems coexisted. There was, on the one hand, that dynamic and evolving blend of some African and Christian beliefs that could be called Afro-Jamaican or Afro-Barbadian or Afro-Antiguan Christianity. On the other hand, there were those African core beliefs that never blended at all (or at least not for a long time) and remained beyond the reach of Christian influence. That which was given primacy at a particular time depended upon the needs of the moment and upon what was considered to be most efficacious. Finally, there is some evidence that the Africans also brought their medicinal practices to the Caribbean. Richard Ligon, for example, reported that

> When they are sick, there are two remedies that cure them; the one, an outward, the other, an inward medicine. The outward medicine is a thing they call Negro-oyle and 'tis made in Barbary, yellow it is as Bees wax, but soft as butter. When they feel themselves ill, they call for some of that, and annoint their bodies, as their breasts, bellies, and sides, and in two dayes they are perfectly well. . . . The inward medicine is taken, when they find any weakness or decay in their spirits and stomachs . . .[32]

In an age when disease struck the human body with predictable regularity, African peoples and others embraced an elaborate set of beliefs about disease and the appropriate remedies for them. Some African societies believed that sickness was caused by the malevolence of an enemy and by powerful forces that operated outside of one's body. Some persons possessed the sorcery and the power to do harm to others by investing certain objects with the capacity to create mischief. To be effective, these objects could either be ingested or one had to come into contact with them in some particular way. The target of such malevolence could adopt appropriate countermeasures, usually by wearing certain objects or performing time-tested rituals.

The belief in the capacity of others to cause one to become ill was, essentially, a religious belief since it ascribed power to certain supernatural forces, acting through particular agents, to do good or evil. The Africans' explanation for sickness and disease and their responses should be seen and understood properly within the context of their cosmology. Disease and sickness had a spiritual basis and therefore required a spiritual response. Under the circumstances, it is important that we do not impose Western – and secular – concepts of disease and treatment on Africans whose understandings were entirely different. Since in the Africans' cultural worlds disease and sickness were the consequences of religious infractions or the malevolence of another, the efforts to restore a sick person to health formed an integral part of religious practice. Religious rituals constituted the means or the agency to good health. Ligon, in the comment that we just cited, may have observed religious specialists at work, trying to wash away the malevolent forces that had caused the illnesses of the persons in question.

We have not, in this discussion, teased out all of the ways in which these early African peoples laid the cultural foundations of the contemporary Caribbean. Sensitive students of the region, however, will readily recognize the traces of the past in the present. To say this, of course, is not to deny the transformations in meanings and practices that have occurred over time. The Caribbean region in myriad ways still possesses Africa's cultural soul even if some are unable to accept that reality. The passage to the Caribbean tested the physical capacities of the involuntary migrants but it did not destroy their humanity or obliterate their cultural memories. Slavery claimed many victims, but a people's creative soul was not one of them.

Notes

1. For a controversial treatment of this question, see Ivan Van Sertima, *They Came Before Columbus* (New York: Random House, 1976). The first person of African descent to arrive for whom there is firm evidence came in 1492 as a member of Columbus's crew. He is believed to have been a free man.

2. The literature on the slave trade has proliferated over the last two decades. For a general discussion of this human traffic see James Rawley, *The Transatlantic Slave Trade: A History* (New York: W.W. Norton, 1981). The best analysis of demographic and distribution questions is Philip D. Curtin, *The Atlantic Slave Trade: A Census* (Madison: University of Wisconsin Press, 1969). Also consult Joseph E. Inikori and Stanley L. Engerman, eds., *The Atlantic Slave Trade: Effects on Economies, Societies and Peoples in Africa, the Americas and Europe* (Durham: Duke University Press, 1992).

3. Public Record Office, Records of the Treasury, no. 70, no. 175. Hereafter cited as PRO, T. 70.

4. Ibid., 26–27.

5. Ibid., 202–10.

6. James Houstoun, *Some New and Accurate Observations, Geographical, Natural and Historical . . . of the Situation, Product and Natural History of the Coast of Guinea* (London, 1725), 34.

7. These are found in the reports from the agents on the coast. See PRO, T. 70.

8. For important discussions of these questions, consult F.M. Snowden, Jr, *Blacks in Antiquity: Ethiopians in the Greco-Roman Experience* (Cambridge: Harvard University Press, 1970); and his *Before Color Prejudice: The Ancient View of Blacks* (Cambridge: Harvard University Press, 1983). See also William McKee Evans, "From the Land of Canaan to the Land of Guinea: The Strange Odyssey of the 'Sons of Ham' ", *American Historical Review* 85 (1980): 15–43; and James H. Sweet, "The Iberian Roots of American Racist Thought", *William and Mary Quarterly* (January 1997).

9. PRO, T. 70.

10. Ibid.

11. Ibid.

12. Igor Kopytoff and Suzanne Miers, eds., *Slavery in Africa: Historical and Anthropological Perspectives* (Madison: University of Wisconsin Press, 1977), 12–24.

13. John Thornton, *Africa and Africans in the Making of the Atlantic World, 1400–1680* (Cambridge: Cambridge University Press, 1992), 172.

14. Ibid., 173.

15. Dena Epstein, *Sinful Tunes and Spirituals: Black Folk Music to the Civil War* (Urbana: University of Illinois Press, 1977), 24–25.

16. Richard Ligon, *A True and Exact History of the Island of Barbados* (reprint, London: Frank Cass, 1970), 48–50.

17. Sir Hans Sloane, *A Voyage to the Islands of Madera, Barbados, Nieves, S. Christopher and Jamaica, with the Natural History of the . . . Last of These Islands* (London, 1707), 39–40.

18. Sterling Stuckey, *Slave Culture: Nationalist Theory and the Foundations of Black America* (New York: Oxford University Press, 1987), 54.

19. Ibid.

20. Ibid.

21. Morgan Godwyn, *The Negro's and Indians Advocate, Suing for Their Admission into the Church . . .* (London, 1680), 33.

22. Sloane, *A Voyage,* 1: lii.

23. Elsa Goveia, *Slave Society in the British Leeward Islands at the End of the Eighteenth Century* (New Haven: Yale University Press, 1965), 156.

24. Epstein, *Sinful Tunes,* 59.

25. See his *Black Odyssey: The Afro-American Ordeal of Slavery* (New York: Vintage Books, 1977).

26. John M. Mbiti, *African Religions and Philosophies* (New York: Praeger, 1970), 146.

27. Colin A. Palmer, *Slaves of the White God: Blacks in Mexico, 1570–1650* (Cambridge: Harvard University Press, 1976), 145–66.

28. Thornton, *Africa and Africans*, 264.

29. Nicholas Creswell, *Journal of Nicholas Creswell, 1774–1777* (New York: Dial Press, 1924), 40.

30. Charles Leslie, *A New History of Jamaica* . . . (London, 1740), quoted in Epstein, *Sinful Tunes*, 305–9.

31. Ligon, *A True and Exact History*, 50.

32. Ibid., 51.

CHAPTER 3

The Invention of
Slave Society

B.W. HIGMAN

Elsa Goveia's significance as a writer of West Indian history is based largely on two classic books. These are *A Study on the Historiography of the British West Indies to the End of the Nineteenth Century* (1956) and *Slave Society in the British Leeward Islands at the End of the Eighteenth Century* (1965). The first of these books, the *Historiography,* was written shortly after she took up a lectureship in the Department of History at Mona, and the preface is dated September 1954. The second book, *Slave Society,* was published later but written earlier. It was based on her London doctoral thesis, completed in 1952 with the title "Slave Society in the British Leeward Islands 1780–1800". These two books by Goveia had quite different subjects. The *Historiography* analysed what earlier historians had said about the West Indies. *Slave Society* dealt with the historical experience of a particular period and place. But the two books shared an underlying concern for the nature of the society in which West Indian people found themselves, and for the historians' approach to their study. In this way, Goveia demonstrated an acute awareness of the relationship between the practice of history writing and the past itself, a relationship always understood in terms of the writer's present.

In this chapter, I want to focus on the central model of Goveia's historical work, the idea of slave society. There are several reasons why the concept is important, and several ways it might be discussed. My main concern will be to try to establish where the slave society concept came from and to ask whether its role in historical interpretation has changed over time. This is why I have called my chapter the "invention" of slave society.

What exactly did Goveia mean by slave society? She defined it at the very beginning of the preface to her book of 1965, wrapping inverted commas around "slave society" to suggest clearly that it was a concept, perhaps one with which her readers would be unfamiliar. She began:

> The term 'slave society' in the title of this book refers to the whole community based on slavery, including masters and freedmen as well as slaves. My object has been to study the political, economic and social organization of this society and the interrelationships of its component groups and to investigate how it was affected by its dependence on the institution of slavery.[1]

Goveia's thesis of 1952 began a little differently, sounding less modern but capturing the same overall idea. She began: "The West India community of the eighteenth century consisted of three main classes of persons – masters, freedmen, and slaves. All these classes, existing as a community, are included under the term 'Slave Society'." This time she used capital letters, as well as inverted commas, to distinguish slave society as a concept. Her aim, she said in her thesis, was to describe "the action and interaction" of masters, freedmen and slaves, "as components of a specific form of society and economic organization – that based upon slavery".[2] In the revision of 1965, Goveia explained that she had "tried to identify the basic principles which held the white masters, coloured freedmen, and Negro slaves together as a community, and to trace the influence of these principles on the relations between the Negro slave and his white master, which largely determined the form and content of the society".[3]

Although Goveia recognized segmentation in the social structure of the West Indian colonies, she contended that "the culture of the Leeward Islands formed a coherent whole". Thus, she said, "the slave society of the Leeward Islands at the end of the eighteenth century was divided into separate groups, clearly marked off from each other by their differences of legal and social status, of political rights and economic opportunity, and of racial origins and culture". The differences between groups were striking, but should not be allowed "to obscure the existence of the community of which they were all a part". In this community, argued Goveia, the "fundamental principles of inequality and subordination based on race and status were firmly impressed upon the lives of all its members". These principles embodied "the necessities of the West Indian slave systems . . . determined the ordering of the separate groups as parts of the community and held them all together within a single social structure".[4]

Goveia made further comment on the definition of slave society in 1970, in her introduction to the first issue of *Savacou* published by the Caribbean Artists Movement. She said there that slave society could be "used to describe either the society made up exclusively of the African and Creole slaves who lived in the West Indies, or else, more generally, the whole society based on slaves, including masters and freedmen as well as slaves". This was a new departure, introducing the possibility of a limited use not found in Goveia's thesis or book. But she emphasized the significance of the "whole society" approach, and noted that disagreement existed about the nature of the "wider slave society".[5] In particular, Goveia challenged the interpretation of Orlando Patterson, whose *Sociology of Slavery* had appeared in 1967. Patterson contended that Jamaica during slavery was so loosely integrated that it could hardly be called a society at all, but was better described as "a collection of autonomous plantations, each a self-contained community with its internal mechanisms of power, than as a total social system".[6] The subtitle of Patterson's book was *An Analysis of the Origins, Development and Structure of Negro Slave Society in Jamaica.* By using the term "Negro Slave Society", Patterson limited his analysis, and he had much less to say about the non-slave elements of slave society than had Goveia.

To summarize, the idea of slave society as defined and developed by Goveia was based on two basic assumptions. The first was that all of the people living in Antigua, for example, belonged to a single society rather than a series of separate components. They were part of the whole community, even in conflict. The second assumption was that it was the social relations associated with the institution of slavery that determined the overall character of these societies. That is why Goveia called the total community a slave society.

In her thesis, but not in her book, Goveia criticized "modern" historians of the British West Indies for their emphasis on the political and economic history of the colonies, and particularly on the activities of the whites. The slaves, she said, had been allowed to enter the story only as economic agents, and the free coloureds hardly at all. Her central contribution to the historiography, as she saw it in 1952, was to study all of these groups and "the forces which held them together as parts of the single entity which was their society".[7] She argued the same case more generally in the conclusion to her *Historiography* of 1956, saying that the West Indian historian's task was to discover the "principle of change" and "to seek, beyond the narrative of events, a wider understanding of the thoughts, habits, and institutions of a whole society".[8] Looking back after nearly half a century, Goveia's advocacy of social history seems uncontroversial, but in 1952 and 1956 it was revolutionary, particularly in the colonial West Indies. In this historiographical context, it is quite appropriate to ask whether it was Goveia who invented the concept of slave society.

Why does it matter how we describe and label the social relations of the period of slavery, and why does it matter where these descriptions and labels come from? The slave society label matters because it contains a particular interpretation of the period of slavery in the Caribbean. By pointing to the centrality of slavery, it gives that institution a determining role in the whole structure. Slavery and enslaved people are not merely elements in a larger colonial society, constructed in the Caribbean, in which European society and culture dominate, and they are not separable from the total system. This model, advocated by Goveia, has its focus in the whole society idea. Its implications are several. In the first place, slave society could not be reduced to smaller units. The idea that the slave plantation producing sugar was a microcosm of the whole society was not acceptable, and the experience of other agricultural units and urban centres had to be part of the picture. Second, the idea that the slave plantation was a total institution was thrown into question, at the same time as the "total" influence of slavery was emphasized. Third, to understand slave society it was necessary to study the free people, the whites and the browns, the masters and the masterless, as well as the slaves themselves. Fourth, slave society pointed beyond colonial and territorial boundaries, to suggest a similarity of experience wherever slavery was dominant, an experience that transcended and perhaps united the people of the West Indies in a common history that was more important than the geographical base of the territory, be it Antigua, Jamaica or Guyana. And it pointed beyond the Caribbean to a much wider world of comparative history and a search for universal models. Fifth, the slave society idea directed attention away from politics and economics towards a more cultural approach, giving the impetus to a related yet different model, the idea of creole society. All five of these implications of the slave society model are vitally significant because they offer a way of describing and understanding the period of slavery that was fundamentally different to that typical of the historiography before 1950, and the working out of these implications has been a preoccupation for West Indian historians over the last fifty years. These are the reasons why I believe the slave society concept is significant.

Why does it matter where the concept comes from? I believe it is always a good thing to check where your ideas have been before embracing them too enthusiastically. It is useful to know what intellectual freight concepts and ideas carry – what hidden agendas – to help understand their inherent hazards and the possible complications that may come from them. In the case of the slave society concept, many of the implications I have just outlined may appear to mirror the social and political preoccupations of liberal West Indian nationalism and integrationism of the late colonial period. Indeed, Goveia closes her *Slave Society* book of 1965 with a clear statement of her hope for a democratic commitment to universal social values, and for "a new sense of community, transcending the geographical and political divisions and the alienations of caste and race that have so far marked [the West Indies'] common history".[9] These contemporary resonances do not, however, provide a satisfying explanation for Goveia's advocacy of the slave society concept as the appropriate model for understanding the West Indian past, and it is necessary to turn to the historiography and its long-term intellectual context to get nearer to an answer.

As far as I am aware, only one writer has previously made a clear statement on the origin of the slave society concept. This is Arthur L. Stinchcombe in *Sugar Island Slavery in the Age of Enlightenment* (1995). In a footnote, Stinchcombe says simply that "the original use was by Finley".[10] Stinchcombe refers to a 1959 article by Moses Finley, a leading historian of the ancient world, entitled "Was Greek Civilisation Based on Slave Labour?"[11] But Finley does not in fact use the term slave society in that paper. He did produce a refined critique of the slave society concept but that came later, in 1968, three years after Goveia had published her *Slave Society*.[12] Perhaps Finley got the idea from Goveia. But he does not say so.

Did the slave society concept start with Goveia herself? Although both her thesis and her book were heavily footnoted, she gives no reference to any source in the immediate context in which she defines and discusses the idea, and leaves no clear clues as to whether she regarded it as original or simply a straightforward use of a term in the mainstream of the historiography. The

capital letters in her thesis, and the inverted commas of her book, do suggest
that she regarded the term as outside the mainstream, but they do not carry
us much further.

Did the slave society concept come from the work of anthropologists and
sociologists, the theorists of society? In the early 1950s, the Jamaican M.G.
Smith and the Trinidadian Lloyd Braithwaite produced historical accounts of
West Indian social structure during the period of slavery, but neither of these
provided the model for Goveia's slave society concept. Smith's article entitled
"Social Structure in the British Caribbean about 1820" was published in *Social
and Economic Studies* in 1953, and Braithwaite's "Social Stratification in
Trinidad" appeared in the same journal in the same year. Goveia used both
of these papers in her book, and gave special notice to the importance of
Smith's ideas.[13] The papers were published after Goveia had completed her
thesis, of course, but perhaps the slave society idea had been communicated
verbally. In the case of Smith, Douglas Hall's recent biography helps to solve
the case. On 18 September 1952, M.G. Smith, fresh from London with his
PhD in West African anthropology, came to the Institute of Social and
Economic Research at Mona, and met Braithwaite and Goveia, describing her
as "a B.G. girl, charming, who has just completed a PhD thesis for London
in eighteenth century W[est] Indian History". Perhaps Smith read the thesis,
or at least heard its title. In any case, by late November 1952 Smith was off
to Grenada and it was there that he wrote his article on social structure.[14]
Although in that article he used the term slave society several times, he used
it differently from Goveia. He used the term only in the section of the paper
dealing with "The Slaves", and for him slave society identified the internal life
of the slave community and distinguished it from "white society", "creole
society" (the local-born population only) and "West Indian society" (the
whole).[15] Thus Smith's use of the slave society concept was limited, and he
preferred to call the whole society that Goveia defined as slave society a "plural
society". Braithwaite never used the term slave society and talked only of
"colonial society" and "island society".

Of the eight "standard modern works" cited by Goveia in 1965 as most
relevant to her work none seems to provide the source for the slave society
concept. Apart from Smith's paper, these works were *The Myth of the Negro
Past* (1958) by the American anthropologist Melville Herskovits; *A West India
Fortune* (1950) and *Merchants and Planters* (1960) by the English historian
Richard Pares; a 1926 article on an Antiguan plantation by the American

historian of slavery, U.B. Phillips; two papers on the British West Indies by
Frank W. Pitman, an American historian, published in 1926 and 1931; and
The Fall of the Planter Class in the British Caribbean (1928) by the American
historian Lowell J. Ragatz.[16] All of these works were listed in the bibliography
of Goveia's 1952 thesis, with the exception of Phillips's paper of 1926, and,
of course, the later publications of Herskovits and Pares. But the bibliographies
of the book and the thesis are differently organized, and the thesis refers to
significant works not mentioned in the book. In her thesis Goveia dismissed
most of the modern works (and by modern she meant anything published
between 1898 and 1950) as not "directly concerned with the subject" she had
tackled. The closest she could find to her topic was Pitman's article called
"Slavery on the British West Indian Plantations in the Eighteenth Century",
published in the *Journal of Negro History* in 1926. Pitman's treatment was
blatantly racist but he did, for the first time, focus clearly on social relations
in the slave community, thus escaping the economic-political-moral framework of earlier studies. Ragatz had called Pitman's paper "the best modern
treatise on the subject". Goveia quoted this assessment in her thesis, but went
on to say that she "found a more stimulating approach in two more recent
works, concerned with related fields of study". These were Gilberto Freyre's
"study of slavery as a social institution in Brazil" and James G. Leyburn's
analysis of "Haitian society as a society of castes". Freyre's book was published
first in Portuguese in 1933, then in Spanish in 1942, and in English in 1946
as *The Masters and the Slaves*. Leyburn's book, *The Haitian People* was first
published in the United States in 1941. Goveia noted politely that, compared
to these two works, Pitman's paper of 1926 "appeared inadequate, and
old-fashioned".[17]

If these works of Freyre and Leyburn were so highly regarded by Goveia
in 1952, did they provide her slave society model? Leyburn, an American
sociologist, certainly did not. But he did talk briefly of a "slave economy" in
the period before the Revolution of 1791 and, more importantly, his was a
"whole society" approach, along the general lines advocated by Goveia.
Generally, however, he focused on what he, like Braithwaite, termed a
"colonial society", a society based on a system of classes which effectively
excluded the slaves. Thus Leyburn's "whole society" comes into its own only
after slavery.[18]

Freyre came much closer to providing the slave society model. Born in
1900 in Pernambuco, the major sugar plantation zone of Brazil, Freyre grew

up in an elite family and studied social anthropology in the United States. In a preface written in 1945 for the English-language edition of *The Masters and the Slaves,* he described his work as a study of "the formation and disintegration of patriarchal society in Brazil, a society that grew up around the first sugar-mills or sugar plantations established by the Europeans in our country, in the sixteenth century". His was a nostalgic vision, but he saw Brazilian culture as the product of a "synthetic principle", a unique blending of people, animals, plants, architecture, techniques, values and symbols, that created "one of the most harmonious unions of culture with nature and of one culture with another that the lands of this hemisphere have ever known".[19] Certainly Freyre pictured the period of slavery in Brazil as a steamy melting pot, a model that related closely to the "whole society" approach of Goveia and Leyburn. But however close he came to the idea, Freyre did not label this Brazilian unity a "slave society". The closest he came was in the first chapter of *The Masters and the Slaves,* concerned with the Portuguese colony of Brazil, which he subtitled "formation of an agrarian slave-holding, and hybrid society".[20] This did not make slavery central in the way intended by Goveia in her slave society concept.

So far, following the clues provided by Goveia in her thesis and books, it might appear that she was indeed the inventor of the slave society model. She certainly did not make that claim, but she did not tell us where she encountered the idea either. The immediate source of the model, probably, is Frank Tannenbaum's book titled *Slave and Citizen* (1946). This influential extended essay came out of a seminar on the comparative history of slavery taught by Tannenbaum and others at Columbia University in New York, beginning in 1938. Tannenbaum opened his discussion with a reference to Freyre and the similarities between Brazil and the US South, emphasizing the different social roles of the "Negro" and the "mulatto" in the two nations.[21] Importantly, Tannenbaum cast his analysis in terms of a "Negro problem", essentially the narrowing of the social gap between the white and black communities, which was much further ahead in Brazil than in the United States. He argued that this could be achieved because, in spite of the strong legal and social contrasts drawn in his book, "the slave systems in Latin and Anglo-Saxon America were not institutions differing absolutely one from the other". Rather, said Tannenbaum, these were differences of degree not of kind, because "the institution of slavery had a logic of its own. Wherever it existed in this hemisphere it worked its way into the social structure and modified the total society." The impact of slavery as an institution was fundamental, spreading much more broadly than suggested by a reading of the slave laws. "In fact," Tannenbaum contended, "so inclusive was the influence of slavery that it might be better to speak, not of a system of slavery in Brazil, Cuba or the United States, but of the total pattern as a slave society."[22]

Here, then, is a clear and explicit statement of the central features of the slave society concept, very much along the lines advanced by Goveia. Tannenbaum went on to expand his thesis, saying that slavery was not separable from the world of the total community but rather suffused every aspect of life. He argued the same case in his 1946 review of *Capitalism and Slavery* by Eric Williams. Tannenbaum said there that "in any society where slavery has been institutionalized . . . it is better to speak of a slave society rather than of slavery, for the effects of the labor system – slave or free – permeate the entire social structure and influence all its ways. If we speak of slavery, we must do so in its larger setting, as a way of life for both the master and the slave, for both the economy and the culture, for both the family and the community."[23] Further, and more contentiously, Tannenbaum argued in *Slave and Citizen* that, "Wherever we had slavery, we had a slave society, not merely for the blacks, but for the whites, not merely for the law, but for the family, not merely for the labor system, but for the culture – the total culture. Nothing escaped, nothing was beyond or above or outside the slave institution; the institution was the society in all of its manifestations".[24]

Tannenbaum also argued that, everywhere in the New World, "a slave system made a slave society, with all of the *mores* of a slave society".[25] This distinction between slave system and slave society is important to earlier and later interpretations. The term "slave system" is used generally to refer to the mechanisms used to control and exploit enslaved people, particularly the institutional framework of theory and practice. So a slave system is something less than a slave society, and not necessarily the driving force of the larger economy or society. Earlier studies of slave systems were close to studies of "slaves and slavery" as elements of a larger whole, be it plantation society or West Indian society. These were "societies with slaves" rather than slave societies.

Overall the description of slave society advanced by Tannenbaum in 1946 is as developed as that stated by Goveia in 1952. This leaves us with a puzzle. It is hard to imagine that Goveia was unaware of Tannenbaum's *Slave and Citizen*, which appeared while she was an undergraduate. Lloyd Braithwaite listed it in his references in 1953, and *Slave and Citizen* was indeed one of the few large-scale theoretical interpretative works relating to Goveia's work available at the time. On the other hand, Goveia did not refer to Tannenbaum in her later study of the West Indian slave laws, which seems equally strange.[26]

Tannenbaum was no more helpful than Goveia in identifying a source for the slave society concept. The idea seems to be constantly reinvented. On the pages in which he outlined the model, Tannenbaum mentioned no earlier writers apart from a subsidiary notice of Freyre. On the other hand, he did cite one much earlier use of the term from 1857. This was the Reverend J.D. Long of Maryland, a traveller in the US South. Long used "slave society" in the context of a discussion of miscegenation, saying female slaves were readily available to their licentious masters and that this was a product of "the very structure of slave society".[27] But Long's discussion did not develop the slave society concept, and might perhaps seem merely to refer to the unequal social relations of master and slave rather than to the larger society.

Who else used the slave society concept before 1950? Eric Williams's *Capitalism and Slavery* (1944) was certainly known to both Goveia and Tannenbaum, and Williams did indeed refer to slave society. But he did so without making the concept do any real work. In the bibliography to *Capitalism and Slavery*, Williams praised the planter Bryan Edwards's *History of the British West Indies*, saying that it was "one of those rare cultural landmarks in a slave society which, unlike the slave society of Greece, despised education and did not reproduce any of the great gifts of Greece to the world".[28] His only other reference to slave society occurs in the first chapter of *Capitalism and Slavery* on "the origin of Negro slavery". There, in a famous passage comparing the spread of sugar and slavery to a relay race, Williams associated plantation slavery with soil exhaustion and the continuing need for fertile fields in new sites. He wrote: "Expansion is a necessity of slave society; the slave power requires ever fresh conquests."[29] In support of this contention, Williams offered references to *The Slave Power* by John Elliot Cairnes, first published in 1862, and to Herman Merivale's *Lectures on Colonization and Colonies* (1839–41). Merivale was a fruitful source of ideas for Williams, but Merivale never employed the term slave society. Williams's use of "slave power" in the sentence just quoted leads directly to the work of the same name by Cairnes, and Cairnes did indeed have a clear and explicit notion of the slave society concept.

Cairnes's book of 1862, *The Slave Power,* was directed at an interpretation of the American Civil War. This was a work of considerable contemporary significance and it may be regarded as the starting point for two strands of thought making more or less use of the slave society concept between the 1860s and the 1940s. The first of these strands was United States historiography in both its conservative and liberal traditions, and the second was Marxist understandings of the mode of production, including the slave mode of production.

Cairnes was an Irish economist, and *The Slave Power* was based on a series of lectures delivered at the University of Dublin in 1861. His choice of North American slavery as a topic, he said, was based on "speculative" or theoretical questions: "to show that the course of history is largely determined by the action of economic causes".[30] Cairnes held a concept of social evolution, and believed that history could be reduced to a science in which historical events formed an orderly succession in accordance with fixed laws. Here the links with Marx and with Darwin become apparent. It is also possible to see here the origins of a theory of slave society. As Adelaide Weinberg argues, Cairnes found that "an economic organization based on slave production in the particular circumstances of the American South carried with it certain typical associations and a predictable historical course".[31] In the United States, said Cairnes, the contest between North and South was "between two forms of society". These were free society and slave society.[32]

Four of Cairnes's nine chapters had "slave society" in their titles. Chapter 3 dealt with the "internal organization of slave societies", chapter 4 the "tendencies of slave societies", chapter 5 the "internal development of slave societies", and chapter 6 the "external policies of slave societies". In the first of these chapters Cairnes offered a definition:

> The constitution of a slave society . . . is sufficiently simple: it resolves itself into three classes, broadly distinguished from each other, and connected by no common interest – the slaves on whom devolves all the regular industry, the slaveholders who reap all its fruits, and an idle and lawless rabble who live dispersed over vast plains in a condition little removed from absolute barbarism.[33]

In some parts of the South, said Cairnes, there existed "a hardy and industrious race" of peasant farmers, but these formed no part of "the economy of slave society" and indeed impaired the strength and symmetry of slave society. It was the three classes – slaves, masters, and poor whites – who made up slave society. Here we may notice some contrasts with the slave society of

Tannenbaum and Goveia. Whereas Tannenbaum and Goveia were inclusive, Cairnes excludes the peasantry. Cairnes's three classes are not the same as Goveia's three, but this difference may be accounted for by differences in the demographic composition of the West Indies and the United States, with the free coloured having a lower profile in the US South. This helps to explain the lack of an integrationist element in Cairnes's model, in contrast to the hybridizing, creolizing tendencies of slave society in Goveia, Tannenbaum and Freyre. But the essential idea of slave society was clearly set out in Cairnes's *Slave Power* of 1862; it formed part of a critique of the institution of slavery from the perspective of political economy that proved persistent in the historiography, through Williams and Goveia to contemporary writers.

True to form, Cairnes does not tell us where he found the slave society concept. But he does cite pro-slavery sources which used the idea. For example, he quotes the *Richmond* [Virginia] *Inquirer* in order to show that the two "systems of society" could not mix, and that slave society is "essentially exclusive of all other forms of social life". According to the pro-slavery *Inquirer,* "Two opposite and conflicting forms of society cannot, among civilized men, co-exist and endure. The one must give way and cease to exist; the other become universal. If free society be unnatural, immoral, unchristian, it must fall, and give way to slave society, a social system old as the world, universal as man."[34] Some Southern slave owners went further in reversing moral rights, describing the Civil War as "the effort of slave society to emancipate itself".[35] These defiant expressions of the early 1860s came from those Cairnes wished to condemn, but it was from these defenders of slavery that he took the slave society concept.

When did the term slave society become a part of the southern pro-slavery argument? It plays a prominent role in the writings of the Virginian George Fitzhugh, editor of the *Richmond Enquirer* for most of the 1850s. Fitzhugh's *Cannibal's All! or Slaves Without Masters* (1856) set up a comparison of the "evils of slave society and of Free Society", arguing that slave society involved slavery to human masters while Free Society meant slavery to capital (these were the slaves without masters). The northern abolitionists, said Fitzhugh, had nothing to offer as a substitute to capitalism other than "Free Love, Communism, or Socialism". He described capitalism as "a cruel master" and said emancipation in the West Indies – which he called the "free negro system" – was a failure. The only remedy he could see for the condition of the English working classes, made poor by the capitalist Industrial Revolution, was enslavement.[36]

Fitzhugh differed from most of his pro-slavery predecessors and contemporaries in that his approach was not political, legal or economic, but rather sociological and psychological.[37] He saw society as a hierarchical organism, developing slowly rather than in revolutionary shifts. He had no time for rationalism, the Enlightenment or the inalienable rights of man. In an earlier book, published in 1854, Fitzhugh had made clear his social bent and his understanding of new disciplines as concerned with pathologies and the curing of social ills. That book was titled *Sociology for the South, or the Failure of Free Society*. He dedicated it to "the people of the South", saying that "on all subjects of social science, Southern men, from their position, possess peculiar advantages when they are under discussion. History, past and contemporaneous, informs them of all the phenomena of other forms of society, and they see every day around them the peculiarities and characteristics of slave society, of which little is to be learned from books."[38] Fitzhugh's idea of slave society comprised all elements of the population, working together in friendly and fruitful cooperation.

It is certain then that the slave society idea did exist before abolition in the United States, and that it appeared first in the public press rather than within the academy. It is also certain that the slave society concept was closely linked to the pathological approach of the first American sociologists, an approach that remained dominant down to World War I. To this extent, it is fair to conclude that slave society was the product of "sociological" thinking, however far its sympathies may be from that of modern practitioners of the discipline.

The very first book published in the United States to use the term "sociology" was titled the *Treatise on Sociology, Theoretical and Practical,* by Henry Hughes. It appeared in 1854, the same year as Fitzhugh's *Sociology for the South*. Hughes was a Mississippi lawyer, and like Fitzhugh he used his theoretical sociology to provide a defence of slavery in the United States. The choice, said Hughes, was between two social orders. One of these was the "free-labor form of society", a liberal free-market, democratic, plural system, indifferent to progress. Hughes thought this both immoral and unscientific. The second social order was what he called "ordered sovereignty" or the "warrantee form of society", the social and political expression of a scientific sociology. This, said Hughes, offered a social system in which progress was guaranteed and regulated by an aristocracy of talent, a model for which already existed in the instruments and codes of the plantation South. But Hughes insisted that "slavery" was a misnomer, and thus called his utopia "Warranteeism" – emphasizing mutual responsibilities and obligations – rather than slave society. However, in 1852 he had foreseen a future "Slavery-Perfect Society", the product of progressive phases of social development. For Hughes, slave society was a kind of utopia.[39]

The models of society advocated by Fitzhugh and Hughes differed in their details, but shared the notion of a moral order underlying human association. Their positive picture of slave society was, of course, separated by a great gulf from that found in Goveia, Williams and even Cairnes. Similarly, the hybridity and creolization fundamental to Freyre's and Tannenbaum's models had no place in the moral order of pro-slavery ideology. But the idea that society must be understood as an organic whole, and that it was the institution of slavery which characterized and controlled the structure and form of that whole society, is common to all of the variations of the slave society concept.

If it is correct to locate the invention of the slave society concept in the US South in the 1850s, then its origin must be explained as a reaction to abolitionism and the idea of free society in Haiti, but more particularly in the British West Indies. The term slave society does not appear, as far as I have been able to determine, in any literature produced during the period before the abolition of slavery in the British West Indies in 1838. This applies to literature in Spanish and French as well as English. Could it have been in common use in everyday speech, among the slaves for example, and never written down? Perhaps, but I would argue that the concept itself seems to have been absent from West Indian thought before 1838, and that there was therefore no occasion for its use in common discourse. Rather, I find that the slave society idea was the creation of later conceptualizers, and that is why I think it appropriate to talk of the "invention" of slave society. It is an invention attempting to give authority and moral respectability to a form of society under attack, and the co-optation of the newly minted scientism of sociology, the science of society, can be interpreted in the same light.

After emancipation, the pro-slavery version of slave society, with its positive picture of plantation slavery, quickly became unpopular. Even when it resurfaced in the early twentieth century, particularly in the work of U.B. Phillips on the American South and L. J. Ragatz and F.W. Pitman on the West Indies, the term "slave society" was rarely employed. Phillips, the master of slave studies in the United States before 1950, talked of the plantation as a "school" in much the same way as Hughes, but the only reference to slave society in Phillips's major work *American Negro Slavery* (1918), occurs in a quote from Cairnes.[40] In this way, as argued earlier, Cairnes becomes the crucial link between the various strands of thought. The second strand of that thought was found in Karl Marx.

Marx's understanding of slavery as a form of exploitation was strongly influenced by his reading of Cairnes, but Marx himself spoke of slave-holding societies rather than slave societies. His followers and interpreters often came to have faith in a simple progression of five distinct stages, each founded on a mode of production: from primitive communism, to slavery, to feudalism, to capitalism, to socialism, in which every stage had to occur in every society and follow one another in the same inevitable order. Although the terms "slave mode of production" and "slave society" served a similar function, it is generally argued that slave society was more comprehensive, taking in a wider range of social relations and coming closer to the idea of social formation (the combined social and economic structures of production).

Marx criticized both slave society and free (capitalist) society because they were both systems of exploitation as well as modes of production in the technical sense, and he located these two formations in a series of stages of social development. In the first half of the twentieth century, scholars identified slave societies in the ancient Middle East, ancient China and the Mediterranean, for example, and there were attempts to establish general laws for all slave societies within the Marxist frame of analysis. The very first book that I have been able to find with the term "slave society" in its title was an English translation of a work by Karl Kautsky, called *Slave Society in Imperial Rome* (1926). Other translations of the same work, however, used the term "slave economy", and this was closer to the original German. In the middle of the twentieth century, the discovery that Marx had in the late 1850s developed the concept of an Asiatic mode of production loosened the hold of the rigid scheme of stages of social development. This made possible a distinction between what came to be called "genuine" slave societies, and societies in which slavery and the slave mode of production existed without dominating those societies. Similarly it was no longer a part of official socialist doctrine that slave society was a universally necessary stage of development.[41]

By the middle of the twentieth century, then, when Goveia was preparing her thesis in London, the slave society concept existed in two separate streams of thought. One of these was the Marxist, in which slave society formed part of a metahistorical interpretation of the development of human societies. The second stream was located in the emerging comparative histories of the Americas, especially in the ideas of Tannenbaum. Broadly speaking, these two streams of thought existed in isolation circa 1950. It was the Marxist stream that first influenced academic historians of the ancient world, particularly through the work of Moses Finley. Goveia was more directly affected by the comparative history stream. Both of these streams of ideas flowed underground for long periods but ultimately connected with the concepts advanced by Cairnes in *The Slave Power* in 1862, and from him to a small group of pro-slavery society theorists in the US South in the 1850s.

It was not until the late 1960s, after Goveia had published her book in 1965, that these two almost separate "inventions" of the slave society concept came together in a broader comparative historiography of slavery. That new historiography came to employ slave society as a fundamental model. Historians of the ancient world frequently came to refer to the literature of modern slavery in the New World, and historians of the Americas sometimes, though less often, referred to the ancient world. Finley's 1968 analysis was strongly influenced by the Marxist model. He proposed a distinction between genuine slave societies and slave-owning societies. This distinction was based primarily on the location and function of slaves in the economy. Finley argued that true slave society existed only where "the economic and political elite depended primarily on slave labor for basic production".[42] Where slavery existed but served no fundamental economic function, there was a slave-owning society but not a slave society. Another way of defining genuine slave societies is demographic. Finley argued that in a true slave society, slaves should make up at least one-third of the total population of a large region for a significant period of time. Some scholars have reduced this limit to one-fifth. It was not an issue that worried Goveia, for most of the territories of the Caribbean meet all of these tests easily, with more than 80 per cent of the population enslaved, essential to the economy and continuing for one hundred to two hundred years. But the Caribbean was exceptional in this regard.

The distinction between slave societies and slave-holding societies has become important, though contentious, in the literature of the last thirty years. Tannenbaum, as we have seen, argued in 1946 that "wherever we had slavery, we had a slave society". Finley, on the other hand, could find just five genuine slave societies throughout the course of human history. These were ancient Greece, ancient Italy, Brazil, the US South and the Caribbean. A number of critics, notably Orlando Patterson, have contended that this definition of slave society is too limiting, preferring an emphasis on slave-holding societies as units of analysis, somewhat in the style of Marx. Keith Bradley, in his book *Slavery and Society at Rome* (1994), observes that the distinction between "genuine" slave societies and those in which slaves were simply present, is a modern rather than a historical distinction and therefore limiting in terms of its ability to comprehend the significance of slavery to contemporaries.[43] We can treat this in two ways. One is to confirm the finding that the slave society concept is very much an "invention" of modern, almost entirely post-slavery, thought, and this might lead to its rejection. The other approach is to accept the modernity of the concept, and to recognize that such invention is an everyday aspect of historiography. What matters is the fruitfulness of concepts, in terms of developing an understanding of the past, as well as a willingness to question constantly. Too often, however, the term slave society has come to be used loosely by historians since Goveia. It is sometimes used interchangeably with the terms "slave system", "slave economy", "slave population", and "slave community", for example, and used to identify the enslaved sector rather than the whole society, in the way preferred by Goveia. Perhaps the term has been devalued as a consequence of its popularity. It is too important, too central, to Caribbean history to be treated this way.

What have I achieved in this chapter? First, I have established a new or alternative origin for the slave society concept. Second, I have pushed its origin back from 1959 to 1854, while readily accepting that even earlier sites may remain to be uncovered. Third, I have found the concept's origin in the United States, in a particular time and place. Fourth, I have located the origin of the slave society concept in pro-slavery thought, in opposition to the idea of "free society". Fifth, I have found the concept's origin in a moral argument over the nature of the ideal society, linked directly to the disciplinary origins of sociology as problem. Sixth, I have traced the movement of the slave society concept from pro- to antislavery thought, and thence to its modern neutralized analytic form. It is my hope that study of the invention of the slave society idea may lead to a more explicit critique and a more careful application of this key concept of Caribbean history.

Notes

1. Elsa V. Goveia, *Slave Society in the British Leeward Islands at the End of the Eighteenth Century* (New Haven: Yale University Press, 1965), vii. Cited hereafter as *Slave Society.*

2. E.V. Goveia, "Slave Society in the British Leeward Islands, 1780–1800" (PhD thesis, London University, 1952), 1. Cited hereafter as "Slave Society".

3. Goveia, *Slave Society,* vii.

4. Ibid., 249–50.

5. Elsa V. Goveia, Introduction, *Savacou* 1 (June 1970): 3.

6. Orlando Patterson, *The Sociology of Slavery: An Analysis of the Origin, Development and Structure of Negro Slave Society in Jamaica* (London: MacGibbon and Kee, 1967), 70.

7. Goveia, "Slave Society", 2.

8. Elsa V. Goveia, *A Study on the Historiography of the British West Indies to the End of the Nineteenth Century* (Mexico City: Instituto Panamericano de Geografia e Historia, 1956), 177.

9. Goveia, *Slave Society,* 338.

10. Arthur L. Stinchcombe, *Sugar Island Slavery in the Age of Enlightenment: The Political Economy of the Caribbean World* (Princeton: Princeton University Press, 1995), 125, n. 1.

11. M.I. Finley, "Was Greek Civilisation Based on Slave Labour", *Historia* 8 (1959): 145–64.

12. M.I. Finley, "Slavery", *International Encyclopedia of the Social Sciences,* vol. 14, ed. David L. Sills (New York: Macmillan and The Free Press, 1968), 307–13.

13. Goveia, *Slave Society,* 235, 319, 340.

14. Douglas Hall, *A Man Divided: Michael Garfield Smith: Jamaican Poet and Anthropologist* (Kingston, Jamaica: The Press, University of the West Indies, 1997), 56, 63–65.

15. M.G. Smith, "Some Aspects of Social Structure in the British Caribbean about 1820", *Social and Economic Studies* 1 (1953): 55–56, 64, 68, 71–73, 75–76, 78.

16. Goveia, *Slave Society,* 340–41.

17. Goveia, "Slave Society", iii.

18. James G. Leyburn, *The Haitian People* (1941; reprint, Westport: Greenwood, 1966), 15, 306.

19. Gilberto Freyre, *The Masters and the Slaves* (New York: Alfred A. Knopf, 1946), xi–xiii.

20. Ibid., 3.

21. Frank Tannenbaum, *Slave and Citizen* (1946; reprint, New York: Vintage Books, 1961), 3–5.

22. Ibid., 117.
23. Frank Tannenbaum, "A Note on the Economic Interpretation of History", *Political Science Quarterly* 61 (1946): 247–48.
24. Tannenbaum, *Slave and Citizen,* 116–17.
25. Ibid., 118.
26. Elsa V. Goveia, *The West Indian Slave Laws of the Eighteenth Century* (Bridgetown, Barbados: Caribbean Universities Press, 1970).
27. Cited in Tannenbaum, *Slave and Citizen,* 123.
28. Eric Williams, *Capitalism and Slavery* (Chapel Hill: University of North Carolina Press, 1944), 266–67.
29. Ibid., 7.
30. John E. Cairnes, *The Slave Power* (New York: Augustus M. Kelley, 1968), vii. All references here are to the 1968 reprint of the 1863 second edition.
31. Adelaide Weinberg, *John Elliot Cairnes and the American Civil War: A Study in Anglo-American Relations* (London: Kingswood Press, 1970), 25.
32. Cairnes, *The Slave Power,* xvi.
33. Ibid., 95.
34. Cited in Cairnes, *The Slave Power,* 183.
35. L.W. Spratt in the *Charleston Mercury,* 13 February 1861, quoted in Cairnes, *The Slave Power,* 397.
36. George Fitzhugh, *Cannibals All! or Slaves Without Masters* (1856; reprint, Cambridge: Harvard University Press, 1960), 8–9, 20, 184, 153–56.
37. C. Vann Woodward, in Fitzhugh, *Cannibals All!,* xxxi–xxxii.
38. George Fitzhugh, *Sociology for the South, or the Failure of Free Society* (1854; reprint, New York: Burt Franklin, 1965), iii–iv.
39. Henry Hughes, *Treatise on Sociology: Theoretical and Practical* (Philadelphia: Lippincott, Grambo and Co., 1854), quoted in Drew Gilpin Faust, ed., *The Ideology of Slavery: Proslavery Thought in the Antebellum South, 1830–1860* (Baton Rouge: Louisiana State University Press, 1981), 240, 270; Arthur J. Vidich and Stanford M. Lyman, *American Sociology: Worldly Rejections of Religion and Their Directions* (New Haven: Yale University Press, 1985), 9–11.
40. Ulrich Bonnell Phillips, *American Negro Slavery* (1918; reprint, Baton Rouge: Louisiana State University Press, 1969), 355.
41. Finley, "Slavery", 312.
42. Ibid., 310.
43. Keith Bradley, *Slavery and Society at Rome* (Cambridge: Cambridge University Press, 1994), 30.

CHAPTER 4

Slavery and the Transformation of Society in Cuba, 1511–1760

FRANKLIN W. KNIGHT

The slave society of the British Virgin Islands was only a small segment of the slave society of the West Indies. But analysis of its characteristics sheds light on the characteristics of plantation slavery and of the "Creole" society in the eighteenth century throughout the islands.

– Elsa Goveia, *Slave Society in the British Leeward Islands at the End of the Eighteenth Century*

Introduction

In the swift passage of time and the seemingly inundating flood of studies on various aspects of slavery that have appeared since Elsa Goveia's landmark study of *The British Leeward Islands at the End of the Eighteenth Century* in 1965, we tend to forget the signal importance of her work.[1] Elsa Goveia's seminal contribution to Caribbean, American and Atlantic diaspora historiography was to encourage scholars to cease the superficial examination of slavery as though it were an artificial, exotic appendage to broader communal, economic and social activity. Instead she enjoined us to consider the society as a whole, as an organic construct in which all the segments were reciprocally and symbiotically connected. Viewing slaves and slavery in isolation – without non-slaves and free society – is akin either to studying sexual differences between male and female without looking at gender, or playing cricket without a wicket.

Elsa Goveia was the first to give currency to the meaningful term "slave society" and in her book she felt constrained to define what she meant: "The term 'slave society'," she wrote in the preface to her work, "refers to the whole community based on slavery, including masters and freedmen as well as slaves. My object has been to study the political, economic, and social organisation of this society and the interrelationships of its component groups and to investigate how it was affected by its dependence on the institution of slavery."[2]

Happily, today, thanks to her effective teaching and example, such an injunction is hardly necessary. Most scholars now believe what she wrote. It is with this consciousness that I would like to examine the evolution of the slave society in the largest island of the Antilles. By looking at this first stage in the evolution of one part of the Caribbean, I hope we can understand something of the variations which later developed.

Above all, I hope that by looking at the genesis of the slave society we can understand that it was not a given, not inevitable in the Caribbean experience. Slavery in the Caribbean was a consciously made societal adoption. The slave society in the Americas was deliberately constructed, slowly and carefully, based on a long experience of trial and error. A study of its construction not only demolishes some myths along the way but also illuminates the distortions that the institution introduced as it warped the relations between people as well as between groups and labour in the region.

Anyone familiar with the particular case of Cuba will, of course, realize that the history of Cuba has always been associated with slavery – at least until the legal abolition of slavery by the royal decree of 7 October 1886 that declared an end to the system of *patrocinado,* the cumbersome apprenticeship apparatus designed in 1880 to terminate slavery gradually.[3] Slavery probably began in Cuba before the first organized Spanish colonial settlement in 1511. Christopher Columbus reported in his journal that one group of indigenous Cubans, the Ciboney or Guanahuatebey, complained that some of them were enslaved by the more numerous local Taino Arawak.[4] When Spanish colonists began their occupation of Cuba in 1511, they were not introducing slavery but merely adding a new dimension to it.

It is proper, therefore, to begin with the realization that throughout the history of Cuba, slavery and free labour have always operated concurrently, though not necessarily in co-equal proportions. The early Spanish colonists enslaved Indians and used purchased African slaves, but most labour was supplied by "encommended" Indians who were technically free. Hence, it would be a gross exaggeration to describe the early communities in Cuba as constituting what would conventionally be described as a slave society.

In some of my earlier writing I have described the experience of European colonization in the Caribbean as manifesting two sets of characteristics: the characteristics of the settler society, and the characteristics of the exploitation society. Both of these types of societies – which represented opposite points on a continuum rather than polar opposites – could be and historically were societies with slaves, where slavery comprised a mode of labour organization.

The settler society was the attempt to recreate the metropolitan society in microcosm. Such was the goal in Spanish Hispaniola after Nicolas de Ovando arrived in 1502 with some fifteen hundred Spanish (and Canary Islanders) and planted the first proper Spanish colony in the New World. A continuation of the southward *Reconquista* in Iberia, the early colonists went out to Hispaniola with the spirit that Bernal Diaz del Castillo, the intrepid soldier of Hernán Cortés, described as present in his fellow warriors in New Spain: they went out, he wrote, "for the service of God and His majesty, to give light to those who were in darkness, and to procure wealth, as all men desire".[5] Hispaniola was orginally designed to be a miniature of Andalucia: a fledgling colony on a hostile frontier.

Similarly, English colonists in Barbados between 1627 and 1650 or French settlers in Martinique and Guadeloupe between 1640 and 1700 desperately tried to establish a form of English and French society in the tropical Caribbean. And recreating European patterns of society was what the colonists in New England, the mid-Atlantic colonies, and the highlands of Mexico and Peru were all trying to do when they first adventured into the Americas.[6]

From the very beginning, despite the preponderance (in some cases) of free labour, slavery was employed as a common labour device throughout the Caribbean. In most cases, the first slaves were non-Europeans: imported, hispanized Africans from Iberia, or indigenous Indians who refused to accept

European domination quietly. Moreover, in the early period of the European experience in the Americas, the distinction between *servant* and *slave* was often blurred, with social mobility being more feasible in settler societies than in the cases of exploitation societies.[7] Early Cuba was typical of this sort of colonizing venture.

By contrast, exploitation societies were consciously designed to maximize the efficient production of tropical staples for export to the European market. The labour force was predominantly an enslaved labour force. Recreating the European society was relegated to a secondary and minor consideration. Unlike the case of the settler colonies, the labour force often numerically overwhelmed the free, white managerial component. The society that eventually emerged in the exploitation colonies was one in which the non-Europeans had an enormous impact on all aspects of social conduct, although the managerial component of Europeans tried to legislate the parameters within which the masses could exercise their creativity.[8]

One way to look at the evolution of Caribbean society, therefore, is to examine the ways in which, in some areas, the colonies moved from examples of settler colonies to examples of exploitation colonies. The implication of this movement or transformation coincided with the changing reality of the political economy of much of the Caribbean between the early sixteenth century and the nineteenth century. It is possible, furthermore, to consider the transformation of society and economy in Cuba between 1511 and 1760 as a transition from a predominantly free-labour society to a predominantly slave society, as a transformation from a standard type of settler society to a modified example of the exploitation society. Put another way, one might describe this change as one from a slave-holding society to a slave society – from a society, that is, in which some people used slaves to accomplish various tasks, to one in which the nature of slave-holding assumed important economic, social and ideological considerations.

It is easy to trace this transformation in Cuba, and to evaluate the impact which the conversion of the dominant mode of labour from predominantly free to overwhelmingly slave had on the society. To do this we can take what little demographic and economic data we have from time to time and subject them, as we would a set of photographs, to some scrutiny to provide a window into the structure of the society at the periods indicated. I will examine Cuba in the sixteenth century, the seventeenth century and the late eighteenth century when the population of the island – or parts of the island – was calculated or estimated. I focus especially on the years 1570–82, 1680–94 and 1760–74. The references I will make to the nineteenth century are merely for purposes of extended comparison.

The Slave-Holding Society in Cuba

In many ways the Spanish expansion to Cuba was a logical and linear continuation of the *Reconquista*. After its initial settlement by Diego Velasquez in 1511, the population of the island grew until the expedition of Hernán Cortés discovered gold in Mexico. After that Cuba rapidly lost population to the mainland, and the exodus was further accelerated after the reports arrived of newer finds of gold and silver in the highlands of Peru. Population figures are hard to find, and those found are far from reliable for most of the early sixteenth century. Nevertheless scattered estimates abound. One can be found in the work of Irene Wright, who estimated the population around 1550 as approximately three thousand – roughly divided between Spanish and non-Spanish in the following order:

vecinos españoles [Spanish heads of household]	322 [x5 = 1610]	= 47.2 per cent
indigenas [free Indians]	1,000	= 29.3 per cent
esclavos negros e indios [black and Indian slaves]	800	= 23.4 per cent[9]

We can make some passing observations about the figures cited in Wright:

1. The normal multiplier factor for converting *vecinos* [male heads of households] into persons was x5, so the 322 *vecinos* would be equivalent to about 1,610 individuals.
2. Indians and slaves surpassed, slightly, the Spanish population.
3. Both Indians and Africans are included in the category of slaves, and together are the smallest component of the population. It is fair to assume, even without further corroborating evidence, that work was accomplished without heavy reliance on a servile class. Of course, in a mainly grazing and truck farming economy, the labour demands would not be excessive for purposes of self-sufficiency. And despite the myth that all the early Spanish were actual or would-be *conquistadores* or *petit* nobility, they must have survived in Cuba based on their own labour

rather than on the wanton exploitation of the local (or imported) population.

4. Even though the numbers are small, the evidence suggests that the society was quite plural, with the ratio of slaves to free being 1:3 while the ratio of whites to non-whites was 1:1. By comparison and contrast, in 1774 Cuba had 1:4.4 slaves to free; by 1841 when the transformation was complete, one of every two individuals was in the non-free category.[10]

5. This early estimate did not include the transient population, then called *estantes,* who, according to one official document, were of semi-permanent status, "many of them merchants who practically lived on the island".

Later in the century we begin to have a much better idea of the population of the island. The Spanish made a crude *empadronamiento,* or count of heads of households, for all their towns in 1570, and this provided a rough profile of the population, Spanish and non-Spanish, which lived within the jurisdictional boundaries of the expanding empire at that time.[11]

According to the *empadronamiento,* Cuba had 240 *vecinos* eligible for military service and bureaucratic functions. This number of *vecinos* was only slightly ahead of that for Puerto Rico (200 *vecinos*) but was considerably less than that for Hispaniola (1,000). The official chronicler of the Indies, Juan Lopez de Velasco, declared that Cuba had lost 60 per cent of its population since 1520, although he provided no basis for his calculation. He did note that the island had one *vecino* for each 480 square kilometres, compared with one per 80 for Hispaniola and one per 45 for Puerto Rico. More important for our purposes is Velasco's notation:

> *Son los vecinos todos pobres y en esta isla como en La Espaniola, se va despoblando en cada dia por haber faltado el oro a causa de haberse acabado los indios, de cuya causa no van Mercaderes a la isla con quien trata sus granerias que comunmente son cueros y algun azúcar.*[12]
>
> [The *vecinos* are all poor and this island, as is the case in Hispaniola, continually loses population owing to the exhaustion of the Indian population. As a result, very little commerce is done with the island, whose principal products are hides and a little sugar.]

Juan Lopez de Velasco, in all probability, got his information from the clergy. A *testimonio de la visita* (official report of a *visita*) made by Juan del Castillo of the diocese of Cuba in 1570 gave extensive descriptions of the ten Spanish towns then in existence throughout the island, as well as the population.

According to the report of del Castillo, the island could hardly have been an attractive place. In a schematic form (mine), the report noted:

Baracoa had eight Spanish *vecinos,* described as *"muy pobres"* (very poor), and seventeen married Indians.

Santiago had thirty-two *vecinos.*

Los Caneyes had twenty Indians.

Bayamo, described as *"el mejor pueblo de la isla, muy sano y de muchas haciendas y tierra muy descubierta"* (the best town on the island, very healthy, with many houses and much cultivated land), had more than seventy Spanish and eighty married Indians.

Puerto Príncipe, now Camaguey, in the centre of the island, had twenty-five poor Spaniards and forty married Indians.

Trinidad had fifty married Indians and no Spanish *vecinos.*

Sabana De Vasco Porcallo, probably now Sancti Spiritus, had then "20 *vecinos,* half Spanish and half of married Indians" – a description which clearly indicates that Indians could become *vecinos,* as we shall see later.

Sancti Spiritus, now Santa Clara, whose church was described as the "richest on the island", had twenty Spanish and twenty married Indians.

Havana had then "more than 60 *vecinos",* and was beginning to dominate the island already.

Guanabacoa had more than sixty married Indians.

In passing we may note that the large number of married, and therefore converted, Indians within the Spanish jurisdiction indicates that not only were the Indians far from being annihilated at this date, but Spanish control of the island was still restricted to relatively small enclaves scattered about the island. It is also clear that the social structure was somewhat fluid for social groups below the category of *vecinos.*

If we assume that all the designated men are *vecinos,* then it is worth pointing out that 56.9 per cent of all the heads of households were Indians. Three towns were entirely Indian: Los Caneyes, Trinidad and Guanabacoa. Indians comprised the majority in three more towns: Baracoa, Bayamo and Puerto Príncipe. Indians were numerically equal to the Spanish in two towns: Sabana de Vasco Porcallo and Sancti Spiritus. Santiago de Cuba and Havana were the only two towns in which the population was entirely Spanish. These two towns together had 41 per cent of the Spanish *vecinos* and 17.2 per cent of all *vecinos*.

In the light of these figures it is hard to agree with the generally accepted opinions that the Indian population had disappeared throughout the Antilles. And they certainly question the notion of the nature and extent of Spanish colonial society when less than 20 per cent of the population living within the confines of the Hispanic colonial state were of Spanish descent. If Indians prevailed in such large numbers within the officially controlled enclaves, then their numbers outside must have been greater, and their demise nowhere as immediate as is generally assumed.

Indeed Juan Lopez de Velasco presented a social stratification of the island's free population which provided the following categories in descending order of importance:

1. *Vecinos;*
2. Sons and dependents of the *vecinos* – bachelor youths (*mozos solteros*)
3. *Vecinos* who live by their labour, and their children;
4. Transients (*estantes*);
5. Free blacks (*negros horros*) – presumably including the mulattos;
6. Indians; and
7. Excluded and presumably falling at the bottom of the social ladder, Indian and black slaves.[13]

We may note in passing that had the last category been important, it would not have escaped observation by Lopez de Velasco and the priests.

Within a decade of this description, the Spanish had begun the reorganization of their American empire.[14] Unable to defend the entire hemisphere – since after 1580 Portugal also was attached to the Castilian kingdom – Spain initiated a policy of strategic withdrawal from the peripheral areas, concentrating on the precious metal–rich mainland and the sea routes connecting the Americas to Iberia. The smaller islands were virtually abandoned for the larger ones, and Cuba assumed greater importance in the realm of empire owing to its strategic geographical location for sailing ships plying the route between New Spain, New Granada and the Old World. The fortifications constructed at Havana and other port towns were necessary defensive measures against the encroachments of rival Europeans and their semi-official bands of privateers.[15]

With the growing naval importance of Havana came a growing demand for labour to build the residences and fortifications and to provide food for the garrisons continually stationed there. Havana slowly grew from a village to a town and from a town to a city, becoming by 1790 the third largest city in the Western Hemisphere, with a total population in excess of forty thousand inhabitants.[16] Obviously, as the need for labour increased the local population could no longer supply both manpower for the military services and food and services for all the permanent and transient residents.

Increasing Stratification of Labour

With the increase in population came an increase in the stratification of the labour force. The society, formerly of a few wealthy *vecinos* and a larger number of common folk, began to accentuate social condition and social distance between castes and classes. Just as with the transformation in Barbados in the middle of the seventeenth century, Cuba underwent great demographic and social change – though such changes were not tantamount to a revolution of any sort.

This is already apparent in the first detailed survey of the male population, done in 1582 with the aim of determining military eligibility.[17] Called the *Padron de vecinos, solteros, estantes, Indios y Negros Horros de la Habana y Guanabacoa,* it listed by name all the able-bodied males in the western sector of the island, with subjective evaluations of some groups. Despite some minor arithmetical errors, the profile provided is truly fascinating. The principal social divisions – and, indeed, the social status categories – remained as they were in 1570, although among the population were included a number of Portuguese, Frenchmen and one individual from Flanders.[18] Altogether the list, which is reproduced in that monumental study by Levi Marrero, *Cuba: economia y sociedad,* has 299 names.[19] In terms of major categories, the breakdown is as follows:

vecinos – 48 (actually 47 names);

mozos solteros, etc.– 14;

vecinos que viven de su trabajo – 69;

estantes de la tierra[20] – 48;

Negros horros – 25;

Indios de la Habana – 39;

Vecinos de Guanabacoa – 56 (given as 11 Spanish and 45 married Indians).

Of the list, the Spanish and Spanish creole element comprised 56.2 per cent of the entire group, or 168 individuals. Hispanized Indians comprised the second largest component, with eighty-four individuals or 28.1 per cent. Mulattos and mestizos accounted for twenty-two persons or 7.4 per cent, while the liberated slaves (*negros horros*) accounted for twenty-five individuals or 8.3 per cent. The combined non-European sector accounted for 131 individuals or 43.8 per cent of the group.

A large number of the males had no occupational listing. That included a fairly large number of the most substantial of the *vecinos,* of whom the military commander of the Fort at Havana stated, "*Los contenidos arriba son los vecinos particulares de que se puede echar mano y tener dellos la confianza*"[21] (Those listed above are the outstanding *vecinos* with whom one can shake hands and in whom one can place one's trust). A number of mestizos and mulattos, although surprisingly no Indians, were included in the artisanal occupations, both as master craftsmen and as apprentices, or as pursuing no trade.

Juan Gallego and Francisco de Santa Maria were two of nine master carpenters, a very important craft in Havana. Francisco de Gongora, Pedro Lopez (probably the son of the listed peasant, Bartolome Lopez) and Francisco de Yibenes were listed as mestizo carpenter apprentices. Domingo de Quejo was a master blacksmith, one of three in the city. Juan de Licao, a name which looks suspiciously Portuguese, was listed as a mestizo apprentice tailor; Juan Mendez, another mestizo, was listed as an apprentice shoemaker.

While this *padron* is only for Havana and its environs, it does present a picture of the social cross-section of the colony at that time. Perhaps the most surprising observation about the *padron* is that although the list contains more than thirty occupations, there is not a single mention of any occupation clearly relating to sugar. The age of sugar had not yet arrived in Cuba. Moreover the picture indicates the correlation between the rise of sugar and the increase in slaves.

Society and Labour in the Sixteenth Century

By the end of the sixteenth century the pace of change began to accelerate – although anything approaching a sugar revolution was still nearly two centuries away. The frontier society was gradually losing both its social democracy and its informal egalitarianism. Throughout the sixteenth century evidence can be found of Indian and African (or at least Afro-Cuban) participation in various aspects of the society, which become rarer during the seventeenth century and virtually disappear during the eighteenth century.

Indians and Africans petitioned the town councils for usufructal grants of land (*mercedes*) for *conucos* (slave gardens) just as free Spaniards or Canary Islanders did, and engaged in raising cattle and growing food crops.[22] Various *padrones* refer to Indians as *vecinos,* suggesting that they had obtained the social acceptability to bear arms and serve in minor official, usually municipal, positions. In March of 1569 an Indian, Alonso, petitioned the Havana *cabildo* for a plot of land, describing himself as *"Alonso, indio, vecino desta villa . . ."* (Alonso, an Indian, a *vecino* of this town). Similar petitions may be seen for Indians from south-west of the province of Havana in 1568 and for the *merced,* Managua in Guanabacoa, for Indians in 1588.

Free Afro-Cubans also petitioned and received grants of *mercedes* during the century. In 1561 Beatriz Nizarda, describing herself as *"de color moreno"* (brown skinned), asked the Havana *cabildo* for a plot of land and was granted *un solar cerca de donde están los demás negros horros* (a plot near where the other free blacks are). In 1577 Hernando de Rojas, described as *un negro horro,* received a *merced* for rearing pigs in Guanabano. Diego de Rojas, described as a *moreno horro,* received a *sitio* for small stock raising near Río Grande; while Francisco Engola (probably an Angolan), who described himself as *horro vecino de Campeche* (a free black, a *vecino* from Campeche), also got a small land grant for raising cattle. These three grants were a significant proportion of the twenty-one granted by the city council in 1577.[23]

The possibility of joining the landed classes or of becoming *vecinos* should not be construed as eliminating the subordinate position into which Indians and other non-Europeans were placed during the century. In 1565 and again in 1566 the city council of Havana repeated restrictions against the hunting of range cattle in the common lands by Indians, mulattos and blacks.[24] And while Afro-Cubans might on occasion have designated themselves loosely as *vecinos,* they were never officially recognized as such.

Nevertheless the structure of the society nearly a century after its reconstitution as a Spanish colony demonstrated a remarkable pluralism, with significant participation in the economy by the non-European element, especially at the level of the occupations. In this respect Cuba varied very little from the pattern of the rest of the Spanish Antilles. Two occurrences, however, deepened the schism between Cuba and its sister Spanish Antilles: the development of Havana as a major city and a major centre of Spanish military power; and the growth of the sugar industry, slowly through the seventeenth and eighteenth centuries, and rapidly after 1760.

Profile of the Colony at the End of the Seventeenth Century

A glance at the demographic profile of the colony at the end of the seventeenth century – in the late 1680s – certainly illustrates graphically the changes in reality and, equally important, *in perception* which were taking place in Cuba. Whites were more important in the organized communities; slaves were visible everywhere; and Indians had begun to disappear statistically, though their numbers remained high.

It is difficult to reconcile the large, often conflicting number of estimates of the population at that time.[25] Bishop Compostela reported to the king at the end of November, 1689 that Cuba and Florida together had a population of "9,066 families and 49,897 persons". He indicated that Florida had "500 families and 1,444 persons" – the neatness of the figures suggests that they were mere guesses. But that leaves 8,566 families in Cuba with approximately 48,453 free individuals. The bishop listed Havana as having 2,686 families and 16,117 persons, which averages slightly more than six persons per family.[26]

A *padron* of Havana in 1691 indicated 2,152 families with 11,940 persons, or 5.5 persons per family. (The discrepancy between the two *padrones* can be explained: the 1691 *padron* was taken of persons within the city walls while presumably the 1689 count was for greater Havana.) What is surprising about the Havana data for that era is the complete absence of any reference to Indians – surprising because Havana had expanded geographically to absorb the town of Guanabacoa, which was an Indian town in 1580, and one of the most populous on the island.

Indeed what appears most surprising from a cursory look at the various *padrones* for the later seventeenth century is the absence of the previous indigenous population of the early towns. With the exception of Bayamo and Santiago, both of which registered a significant population of Indians in 1684, the category of Indians was replaced by that of slaves. Nevertheless in the 1680s approximately 10 per cent of the free population of Bayamo – about four hundred individuals – and 7.3 per cent of the free population of Santiago de Cuba – about two hundred and twenty persons – were Indians. *Villas* (towns) such as Los Caneyes and Jiguaní in eastern Cuba remained entirely or predominantly Indian until the late eighteenth century.

Another observation about the *padrones* of the 1680s is the declining mention of occupation. Race and caste replaced the former indicators of social status, and the presence of slaves made occupational designations less important than before. The work force was slowly becoming universally non-free.

The Impact of the Sugar Industry

The major catalyst for the increased labour demand and the re-evaluation of labour in Cuba came from the sugar revolution of the late eighteenth century. The sugar cane had been brought by Christopher Columbus on his second voyage to Hispaniola, and accompanied the spread of Spanish settlement throughout the region.[27] The early colonists who accompanied Diego Velasquez to Cuba brought the sugar cane, and as early as 1535 a number of hand-operated mills, called *trapiches,* were in operation around Havana. The operations were small, and the product probably only for domestic consumption. In any case while Hispaniola was exporting sugar by mid-century, it was only in the 1580s that the records of the *Casa de Contratación,* or House of Trade, in Seville began to show sugar cargoes from Cuba.[28] In 1581 the *Casa* registered 540 *arrobas* of sugar, or 13,500 lb, arriving in Seville. In 1587 some 450 *arrobas* (11,250 lb) arrived. In 1593, 607 *arrobas* (15,175 lb) arrived; while in 1594 the amount had increased to 2,460 arrobas or 61,500 lb.

The erratic listings of these sugar imports suggest that the amounts did not correspond to annual production figures. The Crown had initiated a program to expand sugar production by extending the privileges enjoyed by the sugar producers of Santo Domingo to Cuba toward the end of the sixteenth century. According to Roland T. Ely,[29] these privileges included a reduction of the tithes by 50 per cent; the protection from seizure for debt of sugar lands, manufacturing equipment, cattle, slaves or factories; and the offering of loans to any prospective sugar producer of up to 40,000 *ducats* for periods extending to eight years.

These incentives appeared inadequate to boost sugar production. The loan system was only a modest success, with no borrower asking for more than 4,400 *ducats* – and most loans being in the range of 500 *ducats*. In order to engage in large-scale sugar production Cubans needed cultivable land, far more labour than was available, and far more ships to send their merchandise to market. In the fifty-two years between 1513 and 1565 only forty-seven ships legally entered the port of Havana, a rate of less than one ship per year, while in the thirty-four years after 1566, 166 ships entered the port officially, a rate of nearly 5 per year. As late as 1756 only twenty-seven vessels entered the port of Havana, and fourteen of those came from Vera Cruz. It is not surprising, therefore, that in 1595 when the Crown granted a *derecho* to Pedro Gomez Reynel to import some thirty thousand Africans within nine years, he surrendered the contract without being able to fulfil the terms. A similar contract awarded to the Portuguese Gonzalo Váez Coutinho failed because of the low demand in Havana.[30]

Gomez Reynel and Coutinho were ahead of their time. It took more than a century for Cuban commerce, based mainly on the export of gold, hides and tobacco, to generate the wealth which could be invested in sugar production. In 1568, the first landed trust, or *mayorazgo,* was founded on the outskirts of Havana by Antonio Recio, one of the city's richest *vecinos.* (Three Recios, Juan Recio, Anton Recio and Martin Recio appear among the *vecinos* of 1582.) By 1595 Vicente Santa Maria built the first *ingenio* (mechanical mill) – as distinct from *trapiche* (manual mill) – at a place called Los Congrejos near Havana. Gradually permission was granted for recipients of *mercedes* to convert their grazing rights into sugar cultivation, and eventually the landed base for large-scale sugar production developed throughout the seventeenth century, employing water and animals to provide the needed power.[31]

Writing to his monarch in 1604, Gonzalo Váez Coutinho (also a Portuguese slave trader and brother of the former Coutinho), deplored the fact that the lack of a large population inhibited in Cuba the exploitation of its vast mineral wealth. He also mentioned, with mildly disguised self-interest, that much wealth could be derived from cultivating sugar with African slaves.[32] Throughout the seventeenth century the population would increase gradually, despite the demographic crisis in Spain, bolstered mainly by the importation of African slaves. Indeed as early as 1608 observers such as Bishop Juan de Las Cabezas Altamirano were beginning to notice the presence of African slaves and the relatively large numbers of Indians outside the confines of Spanish towns.[33] By the end of the century the island had drastically changed from the sleepy, peripheral, miserable collection of straggling colonists of 1582, having overtaken Santo Domingo as the most important port in the Spanish Antilles.

An examination of the *padrones* of 1689 confirms this view.[34] Cuba then had a population of nearly 50,000 persons and a clerical population of 529. More than 50 per cent of this population resided in the western sector of the island, with Havana having 16,117 individuals or 32.2 per cent of the island total. By that time the indigenous Indian population had declined, losing its category of distinctive Indian towns although still representing about 10 per cent of the urban residential population.[35]

The slave trade slowly became a regular source of population augmentation and, of course, labour supply during the course of the seventeenth century. Nevertheless the irregularity of the arrivals and the erratic manner in which evaluation and accounting were done – slaves being calculated erratically by officials as *piezas* (tons), or individuals – indicated that much still had to be learned to produce the efficient transportation and supply system of the later period. The official archival lists show only about five thousand legally imported slaves to Cuba throughout the seventeenth century – most imported from Jamaica in the last decades of the century.[36] The characteristics of the slave population in Cuba – if the sample of 292 working in the copper mines of Santiago de Cuba is any indication – demonstrated a profile unlike that of the later period. Males comprised 53 per cent, females 47 per cent, and 20 per cent of the group were under 14 years old. Moreover a good proportion – 22 per cent of the creole slaves – were mulatto, indicating some longevity and self-perpetuation. By mid-century the mines were petering out; by the end of the century slave prices in various Cuban markets were only about 80 per cent of what they had been at the beginning of the century.[37] Slave-holding was far more generalized in 1700 than in 1600, and slaves were highly visible both as domestic servants and as field hands. But Cuba was far from being a slave society in 1700.

From Slave-Holding Society to Slave Society: The Eighteenth Century

The transformation would be made in the eighteenth century. There would be a revolution in the delivery system for slaves as the individual *asientos* gave way to national monopolies after 1713, and as the Europeans in general developed an efficient, intricate transformation and marketing interrelationship involving Europe, Africa and the Americas.[38]

During the eighteenth century sugar would gradually overtake tobacco and ranching as the preferred economic activity. More and more *trapiches* were built and improved to the point of becoming *ingenios*. More slaves were delivered legally by a system of *asientos* or illegally by the enthusiastic foreign slave vendors from North America, Great Britain and France. A better marketing system, too, enabled the Cuban producers to sell their product – legally in the metropolis if they could, or illegally to anyone if they had to. The Spanish mercantilistic operation collapsed entirely during the eighteenth century, and by the time that limited free trade with neutral powers was legitimized in 1776, the island had already committed itself to the path of the plantation, export-oriented, exploitation society, the appetite for slaves having been stoked by the English capture of Havana in 1763.

Although the full impact of the sugar revolution had not yet been felt in Cuba, the census of 1774 clearly demonstrated the future direction of growth. Thereafter labour meant slaves. For in 1774, in a total island population of 171,620, there were no Indians to be found officially.[39] Nevertheless Indians were petitioning the Crown about diverse matters throughout the 1780s and 1790s. The white population amounted to 96,440 or 56.9 per cent. The intermediate free coloured sector accounted for 36,301 or 20.3 per cent. The slave sector was already 38,879 or 22.8 per cent. The stark, threefold categorization indicated the inexorable transition from a society of cross-cutting social cleavages – the seven categories of the 1570s and 1580s – to one of mutually reinforcing social cleavages. Cuba became, as were the other Caribbean sugar islands, a society of three castes internally subdivided into classes. Race, colour and occupation assumed greater importance as the distinction between the free and the non-free required severe definition in law and in custom. When this was necessary, the mature slave society had arrived.

Throughout the nineteenth century further linear expansion would take place, but the norms of the society would no longer be altered as they were during the seventeenth and eighteenth centuries. By 1841 the second sugar revolution – mainly a technological revolution – had begun. By that time the slave component represented the single largest sector of the population: 436,495 or 43.3 per cent (compared with a white component of 418,291 or 41.6 per cent; and a free coloured component of 152,838 or 15.1 per cent).[40] Even so, it was the beginning of the end of slavery in Cuba.

If we look a bit more closely at the situation in 1774 we can see this sequence quite clearly. In 1774 whites outnumbered non-whites by 21,260. By 1827 the non-whites outnumbered the whites by 82,385. The gap had widened by 1841, with the non-whites outnumbering the whites by 171,042. It was panic time among the whites in Cuba, and the cruel massacre of non-whites allegedly implicated in the Conspiracy of the Ladder was partly the result of this panic.[41] After 1841 manual labour would forever be regarded as menial labour, as the work of "blacks", even when it was being done by Mexican Indians, Chinese and Canary Islanders. But non-whites would never again be allowed to regain the numerical majority in the island. And by that time a new transition from slavery to free labour was already underway, although the majority of Cuban sugar producers refused to countenance it. By 1860 the island had come full circle and free labour was resuming its previous importance. But the conditions of the sixteenth and seventeenth centuries could not be recaptured.

Conclusions

We can now consider some of the implications of slavery and the social transformation in Cuba.

1. While the process of converting to a standard quasi-monoculture comparable to the English and French Caribbean was much slower, the end product was quite similar. Sugar and slavery had the same overall effect in Cuba as elsewhere. But the lag in arriving at the stage of the sugar revolutions meant that the social and demographic impacts would be mitigated. The settler society was never inundated demographically in Cuba as in the other islands and territories, and the relatively late arrival of the African population meant that the free population retained at all times the "critical mass" necessary to maintain a coherent, complex culture. At no time in the history of Cuba did the non-free swamp the free as was the pattern throughout most of the other islands.

   In the demographic revolution which occurred as a result of the conquest, occupation and later development of the island, the indigenous population did not perish immediately and without a trace. They did not vanish. They survived, and they survived in substantial numbers.

   As late as 1793 Indians from the town of Jiguaní, south-east of Bayamo, were still in litigation to recover lands they alleged were confiscated by wealthy families from Bayamo and Santiago de Cuba.[42] Indians, however, lost their corporate and political identity, and by the late eighteenth century had lost most of their cultural identity as well. This is hardly surprising, since Spanish policy after the sixteenth century offered the choice of conversion and hispanization or elimination – by slavery if possible, by war and disease if necessary.

Nevertheless the advent of sugar and slavery converted national and regional identifications into oversimplified categories of race, colour and civil status – accentuating caste at the expense of class and condition. By this process acculturated Indians were appropriated into the "white" category, probably by virtue of somatic norm proximity rather than any conscious attempt at cosmopolitanism. At the same time, the increase in the subordinated African population sharpened the identity and distinction between denominated white and non-white. Still, after the seventeenth century Cuba reversed its population loss to the mainland and became a net importer of people, albeit from Africa.

2. Economically the wealth of the island came increasingly to be identified with sugar production, as the mixed economy based on mining, grazing and tobacco farming yielded to concentrated demands of capitalist land-enclosing constructs. Land and slaves assumed ever greater importance as valuable economic assets, essential prerequisites for success in the colonies.

3. The rising population and wealth had profound political repercussions which I have not developed here. Havana used its strategic and administrative position to extend its hegemony over the rest of the island, destroying the political equality of the smaller towns' councils in the process and concentrating in its hands the *de facto* authority to represent the interests of the entire island in Spain. Santiago de Cuba valiantly retained its identity, partly because of geography and the state of transportation technology, until the late nineteenth century.

4. Occupations, formerly fluid, began to assume – as they had elsewhere in the Caribbean – connotations of race, colour and social condition. Occupational stereotyping became the order of the day. As mentioned before, manual labour became identified with non-whites and carried menial connotations. So it was in Barbados as early as 1650 and so it came to be in Cuba in 1750.

5. Sugar, the plantation and slavery provided the inescapable combination which fashioned, changed and distorted the linear continuation of European settler society in the Caribbean, but in so doing they reinforced a common trajectory from which the region has not yet successfully

escaped. Caribbean culture and society – and most especially Cuban culture and society – simply cannot be understood without this important reference point.

Notes

1. Elsa V. Goveia, *Slave Society in the British Leeward Islands at the End of the Eighteenth Century* (New Haven: Yale University Press, 1965).
2. Goveia, *Slave Society*, vii.
3. Hortensia Pichardo, *Documentos para la historia de Cuba*, 3 vols. (Havana: Ciencias Sociales, 1971), 1: 413–21. The best study of the disintegration of slavery is Rebecca J. Scott, *Slave Emancipation in Cuba: The Transition to Free Labour, 1860–1899* (Princeton: Princeton University Press, 1985). See also Arthur F. Corwin, *Spain and the Abolition of Slavery in Cuba, 1817–1886* (Austin: University of Texas Press, 1967).
4. The evidence for pre-Hispanic slavery in the Caribbean is sketchy. It derives from the Las Casas reading of the logs of Columbus, now lost, in which he refers to an enslaved group in Cuba and Hispaniola. See Carl Sauer, *The Early Spanish Main* (Berkeley: University of California Press, 1966), 185.
5. Bernal Diaz del Castillo, *The True History of the Conquest of Mexico,* trans. Maurice Keatinge (London, 1800; facsimile edition, La Jolla, California: Renaissance Prints, 1979), 502. Varying translations of this text appear elsewhere, for example in John Parry, *The Age of Reconnaissance, Discovery, Exploration and Settlement, 1450–1650* (New York: World Publishing, 1963), 19.
6. See Nicholas Canny and Anthony Pagden, *Colonial Identity in the Atlantic World, 1500–1800* (Princeton: Princeton University Press, 1987).
7. Richard Ligon, *A True and Exact History of the Island of Barbados* (London, 1657).
8. I have developed this point in *The Caribbean: The Genesis of a Fragmented Nationalism* (New York: Oxford University Press, 1978) and "Patterns of Colonial Society and Culture: Latin America and the Caribbean, 1492–1804", in *South Atlantic Urban Studies,* ed. Jack R. Censer, N. Steven Steinert and Amy M. McCandless (Charleston: University of South Carolina Press, 1978), 3–23.
9. Irene Wright, *The Early History of Cuba, 1492–1586* (1916; reprint, Westport: Greenwood, 1970), 194; and Fernando Portuondo, *Historia de Cuba*, 8th ed. (Havana: Instituto Cubano del Libro, 1965), 91–92.
10. Franklin W. Knight, *Slave Society in Cuba During the Nineteenth Century* (Madison: University of Wisconsin Press, 1970), 22.
11. See Levi Marrero, *Cuba: economia y sociedad,* 14 vols. (Madrid: Playor, 1974–89), esp. vol. 2.

12. Ibid., 2: 325.
13. Ibid., 329.
14. Archivo General de Indias (Seville), Sección de Santo Domingo, Legajo 2070. Real cedula de 21 de noviembre de 1590; Francisco Castillo Melendez, *La defensa de la isla de Cuba en la segunda mitad del siglo XVII* (Seville: Diputacion Provincial, 1986), 99–101.
15. Marrero, *Cuba*, vol. 2; Carla Rahn Phillips, *Six Galleons for the King of Spain: Imperial Defense in the Early Seventeenth Century* (Baltimore: Johns Hopkins University Press, 1986).
16. Knight, *Slave Society*, 22.
17. Marrero, *Cuba*, 2: 332–34.
18. Foreigners were not surprising in the Spanish New World, or for that matter in Spain. See Ruth Pike, *Enterprise and Adventure: The Genoese in Seville and the Opening of the New World* (Ithaca: Cornell University Press, 1966).
19. Marrero, *Cuba*, 2: 332–36.
20. Curiously described as *"sin casa ni mujer, ni hacienda, ni padres, ni madres, personas sin prendas en esta villa"* (without home, without wife, without property, without fathers, without mothers, persons without links in this town).
21. Marrero, *Cuba*, 2: 332.
22. Ibid., 76–78.
23. Ibid., 78.
24. Ibid., 98–99.
25. See Ibid., 3: 52–64.
26. Ibid., 64.
27. Pike, *Enterprise and Adventure,* 59–61.
28. AGI (Seville), Santo Domingo, Legajos 71, 116.
29. Roland T. Ely, *La economia cubana entre las dos Isabeles, 1492–1832,* 3d edition (Bogota: Aedita editores, 1962), 25–27.
30. Enriqueta Vila Vilar, *Hispano-America y el comercio de esclavos: Los asientos portugueses* (Seville: Escuela de Estudios Hispanoamericanos, 1977), 24–25.
31. Marrero, *Cuba*, 3: 212–16.
32. Quoted in Marrero, *Cuba*, 3: 7. The original is in AGI, Santo Domingo, 451.
33. Marrero, *Cuba*, 3: 17–19.
34. These *padrones,* scattered in AGI Santo Domingo 150 and AGI Contaduría 1160, have been summarized in Marrero, *Cuba*, 3: 52–65.
35. It is difficult to determine whether the decline of the Indian population is as real and dramatic as the *padrones* suggest, or the increase in Spanish and African manpower meant that the Spanish could now attend to defence without the support of the Indians.

36. This is an indication of the illegal trade volume, since the import figures do not correlate with the slave population in Cuba or throughout the region. See Vila Vilar, *Comercio*; Marrero, *Cuba*, 3: 40.

37. Marrero, *Cuba*, 3: 32–45.

38. See Colin A. Palmer, *Human Cargoes: The British Slave Trade to Spanish America, 1700–1739* (Urbana: University of Illinois Press, 1981).

39. Kenneth F. Kipple, *Blacks in Colonial Cuba, 1774–1899* (Gainesville: University Press of Florida, 1976), 25–27.

40. Knight, *Slave Society*.

41. Robert Paquette, *Sugar Is Made with Blood: The Conspiracy of the La Escalera and the Conflict between Empires over Slavery in Cuba* (Middletown, Conn.: Wesleyan University Press, 1988), 125.

42. Litigation by Indians may be followed in AGI (Seville), Santo Domingo, Legajos 1600–22, especially Legajos 1618–22.

CHAPTER 5

Planters, Farmers and Gardeners in Eighteenth-Century Jamaica

DOUGLAS HALL

I am grateful for the opportunity to share in this memorial to the work and the person of Elsa Goveia. I am also happy to be once again briefly stamping on familiar territory.

I must, however, begin with excuses. I propose to say something about the horticultural interests and endeavours of planters, farmers and gardeners in Jamaica in the eighteenth century – but I am neither botanist nor horticulturalist, and, even though living in rural Westmoreland, I am not even a "herbalist" in the current sense of the word. As a learner-farmer with a preference for small livestock over plants I am limited to expressing interest rather than expertise in the topic.

You may well wonder why I chose it. There are two reasons. First, historians of eighteenth-century Jamaica (or the West Indies for that matter) have for obvious reasons given emphasis to examinations of one or other aspect of the slave-supported sugar estate economy and society. Because that part of our history is relatively well documented in official records and in the correspondence and papers of the sugar planters, in our early rush to the gold mines of information we took the larger veins and did not search for the smaller, though perhaps equally rich, capillaries of data.

So our accounts have tended to be a little lopsided, and I suspect that we have much more to discover about the ways in which individuals thought, behaved and interacted in our slave societies.

My second reason is that within the past fifteen years or so, and largely as a result of the inspiration of teachers like Elsa Goveia, the number of people engaged in West Indian historical research has increased and the volume and the competitiveness of enquiry have grown. Guided both by the work of bibliographers and archivists, such as Kenneth Ingram and Clinton Black, and by a keener nose-scent for information, some of the more recent research has begun to tap the capillaries.

Recent work by historians of English agriculture has raised questions about the relative contributions of the large landowners, the smaller country squires and the tenant farmers to the introduction of agricultural and horticultural improvements. There is now a reconsideration of the history of English agriculture based on the examination of previously neglected materials such as farmers' account books, inventories, diaries, correspondence, and other papers.[1] I mention this because we are now beginning, in the writing of our own history, to follow a similar revisionist path. For instance Professor Edward Brathwaite, Professor Barry Higman, Verene Shepherd and others have pointed to the importance of the previously neglected small settlers in the eighteenth and early-nineteenth-century Jamaican countryside.

Brathwaite reminds us that the Jamaica Assembly in 1792 estimated that there were about four thousand resident cultivators on properties not exceeding five hundred acres each, and that "their contribution to the society was not negligible".[2] Higman, distinguishing between estates, plantations, pens and settlements, points out that "the small, strongly diversified unit was both common and widely dispersed, even if it did not dominate the economy or the slave population".[3] His acknowledged difficulty in distinguishing clearly between pens and settlements, and his demonstrated preponderance of properties called settlements in Hanover and Western Jamaica, are nicely supported by an advertisement put out in the mid-1780s by a resident proprietor, Mr Thomas Thistlewood, from whose diaries I shall soon be quoting heavily.[4] The advertisement began: "To be sold in the parish of Westmoreland, a small Settlement, known by the name of Breadnut Island Pen . . . containing 160 acres."

In his diaries Mr Thistlewood shows that, as in rural eighteenth-century England, where the country squire's daily round was enlivened by going to the races, playing cricket, shooting, fishing, and gardening, so too was the life of planters, farmers and even of slaves in eighteenth-century Jamaica. I am going to put before you some evidence of the existence in Jamaica in the second half of the eighteenth century of a strong horticultural interest which, not surprisingly, engaged the farmers or smaller landowners whose income was in part derived from sales in the local markets, but which also attracted the attention of sugar planters and of slaves.

Descriptions of the English countryside in the eighteenth century tell of the estates of the large landowners who (unlike the West Indian plantocracy of the time) rented out their land to tenant farmers and derived their income from rents and other charges on their tenants. On the English estates stood the residences – the halls or manor houses – of the proprietors with their surrounding woodlands, parks and ornate gardens.[5] The stately homes of England were not architecturally reproduced in Jamaica, but the resident plantocracy demonstrated a desire to emulate the lifestyle of their rural English counterparts. In one aspect in particular – gardening – planters large and small were engaged with some enthusiasm. This horticultural interest was not of local birth. It followed a surge of activity in England where, between about 1720 and 1850, English horticulturalists broke away from continental philosophies and practices and established a new horticultural landscape in which the formal, geometric and strikingly ornate patterns copied from European gardens yielded to emphases on enchanting disorder, and attempts to evoke natural beauty rather than to try to beautify nature.[6] This horticultural interest rested on practical as well as on aesthetic foundations. In botanic gardens at Kew, Chelsea and Edinburgh, plants brought in from all over the world were examined for their economic potential as much as for botanical interest.[7]

In terms of the mercantilist theory prevailing through most of the eighteenth century, a nation's wealth came from a favourable balance of trade which would bring in settlements in coin and bullion from debtor nations. If a country or an empire could be made more and more self-sufficient it would clearly have to spend less on imports, and would earn by exports to those less self-sufficient. As one of the early mercantilist writers put it, "The ordinary means therefore to increase our wealth and treasure is by Forraign Trade, wherein wee must ever observe this rule; to sell more to strangers yearly than we consume of theirs in value."[8]

In 1762 the Society of Arts in England "made available a premium to anyone establishing a nursery or botanic garden on the island of St Vincent for the propagation of useful plants and the reception of transported varieties from Asia". Three years later a garden was begun on twenty-five acres of land near Kingstown, the capital. The choice of St Vincent is probably explained by the fact that it was not then a developed sugar island, and had just been acquired by the British from the French. Sir Joseph Banks, of the Society of Arts in England, also began a wide correspondence with planters in the West Indies and elsewhere, offering support in any attempts they might make to obtain exotic plants.[9]

In Jamaica, large estate owners who were residents kept large flower and fruit as well as kitchen gardens in English fashion. Mr Thistlewood, who arrived in Jamaica in 1750, was soon after employed by a wealthy Westmoreland/St Elizabeth planter, Florentius Vassall, as overseer on his cattle pen at Vineyard, between Lacovia and Black River. The Vineyard house was a rather nondescript affair – Vassall, when in Jamaica, resided in Westmoreland – but the garden near the house contained a variety of citrus, a grape arbour (this apparently was a favourite in the eighteenth century planters' gardens) and many other fruit trees, shrubs and flowers. On Tuesday April 16, 1751 he recorded that Captain Colart of the ship *Boston* had brought for Mr Vassall various wines and two tubs of English fruit trees. These would go to Westmoreland. Vassall, as we shall see, was only one of many importers of plants and seeds. Thistlewood himself set up a business in it, importing mostly but not entirely from England – sorting, cataloguing and sending catalogues and samples to prospective buyers.

In the *Hortus Eastensis*,[10] the catalogue of plants in the much-mentioned garden of Hinton East at Spring Garden (at Gordon Town) in the later eighteenth century, there are twenty-one people named as having been the first to bring into Jamaica plants to be found growing in that garden in 1793. Foremost among them were Hinton East himself (he had died in the previous year) and Matthew Wallen, who had an equally well-known garden at Cold Spring (on the St Andrew/Portland border near Hardwar Gap). Hinton East was a creole of English parents. A lawyer, he was from time to time judge advocate general, receiver general, and an elected member for Kingston in the island assembly. In 1770 he began to establish his private botanic garden at Spring Garden and to import and export seeds and plants. Matthew Wallen, equally known for his botanical interests, was a member of assembly in several years between 1750 and 1790 representing the Parish of Port Royal, which in those days stretched inland up into the Liguanea mountains where his garden was established.[11] But Thistlewood's name does not appear in the *Hortus Eastensis*. He was, after all, an overseer and then a small settler far in the west. A little more surprising is the fact that he made no mention of East or of Wallen, though it is very unlikely that he did not know of them.

In 1774, aware of the British precedent and moved by the persuasions of people in Jamaica and in England, and perhaps by the news that the botanic garden in St Vincent was then in a state of decline, the Jamaica Assembly (a body controlled by the planter interests) established a botanic garden at Bath in St Thomas, and acquired Enfield, adjoining East's Spring Garden, with intention to set up another one there. That proposal, however, came to nothing, and twenty years later in 1794, following the death of Mr East, the Assembly acquired Spring Garden itself: "with thirty-nine Negroes belonging to it, many of whom are valuable gardeners, for the sum of £5,000 currency, and there being a commodious dwelling-house and offices thereon, together with a botanic garden containing a numerous collection of very valuable plants".[12]

The man in charge of the early operations at Bath was Dr Thomas Clarke, arrived from England in 1777. Like many of the eighteenth century botanists he was a medical man, primarily interested in medicinal and pharmaceutical plants, of which he was himself an outstanding collector. In charge at Spring Garden was Mr James Wiles, a botanist who had arrived at Port Royal in February 1793 with Captain Bligh in the ship *Providence,* bringing 346 breadfruit plants.

After a period of decline the botanic garden at St Vincent was brought back into operation in 1785 under the direct control of the British War and Colonial Office, and breadfruit plants were also delivered there.[13]

In Jamaica the plants were distributed by the Botanic Gardens Committee of the Assembly as follows:

- Sixty-six to the botanic garden at Bath. The land space available there was too small, so Dr Dancer, another medical man interested in plants, gave an additional piece of adjoining land.
- Thirty to Spring Garden, not yet purchased by the Assembly, but with the assistance of Mr Lynch who was acting for the heirs of Hinton East [was negotiating to do so].
- Eighty-three to be distributed by an agent in Kingston to individuals in the County of Surrey.

- Eighty-four through an agent in Port Henderson to people in Middlesex, and
- Eighty-three to persons in the County of Cornwall through an agent in Savanna-la-Mar. Of that number, twelve plants went to St Elizabeth, fifteen to Westmoreland, sixteen to Hanover, eighteen to St James and twenty-two to Trelawny.

Sir Joseph Banks, who had been instrumental in Captain Bligh's expeditions, was not forgotten. The Botanic Gardens Committee, assisted by Mr Wallen, Dr Dancer and Dr Broughton (the compiler of the *Hortus Eastensis*), had put together a collection of plants requested for His Majesty's garden at Kew.[14]

It had never been a one-way traffic. Hinton East, in a long letter of July 1784, acknowledged receipt of a letter from Banks "with two seeds of the moving plants enclosed. It affords me great pleasure [he wrote] to inform you that I have for a considerable time past, been in possession of this plant which thrives abundantly in my garden." With his reply East sent to Sir Joseph seeds of Jamaican and French colonial origin.[15] Theirs was by no means the only such correspondence.

The private horticultural correspondence was also international. Again, my examples come from the Thistlewood diaries; but, as the entries will later indicate, he was not unique in his interest. In January 1763 he sent to his then employer, John Cope, "a honey water melon, raised from seed, from Martinico". Unfortunately he did not say how he had obtained the seeds. In 1770 he sent a small cake of annatto and a small bottle of annatto seeds to England and asked that enquiries be made about the price they might command. In February 1779, and this was not the only occasion, he went out collecting seeds of the sensitive mimosa ("dead-and-wake" or "shame-me-lady") which he sent to his friend and corresponding agent in England, Mr Hewitt at Brompton, near London. In March 1772 he shipped seeds of poinciana, Barbados pride, Spanish carnation, ringworm bush and four other plants to a D. Lowther in England (another medical botanist perhaps). With them went references to historical and botanical publications in which some were mentioned.

On the official level botanical collection was competitive. On a visit to England in September 1784, Matthew Wallen told Banks a story of how in the recent war with America a French ship carrying breadfruit plants from Mauritius to the French West Indies had been intercepted by the English, and the French crew had destroyed "as many plants as possible to prevent them falling into British hands".[16]

Perhaps they had not entirely succeeded, for a few years after that event and seven years before Captain Bligh arrived in Jamaica, Mr Thistlewood recorded, in early January 1786: "In the morning received a note from Mr Rose by a Negro with a box of plants. Gave him 2 bitts [about 1s. and 3d.]. Wrote Mr Rose and sent Sukey, Franke, and Maria for the remaining ones, Plants received – Breadfruit, mango, camphor [camphire], Madeira peach or Clingstone of America, Lichee or Persian Plum . . . [and a variety of seeds]."

The next day he recorded the heights of the plants: the mango 15 inches, the lichee 11 inches, the peach 6½, and the breadfruit 18 inches with four leaves.

Hinton East, two years before in his letter of July 1784 to Sir Joseph Banks, had said, "one of the mango trees is now bearing for the first time and the fruit promises to be very large". (The mango, we are told, had been first brought in and planted in his garden in 1782 so this plant would have been about two years old.) But to go back to Mr East:

I have [also] two or three plants which came from the Isle de Bourbon supposed by some to be the breadfruit, but I am extremely doubtful, as they do not in the shape of them by any means correspond with the account and drawings given by Mr Ellis. The acquisition of that kind of breadfruit would be of infinite importance to the West India islands in affording, exclusive of variety, a wholesome pleasant food to our Negroes . . .

Perhaps Mr East was right. Perhaps Mr Ellis' descriptions and drawings were not. Nonetheless Sir Joseph Banks, who as a young man had sailed with Captain Cook and been introduced to the breadfruit in the South Seas, was open to persuasion and ready to support an attempt to bring the plants into the British Caribbean. In 1786 Mr East visited Banks and they discussed the possibilities.[17] (Note a coincidence of names: Mr East's Spring Garden, Mr Wallen's Cold Spring, and Sir Joseph's country residence in England, Spring Grove. Perhaps botanists, like sweet lovers, love the spring.) Be that as it may, it was in the following year, 1787, that Captain Bligh set out in the ship *Bounty* towards the famous mutiny. Then, in the early 1790s, came his second attempt in the ship *Providence* with her escorting brig *Assistance*. The names of the vessels were of Sir Joseph Bank's choosing.[18] He clearly viewed it as a rescue mission.

The mango story contains no qualifications such as Mr East's doubts about his breadfruit plants. We are told that the mango plant and other exotics first arrived in Jamaica in 1782; ". . . brought in by Captain Marshall of Rodney's squadron [it] was first planted in Hinton East's botanic garden, in Liguanea".[19] The *Hortus Eastensis* tells the same.

Let us go back to Mr Thistlewood:

> Monday 20th September, 1773 [nine years before Captain Marshall]. Planted in [my] New Garden eleven Bengal peach stones and two mango stones. Note! one of the mango stones is about 4 inches long, 2 broad, and eight-tenths thick. Both furrowed lengthways. Enclosed in wax from 2 to 3 tenths thick, and this wrapped up in a waxed cloth. Seemed pretty fresh.

He does not say where he got them; and, in fact, they did not germinate.

Mid-January 1779, still three years before Captain Marshall: Thistlewood and his lawyer friend Robert Chambers of Savanna-la-Mar visited Friendship and Greenwich, belonging to our earlier acquaintance Florentius Vassall. Next morning, with the overseer Mr Bodington, they "rode about a mile and a half to see the young mango tree. It is in a plantain walk considerably to the North East of Greenwich works, in a fine rich soil, at about 20 feet distance from the Cabaritta river. This young tree is now about 2½ feet high." Fifteen months later, in March 1780, they went back to see it, now "about 8½ feet high, has branches out at 7 feet, seems thriving".

We know that Mr Vassall imported plants. Perhaps we owe our first mango tree to him. In such details we can now begin to revise some of the little we have of our horticultural history, or would it be our arboricultural history.

I have not fully and minutely compared the *Hortus Eastensis* with Mr Thistlewood's list of plants "growing" in his garden in October 1770, the year in which Mr East began his garden, or his later list of 1775, nine years before his death; but here are a few examples of difference during the time at which various plants are acknowledged to have first been brought to Jamaica.

According to *Hortus Eastensis,* the horse chestnut was brought from Asia by a Mrs Brodbelt in 1770; the amaryllis, eight sorts from various places including the Americas, China and South Africa between 1770 and 1789; the wallflower, by Wallen. In 1772; the amaranthus, three sorts, from the East Indies in 1773; the common oak from Britain, by Wallen in 1773; four sorts of cypress, from various sources, by Mr East and two other gentlemen – Mr Thame and Mr Salt – at different times between 1773 and 1789; the walnut from Persia by Wallen in 1774; the white mulberry from China by Mr East in 1784. All of these were listed by Thistlewood as "growing" in his gardens in 1770. He had only one cypress and one sort of amaranthus; but he had two sorts of amaryllis, one of which had been given to him by John Cope of Egypt estate.

Compared with the gardens of East, Wallen, and no doubt others, Thistlewood's was small, but that made him no less enthusiastic or competent a gardener. He was of a farming family in Lincolnshire in England, and he counted gardeners among his relatives and friends. Before coming to Jamaica he had sailed in the service of the East India Company and had then indicated his interest. In October 1748, for instance, he had visited Mr James Scott, of Turnham Green near London, and "was all over his gardens. . . . I gave Mr Scott sundry nuts, berries, seeds, &c I had collected abroad and brought out for him".

Thistlewood's uncle, John Longstaff, was gardener at Stainfield Hall in Lincolnshire. Thomas Harrison Butler and Treddaway Butler, gardeners at Pandon in the same county, were his friends. With them, he had been all over their gardens. And here in Jamaica, though he served many years as an overseer on sugar properties, it was as a gardener that he made his unquestioned reputation in his parish.

In March 1761, while still an overseer, he was visited by Dr Anthony Robinson, another medical botanist, who was paid by the Society of Arts, through the governor of Jamaica, £200 a year for "collecting curiosities and making remarks, &c. &c. in this country". They became good friends and Robinson gave Thistlewood lessons "in drawing birds, plants, &c.".

Some of Dr Anthony Robinson's drawings are to be found in the manuscript collection of our National Library. Edward Long wrote of him:

> The late Dr. Anthony Robinson [he died in early 1768] made a collection of several hundred figures and descriptions of Jamaica plants and animals. . . . This work, if it should ever be given to the public will be found to correct many errors in Sloane and Brown, who, compared with him, were in various instances very superficial observers, or ill-informed.[20]

Long and Robinson had been friends, and perhaps Long's appraisal was overdone, but the Jamaica Assembly recognized Robinson's work.

He had succeeded in making a vegetable soap and in making a sago flour from a local species of the sago palm. Shortly before his death the Assembly had voted him a hundred pistoles (about £200 currency) with a promise of more. According to Edward Long, Robinson's sago product was "equal in its alimentary qualities to what comes from the East Indies". The East Indian sago palm is recorded to have been first introduced in 1775 by Dr Clarke, who is also credited with bringing the first ackee plant from West Africa in 1778, and many others.

Robinson had clearly recognized Thistlewood's interest and industry as a gardener, even as overseer on a sugar estate he gardened. In March 1760, for example, he planted in the kitchen garden at Egypt cauliflower, broccoli, cabbage, lettuce, parsley, spinach and beets. Even then he was importing plants and seeds, growing them, cataloguing them, and selling by advertisements in the local taverns, by sending samples to the surrounding proprietors and others, and even by sending out slaves with baskets of seeds, flowers and vegetables to go higglering.

"Wednesday 20th January, 1762. I have now a white narcissus in full flower in the garden, a pretty large bunch of 12 or 13 flowers in it. This is probably the first that even flowered in this island. It opened about a week ago." In the following week he noted that another bunch opened. Under Narcissus the East catalogue lists three sorts, all brought from southern Europe by Mr Thame in 1773.

"Thursday 17th May, 1770. Sowed a bed of Battersea asparagus seeds. . . . This day flowered an English pink (of a beautiful red) in my garden, which is the first I have seen, or heard of, to have flowered in the island. The plant is flourishing and will have many flowers." Under the generic heading *Dianthus,* the East catalogue lists three varieties of pink first brought in from continental Europe, China and England by Mr Wallen, all in 1772. Mr Thistlewood, remember, had shipped Spanish carnation seeds to Dr Lowther in March of that year.

"Sunday 22nd September, 1776. The honeysuckle (trumpet) or woodbine, in my garden is now in flower, and is perhaps the first and only one ever in this island yet." But in this case probably not, for the East catalogue shows importations in 1773 and perhaps before.

Interestingly, in *An Account of Jamaica* published in 1808, James Stewart remarked, "The Woodbine or honeysuckle, is unknown here."[21] Quite possible, for many of the imported plants died out altogether and some, failing at first, were subsequently reintroduced with greater success.

The sources of Mr Thistlewood's supplies are interesting because they indicate his activities as an importer, and illustrate the horticultural interests of local people – estate owners, settlers and slaves. His external sources were chiefly in England and North America. In his 1775 catalogue of over three hundred plants in his garden, about sixty had come from England, about twenty-five from North America, and the rest he had obtained locally from other gardeners or collected in fields and waysides. Some examples follow:

- In May 1770 he exchanged seeds and plants with Mr Hayward of Hatfield near Savanna-la-Mar, at whose gate slaves regularly held a Sunday market. Hayward was in business in Savanna-la-Mar.
- In January 1773 John Ricketts of Canaan and Ridgeland, a large proprietor, "Gave me an advertisement of Trees, &c. sold by William Prince, near New York".
- June 1774: "Returned Dr. Panton's [copy of] Milne's Botany; also gave him some borage, celery, curled parsley and cardoon seeds."
- In the same month he planted rose-apple seeds brought from Kingston for him by a Mr Peter Richardson, and Abbay or Macca-fat nuts sent to him by a Mr Duncan.
- In January 1775 Mr Matthew Bowen, from the Bluefields area gave him "a great variety of flower seeds sent him from North America by Mr Gooden". Mr Gooden was Thistlewood's next-door neighbour at Kirkpatrick Pen, now called Llandilo.
- February 1777: "Received a letter from William Mure, Esq. of Saxham Estate in Hanover, with 3 plants of the bamboo cane and a cutting of the coral tree. Wrote to him and sent him 6 young cypresses, 6 sarsaparilla plants, 2 malabar nuts, 6 cuttings of the African rose and 6 ditto of the Cyprian fig, some melongene, changeable rose and musk, ochro seeds, also a red bean of a different sort from his."

The rose-apple planting of four years before seems to have succeeded, for in June 1778, Thistlewood rode to Mr Beckford at Hertford, another large proprietor, and "gave him the rose-apples". Beckford, in return, gave geranium slips, jonquil roots and other flower seeds.

There were others: John Cope, William Lewis at Cornwall, Mr Meyler of Meylersfield, all large landowners; overseers such as Mr Bodington whom we have already met on a journey to a mango tree; small settlers like William Pommells in Westmoreland and the Brownes at Dettingen in St Elizabeth, both indigo planters who also had gardens; John Scott at Cave who "has plenty of pot herbs, bees, &c and locks his gates. Has a very fine house." There was also Francis Scott, a young gardener (perhaps related to John Scott of

Turnham Green) who was sent out into Thistlewood's care. He moved into sugar overseership first at Retrieve, on the road to Negril, then at Ackendown on the road to Black River, but he continued his gardening and was a regular visitor at Thistlewood's pen.

And what of the slaves? There were thirty-nine slaves sold with Mr East's garden, and some were said to be gardeners. They had to be. Thistlewood's slaves and others also laboured in the gardens of their owners. The question is whether they ever gardened on their own account or were even interested in the products of the gardens. There is some evidence that they did and were.

Dido was a slave belonging to John Cope – owner, with his wife, of Paradise, Salt River and Egypt estates. Dido had for several years worked under Thistlewood (in more than one sense of the term) in the garden at Egypt. In December 1767 when he had just moved into his own recently acquired pen or settlement, she sent him "thyme, sage and rosemary" which he planted. In January she sent another gift: "In the evening, planted 25 cabbage plants in the garden which Dido sent me from Paradise."

These were not the only recorded occasions nor was Dido the only slave-donor, but the instances were not many and the donors were all people who had worked with Thistlewood at some time or another. After his death in 1786 his land and slaves were sold, and although I have found no advertisement of them as gardeners, some of them certainly had considerable horticultural practice.

In February 1768, following the arrival of one of his many shipments of plants from England, Thistlewood, Dick, Maria and Coobah were "employed planting the English trees" and putting out narcissi, tulips, lucerne, clovers, timothy grass, sainfoin, turnips, cabbages, parsley, borage, burnett, angelica and many others. In October 1770, he planted in a provision ground, in addition to the usual food staples, potato slips, sugar beans and alligator pear seeds.

In July 1774 he recorded (it was on a Saturday), "Gave my Negroes today [that is, to work on their own account]. Gave them plenty of cabbage, savoy and broccoli plants to plant in their grounds." Perhaps the slaves threw the plants away, but I doubt it. Thistlewood was too careful a man to have given them plants expecting them to be destroyed. Then, as now, there was a market for such produce. Thistlewood himself sold to slaves as well as to wealthier buyers.

He records having sold tobacco which was "taken at different times for garden stuff to various sorts when they could not sell it for money" – "they" being the slaves he sent out on the road with produce. On the other side of the coin, he sometimes took payment in garden produce: "Two water-hens, some green peas, radishes, and a large land-turtle which I took in payment from Egypt Negroes for work [sewing and dressmaking] done by Phibbah." (Phibbah was one of John Cope's slaves whom Thistlewood had hired at £18 a year so that she could continue to live with him when he left Mr Cope's employment. She outlived him, and in his will he made provision for her to purchase her freedom, acquire a small house and land, and two slaves of her own.)

Information about the gardening activities of the slaves is plentiful if not precise. Edward Long, describing the Kingston market in the 1770s wrote:

> Here are found not only a great variety of American, but also of European vegetables: such as peas, beans, cabbage, lettuce, cucumbers, french beans, artichokes, potatoes, carrots, turnips, radishes, celery, onions, etc. These are brought from the Liguanea mountains, and are all excellent in their kind.[22]

A few years later Bryan Edwards said the same sort of thing. He spoke of the Kingston and Spanish Town markets being "supplied with cabbages, lettuce, carrots, turnips, parsnips, artichokes, kidney beanes, green peas, asparagus, and various sorts of European herbs, in the utmost abundance" from the mountain areas.[23] And there were others, residents and visitors, who recorded similar descriptions. Some of this produce probably came from the kitchen gardens of the plantocracy, but there can be little doubt that most of it came from the gardens of the smaller settlers and the slaves.

There are, I suppose, three reasons for horticultural pursuits: planting for propagation, observation and experiment; planting for pride in the ownership of a beautiful garden; and planting for profitable sale in the market. The first is the business of the botanist and true horticulturalist; the second of the relatively well-to-do landowner who can afford the luxury; and the third of the market gardener. The categories, obviously, are not mutually exclusive. Still, it seems a fairly safe generalization that in the first category we would find the officially appointed or recognized botanists and gardeners; in the second, the larger and wealthier land and householders; and in the third, the smallholders who lived by the produce of their provision grounds and gardens.

But those whose livelihood depended solely on gardening for sales in the local market lived small. Thistlewood's income from his gardens was only one source. He imported goods for sale, he exported local produce such as rum and logwood, he earned commissions on business executed for absentees, he hired out his slaves, and there were other little extras such as earnings from Phibbah's sales of sewing and baking. From his pen, the produce of his gardens was only one item. He raised cattle and sheep, he shot and sold wildfowl and he sold grass. Grass, remember, was a profitable item in the eighteenth century. Before the steam and the internal combustion engines the grass seller was the equivalent of our present-day gasoline retailer.

Bryan Edwards informed us that one acre of grass would maintain five horses for a year, allowing 56 lb of grass a day to each.[24] Thistlewood reckoned that a horse would eat three bundles a day at 7½d. a bundle. If they were on par, the common bundle must have weighed about 18 to 19 lb.

I hope that I have now sufficiently indicated the existence in Jamaica in the second half of the eighteenth century of an active horticultural interest among the professional and amateur botanists, the large plantocracy, the smaller farmers and settlers, and, though for obvious reasons to a lesser extent, the slaves.

Of the professionals, the subsequent story is one of decline. In 1796 the Botanic Gardens Committee of the Assembly noted that the ornamental aspect of the garden at Spring Garden had been neglected by Mr Wiles, who had given greater attention to the propagation and distribution of new plants.[25] This is not surprising. Mr Wiles had arrived with Captain Bligh and the breadfruit.

In 1807 the Assembly sold Spring Garden. One later explanation vaguely referred to "domestic troubles" and "want of due appreciation of the value and nature of botanic gardens".[26] But by 1807 there was not much more in the way of new plants to be propagated and distributed on a large scale.

The Bath garden, small, subject to flooding and difficult of access, went into decline. In 1862 the government established the Castleton garden, meant to replace Bath.[27] In 1888 James Anthony Froude (not a lovable commentator, but in this remark apparently reasonable) observed in 1888: "There were lovely flowers of course, and curious plants and trees . . . but I expected to find, and I did not find, some useful practical horticulture going on. They ought for instance, to have been trying experiments with orange trees . . . [but] . . . they neither bud nor graft."[28] The private gardens of the wealthier residents remained, but were less numerous as estates went into ruinate in the harder economic days of the nineteenth century. But Lady Nugent, at the very beginning of that century, wrote of lovely private gardens in several places she visited: Clifton in the Liguanea mountains, Papine estate, Mr Simon Taylor's property in Portland, Windsor in St Elizabeth and Porus.[29]

Even Mr Froude, in 1888, found some private gardens that he enjoyed. Nor were the private efforts to maintain exchanges of plants completely ended. In the manuscript notebooks of Stephen Cave, to be found in the National Library of Jamaica, he mentions sending parcels to England containing seeds, roots, curiosities, sticks and other items; and he gives evidence of exchanges of correspondence and materials with other persons in Jamaica and in the Leeward Islands and Barbados.[30] That was in the late 1840s; we know also of gardens maintained in the later nineteenth century by caring residents who planted for pride rather than for propagation or profit.

In the early 1840s the Baptist missionary James Phillippo commented:

> Horticulture, indeed, has been wholly disregarded except by a few individuals who have formed themselves into a society in Kingston; and missionaries, who have endeavoured to give an impulse to these pursuits among the peasantry of the new townships. Hence, with the exception of the neighbourhood of the towns of the south side of the island very few European vegetables are produced, although in all the highlands of the country they would flourish in the greatest abundance, and attain the highest perfection.[31]

The peasantry, of course, were the former slaves. Removed from the provision grounds and gardens of the slave owners of previous years, those who still had access to land would have been planters for profit. They were not botanists, though they might have been gardeners, and they lacked the resources of land and capital to allow them to plant extensively for pride. No wonder then that they continued their market gardening of the exotic esculents, as they were called, mainly in areas adjacent to the larger towns. Moreover their production of the more delicate exotics, which needed special care and skill in their cultivation, would have tended to decline through lack of horticultural knowledge – as distinct from horticultural practice – and lack of capital to maintain stocks of seeds and plantlets.

The Thistlewoodian gardeners, too, would have had a harder time surviving. The official British view, that it would be desirable to grow whatever could be grown within the imperial territories, declined as mercantilist policies yielded to free trade policies designed to earn wealth by buying in the cheapest and selling in the dearest markets, whether British or foreign. This affected the history of the botanic gardens, and it also affected those private persons who had been encouraged to import and export horticultural materials.

More immediately, they would have been affected by the abolition of slavery and the institution of wage labour. Thistlewood, for example, may be said to have in some degree subsidized his horticulture by the hiring out of his slaves to neighbouring sugar estates, and by his other enterprises.

In the eighteenth and for most of the nineteenth century, horticultural production for profit was limited by the size of the local market. Before the introduction of the steamship, refrigerated cargo space, the internal combustion engine, the aeroplane, and the more rapid means of communication by cable and wireless, the export marketing of perishables was not a practical proposition. Even where decline did not set in, growth was inhibited by the limitations of the prevailing technology.

Recent revivals in horticultural enterprise, encouraged by the quicker means of communication and transport now available, have tended to bring back into prominence attempts to plant for profit and to plant for propagation.

In the nineteenth century the sugar barons went into decline. Little did Matthew Wallen suspect in the later eighteenth century, when he brought the first *cannabis sativa* from India, that he was sowing the seeds of the profit-seeking baronetcy of the later twentieth century.

In this account I have made much use of the diaries of one man only – but, as I have shown, he wrote about others too. His records indicate a much wider range of agricultural and horticultural interest and engagement among sugar planters and others in the western parishes than we have hitherto acknowledged. In the east, going by Dr Broughton's catalogue, there were no fewer than twenty-one persons engaged in the importation of plants and seeds – and remember that these recorded importations related only to plants growing in Mr East's garden at the time of his death.

How much more might we have discovered if Mr Wallen and Dr Clark and others had left us similar catalogues or diaries. Perhaps there are some, still hidden somewhere. I know that I have neither swamped you with scholarship nor surprised you with startling revelation. I hope, though, that I have raised your interest and your curiosity.

Life in our slave society of the eighteenth century went beyond master-driver-slave-and-whip, and sugar-rum-and-molasses. Those skeletal and therefore basic shaping aspects of our history are now being fleshed out, and I suspect that we shall find, in sources yet undiscovered or overlooked, much to qualify and much to enhance our understanding of our past, that is to say, our understanding of the attitudes, interests and activities of our ancestors, slave and free.

Notes

1. See G.E. Mingay, *English Landed Society in the Eighteenth Century* (London: Routledge and Kegan Paul, 1963); and also "The Agricultural Revolution in English History: a Reconsideration", in *Essays in Agrarian History,* ed. W.E. Minchinton (London: David and Charles, for the British Agricultural History Society, 1968).
2. Edward Brathwaite, *The Development of Creole Society in Jamaica, 1770–1820* (Oxford: Clarendon Press, 1971), 146–50.
3. B.W. Higman, *Slave Population and Economy in Jamaica, 1807–1834* (Cambridge: Cambridge University Press, 1976), 30–35.
4. The Diaries of Thomas Thistlewood, 1748–86. Manuscript original (in the Lincolnshire County Archives) the property of Lord Monson, whose permission I have received to use them in research and publication. Wherever I have quoted from them I have given indication of the date of the entry in the diaries.
5. T.S. Ashton, *An Economic History of England: The Eighteenth Century* (London: Methuen, 1955), 34–35.
6. Miles Hadfield, *A History of British Gardening* (London: Spring Books, Hamlyn, 1969), chapters 5, 6.
7. David Mackay, "Banks, Bligh and Breadfruit", *New Zealand Journal of History* 8, no. 1 (April 1974): 61–77.
8. Thomas Mun, *Englands Treasure by Forraign Trade* (1664; reprint, Oxford: Blackwell, 1967), 5.
9. Mackay, "Banks, Bligh and Breadfruit", 61–67.
10. Arthur Broughton, MD, comp., *Hortus Eastensis* (Kingston, Jamaica, 1792). The catalogue is reproduced in Bryan Edwards, *History of the West Indies,* vol. 3, 5th ed. (London, 1819), 367–407.
11. W.A. Feurtado, *Official and Other Personages of Jamaica, from 1655 to 1790* (Kingston, Jamaica, 1896), 30, 98.
12. *Journals of the Assembly of Jamaica* IX (27 November 1793): 247–49. See also Alan Eyre, *The Botanic Gardens of Jamaica* (London: André Deutsch, 1966), 15–20.
13. Mackay, "Banks, Bligh and Breadfruit", 61–67.
14. *Journals of the Assembly of Jamaica* IX (27 November 1793): 247–49.

15.   East manuscript 566, National Library of Jamaica.
16.   Mackay, "Banks, Bligh and Breadfruit", 61–67.
17.   Ibid.
18.   Ibid.
19.   Frank Cundall, *Historic Jamaica* (London, 1915), 25.
20.   Edward Long, *The History of Jamaica,* vol. 2 (1774; reprint, London: Frank Cass, 1970), 135.
21.   Anon. [J. Stewart], *An Account of Jamaica and Its Inhabitants* (London, 1808), 106. Some of Dr Robinson's drawings are in manuscript 178 in the National Library of Jamaica.
22.   Long, *History of Jamaica,* 2: 105.
23.   Edwards, *History of the West Indies,* 1: 254–55.
24.   Ibid., 253.
25.   *Journals of the Assembly of Jamaica* IX (23 April 1796): 507.
26.   Cundall, *Historic Jamaica,* 28.
27.   Eyre, *Botanic Gardens,* 22.
28.   James Anthony Froude, *The English in the West Indies* (London, 1888), 211.
29.   Maria Nugent, *Lady Nugent's Journal of Her Residence in Jamaica from 1801 to 1805,* ed. P. Wright (Kingston, Jamaica: Institute of Jamaica, 1966), 25, 28, 74, 94, 96.
30.   Stephen Cave, manuscript 18, National Library of Jamaica, 116.
31.   James Phillippo, *Jamaica: Its Past and Present State* (London, 1843), 97, 98.

CHAPTER 6

The Post-Slavery Labour
Problem Revisited

WOODVILLE K. MARSHALL

The title has been chosen for three reasons. First Douglas Hall, a former colleague and mentor, visited the question in 1978. However since then more work touching on the question has been published, and a debate has started between some scholars on *approaches* to the question and interpretation of the issues. As a result Hall's own reconsideration is now being reassessed. The second reason is that the post-slavery "labour problem" is a key issue in modern West Indian history. It is perceived as a vital part of those processes of adjustments and reconstruction which help to explain social formations to which we can link ourselves. Therefore a clear comprehension of the issues involved in the labour problem might bring into sharper focus developments like the emergence of peasantries and free villages, mass immigration, persisting out-migration and rural-urban migration and the fortunes of the plantation. However this apparent importance is not at all reflected in the historical literature, which is not in general distinguished by a search for quantifiable data, close analysis or sophisticated manipulation of numbers – all of which characterize the best of our slavery studies. Nor, despite Douglas Hall's efforts, has there been until fairly recently the type of controversy which has stimulated scholarship on the demography of slavery, the presence or absence of a creole society, the nature and extent of slave resistance. The third – and least important – reason is a personal one. One of my slight contributions to the discussion has been a departure point for one contributor to the recent debate, Nigel Bolland; and comments in the same piece have elicited some critical comment from another participant, Michel-Rolph Trouillot. Therefore, since in these matters I might be considered more a historiographer than a historian, I am probably well placed to assess both the research output and the state of the debate.

In this chapter, then, I propose to do two things: first to summarize the issues in the recent debate in order that the different approaches and interpretations can be identified; and second to outline what I consider the crucial questions that must be addressed in order that the several issues might be better illuminated and that relevant information may be retrieved and analysed.

I

Douglas Hall has already provided an adequate summary of the "impressions" which the literature up to 1978 conveys. Without making any issue of the methodological and conceptual sophistication displayed by the various purveyors of these impressions, I draw attention to Hall's terminology. "Impressions" suggests strongly that the subject was underexplored. Hall summarizes these impressions in this way:

> that the majority of ex-slaves wished to remove themselves from the estates on which they had suffered so much in the days of bondage; that the ex-slaves were, apparently, with some reluctance, forced to leave the estates because of the harsh attitudes and demands of their masters, the ex-slave owners; and, in either case, that the movements clearly depended on availability of land.[1]

In other words, historians (up to 1978) were *agreed* on the existence of a general desire among ex-slaves to desert the estates at emancipation, and on the role that availability of land played in the realization of this desire; but they did not agree about the reasons for the commitment to estate desertion. Some suggest that "pull" factors are crucial; for others, "push" factors are decisive.

Hall himself, the author of outstanding post-slavery studies of Jamaica and of the Leeward Islands, clearly identified with the "push" explanation. In his

1978 article he clearly summarized the case which had been hinted at first by William Sewell in 1859, was more fully articulated by George Cumper in 1954, and has been given empirical foundation by myself in 1977 and by Swithin Wilmot in 1984. Hall wrote:

> The movement of the ex-slaves from the estates was not a flight from the horrors of slavery. It was a protest against the inequities of early freedom. It is possible that, had the ex-slaves been allowed to continue in the free use of gardens, house and grounds, and to choose their employers without reference to that accommodation, there would have been very little movement of agricultural labour at all from the communities apparently established on the estate during slavery.[2]

This argument is obviously based on some evidence of estate desertion, on the nature of employers' labour recruitment and retention policies, on ex-slaves' insecurity of occupancy, and on ex-slaves' limited ability to influence the price of labour and the rent for small portions of estate land. The argument also implies the existence of real options. The ex-slaves could stay or go; but if forced to go they did not have to worry about finding the base of subsistence in non-plantation employment. Immediately, we can recognize that some issues need clarification. When and for how long did this exodus from the estates manifest itself? How large was it? How can one *establish* that employers' coercive policies did conspire to push the ex-slaves off the estates? Were non-plantation employment opportunities available in sufficient quantity to satisfy the demands of the army of displaced plantation workers?

While this "push" interpretation is of relatively recent origin, the "pull" interpretation is as old as the slavery abolition question itself, and is therefore the staple of the historiographical tradition. Briefly, this interpretation suggests that a mix of psycho-cultural and objective factors were critical: ex-slaves, because of the experience of slavery, possessed a long-standing antipathy to the plantation and all its works *and* a "natural" desire to exploit the abundant land outside the plantation for a "simple" peasant-type existence. This was the view propounded by officials in the Colonial Office, by some abolitionists, and naturally by the slave owners as soon as slavery abolition became a practical possibility. All accepted that the lure of the available land would destroy the blacks' "inclinations to industry" and therefore remove all possibility of the plantation retaining an adequate labour force. These fears and suppositions received theoretical formulation in 1841 when Herman Merivale, an Oxford professor (and later permanent under-secretary of state for the colonies) published his magisterial *Lectures on Colonization and Colonies*. It was he who invented that threefold classification of the post-slavery labour situation which, sometimes without due acknowledgement, keeps resurfacing in the later literature. For Merivale, there would be no labour shortage in the old, small and heavily populated islands like Barbados, Antigua and St Kitts. However there might be a problem of labour shortage in those larger colonies where most of the fertile land was already in cultivation but where less valuable land was still available (Jamaica, for example). But there would most certainly be a major problem of labour shortage in those fairly large, thinly populated territories which offered possibilities for smallhold settlement (Guyana, Trinidad and Dominica, for example). There are obvious similarities between this classification and those used by W.L. Mathieson in the 1920s and 1930s, and the high, medium and low density categories popularized by W.A. Green since 1976. Clearly this interpretation, as enunciated by Rawle Farley, by W.E. Riviere and by Green himself,[3] draws some of its inspiration from the theorists (E.G. Wakefield, H.J. Nieboer and E.D. Domar) who suggested an incompatibility between the viability of large-scale plantation enterprise and the existence of open resources.

But the longevity of the explanation has not secured adequate answers to several questions. Can non-plantation residence be equated with withdrawal from plantation labour? Were the ex-slaves, already deeply involved in the provision ground/marketing system, likely to sacrifice their social and economic investment in the provision grounds and huts, in the support system of the slave villages? Would not decampment to the bush have robbed them of vital proximity to market, casual wage employment, church and school?

II

Three scholars, W.A. Green, O.N. Bolland and Michel-Rolph Trouillot, have recently contributed some overdue complexity to the issue and injected controversy into the discussion. Green clearly had no intention of promoting controversy when he published his *British Slave Emancipation* in 1976. In this first synthesis to be attempted since Mathieson's pioneering volumes of the 1920s and 1930s, Green merely put some statistical gloss on the Merivale/Mathieson threefold classification to bolster his assertion that the *determinants* of the post-slavery labour situation were population density and land availability. To the extent that planters' labour recruitment policies entered the equation, these were *responses* to the absence of a disciplined labour force, itself a product of a high land to man ratio. Therefore Green can be seen as giving the "pull" explanation a strong endorsement. What makes him important to our discussion is, first, that his book has become a standard work on post-slavery adjustments, and second, that his interpretation has embroiled him in controversy with Nigel Bolland.

Bolland, in articles published in 1981 and 1984,[4] roundly criticized Green's conceptualization as deterministic, monocausal and reductionist. The basis for his criticism was both empirical and conceptual. Belize, which Bolland had intensively studied, though a classic low-density territory in the Green classification, did not, according to Bolland, experience the severe dislocation in labour supply after slavery abolition which the classification had decreed. This led Bolland to recognize and argue that labour power was not suddenly freed in 1838 but, like land resources, was still subject to real constraints of persisting power structures; land availability was not determined by population density, for a real land monopoly could coexist with low population density and "the dialectical inter-relationships between land, labour and population within a particular historic mode of production" are the keys to explanations of the post-slavery labour question. In other words, Bolland suggests that the issue is more complex than Green makes it out to be: that the factor of the power of elite groups cannot be ignored; and that the application of dialectical theory rather than the static concepts of population density and land availability would better inform us about the adjustment processes in the post-slavery British Caribbean.

Green's replies to these charges are unconvincing because they lack specificity. He questions Bolland's methods but hardly attempts to answer Bolland's specific criticisms. Principally, he argues that the utilization of dialectical theory would not improve the comprehension of the post-slavery reality because the theory suggests duality when, paraphrasing W.L. Burn, there were *three,* not two, alternative development strategies available to the British Caribbean. Therefore the dialectical theory approach "narrows West Indian History and neglects its multiple subtleties, richness and variation".[5]

How Greene's rhetorical flourish defends land availability as a determinant of the labour situation is not clear, but will presumably become clearer when his next book or article appears. However the clash of opinion is important for underscoring some conceptual and methodological issues. It focuses attention on possible imprecision in the use of terms like "free society", "free labour", "land availability", and therefore raises questions about some established assumptions. At the empirical level we are forced to recognize, as Green points out, that the labour question involved not only planters and ex-slaves but also officials (in the Colonial Office and on the spot) and some of the abolitionists. Most of these, while not possessing a clear vision of post-slavery society, knew what they did *not* want: neither a re-creation of a new form of slavery nor a collapse of the plantation; and they did try to use what influence they possessed to construct a middle way.

The conceptual and methodological issues are addressed, perhaps more cogently than any other contributor, by Michel-Rolph Trouillot. But it is somewhat unfortunate that, in his 1984 and 1988 contributions, he seems unaware of Bolland's criticisms of the Green argument, because his own criticisms of much of the literature are equally fundamental and generally run in the same direction as Bolland's. Let me quote him:

> The assumptions that have influenced the debate about "the flight from the estates" include an idealist perception of "Freedom" and "Slavery" that implies the irrelevance of a firm "time base," and a mechanical approach to causality; that Caribbean societies, particularly the British territories, shared basically common experiences; that the socio-economic reality of the plantations within the territories need not be differentiated on the basis of size, crops, or variations in labour process; that an existential homogeneity characterized the lives of Caribbean slaves.[6]

This damning indictment, from which only a few scholars are exempted, is illustrated, perhaps too briefly, by reference to some of the literature. For example, Trouillot notices that, though there can be no literal interpretation of the notion of freedom because it is a notion actualized in positive or negative terms, both Gisela Eisner and Douglas Hall do precisely that. They argue that, had the ex-slaves been assured of attractive wages and conditions of employment, there is no reason to suppose that they would not have remained on the estates. For Trouillot this is an unfounded assumption: there can be no reason to believe that ex-slaves "shared a trade-unionist-like interpretation of freedom". If freedom had been actualized by slaves and ex-slaves as land ownership, as it might have been, then high wages would still have been unattractive to them. Other examples illustrate a mechanical approach to causality, weak methodology in the attempts to penetrate the individual consciousness about the horrors of slavery, looseness in the framing of assumptions, and the use of assumptions and arguments which relate to different periods of time. Therefore he recommends what could be our text: "Along with the requirement of theoretical bases, scholars need to study particular societies in order to flesh out, as richly as possible, the events or the facts on the ground."[7]

But how does Trouillot apply his own method in his study of Dominica, and with what results? He does exhibit care in the framing and testing of assumptions, particularly on the ex-slaves' labour practices during the first four months of emancipation, and this is clearly an important advance. However his failure to produce (or collect) hard evidence beyond these four months on the ex-slaves' activities, particularly the incidence of squatting, must raise a question about both the validity of the larger conclusions and the consistent use of a firm time base. His findings, unlike Bolland's, do give some comfort to the adherents of the "pull" explanation. A sample of forty-one estates reveals that about half of the former slaves deserted the plantations *immediately* at emancipation. Though some of them did return, the reduction in the labour force was nearly 40 per cent. But in the main, his conclusions strongly support a complex explanation: rather than "push" or "pull", the patterns of employment and labour withdrawal were influenced by historical continuities and by a determined search on the part of the ex-slaves for their own advantage. These were expressed in a commitment to a *peasant labour process,* an attempt by the ex-slaves to ensure that post-slavery employment practices featured flexibility in the allocation of labour time and permitted provision ground cultivation. Consequently they demonstrated a marked preference for employment on estates which permitted share-cropping and labour-rent practices.

How then does the question stand? In purely quantitative terms, the "pull" explanation dominates the literature, but it has been severely weakened by Bolland's largely unanswered onslaught on Green. The "push" explanation, particularly as articulated by George Cumper, Douglas Hall, Swithin Wilmot and Verene Shepherd, is steadily gaining ground, mainly because it is being provided with a firm empirical base. However the important advance has been the complex explanation propounded by Bolland and Trouillot; and this is likely to become dominant because it is based on analytical rigour, abandonment of mono-causal explanation, appreciation of the influence of continuities, and attempts at quantification.

III

I hope to illustrate how this last approach could enable us to come to grips with vital issues like the labour requirements of the estates, the number of ex-slaves involved in flight or desertion, the size of the shortfall in plantation labour, the timing of the desertions, and the differential rates in desertion.

The Labour Problem

Let us begin, at the lowest level of analysis, with the term "the labour problem". This may be a loaded term. It suggests a particular perspective: a labour problem of a particular sort had to exist once the slaves were freed. This was evidently the view of the planters, of the Colonial Office, of the abolitionists; all of them said so, and in this regard their actions matched their words. But we do not need to be saddled with the ethnocentric and racist baggage that was involved in that formulation. Rather we need to pay attention to a few small points.

First, a new labour system had to be created at full emancipation. This could be classified as a problem only to the extent that those who took responsibility for fashioning it had little or no experience in that area. Second, there was variation in labour supply between the different territories. In some territories (Guyana, Trinidad, Dominica, St Lucia) there were clear signs of labour shortage before emancipation. Therefore in these territories there existed a condition of potential labour shortage which emancipation could aggravate. This was a problem for employers but not immediately one for ex-slaves.

In some other territories (Barbados, Antigua, St Kitts), high population density, small size and the pervasiveness of the plantation culture suggested that a sufficiency of potential labourers was present. In these territories there would be no obvious problem about labour recruitment. However these same conditions could create a persisting problem for potential labourers. They would face the distinct possibility of low wages, limited opportunities for non-plantation employment and, consequently, a relatively lower standard of living. How they attempted to respond to these conditions – by industrial action, by emigration, and so on – are issues worthy of investigation.

Third, a labour problem could exist if the terms and conditions of employment in any territory or group of territories did not match the expectations of the potential labourers, particularly in situations where some choice in employment was available. Such a problem could be classified not as a problem of labour shortage, but as a problem of labour relations.

Models for Employers' Labour Recruitment and Retention Policies

The literature, while reasonably full on the details of the planters' labour and retention policies, is largely silent on the models for these policies. But models were apparently used, because there is an impressive similarity in what the legislators attempted in terms of vagrancy legislation, contracts for general hiring, conditional tenancy and police establishment. If we can locate the models perhaps we will gain additional opportunities to understand the mind-set of the employers, to recognize the extent of the flexibility they may have possessed, and to check the extent to which they were affected by environmental factors. Did employers opt for what is loosely termed "coercion" because that was what they were familiar and comfortable with? Did they look outside to Haiti, the first emancipated plantation colony, to see what they should or should not do? Did they look to Britain to copy the Irish cottier system or the English tied labourer system?

Obviously, the search should start with Antigua, the first "fully free" British Caribbean territory, which established the post-slavery labour legislation that was later copied by other British Caribbean territories. But a perusal of that colony's legislation does not yield any clear answer. Douglas Hall asserts that Antigua's Contract Act of 1835 was based on "English agricultural practice at the time".[8] This is not particularly helpful because both the text of the act and the governor-in-chief's dispatch make the identical statement; so we are still in the dark about why current English agricultural practice should be regarded as relevant to the Caribbean situation. But some clues do exist. The projections made by the staff of the Colonial Office, the emancipation plans hatched by abolitionists, and the suggestions that the West India Committee made to the Colonial Office, are almost all of a piece: regulation and restriction of the blacks' freedom in the interest of regular plantation labour. Therefore the adoption of mechanisms which ranged from the transplantation of the social structure of rural England (landlord, tenant and labourer), to the Irish labour system, to variations of Boyer's Rural Code, was being proposed. If, therefore, emancipation plans involved vagrancy legislation (patterned on

Britain), strong police establishments (patterned on Ireland), and limited right of occupancy of house and ground, then it may be safe to say that coercion of ex-slaves was intended, and that a model of sorts was provided.

But this point could be modified if there is clear proof that employers were prepared to embark on a programme of rationalization in labour use. Douglas Hall and Kusha Haraksingh have argued that emancipation offered employers opportunities for a drastic *trimming* of the labour force – its reduction to the "effectives", about 60 per cent of the plantation labour complement, by dispensing with the services and particularly with the maintenance of the aged, the infirm, the infants, and/or by deliberate exploitation of the seasonal demands of the plantation's labour cycle. The coercive policy based on conditional tenancy suggested a retention on the plantation of most of the former slaves, but implementation of labour rationalization policy would have meant selective recruitment. Some attempt must be made to reconcile these positions. One possibility is that rationalization in labour use was the employers' preferred approach, but their fears about not being able to recruit a sufficient quantity and quality of labour when that was required dictated the adoption of the coercive policy.

Size of the Adequate Labour Force

The size of the adequate labour force is a related and important question. It is important because the literary sources from the early 1830s are full of gloomy forecasts and, later, of repeated confirmations of short labour supplies, of irregular attendance, of extreme difficulty in completing the cycle of field preparation, cultivation of sugar cane and sugar manufacture on estates in Trinidad, Guyana, Jamaica and the Windward Islands. It is important, too, because some historians repeat in equally loose fashion the claim that the labour force in several territories was inadequate or in short supply. They never show how many labourers were required, what the extent of the deficit may have been, or what criteria should inform the establishment of either the adequate or the optimal size of the labour force.

We need precision here. Should the slavery criteria of so many labourers to an acre of cane land be employed? But if the factors of rationalization and seasonality are included would the estimates not be drastically reduced? Further, might we not expect increases in productivity now that the incentives of money wages and opportunities to control allocation of labour time had replaced force and the threat of force as the stimulus to regular labour? This factor of increased productivity is vital to any calculation of minimal or adequate levels of labour provision for estates. The experience of task work, rather than day work or gang labour, seemed to demonstrate that blacks' productivity may have increased by as much as 50 per cent. Employers were complaining of labour shortage while claiming that labourers completed the task (or a day's labour) in four-and-a-half or five hours, and that in some cases they actually completed two tasks in one day! Clearly, if employers could have harnessed this increased productivity to the satisfaction of their own labour needs, no problem of labour shortage would have existed. Is it not possible, then, that planters' persistent complaint about irregular and short labour supplies was often the articulation of their chagrin at discovering the extent to which blacks had hoodwinked them during slavery by exhibiting perform-ance levels far below their capabilities?

The point is that measuring labour shortage is not the simple matter of contrasting the estate's slave list of 1830–38 with the estate's pay list of 1839–42. A pay list showing a 50 per cent reduction in numbers could represent a far stronger labour force in terms of productivity. Therefore if we construct a measure for the adequate labour force, we can make credible statements about the *dimensions* of labour shortage or surplus and about the level and kind of incentives that may have been required to either retain labourers on the plantation or attract them back to it. Even more to the point, such a base should enable us to better understand the objectives that employers sought to achieve, first in making estimates of the number of immigrants that were required and, later, in supporting continued immigration well after their own projections seemed to have been met.

Ex-Slaves' Reaction to the Employers' Coercive Policy

Ex-slaves' responses to the employers' drive for "steady and continuous" labour bring into focus aspects of the dialectical interplay which Bolland highlights. There is an apparent collision between what the ex-slaves expected from the plantation and what the employers wanted from the labourers. Ex-slaves wanted *continued* access to provision grounds and accommodation which were technically the property of their employers, and were prepared in turn to sell a *portion* of their labour to the estates on which they were located at a price they hoped to influence. The employers insisted that they wanted daily labour at stipulated wages, and labour immobilized by conditional tenancy or labour rent. Collision could and did occur because both sides said that their demands were non-negotiable. All this is now fairly clearly established through the work of Cumper, Hugh Paget, Douglas Hall, Swithin Wilmot, Trouillot and myself.

What is not so clearly established, however, is the full nature of the labourers' terms and the reasons for their apparent militancy. To do this we should follow Mintz and Trouillot and stress the continuities between slavery and post-slavery, particularly as they were sustained in that set of attitudes, ideas and practices that were interwoven into the provision ground/marketing system. If Mintz is accurate in claiming that the slaves' proto-peasant activity disposed them to equate freedom with own-account activity because proto-peasant activity represented one of their few corners of genuine independence, then it may be reasonable to project this mind-set on to the players in the post-slavery situation. This is not to suggest, as Mintz sometimes does, that the mindset led naturally and inevitably to a rejection of the plantation and to an embrace of full peasant activity. Rather the suggestion is that these attitudes and practices influenced the ex-slaves, particularly in the early years of post-slavery, in the direction of a *re-allocation of labour time* in order to accord priority to own-account activity. For this point to be firmly established, we need detailed analysis of the provision ground/marketing system, fuller information on the bargaining that ex-slaves and their unofficial representatives conducted with employers in the first months of full emancipation, and knowledge of the precise terms on which agreements were struck.

Next we must try to see whether there is a tidy fit between labour withdrawal and breakdown in wage "negotiations", or between labour withdrawal and the imposition of a particular policy of labour retention. We already have highly suggestive evidence from Jamaica and the Windward Islands for the 1839–42 period and from Guyana for 1842 and 1848. But we clearly need larger supplies of information on the *extent* and the *timing* of the withdrawals. I would suggest that close scrutiny of stipendiary magistrates' reports, plantation account books and newspapers will produce the corroboration that is required.

Push versus Pull

I suggest that "push" factors cannot be sharply distinguished from "pull" factors, even if we do manage to retrieve convincing evidence of industrial dispute linked to estate desertion. The existence of "pull" factors can be posited, not on the remembered horrors of slavery (for which we have no Stone Poll to guide us), but on those proto-peasant activities which are an element in the "push" factors. In other words, while there is probably no simple linear progression from proto-peasant activity in slavery to full peasant existence in full emancipation, the possibility does exist that the desire for economic activity and a lifestyle free from constant hassle and conferring full choice over the allocation of labour time may have impelled those who could afford to make the conversion to do precisely that as soon as full emancipation provided options in residence and employment. Others not so well placed may have followed suit when cash and land became available to them. Or, "push" and "pull" may have reinforced each other. To establish the primacy of "pull" over "push", evidence of immediate and substantial estate desertion not connected to any apparent tension in labour relations would have to be presented. This has not been convincingly done by any of the "pull" adherents; and it will be almost impossible to document estate desertion that did not coincide with industrial unrest, because industrial tension and unrest were a persisting feature of early post-slavery. Our present supplies of information therefore give more weight to "push" than "pull".

Land Availability

Whether "push" or "pull" is critical, we have to confront the land availability issue. Obviously, as Bolland cautions, we cannot see the issue as one of man to land ratio. We must be precise about the amount that was available for alienation, about the type of land that was alienated (Crown land, abandoned land or estate land) and particularly about the methods of alienation. Land had to be acquired legally (by purchase, lease or share-cropping agreement) or it may have been appropriated illegally. Squatting does not seem to have occurred to any extent. Only from Trinidad and Dominica do we get reports of extensive squatting. Even in these cases the evidence is somewhat suspect. It is provided by the planters themselves, many of whom did not scruple to encroach on Crown lands and vacant successions. Further, the alleged squatting did not in general involve decampment to the bush. In Dominica it seemed to be limited to Crown lands on the coast which had already attracted planters' encroachment. In Trinidad the "squatting" occurred on the estates' backlands. Indeed, the possibility exists that what was being denounced as squatting in this territory and elsewhere was the incidence of resident labourers emphasizing own-account activities: that is, short-changing their nominal employers through irregular attendance while devoting most of their labour time to provision ground cultivation.

The alternative, legal alienation of land, could be brought into play only through the operation of a land market. In other words, an agency of transfer had to exist *before* the land supplies, either outside or inside the plantation, could be legally exploited by those "pulled" or "pushed". Therefore the task here is to identify clearly who the agents were and what their motivation may have been. Some attention has properly been paid to the activities of Nonconformist parsons in this regard, but precious little has been paid to the other actors – to the landowners (planters) who sold land to the Nonconformist missionaries for subdivision, to those planters who created "proprietary villages" through subdivision of small portions of their estates, to the land speculators (real estate agents) who can be identified as early as the 1840s. Were these individuals mainly interested in a quick cash return from the sale of marginal lands? Were they sympathizing with an expressed land hunger? Were they working out individualistic labour recruitment and retention policies? Was there pressure on them to maintain planter solidarity on the limitation of ex-slaves' employment opportunities?

IV

To sum up, while I am not totally satisfied that Trouillot's work is completely free from the deficiencies he excoriates in others, I generally accept his suggestions for a research agenda and methodology:

- There must be greater precision in the framing of the research questions, and rigour must be applied to analyses of data.
- The continuities represented by provision ground cultivation and marketing of surpluses, as well as by plantation residence, must be fully recognized, and these must be handled with some discrimination. While it may be tempting to move on the straight line of resistance – from proto-peasant activity in slavery to full peasant existence and rejection of the plantation in freedom – it is possible that the continuities may represent either an element of cultural determinism, or the recognition of advantage, or both.
- We need a proliferation of microstudies for territories, parishes and individual estates, based on those sources – estate accounts, newspapers,

stipendiary magistrates' reports, court records – which could enable us to retrieve the details of recruitment policy, the extent of fluctuation in pay lists, attendance and wage levels, the components of the labour force, the timing of permanent withdrawal. In other words, we need to extend fiftyfold the work on Worthy Park and Fort George Pen in the production of parish-based studies of the type that Swithin Wilmot and Verene Shepherd have begun. Only then will we be able to say that the flight from the estates has been properly considered and that we can comprehend the nature of the post-slavery labour problem.

Notes

1. Douglas Hall, "The Flight from the Estates Reconsidered: The British West Indies, 1838–42", *Journal of Caribbean History* 10 and 11 (1978): 8.
2. Ibid., 23.
3. R. Farley, "The Rise of the Village Settlements of British Guiana", *Caribbean Quarterly* 3, no. 2 (1953); R. Farley, "The Rise of a Peasantry in British Guiana", *Social and Economic Studies* 2, no.4 (1954); W.E. Riviere, "Labour Shortage in the British West Indies after Emancipation", *Journal of Caribbean History* 4 (May 1972); W.A. Green, *British Slave Emancipation: The Sugar Colonies and the Great Experiment 1830–1865* (Oxford: Clarendon Press, 1976); W.A. Green, "The Perils of Comparative History: Belize and the British Sugar Colonies after Slavery", *Comparative Studies in Society and History* 26, no. 1 (1984); W.A. Green, "Was British Abolition a Success? The Abolitionist Perspective", in *Abolition and its Aftermath: The Historical Context 1790–1916*, ed. D. Richardson (London: Frank Cass, 1985); W.A. Green, "The Creolization of Caribbean History: The Emancipation Era and a Critique of Dialectical Analysis", *Journal of Imperial and Commonwealth History* 14, no. 3 (1986).
4. See O.N. Bolland, *The Formation of a Colonial Society: Belize from Conquest to Crown Colony* (Baltimore: Johns Hopkins University Press, 1977); O.N. Bolland, "Systems of Domination after Slavery: the Control of Land and Labour in the British West Indies after 1838", *Comparative Studies in Society and History* 23, no. 4 (1981); Bolland, "Reply to William A. Green's 'The Perils of Comparative History' ", *Comparative Studies in Society and History* 26, no. 1 (1984).
5. Green, "Creolization", 162.

6. Michel-Rolph Trouillot, "Labour and Emancipation in Dominica: Contribution to a Debate", *Caribbean Quarterly* 30, nos. 3 and 4 (1984): 74.

7. Ibid., 76.

8. Douglas Hall, *Five of the Leewards, 1834–1870* (St Lawrence, Barbados: Caribbean Universities Press, 1971), 36, 38.

Further Reading

Adamson, A.H. *Sugar Without Slaves: The Political Economy of British Guiana, 1838–1900.* New Haven: Yale University Press, 1972.

Barrett, Ward. "Caribbean Sugar Production Standards in the Seventeenth and Eighteenth Centuries". In *Merchants and Scholars: Essays in the History of Exploration and Trade,* edited by J. Parker. Minneapolis: University of Minnesota Press, 1965.

Bolland, O.N. *The Formation of a Colonial Society: Belize from Conquest to Crown Colony.* Baltimore: Johns Hopkins University Press, 1977.

———. "Systems of Domination after Slavery: the Control of Land and Labour in the British West Indies after 1838". *Comparative Studies in Society and History* 23, no. 4 (1981).

———. "Reply to William A. Green's 'The Perils of Comparative History' ". *Comparative Studies in Society and History* 26, no. 1 (1984).

Craton, M. *Searching for the Invisible Man: Slavery and Plantation Life in Jamaica.* Cambridge: Harvard University Press, 1978.

Cumper, G.E. "Labour Demand and Supply in the Jamaican Sugar Industry 1830–1950". *Social and Economic Studies* 2, no. 4 (1954).

Eisner, Gisela. *Jamaica, 1830–1930: A Study in Economic Growth.* Manchester: Manchester University Press, 1961.

Eltis, D. "Abolitionist Perceptions of Society after Slavery". In *Slavery and British Society 1776–1846,* edited by J. Walvin. Baton Rouge: Louisiana State University Press, 1982.

Farley, R. "The Rise of the Village Settlements of British Guiana". *Caribbean Quarterly* 3, no. 2 (1953).

———. "The Rise of a Peasantry in British Guiana". *Social and Economic Studies* 2, no. 4 (1954).

Green, W.A. *British Slave Emancipation: The Sugar Colonies and the Great Experiment 1830–1865.* Oxford: Clarendon Press, 1976.

———. "The Perils of Comparative History: Belize and the British Sugar Colonies after Slavery". *Comparative Studies in Society and History* 26, no. 1 (1984).

———. "Was British Abolition a Success? The Abolitionist Perspective". In *Abolition and its Aftermath: The Historical Context 1790–1916*, edited by D. Richardson. London: Frank Cass, 1985.

———. "The Creolization of Caribbean History: The Emancipation Era and a Critique of Dialectical Analysis". *Journal of Imperial and Commonwealth History* 14, no. 3 (1986).

Hall, Douglas. *Free Jamaica 1838–1865: An Economic History*. New Haven: Yale University Press, 1959.

———. *Five of the Leewards 1834–1870*. Bridgetown, Barbados: Caribbean Universities Press, 1971.

———. "The Flight from the Estates Reconsidered: The British West Indies, 1838–42". *Journal of Caribbean History* 10 and 11 (1978).

———. "Fort George Pen, Jamaica: Slaves, Tenants and Labourers". Paper presented at the Eleventh Conference of Caribbean Historians, Curaçao, 1979.

Haraksingh, K. "Sugar Estates and Labour in Trinidad 1838–1845". Paper presented at the Eleventh Conference of Caribbean Historians, Curaçao, 1979.

Higman, B. *Slave Populations of the British Caribbean 1807–1834*. Baltimore: Johns Hopkins University Press, 1984.

Marshall, W.K. "The Ex-Slaves as Wage Labourers on the Sugar Estates in British Windward Islands, 1838–1846". Paper presented at the Eleventh Conference of Caribbean Historians, Curaçao, 1979.

———. " 'Commentary One' on Slavery and the Rise of Peasantries". *Historical Reflections* 6, no. 1 (1979).

———. "Apprenticeship and Labour Relations in Four Windward Islands". In *Abolition and its Aftermath: The Historical Context 1790–1916*, edited by D. Richardson. London: Frank Cass, 1985.

———. "Provision Ground and Plantation Labour in Four Windward Islands: Competition for Resources?" *Slavery and Abolition* 12, no. 1 (May 1991).

Mathieson, W.L. *British Slavery and its Abolition, 1828–38*. London: Longman, Green and Co., 1926.

———. *British Slave Emancipation, 1838–49*. London: Longman, Green and Co., 1932.

Merivale, H. *Lectures on Colonies and Colonization*. London: Longman, Green, 1841.

Mintz, S.W. "The Question of Caribbean Peasantries". *Caribbean Studies* 1, no. 3 (1961).

———. *Caribbean Transformations*. Chicago: Aldine, 1974.

———. "Caribbean Marketplaces and Caribbean History". *Nova Americana* 1 (1978).

———. "Was the Plantation Slave a Proletarian?" *Review* 2 (1978).

———. "Slavery and the Rise Of Peasantries". *Historical Reflections* 6, no. 1 (1979).

Mintz, S.W., and D.G. Hall *The Origins of the Jamaican Internal Marketing System.* Yale University Publications in Anthropology, 57. New Haven: Yale University Press 1960.

Murray, D.J. *The West Indies and the Development of Colonial Government, 1801–34.* Oxford: Clarendon Press, 1965.

Paget, H. "The Free Village System in Jamaica", *Caribbean Quarterly* 1, no. 4 (1954).

Patterson, H.O. "The Structural Origins of Slavery: A Critique of the Nieboer-Domar Hypothesis from a Comparative Perspective". In *Comparative Perspectives on Slavery in New World Plantation Societies,* edited by V. Rubin and A. Tuden. New York: New York Academy of Sciences, 1977.

Riviere, W.E. "Labour Shortage in the British West Indies after Emancipation", *Journal of Caribbean History* 4 (May 1972).

Sewell, W.E. *The Ordeal of Free Labour in the British West Indies.* London: Harper, 1861.

Shepherd, Verene. "The Effects of the Abolition of Slavery on Jamaican Livestock Farms (Pens), 1834–1845". *Slavery and Abolition* 10, no. 2 (1989).

Trouillot, Michel-Rolph. "Labour and Emancipation in Dominica: Contribution to a Debate". *Caribbean Quarterly* 30, nos. 3 and 4 (1984).

———. *Peasants and Capital: Dominica and the World Economy.* Baltimore: Johns Hopkins University Press, 1988.

———. "Discourses of Rule and the Acknowledgement of the Peasantry, in Dominica, WI, 1838–1928". *American Ethnologist* 16, no. 4 (1989).

Wakefield, E.G. *A View of the Art of Colonization.* London, 1849.

Wilmot, S. "Emancipation in Action: Workers and Wage Conflicts in Jamaica, 1838–1848". Paper presented at the Sixteenth Conference of Caribbean Historians, Barbados, 1984.

Wood, D. *Trinidad in Transition: The Years after Slavery.* Oxford: Oxford University Press, 1968.

Young, A. *Approaches to Local Self-Government in British Guiana.* London: Longman, Green, 1958.

Liberated Africans in Nineteenth-Century Guyana

MONICA SCHULER

The struggle of former slaves to make a secure living and to control when and how they worked is a major theme of African history and the African diaspora in the nineteenth and early twentieth centuries. As Frederick Cooper perceptively observed in his 1980 study of emancipated slaves in Zanzibar and Kenya, former slaves "did not wish to be either slaves or proletarians". Their solution was to combine wage labour with independent farming.[1] This solution is familiar to West Indians who know the history of slaves emancipated by the British and French parliaments in 1834 and 1848. Less familiar are the experiences of some fifty-two thousand African latecomers, voluntary and involuntary immigrants sent by the British and French to the Guianas and West Indies between the 1840s and the1860s. Although planters and colonial officials intended to use this immigrant labour to subvert the independence of emancipated slaves, the African newcomers followed the ex-slaves' example instead.

Note: "Guyana" will be used throughout this chapter to refer to British Guiana.

The Guyanese branch of liberated African migration, the subject of this paper, was a relatively minor population movement involving only 13,563 people.[2] Historians, assuming that the new African arrivals were rapidly assimilated into Afro-Guyanese society, have given liberated Africans only cursory attention.[3] Yet considering that the colony's mostly Afro-Guyanese population was only 98,000 at emancipation, that more liberated Africans migrated to Guyana than to either Jamaica or Trinidad, and that relatively few returned to Africa, the African newcomers must have played a significant role in Afro-Guyanese society. Indeed their history provides valuable perspectives on post-emancipation Guyana. In particular, by examining the problems faced by African immigrants in the monocultural economy and flood- and drought-stricken Guyanese environment of the 1840s and 1850s, and their roles in two pivotal events, the 1848 sugar strike and the 1856 anti-Portuguese riots, we derive new insights into Creole-immigrant interaction and conflict.

After Britain abolished its slave trade in 1808 and mounted a diplomatic and naval campaign to end the United States, French, Spanish, Portuguese and Brazilian trades, mostly British naval squadrons diverted an estimated 160,000 Africans from the slave trade. Between 1810 and 1864 Britain transported large numbers of recaptive Africans to British dependencies as well as to Portuguese Angola; Havana, Cuba and Rio de Janeiro, Brazil. There British vice admiralty or international mixed commission courts condemned the ships and liberated their slaves – hence the name "liberated Africans". Where Guyana is concerned, the most important liberated African depots were those in Sierra Leone, West Africa and the South Atlantic island of St Helena. A British-Brazilian court of mixed commission at Rio de Janeiro also relayed captured Africans to Guyana, and Guyana planters recruited a small number in the Bahamas. In these reception areas, liberated Africans were apprenticed or indentured to local employers, settled on the land, or recruited into military regiments – that is, until Jamaican, Trinidadian and Guyanese planters became interested in them.[4]

With a population of only 98,000 at the end of slave apprenticeship in 1838, Guyana's relative labour scarcity and land surplus enabled well-organized plantation labourers to bargain successfully with employers over wages and hours.[5] Employers hoped that immigration would give *them* the upper hand. Britain's involvement with slave trade suppression made liberated Africans an obvious source of new labour for the plantations.

The majority of liberated Africans arrived in Guyana from Sierra Leone between 1841 and 1851, from St Helena between 1842 and 1865, from Rio de Janeiro between 1841 and 1852, and from Nassau, New Providence between 1837 and 1846. Other Africans were recruited from the Kru coast of Liberia between 1845 and 1853, and from the Cape Verde islands of West Africa in the 1850s. Liberated African *residents* of Sierra Leone and the Kru of coastal Liberia were *voluntary* immigrants. Recently recaptured Africans recruited from reception depots in Rio, St Helena and Sierra Leone, however, had little say in their emigration, and were *involuntary* immigrants.[6]

For the first seven years of African immigration Africans, especially Sierra Leonians and Kru men, were relatively successful at controlling where and how they worked in Guyana. They faced at most one-year indentures, generally with employers of their own choosing. In theory Africans were to be evenly distributed among the three counties of Berbice, Demerara and Essequibo. In practice, however, this proved difficult to enforce on Sierra Leonians and Kru, who chose employers "by the advice of . . . friends" already in Guyana. Until 1848 many Africans, like the Portuguese, changed employment as their interests dictated – a situation that planters had intended immigration to halt, rather than to perpetuate.[7]

Although wages may have been a factor in such mobility, they were not necessarily the main motive. Some Africans moved because of poor housing,[8] and many more moved to be with shipmates, shifting from place to place, as a perceptive immigration agent general put it, "until they meet in sufficient numbers to form a society amongst themselves".[9]

Planters who lost labourers for these reasons looked to tougher immigration laws to stabilize the immigrant labour force. In 1848 three-year voluntary indentures existed; in 1854 the Colonial Office approved compulsory three-year contracts.[10] By 1863 the continued tendency of indenture-expired Africans to leave full-time estate labour and to acquire land led to an extension of indentures to five years, with the proviso that Africans be granted small allotments near plantations or existing Creole villages. But the new law came too late to have any significant impact, because relatively few Africans arrived between its passage and the end of African immigration in 1865.[11]

Africans were quite successful in forming societies "amongst themselves". They bought land on the open market, complained to the governor about the high cost of land transactions, and petitioned for government land grants. They joined Christian churches, sent their children to school, and passed on their languages, music and stories to their children and grandchildren. Oral traditions and written reports suggest that many Africans settled first in their *own* villages, sometimes on the outskirts of existing Creole communities or plantations, before moving into Creole villages where they tended to locate in ethnic quarters. As in Jamaica and Trinidad, Yoruba from southwest Nigeria and Central Africans, generally referred to as Kongo, seem to have predominated.[12]

A small Kongo village existed at Overwinning, Berbice, tucked behind the village of Islington on Providence estate.[13] Around 1854, seventy to eighty thriving Yoruba recaptives employed on Blairmount estates, Berbice, moved their houses from land they had purchased on the east bank of the Berbice river to the post-emancipation village of Ithaca to be nearer to their London Missionary Society (LMS) congregation.[14]

Land purchases did not always proceed smoothly, as twenty-one African shareholders discovered in 1868 when their headman was duped into overpaying for a portion of L'Esperance, a former coffee plantation on the upper Berbice River. The purchasers also found prohibitive the expense of advertisements, title transfers and several fifty-mile trips to a court where the judge never appeared.[15]

Many Africans worked on West Coast Demerara estates, and by 1860 Africans were the main supporters of Ebenezer LMS chapel at Blankenburg.[16] Many settled in the West Coast Demerara Creole village of Stewartville, also in the Ebenezer chapel district. From Stewartville, four Sierra Leonians petitioned twice in 1874 for a grant of Crown land on Hog Island, Essequibo, to cultivate rice.[17]

Canal No. 1, a former coffee district on the west bank of the Demerara River, attracted many immigrants. By 1849 the Canal's population began to increase and diversify as Africans, Portuguese and Indians, as well as Guyanese, attracted by low land prices and low rents, purchased or rented farms ranging from a few to twenty acres for plantain, provisions, coffee and rice cultivation. Some Africans, notably a group from Blankenburg, moved even before their indentures expired.[18] By 1856 the south bank of the canal, uninhabited since the last years of slavery, had villages on estate fronts for three miles from the canal mouth. Bagotville village, with a population of three thousand, had several hundred Africans and an equal number of Portuguese. By 1859 as newcomers continued to enter the canal, young Guyanese departed to seek estate work on the coast.[19]

Africans, predominantly Yoruba and Kongo, could be found not just in Bagotville, but all along the canal.[20] In 1867 Yoruba comprised the majority at Vauxhall.[21] Yoruba also predominated at L'Heureuse Aventure ("Sabakay"), Beauvoisin and L'Oratoire, which was known as "Oku Town". By 1886 sixteen Yoruba owned the former plantation Soesdyk at the far end of the canal.[22] Mother Bednigo, a Yagba Yoruba who had been kidnapped and sold into slavery and who arrived in Guyana in 1850, was one of a small number of Canal No. 1 Africans still alive in the early part of the twentieth century. According to a Canal No. 1 visitor, the Yoruba evinced "a national spirit". People worked hard and helped one another. Elders acted as judges in most local disputes, their aim being reconciliation rather than punishment.[23]

The canal's Kongo settlers do not seem to have thrived like the Yoruba. By 1881 forty-four Kongo people rented or owned land at Geneve estate while working at Le Desir or West Coast Demerara estates. The Kongo lost control of Geneve, however, because they could not pay their drainage rates, and Geneve's local name became "Congo Heart Burn".[24]

On the east coast of the Demerara, a prime sugar region which acquired African labourers from the first year of immigration, Africans could be found on many estates and in the freehold villages of Victoria, Buxton, Beterverwagting and Plaisance.[25] In 1851 forty-five African immigrants were among the four hundred residents of No. 50 village, also known as Leeds, on the Courentyne coast, Berbice, where compatriots from the Berbice River estates used to visit them at Christmas. Leeds villagers planted corn and rice and raised cattle, goats and pigs. We know about them, their "illicit trade" (they apparently avoided paying commercial licence fees), and the Minje-Mama dance and obeah which had "long existed" at No. 50 village, because the *Berbice Gazette* complained in 1851 that planters were not importing Africans merely "for the formation of such settlements".[26] When drought afflicted the Courentyne coast in 1869, Leeds men migrated to Nickerie River plantations in neighbouring Suriname to keep their families from starving.[27] Many Leeds Africans joined the Church of England.[28] These examples (and there are many more) show Africans attempting to shape their own existence in the shadow of the plantation but free from its control.

Planters did not concede control willingly, however. In addition to lengthening the Africans' indenture terms, planters used religion and education as forms of social control. Even before large-scale immigration, and mostly at the prodding of Guyanese labourers, estate management had begun to perceive rural schools as a means of labour stabilization. Many planters, as well as the government, subsidized church-run estate schools for immigrants, including Africans. Some Sierra Leonians were already Christians when they arrived in Guyana and naturally gravitated to the churches. The Anglican parish clergy, the Anglican Society for propagation of the Gospel, and the more independent LMS and Plymouth Brethren all proselytized among liberated Africans and undertook the education of juveniles and adults in evening, day and Sunday schools. In varying degrees, Christian ministers perceived liberated African education not only as a benefit to the Africans themselves, but also as means of acculturating them so that they would not "contaminate" the Guyanese. Church of England ministers tended to sympathize with planters' demands for labour and used education to persuade African newcomers to choose regular estate employment.[29]

African immigration had a pervasive impact on the existing labour force. Creole labourers' first reaction to African newcomers was encouraging, despite the negative impact that immigrants had on the labour market. The local population had older people from the immigrants' own ethnic groups who proved helpful and supportive. They adopted youths and children and taught them the language and customs of Guyana. On plantation Rosehall, Canje, an old Kongo man, played his drum for newcomers. On Vreed-en-Hoop African newcomers were so suspicious that they would drink water only after the locals did so.[30] On plantation Bathsheba's Lust, Essequibo, Creoles, perhaps remembering the times when planters had threatened eviction at harvest time, dissuaded Africans from cultivating their provision grounds; they claimed that the planter would never permit them to reap anything.[31]

Conflict between locals and African immigrants seems to have been minimal, but two occurrences have been documented. The first was an unexplained violent fight in 1849 between Creoles and Africans on Mara, a Berbice River estate, which had to be broken up by the police; the second, a Kru attack on residents of Cummingsburg, Georgetown in 1858, prompted the police observation that the Kru were "a terror to the peaceable inhabitants".[32]

Planters intended immigration to have an impact on work and wages, but in the beginning liberated Africans seem to have worked for the same wages as local plantation labourers. In the first year of immigration (1841–42), they earned approximately 50 cents per day in the factory, 33 cents for a weeding task of seven and a half hours, and 42 cents for cane cutting. In Essequibo sugar factory labourers also received one free meal per day. As a result of drought, demand for plantation work declined, and by 1845 wages fell 15 to 20 per cent in heavily populated areas.[33]

In view of this early wage parity, African immigrants' value to planters is hard to calculate. The importance of African labour varied from one district to another and seems to have been related to the availability of other types of labour. In districts like Berbice, where Africans constituted the main immigrant labour force in the 1840s, European observers believed African competition disciplined local labourers by reducing wage rates and forcing locals to work harder.[34]

By the late 1840s the Afro-Guyanese working class as a whole could feel the impact of immigrants. Portuguese immigrants had displaced Guyanese as porters, carters, jobbers and shopkeepers. Women and children, who had withdrawn from field labour after emancipation, had to return to work, but the lighter tasks they and Guyanese youths performed were precisely the jobs assigned to Indian immigrants. Thus women, children, the elderly and youths all found wages for their tasks driven down by immigrant competition. As immigration forced plantation wages downward,[35] Guyanese men began to form itinerant labour gangs specializing in more strenuous types of labour. They often travelled great distances in search of districts with a labour shortage, where plantations would be willing to employ them at higher wages. Women and youths were also forced into migrancy. By late 1845 Berbice River villagers, including women, commuted an average of twelve to thirty miles from home bases like Zuid Holland; they worked on plantations like Mara and Ma Retraite during the week and returned to their homes on weekends. Others moved to different counties to find jobs.[36]

Continued dependence on world sugar markets rendered both labourers and planters vulnerable to market changes. In 1846 a sugar crisis resulted from British passage of the Sugar Duties Act, which revoked tariff protection of British West Indian sugar. A British financial panic ensued in 1847, Guyana labourers lost confidence in local banks, and planters hired more indentured immigrant labour and cut wages from 25 to 50 per cent.[37] These developments affected Africans who were already in the colony in much the same way that they affected Guyanese labourers, for both groups operated as free agents in the plantation labour market.

The post-1846 economic crisis in general, and the wage reduction in particular, demonstrated the fragility of labourers' independence and precipitated a Creole and liberated African exodus from plantations and an unsuccessful sugar workers' strike in 1848.[38] The most common explanation for the failure of the 1848 strike is the presence of increasing numbers of immigrants, largely Indians, as alternatives to Creole labour. Yet immigrants themselves did not always find work, and they experienced hardships as a result of the sugar crisis and strike. For instance, bankrupt planters stopped providing food supplies to some Indians, and some were reportedly starving in West Coast Demerara by mid-January 1848, "having nothing to subsist on but roots and wild fruit". In Essequibo, "scores" of jobless Indians depended on charity from "the cottages of . . . [Creole] labourers".[39] Still others suffered from "the seasoning sickness" which usually afflicted newcomers. In Essequibo, at least, immigrants did little more than keep cane fields from being overrun with weeds.[40]

The situation of African (and Madeiran) labourers in 1848, both voluntarily indentured and unindentured, was probably little different from that of Indians. Unindentured Africans had no guaranteed food or supplies, and the approximately one thousand mostly sickly newcomers who arrived between April 1847 and April 1848 would have been in no condition to do much work or to cultivate and harvest provisions to weather the strike.[41] Both the sick and the well would have been dependent on the plantation, and the latter would have little choice but to work. This may explain why Africans as well as Indians performed what little work was done in Canje, Berbice, during the strike, and why, by 5 February, African, Indian and Madeiran immigrants on the Essequibo coast and Tiger, Wakenaam and Leguan islands were "everywhere at work at the reduced rate".[42]

Some Africans *did* strike, however. In the Mahaica-Abary district only a portion of the African labourers worked in January and February.[43] African employees struck on Highbury, East Bank, Berbice River but resumed labour by the end of January even though most of their Guyanese neighbours remained off the job.[44] Africans, who comprised most of the immigrants on Mara and Ma Retraite estates further up the east bank of the Berbice River, supported the strike until April.[45]

The economic crisis that precipitated the strike also made it hard to sustain. Sugar prices were depressed, plantation bills and plantation wages had been in arrears since November 1847, and no one – not urban merchants, nor rural shopkeepers, nor consumers – had much cash on hand for food purchases. The result was a chain of circumstances that reduced the imported food supply in shops, increased the demand for local produce, and drove up prices of staples such as bread and plantains by 50 per cent. North American ships arrived and departed with their food cargoes intact because merchants could not pay for them,[46] and shopkeepers in Essequibo, and probably elsewhere, denied credit to strikers.[47]

The solidarity, organization and militancy that had assured workers' success in an earlier strike in 1842 were insufficient to secure a strike victory in the peculiar circumstances of 1848. Factors beyond the control of Guyanese labourers – the post-1846 economic crisis, and the advent of immigrants, including Madeiran village shopkeepers – produced cracks in the united front Guyanese villagers had painstakingly developed through enslavement, apprenticeship and the first few years of "freedom". Immigrants had not shared that experience, and Madeirans were not part of plantation kinship networks and were unfamiliar with the 1842 strike, when "those who had no means were supported by those who had". They did not know that the 1841 strike committee had maintained discipline by administering an oath which bound strikers to "chop" strikebreakers.[48]

If hard pressed Portuguese shopkeepers refused credit, they might have been perceived as transgressing the local social code. Moreover in the 1847 economic crisis, panicked labourers sold their banknotes to Portuguese shopkeepers at a 20 per cent loss. Government restoration of the banks' solvency came too late to benefit the labourers, and large Afro-Guyanese crowds attacked Portuguese shops in New Amsterdam in 1847.[49] In March 1848, after several months of futile striking, Creoles broke into a number of Portuguese shops in East Bank, Berbice and seized food and cash.[50] The strikers were defeated by April 1848.

Inclement weather clouded the rest of 1848 and compounded the hardship brought about by economic crisis. In East Coast Demerara, heavy rains destroyed food crops and "brought many families into great difficulty".[51] On the Courentyne coast, Berbice, rain and the buildup of mud in canal mouths caused flooding which destroyed smallholders' crops.[52] In Canje, Berbice, many, especially the elderly and children, reached the point of starvation.[53] School enrolments dropped everywhere, because either children had to work or parents could not afford school fees.[54] Seasonal internal labour migration and farm purchases and rentals accelerated as labourers searched for economic security.[55] Crimes such as theft increased.[56]

Not surprisingly, people sought protection and remedies for their misfortunes. Immigrant African obeah practitioners, especially the Kru, were kept busy, even by the Roman Catholic Portuguese, who became regular clients.[57] Alarmed at this development, the authorities passed an obeah repression ordinance in 1855, making it illegal to practice obeah or consult an obeah practitioner.[58]

By the 1850s various social groups had staked out positions in plantation society. All groups farmed. Creoles, Africans, Asians and some Portuguese laboured on estates. Many Portuguese specialized in trade. All competed for scarce resources made even scarcer by planter and state policies and by the continuation of Guyana's drought cycle. And in February 1856, when another drought intersected with competition, anti-Portuguese violence erupted again.

The 1856 attacks were pivotal both in the fortunes of Afro-Guyanese and in the entrenchment of immigration as an instrument of labour control. The events of February 1856 are well known: a middle-class coloured man, John Sayers Orr, who had established a reputation for anti-Catholic demagoguery in North America and Scotland, returned to Georgetown and attracted an Afro-Guyanese audience sympathetic to his anti-Catholic, anti-Portuguese street-corner and marketplace oratory. When some Portuguese retaliated, Orr was arrested for unlawful assembly, and on 16 and 17 February his supporters attacked Portuguese shops in Georgetown and seized their contents.

A rumour circulated that the governor had authorized the expulsion of Portuguese and destruction of their shops.[59] By 18 February most rural Portuguese shops had been broken into, their contents seized and large casks of liquor dumped. Portuguese homes were looted. In Canal No. 1, people levelled Portuguese provision grounds and butchered and carried away livestock. A Guyanese-owned shop in Bagotville was left untouched, however.[60] The attacks ceased between 20 and 25 February.[61]

These events have traditionally been portrayed as both class- and nativist-inspired. In their hardship, Afro-Guyanese failed to consider the taxes that made retail prices high, the risky nature of retail shopkeeping, and the existence of many poor Portuguese in their midst. Instead they complained that Portuguese shopkeepers had become wealthy through monopoly, price gouging and other sharp practices, and they demanded the expulsion of Portuguese to prevent further displacement of natives from land, jobs and the retail trade. An Afro-Guyanese syndicate tried and failed to establish Creole-owned shops.[62]

But Creole nativism and jealousy and John Sayers Orr's activities in Georgetown do not satisfactorily explain the timing and intensity of the *rural* outbreaks, nor why African, Barbadian and Indian immigrants participated in the attacks.[63] In Canal No. 1, with several hundred each of African and Portuguese immigrants, for example, *Guyanese* led the anti-Portuguese attacks, but mostly *Africans* seized shop goods.[64] In West Coast Demerara, Barbadian men allegedly instigated raids on shops, but perpetrators included women, children, Africans and in some cases East Indians.[65] On the East Coast of Demerara, the Kongo on La Bonne Intention estate were allegedly more militant than the Creoles. Indeed they made threats not only against the Portuguese but against all white people.[66] To explain this complex ethnic involvement, conditions in rural Guyana in the months preceding the February disturbances must be taken into account.

As in the 1840s, natural disasters seem to have been an important factor in the 1856 disturbances. The populous East Coast Demerara area, after being flooded by high tides in 1855, suffered from a drought in 1856 which persisted beyond the riots, caused a water shortage, made vegetables scarce, and sent children travelling from two to four miles at midnight to fetch dirty water by stealth from estate trenches. Residents experienced much sickness as a result.[67] West Coast Demerara had been undergoing a drought for three months before the attacks on Portuguese property. At Blankenburg the LMS missionary James Scott reported that only muddy water was obtainable for washing and drinking, and that had to be fetched from a mile away. Provision grounds became unproductive and sugar estate work scarce; as a result, Canal No. 1 farmers found it hard to pay monthly rents and provide for their families. In West Coast Demerara as a whole, those reliable barometers of peasant and labour solvency – the Sunday church collections – decreased sharply.[68]

In 1856, as in 1848, wages dropped and food prices rose sharply. Because of these conditions, more West Coast Demerara labourers began to rent farms in Canal No. 1, only to encounter drought and unproductive farms.[69] They would have become dependent on food from retail shops at a time when shopkeepers may have tried to minimize risk by refusing them credit.[70] Unfortunately, the 1856 credit situation is unknown. To compound the privation, measles and dysentery struck Canal No. 1 around the time of the riots.[71]

Although the anti-Portuguese feeling of 1856 undoubtedly had other deep-seated causes, drought and its complications may have transformed old resentments into shop raids. Drought explains why African immigrants who were primarily farmers became so integrally involved in the Canal No. 1 attacks, an involvement which many have overlooked. Their actions in February suggest that they did not have sufficient food, and that the only way to obtain some without cash or credit was to break into retail shops. In every case where Reverend Charles Rattray of Canal No. 1 observed Africans and Creoles carrying off goods from Portuguese farms, homes or shops, those goods consisted of food. Men and women walked past the missionary's residence carrying "unskinned pieces of cows and hogs on their backs . . . the blood dripping down their bodies".[72]

Drought also explains why East Indians who had taken up rice farming in Canal No. 1 in 1853, and who were undoubtedly in the same predicament as Africans there, also participated in the raids.[73] On Wakenaam Island, Essequibo, and Plantation Hague, West Coast Demerara, some indentured immigrants, notably Kru, also attacked shops or picked up stolen goods, while others did not. It would be useful to know the extent of their dependence on Portuguese retail shops, but we do not. On a few estates in Wakenaam Island, Essequibo and Vergenoegen, West Coast Demerara, East Indians were successfully mobilized to protect the Portuguese. Robert Moore theorized that since East Indians banked their savings in Portuguese shops, they would not have wished to destroy them. The Kru, on the other hand, appear to have followed the old Guyanese practice of burying their savings in holes under their houses and may have had no similar stake in Portuguese security.[74]

The active role played by women and youths in anti-Portuguese speech-making, in removing goods from shops, and in pelting the police with bottles and bricks outside Vauxhall Courthouse, Canal No. 1, also requires explanation.[75] As the people most displaced from estate labour by immigrants, women and youths would have been affected doubly by wage cuts and price increases. As food cultivators and preparers (women actually did much of the farming while men worked on estates), and as nurses of hungry and sick children, Guyanese and African women were in the thick of Guyana's socioeconomic problems, and it would have been surprising if they had *not* taken such an active role in food-procuring sorties against shops.

Break-ins and thefts from the homes of some well-to-do Afro-Guyanese around Queenstown, Essequibo on 21 February 1856 also require an explanation.[76] In Canal No. 1, where "hardly any black man has succeeded with a retail shop, on his own account", some Guyanese entrepreneurs had built and leased houses to Portuguese for retail shops. This symbiotic relationship between Portuguese shopkeeper-renters and Afro-Guyanese landlords may well explain attacks on some Afro-Guyanese residences as well as the restraint shown by "respectable" Guyanese and their willingness to shelter beleaguered Portuguese.[77]

The shop attacks did not challenge the ultimate oppressors – the plantation and colonial system – nor could they halt drought, which intensified and scorched the fields of planter and small farmer alike. Estate jobs became scarcer, the already limited food supply was further depleted by the riot's destruction, and few people had cash to buy the food that was recovered and restored to the shopkeepers. Heavy rains succeeding the droughts destroyed agriculture further.[78] The following year brought cholera,[79] and 1858 saw passage of a special tax to reimburse the Portuguese for losses incurred in 1856.[80] Continued East Indian arrivals caused a labour surplus which made it increasingly difficult for Africans and others to find work.[81]

With such hardships, it is not surprising that African interest in repatriation surged in 1858. Opportunities for transportation to Africa were scarce however, and Guyanese authorities were not interested in assisting their return, for African immigration had declined and then ceased altogether in 1865 after only forty-two Africans arrived.[82] The government accepted responsibility for repatriating only 990 people, of whom only 573, mostly Kru and Sierra Leonians, returned at government expense between 1843 and 1853. An unknown number managed to arrange their own passages between 1858 and 1864.[83]

Most African immigrants, with the occasional exception of the Kru, interacted cordially with Creoles, and sometimes allied with them against planters and other immigrants. Africans' relations with Indians and Madeirans remain to be explored. Like Creoles, Asians and Madeirans, Africans bought or rented land, combined farming with wage labour, and formed their own self-regulating communities along ethnic lines, thus reinforcing African cultural traits in Guyanese society. African immigrants successfully undercut planters' attempts to use them as a means of forcing Creoles – and liberated Africans themselves – into wage slavery, but few achieved more than a modest subsistence.

Abbreviations Used in Notes

Ber.	Berbice County, Guyana
BG	British Guiana
CLEC	Colonial Land and Emigration Commissioners, London
CO	Colonial Office
CWM	Council for World Mission
Dem.	Demerara County, Guyana
GNA	Guyana National Archives
LMS	London Missionary Society
PP	Parliamentary Papers
USPG	United Society for the Propagation of the Gospel

Notes

1. Frederick Cooper, *From Slaves to Squatters: Plantation Land and Agriculture in Zanzibar and Coastal Kenya, 1890–1925* (New Haven: Yale University Press, 1980), 4.
2. Central Africans are likely to have been undercounted by Sierra Leone and Guyana officials. James Crosby, "Statement of the Total Number of Immigrants Introduced into the Colony of British Guiana from the 1st Jan. 1835 to the 31st Dec. 1864", 4 January 1865, CO 111/350, has a total of 13,264 liberated Africans. My total is higher than Crosby's by 299 despite my exclusion of 91 Africans who arrived in 1838, 819 from Nassau (1837–46) and the Cape Verde islands (1856, 1858). However, I added 391 from slavers condemned locally, and the final 42 who arrived from St Helena in 1865. Liberated African ethnic statistics were compiled from governors' dispatches in the CO 267 (Sierra Leone), CO 111 (British Guiana), CO 247 (St Helena), and CO 386 (CLEC) in the Public Record Office, Kew; *The Trans-Atlantic Slave Trade* Database, no. 2177; and from correspondence and newspapers in the Guyana National Archives, Georgetown (GNA). In 1919 the Guyana archivist published an article based on government records. See J. Graham Cruickshank, "African Immigrants after Slavery", *Timehri*, 3d ser., 6 (September 1919): 77. (Reprinted in David A. Granger, ed., *Scenes from the History of the Africans in Guyana* [Georgetown: Free Press, 1999], 21–37.)
3. See Walter Rodney, *History of the Guyanese Working People, 1881–1905* (Baltimore: Johns Hopkins University Press, 1981); Alan H. Adamson, *Sugar without Slaves: The Political Economy of British Guiana* (New Haven: Yale University Press, 1972); Brian L. Moore, *Race, Power and Social Segmentation in a Colonial Society: Guyana After Slavery, 1838–1891* (New York: Gordon

and Breach, 1987); Robert James Moore, "East Indians and Negroes in British Guiana: 1838–1880" (PhD thesis, University of Sussex, 1970); Mary Noel Menezes, RSM, "The Winged Impulse: The Madeiran Portuguese in Guyana, An Economic, Socio-Cultural Perspective", *Guyana Historical Journal* 1 (1989): 21–23.

4.   The following works deal with liberated Africans and African immigration: Johnson U.J. Asiegbu, *Slavery and the Politics of Liberation, 1787–1861: A Study of Liberated African Emigration and British Anti-Slavery Policy* (London: Longman, 1969); François Renault, *Libération d'esclaves et nouvelle servitude: les rachats des captifs africains pour le compte des colonies françaises après l'abolition de l'esclavage* (Abidjan: 1976); Joseph G. Moore, "Religion of Jamaica Negroes: A Study of Afro-Jamaican Acculturation" (PhD diss., Northwestern University, 1953); Monica Schuler, *"Alas, Alas, Kongo": A Social History of Indentured African Immigration into Jamaica, 1841–1865* (Baltimore: Johns Hopkins University Press, 1980); Monica Schuler, "The Recruitment of African Indentured Labourers for European Colonies in the Nineteenth Century", in *Colonialism and Migration; Indentured Labour Before and After Slavery,* ed. P.C. Emmer (Dordrecht: Martinus Nijhoff Publishers, 1986), 125–60; Monica Schuler, "Kru Emigration to British and French Guiana, 1841–1857", in *Africans in Bondage: Studies in Slavery and the Slave Trade,* ed. P.E. Lovejoy (Madison: African Studies Programme, University of Wisconsin, 1986), 154–201; Andrew T. Carr, "A Rada Community in Trinidad", *Caribbean Quarterly* 3 (1953): 35–54; David Trotman, "The Yoruba and Orisha Worship in Trinidad and British Guiana: 1838–1870", *African Studies Review* 19 (1976): 1–17; S. Manning, "The Yorubas of Carapachaima, Trinidad Pre-1910", in *The Pan-African Connection: From Slavery to Garvey and Beyond,* ed. T. Martin (Cambridge, Mass.: Schenkman Publishing), 217–18; Maureen Warner-Lewis, *Guinea's Other Suns: The African Dynamic in Trinidad Culture* (Dover, Mass.: Majority Press, 1991); Peter T. Dalleo, "Africans in the Caribbean: A Preliminary Assessment of Recaptives in the Bahamas 1811–1860", *Journal of the Bahamas Historical Society* 6 (October 1984): 15–24; Howard Johnson, "The Liberated Africans in the Bahamas, 1811–1860", in *After the Crossing: Immigrants and Minorities in Caribbean Creole Society,* ed. H. Johnson (London: Frank Cass, 1988), 16–40; Rosanne Marion Adderly, " 'New Negroes from Africa': Culture and Community Among Liberated Africans in the Bahamas and Trinidad 1810 to 1900" (PhD diss., University of Pennsylvania, 1996). Before emancipation, Guyana had a British Vice-Admiralty Court to which captured slave ships were sent; the recaptives were apprenticed to planters. (Minutes of Evidence, Examination of Commander William O'Bryen Hoare, RN, 1 June 1848: Third Report, Select Committee on the Slave Trade, PP 1848 [536]: 34.) For

liberated African immigrants from Bahamas, see Long notebooks, University of Guyana Library. CO 111/242, separate, Henry Light to Lord Stanley, 25 March 1847 encl. Immigration Table from 1 January 1835 to 31 December 1846.

5. Monica Schuler, "Plantation Labourers, the London Missionary Society and Emancipation in West Demerara, Guyana", *Journal of Caribbean History* 22 (1988): 104–7; Adamson, *Sugar,* 38–43. Planters believed that a larger labour force would enable them to dominate the labour market.

6. George W. Roberts, "Immigration of Africans into the British Caribbean", *Population Studies* 8 (March 1954): 260; CO 111/242, separate, Light to Stanley, 25 March 1847; and CO 111/284, "Table Showing the Number of Immigrants Introduced into British Guiana under Colonial Bounty and at the Public Expense from the Taking of a Census on 15 Oct. 1841 to the Taking of a Census on the 31 Mar. 1851"; Long notebooks on Immigration from Nassau, 1837; W. Russell, "Rice", *Timehri* 4 (June 1886): 101–2.

7. Moore, "East Indians and Negroes", 68. Indians, like Africans, were *required* to sign one-year indentures but could voluntarily sign three-year indentures until 1848 when the legislature attempted to enforce three-year indentures; these were apparently disallowed by the Colonial Office, however (Moore, *Race,* 165–66; CO 111/164, no. 164, Light to Stanley, 3 December 1841; CO 111/190, no. 77, Light to Stanley, 19 April 1842, encl. "Monthly Return of Emigrants, 1 April 1842"). A letter to the *Royal Gazette* claimed that the first African immigrants could change employers "at a moment's notice". See "A Lover of Justice", letter to the editor, 31 May 1841, *Royal Gazette of British Guiana* XXXVI, no. 5458 (1 June 1841): 2.

8. CO 111/179, no. 107, Light to Lord John Russell, 21 August 1841, encl. "Monthly Return of African Immigrants Located in District H, 1 Aug. 1841".

9. Although it has been claimed that Portuguese were the only immigrants to avoid indenture, liberated Africans also avoided it for many years. For Africans, see CO 111/219, no. 16, Light to Stanley, 28 January 1845, encl. William Humphrys to Light, 15 January 1845; CO 111/190, no. 78, Light to Stanley, 21 April 1842, encl. James Hackett to H.E.F. Young, 22 April 1842; CO 111/205, no. 66, Light to Stanley, 13 May 1842, encl. Wolseley to Light, 10 May 1843; CO 111/232, separate, Light to W.E. Gladstone, Blue Book Report, 31 March 1846 encl. Rev. Thomas Bell to Light, 12 January 1846. For the Portuguese, see Moore, *Race,* 140–41.

10. Adamson, *Sugar,* 54–55, 109. Immigration Ordinance no. 22, 1850 required an initial one-year indenture of Africans to be followed by a second year's indenture under the same or a different employer (GNA, no. 87, E. Carbery to W.B. Wolseley, 17 February 1851). The 1854 Immigration Ordinance (No.7) required a five-year industrial residence for adults – an initial

three-year indenture followed by two one-year contracts which could be commuted for a fee – but it required children under age fifteen to be indentured up to age twenty (GNA, James Crosby to William Walker, 21 November 1863 and 1 February 1864). Ordinance no. 2 of 1856 required immigrants under age fourteen to be indentured to age eighteen. J. Graham Cruickshank, "African Immigrants After Freedom", *Timehri*, 3d ser., 6 (September 1919): 82.

11. CO 111/341, no. 115, Francis Hincks to Duke of Newcastle, 29 June 1863; GNA, BG no. 743, Newcastle to Hincks, 10 November 1863, encl. T.W.C. Murdoch to F. Rogers, 27 October 1863. For comparison with Jamaican indentures, see Schuler, *"Alas, Alas, Kongo"*, 51–53. Only 432 Africans, all from St Helena, arrived in 1864 and 1865. See CO 386/188, "British Guiana 1860, African Emigration".

12. Adamson, *Sugar*, 48, implies that most Africans slipped unnoticed into Creole villages, but the record suggests otherwise. See, for example, J. Graham Cruickshank, "Among the 'Aku' (Yoruba) in Canal No. 1, West Bank, Demerara River", *Timehri*, 3d ser., 4 (June 1917): 70–82. Guyanese can still identify the Aku (Yoruba), Kongo and Fula quarters in some villages (interviews with descendants of liberated Africans, 1980, 1985). Schuler, *"Alas, Alas, Kongo"*, and Warner-Lewis, *Guinea's Other Suns,* and Adderly, " 'New Negroes from Africa' ", contain comparative information on Yoruba and Kongo in Jamaica and Trinidad.

13. L. Crookall, *British Guiana; or, Work and Wandering Among the Creoles and Coolies, the Africans and Indians of the Wild Country* (London: T. Fisher Unwin, 1898), 108–9.

14. CWM, BG–Ber., James Roome to A. Tidman, 6 October 1854, and 4 April 1856. The Yoruba in question probably arrived on two voyages of the Berbice planters' chartered ship *Roger Stewart* in May and September 1845, and the *Margaret* in March 1846. For the *Roger Stewart* see CO 111/223, no. 127, Light to Stanley, 14 June 1845, encl. William Munro, MD, to Humphrys, 20 and 23 May 1845; CO 111/225, no. 214, Light to Stanley, 3 October 1845, encl. Munro to Humphrys, 22 September 1845, and Munro, "Distribution of Immigrants per Roger Stewart". For the *Margaret,* see CO 111/225, no. 213, Light to Stanley, 3 October 1845, encl. Humphrys to Young, 1 October 1845; GNA, Immigrants on Plantation Rose Hall, 1845–1850.

15. GNA, Petition of Shareholders, L'Esperance Village, 25 February 1869, and Minute on Petition of Peter Johnson, Christian Fortune, et al., 2 March 1869.

16. CWM, BG–Dem., Charles Rattray to Tidman, 9 February 1853, 22 February 1854, 25 February 1856, 11 March 1859; James Scott to Tidman, 20 February 1854, 23 February 1860.

17. GNA, Daniel Ross et al., Petition for Land, 19 August 1874.

18. The Blankenburg Africans were supposed to sign a second year's indenture, but moved to Canal No. 1 instead. The governor demanded that the stipendiary magistrate return them to Blankenburg (GNA, Sandiford to Walker, 11 and 24 August 1852; Henry Barkly, Minute, 14 August 1842).
19. CWM, BG–Dem., Rattray to Tidman, 21 March 1849, 10 January 1852, 9 February 1853, 22 February 1854, 25 February 1856, 11 March 1856; GNA, Sandiford to Walker, 11 and 24 August 1852; Barkly, Minute of 14 August 1842; Moore, "East Indians and Negroes", 160.
20. Theresa Thomas, interview with author, Bagotville, 1980.
21. GNA, Rattray to Francis Hincks, 10 February 1868.
22. Cruickshank, "Among the 'Aku' ", 74–75; J.A. Veerasawmy, "The Noitgedacht Murder", *Timehri*, 3d ser., 6 (September 1919): 115.
23. Cruickshank, "Among the 'Aku' ", 75; and Cruickshank, "An African Dance in the Colony", Supplement to the *West India Circular* 29 (14 February 1924): 809.
24. GNA, "Memorandum of Canal No. 1, 1881, North Side and South Side", enclosed in T.F. Mordle to Young, 12 July 1881; Cruickshank, "Among the 'Aku' ", 74; interviews, Bagotville, 1980. Although some Indians had taken up rice farming at Vive la Force in Canal No. 1 in 1853, it was not until the empoldering of the canal began around 1891 that significant numbers of Indians were attracted to the area; see J.A. Veerasawmy, "Noitgedacht Murder", 115; Moore, "East Indians and Negroes", 235. Kongo or other Angolan descendants were interviewed in Wakenaam as well as East Coast Demerara and West Coast Berbice in the 1980s.
25. African immigrants' village locations may best be documented from missionary correspondence. See, for instance, Horace Edward Wickham, Report, 1 January 1853, and Henry John May, Report, 6 January 1854, 31 December 1855, USPG, Box 1769, BG, etc.; May to Ernest Hawkins, 22 January 1862, USPG Missionary Reports, 1861, North America, etc.
26. CO 111/280, no. 17, Barkly to Grey, 29 January 1851 and encl. "Effects of Spiritual Destitution", *Berbice Gazette,* 20 January 1851.
27. W.T. Veness to W.T. Bullock, 16 July 1869, E24 USPG Missionary Reports 1868–69, North America, etc. Leeds was only fifteen miles from Skeldon and Eliza and Mary estates but had no road, and visitors from Skeldon had to travel by boat for at least three hours, then wade knee-deep through soft mud for over an hour to the shore (Veness to Hawkins, 13 January 1862, E14 USPG Missionary Reports 1863, North America, etc., and Veness Report to SPG, 1 October 1870, E25 USPG Missionary Reports 1869–70, Canada, etc.).
28. Africans comprised a majority of the seventeen Leeds residents confirmed in October 1869. Veness Report to SPG for quarter ending 31 December 1869, E24 USPG Missionary Reports 1868–69, N. America, etc.; Veness to

Bullock, 20 November 1871, E26 USPG Missionary Reports 1870–71, Canada, etc.

29. Schuler, "Plantation Labourers", 95–97. CO 111/232, separate, Light to Gladstone, separate, Blue Book Report, 31 March 1846, encl. Bell to Light, 12 January 1846. See also John Freeman, Report to SPG, 8 February 1853, USPG Box 1769, BG, etc.; Benjamin Spooner to SPG 6 Feb. 1853, USPG Box 1769, BG, etc.; Charles Conyers to Hawkins, 12 February 1857, SPG Missionary Reports 1856, N. America, etc.; M.B. Johnson to Hawkins, 13 August 1855, 18 February 1856, USPG 1769, BG etc.; Lambert McKenzie, Report to SPG, 3 January 1856, USPG Box 1769, BG etc.; "Diocese of Guiana, Church, Chapel and School List 1857", enclosed in Circular Letter of Bishop to Clergy, 22 Dec. 1857, SPG PFP Letters Received (Originals) BG 1850–59; W.A. Brett to Bullock, 5 January 1863, and Veness to Hawkins, 13 January 1862, E14 USPG Missionary Reports 1863, N. America, etc.; Veness to Bullock, 16 July 1869, Veness, Report to SPG for Quarter Ending 31 December 1869; Veness, Report to SPG, 1 Oct. 1869, and Report to SPG for Quarter Ending 31 Dec. 1869, E24 USPG Missionary Reports 1868–69, N. America, etc.; Veness Report to SPG, 1 October 1870, E25 USPG Missionary Reports 1869–70, Canada, etc.; Veness Report to USPG, 30 Sept. 1871, Veness to Bullock, 20 Nov. 1871, E26 USPG Missionary Reports 1870–71, and 1870–71A, Canada, etc.; CWM, BG–Ber. James Roome to Tidman, 6 October and 4 April 1856. James Nott, an Anglican-educated Sierra Leonian, became a Plymouth Brethren minister in Essequibo – see Henry Case, *On Sea and Land, On Creek and River: Being An Account of Experiences in the Visitation of Assemblies of Christians in the West Indies and British Guiana* (London: Morgan and Scott, 1910) 97–98.

30. Cruickshank, "African Immigrants", 83.

31. CO 111/179, no. 107, Light to Russell, 21 August 1841, encl. "Monthly Return of African Immigrants Located in District G. Essequibo, 1st Aug. 1841".

32. GNA, Robert King to Walker, 13 August 1849; William Grando et al. to P.E. Wodehouse, 8 June 1858, and William McNulty to Walker, 12 June 1858.

33. CO 111/190, no. 77, Light to Stanley, 19 April 1842, encl. "Monthly Return of Emigrants, 1 Apr. 1842"; Moore, "East Indians and Negroes", 140–41, 144.

34.   CO 111/232, separate, Light to Gladstone, Blue Book Report, 31 March 1846, encl. Bell to Light, 12 January 1846.

35. Matthew James Higgins, ed., *Eight Years in British Guiana; Being the Journal of a Residence in that Province, from 1840 to 1848 . . . by Barton Premium, A Planter* . . . (London: Longman, Brown, Green and Longman, 1850). Governor Barkly calculated that "wages had been halved since 1841" and would not rise again (Moore, "East Indians and Negroes", 159–60).

36. CO 111/226, no. 238, Light to Stanley, 2 November 1845, encl. W.
     Sandiford, District L, Ber., "Report on the State, Condition and Prospects of
     the Labourers . . . from Plantation Op Hoop van Beter to Herstelling", 28
     Ocober. 1845. See also CWM, BG–Dem., Scott to Tidman, 3 May 1848, and
     13 February 1849, Thomas Henderson to Tidman, 1 March 1849; also
     Rattray, "Report of the Station at Canal No. 1 for 1848"; CWM, BG–Ber.,
     Samuel Haygood to Tidman, 29 August 1848.
37. Both the strike's duration, usually dated from January to March 1848, and the
     rate of wage reductions, usually quoted as 25 per cent, actually varied from
     district to district. For instance in District I, West Coast and West Bank,
     Berbice, Creoles stopped most estate work as early as November 1847 when
     planters could not pay bills and wages, and did very little estate work until the
     end of March. By the end of April less than half were at work (GNA, no. 24,
     Norton to Walker, 27 April 1848). In West Coast Demerara, where work
     ceased as early as December 1847 and resumed before the end of February,
     planters tried to reduce wages by "50 percent or more" (CWM BG–Dem.,
     Scott to Tidman, 13 January 1848, and 13 February 1849). Reverend Rattray
     gave the strike's inception as 1 January 1848 and wage reductions "in some
     places" at 50 per cent (Rattray to Tidman, 18 February 1848). Not all
     planters reduced wages. In one Essequibo district, for instance, representatives
     of seven estates continued to pay the former rates, thus making it impossible
     for planters on the nearby Arabian Cost to enforce wage reduction without the
     labourers striking (GNA, no. 37, Carbery to Walker, "Report on the State of
     District G", 5 February 1848). See also Moore, "East Indians and Negroes",
     51–52; Examination of Matthew James Higgins, 1848, Minutes of Evidence,
     Third Report, Select Committee on the Slave Trade, PP 1844 (536): 67.
38. Labourers purchased over one hundred freeholds in District G Essequibo and
     in Berbice in 1847: see Carbery to Walker, 30 April 1848; CO 111/254, no.
     20, Walker to Grey, 13 June 1848, encl. "Return of All Lots of Land
     Transported and Advertised to be Transported in the County of Berbice
     during the year 1847". In some cases, such as Woodley Park, West Coast
     Berbice, workers wished to cultivate sugarcane on halves; see GNA, Norton to
     Walker, no. 27, 27 April 1848, and C.H. Strutt to Walker, no. 27, 23
     February 1848. On Leguan Island, Essequibo, however, where every estate
     had from 80 to 150 Indian and Portuguese labourers, planters were
     independent of Guyanese workers and forced them into leaving or accepting
     unfavourable sharecropping arrangements. See CO 111/249, no. 32, Light to
     Grey, 18 February 1848; CWM, BG–Dem., John L. Ferrier, "Report for
     Leguan Station for Year 1848", and Ferrier to Tidman, 4 May 1849. In
     Jamaica a similar departure from estates occurred about the same time; see
     Schuler, *"Alas, Alas, Kongo"*, 62–64.

39. Moore, "East Indians and Negroes", 51–52; CWM, BG–Dem., Scott to
      Tidman, 13 January 1848; CO 111/254, no. 20, Walker to Grey, encl.
      Stipendiary Magistrates' Reports, 1848, Carbery to Walker, 30 April 1848.
      Most of these "squatters and beggars" were Madrasees of whom only 2,736
      out of 3,985 arrivals between 1845 and October 1847 remained estate
      residents. Adamson, *Sugar*, 48–49.

40. Adamson, *Sugar*, 49. For reports on immigrant labour during the strike see
      CO 111/252, no. 61, Light to Grey, 4 April 1848, encl. Walker, "Abstract
      Report of Progress of Resumption of Creole Labour in This Colony During
      the First Three Months of 1848", 4 April 1848. In West Coast, Essequibo, for
      instance, immigrants' sole function during the strike was cane field weeding.
      CO 111/254, no. 20, Walker to Grey, encl. Stipendiary Magistrates' Reports,
      1848, Carbery to Walker, 30 April 1848. Examination of Matthew James
      Higgins, 1848, Minutes of Evidence, Third Report, Select Committee on the
      Slave Trade, PP 1844 (536): 67. CO 111/249, no. 32, Light to Grey, 18
      February 1848, encl. "Abstract of Reports Made to the Governor on the State
      of the Rural Districts of This Colony from 24 Jan. to 17 Feb. 1848", D.
      MacLennan and W.J. Sandiford.

41. They arrived from Sierra Leone on the *Growler* in August 1847, and on the
      Arabian and *Helena* in February and April 1848, respectively; from St Helena
      on the *Bellairs* in April 1847 and the *Sea Park* in March 1848, and on the
      Price Regent from the Kru coast in May 1847. See CO 111/245, no. 158, 13
      August 1847 and no. 174, Light to Grey, 30 August 1847 with enclosures;
      GNA, Minutes of Inquiry, 20 March 1848, enclosed in A. Lyons to Walker,
      30 March 1848; Humphrys to Walker, 25 March 1848; John Johnston to
      Walker, "Report on Arrival of Brig *Helena*", with enclosures, 19 April 1848;
      CLEC General Reports, PP 1847–48 (961) XXVI, 23, and PP 1850 (1204)
      XXIII, 141; CO 111/244, no. 112, Light to Grey, 2 June 1847 with enclosures.

42. CWM, BG–Ber., Haywood to Tidman, 29 August 1848; CO 111/249, no.
      32, Light to Grey, 18 February 1848, encl. "Abstract of Reports Made to the
      Governor on the State of the Rural Districts of This Colony from 24 Jan. to
      17 Feb. 1848", George Ball, District A Upper, Dem. GNA, no. 27, Carbery
      to Walker, 5 February 1848, "Report on the State of District G", and
      Goodman to Walker, 1 May 1848.

43. CO 111/249, no. 32, Light to Grey, 18 February 1848, encl. "Abstract of
      Reports Made to the Governor on the State of the Rural Districts of This
      Colony from 24 Jan. to 17 Feb. 1848", George Ball, District A Upper, Dem.

44. CO 111/249, no. 32, Light to Grey, 18 February 1848, encl. "Abstract of
      Reports Made to the Governor on the State of the Rural Districts of This
      Colony from 24 Jan. to 17 Feb. 1848", Strutt, Districts K and L Berbice.

45. GNA, Strutt to Walker, no. 27, 23 February and 1 March 1848.

46. CWM, BG–Dem., Scott to Tidman, 13 January 1848.

47. CO 111/249, no. 32, Light to Grey, 18 February 1848; GNA, no. 24, Norton to Walker, 27 April 1848.

48. Rev. Robert Duff, *British Guiana: Being Notes On a Few of Its Natural Productions, Industrial Occupations, and Social Institutions* (Glasgow, 1866), 141–42; Moore, *Race,* 151. In 1841 a government medical officer wrote that "the numerous connections and friendships formed during a period when they were restricted to labour on particular estates" made estate work gangs like "large families". See CO 111/181, E.L. Smith, MD, to Young, 6 December 1841, enclosed in no. 175, Light to Stanley, 18 December 1841. See Schuler, "Plantation Labourers", 94, for further discussion of estate social structure. Also Moore, "East Indians and Negroes", 50–51.

49. Menezes, "Winged Impulse", 23.

50. The 1848 incidents occurred at Sisters Village, Light Town (also known as Highbury Village or Victoria), and L'Entreprise estate (near Mara), on the east bank of the Berbice River. Strutt, the stipendiary magistrate, who knew the East Bank Berbice African immigrants, identified the attackers as Creole (CO 111/252, no. 60, Light to Grey, 4 April 1848, encl. Thompson to Walker, 25 March 1848; Strutt to Walker, 22 March 1848; J. Van Waterschoodt to Walker, 27 March 1848; Robert King to Walker, 22 and 24 March 1848).

51. CWM, BG–Dem., Henderson to Tidman, 3 July 1848.

52. CWM, BG–Ber., Daniel Kenyon to Tidman, 27 February 1849.

53. CWM, BG–Ber., Haywood to Tidman, 29 August 1848.

54. CO 111/264, Goodman, 7 February 1849, "[Stipendiary Magistrates'] Consolidated Return, half year ending 31 Dec. 1848". CWM, BG–Dem., Henderson to Tidman, 3 July 1848 and Rattray, "Report of the Station at Canal No. 1 for 1848". CO 111/254, no. 20, Walker to Grey, 13 June 1848, encl. Stipendiary Magistrates' Reports, James A. Beamish to Walker, 2 May 1848.

55. GNA, no. 24, Norton to Walker, 27 April 1848; CWM, BG–Ber., George Pettigrew to Tidman, 31 October 1848; GNA, Strutt to Walker, no. 36, 24 April 1848; CWM, BG–Dem., Rattray to Tidman, 18 February 1848, and "Report of the Station at Canal No. 1 for 1848"; Ferrier to Tidman, 4 May 1849; Henderson to Tidman, 3 July 1848.

56. CO 111/264, Goodman, 7 February 1849, "[Stipendiary Magistrates'] Consolidated Return, Half Year Ending 31 Dec. 1848". CWM, BG–Ber., Haygood to Tidman, 29 August 1848.

57. CWM, BG–Dem., Rattray to Tidman, "Report of the Station at Canal No. 1 for 1848"; Rattray to Tidman, 4 March, 4 May, 1850, 27 March 1851; Rev. Barrett Evidence, Third Report, Select Committee on the Slave Trade, 1848,

PP 1848 (536): 142. CWM, BG–Ber., Haygood to Tidman, 29 August 1848. In the 1950s, memories of Kru obeah men and boatmen echoed in Canal No. 1 residents' belief in fierce water spirits called "Kroomen", male counterparts of the Water-mamas, who sit on river rocks, drag men out of their boats, or attempt to capsize them. See E.P. Skinner, "Ethnic Interaction in a British Guiana Rural Community: A Study in Secondary Acculturation and Group Dynamics" (PhD diss., Columbia University, 1955), 258.

58. C. Grenville, *Local Guide* (Georgetown, 1863), 324–25.
59. Michael Craton, "Continuity Not Change: The Incidence of Unrest among Ex-Slaves in the British West Indies 1838–1876", *Slavery and Abolition* 9 (September 1988): 146–48; V.O. Chan, "The Riots of 1856 in British Guiana", *Caribbean Quarterly* 16 (1970): 39–50; Menezes, "Winged Impulse", 23.
60. CWM, BG–Dem., Rattray to Tidman, 25 February 1856.
61. CWM, BG–Dem., Rattray to Tidman, 25 February 1856. GNA, Humphrys to Walker, 28 February 1856.
62. Moore, "East Indians and Negroes", 236–37. Moore, *Race,* 140–51 includes details of the offending Portuguese business practices. Menezes, "Winged Impulse", 21–23.
63. CWM, BG–Dem., Scott to Tidman, 19 May 1856; Moore, "East Indians and Negroes", 235.
64. CWM, BG–Dem., Rattray to Tidman, 25 February 1856.
65. CWM, BG–Dem., Scott to Tidman, 19 May 1856.
66. GNA, Robert Hinds, *Royal Gazette* Office, to Walker, 19 February 1856.
67. Moore, "East Indians and Negroes", 162. Wickham to Hawkins, 1856, n.d., USPG Box 1769, BG, etc.; Conyers to Hawkins, 12 February 1857, USPG Missionary Reports 1856, N. America; etc; CWM, BG–Dem., Henderson to Tidman, 9 April 1856; Scott to Tidman, 6 March 1856.
68. CWM, BG–Dem., Scott to Tidman, 22 February 1856; Rattray to Tidman, 9 April 1856.
69. CWM, BG–Dem., Scott to Tidman, 13 January 1848 and 8 February 1856. Moore, "East Indians and Negroes", 160.
70. CWM, BG–Dem., Scott to Tidman, 13 January 1848. See the 1869 Courentyne drought when Leeds villagers had nothing to eat but herbal broth (Veness to Bullock, 16 July 1869, E24, USPG Missionary Reports 1868–69).
71. CWM, BG–Dem., Rattray to Tidman, 9 April 1856.
72. CWM, BG–Dem., Rattray to Tidman, 25 February 1856.
73. Moore, "East Indians and Negroes", 235.
74. Sixty Kru from Moor Farm, Wakenaam, attacked shops; see GNA, J. Ross to W. Walker, 7 March 1856 and J. Gardiner Austin Report, 3 June 1856. For other Kru involvement, see GNA, Peter Walmer and Tom Dollar to P.E.

Wodehouse, 18 March 1856; J. Brummell to Walker, 22 March 1856. Moore,
"East Indians and Negroes", 235. See also Moore, *Race,* 146, for a discussion
of Portuguese banking and pawnbroking activities.

75. CWM, BG–Dem., Scott to Tidman, 22 February and 19 May 1856, and
     Rattray to Tidman, 25 February 1856.
76. GNA, Humphrys to Walker, 22 February 1856.
77. CWM, BG–Dem., Rattray to Tidman, 25 February and 3 March 1856;
     Henderson to Tidman, 25 February 1856. Although some Christian
     missionary church "hearers" were convicted as participants in the riots,
     church *members* generally refrained from shopbreaking and looting and even
     sheltered Portuguese. According to Reverend James Scott, this did not mean
     that they disapproved of the raids, for they considered the Portuguese
     intruders and would have been pleased if the riots had succeeded in ousting
     them. See Johnson to Hawkins, 3 March 1856, USPG Box 1769, BG etc.;
     CWM, BG–Dem., Henderson to Tidman, 23 and 26 February 1856, Rattray
     to Tidman 3 March 1856; Scott to Tidman, 6 March, 19 May 1856.
78. CWM, BG–Dem., Scott to Tidman, 6 March and 9 and 23 April; Henderson
     to Tidman, 9 April 1856; Rattray to Tidman, 8 August 1856.
79. Conyers to Hawkins, 12 February 1857, E1, USPG Missionary Report 1856,
     North America etc.
80. CWM, BG–Dem., Rattray to Tidman, 10 March 1858.
81. Schuler, "Kru Emigration", 179.
82. The *Athletae* carried forty-two Central Africans from St Helena in March
     1865. See GNA, Crosby to Walker, 22 March 1865, encl. J.W. Thompson to
     Crosby, 17 March 1865; CO 386/188, British Guiana 1860, African
     Emigration.
83. Schuler, "Kru Emigration", 172, 179; CO 111/270, no. 168, Barkly to Grey,
     17 November 1848; CO 111/284, no. 170, Barkly to Grey, 27 Nov. 1851,
     encl. Humphrys, "Table Shewing the Number and Description of People
     Who Have Been Allowed to Return to Their Native Country at the Expense
     of the Colony"; GNA, "Statement of the Number of Persons Who Have Been
     Introduced into . . . British Guiana under Promise of Free Return Passage,
     and the Number Who Have Left At the Expense of the Colony"; CO
     111/319, no. 39, Walker to Stanley, 8 April 1858 and enclosure, C. Williams
     to Acting Government Secretary, 7 April 1858. GNA, Jim Francis, Tom
     Reed, William Anson and Billy Nelsom to William Walker, 21 March 1858;
     Matthew Atkins, William Thomas et al. to Walker, 21 April 1858. Thomas
     Daker to Wodehouse, 12 August 1859; Crosby to Walker, 1 September 1859;
     John London et al. to Wodehouse, 28 August 1859; John Davis to
     Wodehouse, 15 August 1859; Henry Morgan to Wodehouse, 13 August
     1859; David Thomas et al. to Francis Hincks, 15 Sept. 1862 and appended

Crosby minute, 15 September 1862; A.F. Gore to Crosby, Friday [1862], and Crosby to Gore, 19 Sept. 1862. Susanna Bucknor to Hincks, 11 March 1868; CWM, BG–Dem., Rattray to Tidman, 11 March 1859, Scott to Tidman, 7 March 1861. In 1871, an immigrant of 1841 applied for passage on an African troop transport (GNA, Lawrence Barkly to John Scott, 6 October 1871). As late as 1882 Africans in Bagotville, Canal No. 1, were still attempting to return to Africa; see *Demerara Daily Chronicle* (Mail Edition), 4 September 1882. My thanks to Mary Noel Menezes, RSM, for supplying this reference.

Gender Paradigms

CHAPTER 8

Women and Resistance

"Herstory" in Contemporary Caribbean History

BLANCA G. SILVESTRINI

Introduction

The history of all times, and of today especially, teaches that . . . women will be forgotten if they forget to think about themselves.

– Louise Otto, *Speech of a German Girl*, 1849

I am pleased to be part of this collection honouring Elsa Goveia's memory. The invitation to deliver the Elsa Goveia Memorial Lecture on Caribbean history is perhaps the highest honour a Caribbean woman historian can receive. Elsa Goveia meant many things to me (as well as to other women historians). She was the standard of excellence, the role model, the teacher, the scholar, the woman to whom I looked with admiration when I was taking my first steps in these endeavours in 1972. The invitation, therefore, gives me an opportunity to reflect on some of the themes for which she stands in our memory.

I will follow Elsa Goveia's path in addressing some issues of Caribbean social history and historiography. But responding to the challenge of being part of a different generation, I will discuss those historiographical and conceptual themes through the prism of the history of Caribbean women.

The topic of my presentation – women and resistance in contemporary Caribbean history – is a microcosm of the broader theme of the different roles that Caribbean peoples have had in the views of historians. I was almost tempted to title this chapter "Caribbean Peoples as Subjects, Objects, Participants, and Creators", because one of my main goals is to examine, through looking at women's issues, the ways historians have viewed Caribbean peoples in the last twenty years. Indeed my proposal for the study of women's history also applies to the study of men's history. Themes, methodologies and perspectives on the histories of both women and men will come together to inform the histories of Caribbean peoples.

Twenty years ago, while talking with my grandmother about her experiences as a needleworker in western Puerto Rico, I began framing some of the questions that now guide this paper. Like thousands of other women in the 1920s and 1930s, she was a worker, a mother of five children, widowed at forty, an organizer, a church leader, a good neighbour and a conscientious citizen. She had made the transition from home to factory work. How did she do it? What kind of world did she construct for her children? On whom and on what could she depend for support in facing the everyday challenges of surviving through those depressed years? Did she suffer from some of the changes introduced by the new metropolitan power dominating the country? Did she resist? And what form did that resistance take? Why was she attracted to politics, especially since she was barely literate? How, in short, did she understand and explain her past?

My grandmother was like thousands of other women, but I found little in history that addressed her experiences. Even the role of working women in Puerto Rican politics, in which they had been active since the nineteenth century, was scarcely mentioned. We know that until quite recently "women have been invisible in the conventional historical record, they have been 'hidden from history' ".[1] I found a great gap between scholarly knowledge and people's experiences.[2] In this chapter I will suggest some historiographical and methodological reasons for this gap, and show how women's experiences can serve as living testimonies of the historical process.

Women and the Borderlands of History

Gloria Anzaldúa, in an extraordinary passage in her book *Borderlands/La Frontera,* describes the historical path of Mexican migrant women:

> For 300 years she has been a slave, a force of cheap labour, colonized by the Spaniards, the Anglo, by her own people . . . . For 300 years she was invisible, she was not heard . . . . She remained faceless and voiceless, but a light shone through the veil of silence . . . . The spirit of the fire spurs her to fight for her own skin and a piece of ground to stand on, a ground from which to view the world – a perspective, a home-ground where she can plumb the rich ancestral roots into her own ample mestiza heart.[3]

Women have lived in the borderlands for a long time – the borderlands of society and of history. Their everyday lives, their multiple forms of resistance, their ways of understanding and changing the world have been devalued and considered insignificant. Until very recently, in spite of the many roles played by women, they were defined by their relationships to men – as wives, sisters and mothers of men. A woman's primary functions and roles were dictated by the family of which she was a member. Records traditionally used by historians witness the silence about women's participation in other activities. "They have earned wages. They have generated additional income for their families. Weeding, reaping, sewing, knitting, cleaning others' homes, raising others' children, working in factories or offices, women's labour has made the continuance of their families possible."[4]

Caribbean women have had multiple responsibilities not documented in the historical records. Either their work was not recognized as such at the time or it was valued less highly than men's not only in economic but also in social terms. Some women managed to be recognized for their accomplishments, and these are the ones we proudly display today in our "catalogue of important women". But the experiences of the great majority of Caribbean women are still outside the realms of history. The field of women's studies in the Caribbean has grown steadily in the last twenty years. Group efforts to elucidate women's participation in contemporary Caribbean societies have been of particular significance. The Women in the Caribbean Project of the University of the West Indies, for example, has not only opened new avenues for scholarship with its two-volume publication on women in the Caribbean, but also has provided the groundwork for future studies. The issues of *Social and Economic Studies* devoted to reporting on the preliminary results of the project include an extensive discussion of the methodological assumptions and theoretical framework of the studies of the project.[5] Similarly, the Centro de Estudios de la Mujer of the University of Puerto Rico in Cayey has published an interdisciplinary volume that brings together some of the diverse research done on Puerto Rican women.[6]

As in other instances, Caribbean women scholars are "faced with the situation that knowledge of women's experiences in the region has been filtered through studies and methodological tools designed, conducted and interpreted by males".[7] Therefore the work of the projects noted above is encouraging because it pays attention to women's own definitions of the world, with methodologies that are particularly sensitive to women's modes of thinking. Also these groups bring together women scholars from a variety of fields to produce the kind of innovative research required to fill the gap between our understanding of male experience in Caribbean societies, as history has traditionally been defined, and our need for a picture of Caribbean societies that includes the experience of women of different social classes, ages, ethnicities and races.

Indeed we have come a long way toward understanding women's changing roles, particularly as related to contemporary Caribbean society. Nonetheless, in relation to the progress made in other social sciences, historical studies on Caribbean women are lagging.[8] I still do not find the answers to many questions about my grandmother's generation. Why is that? What kind of history are we still writing that cannot accommodate her story? Is it possible that by our definition of history as a field we exclude the study of large portions of the population either because we do not have the "appropriate" sources or because the methods needed to explore these topics do not belong to the realm of what historians commonly do?

Almost half a century ago, Suzanne Langer cautioned that

> Every age in the history of philosophy has its own preoccupation. Its problems are peculiar to it, not for obvious reasons of intellectual growth . . . but by a subtle common factor which may be called their "technique". It is the mode of handling problems, rather than what they are about, that assigns them to an age. . . .
>
> The "technique", or treatment, of a problem begins with its first expression as a question. The way a question is asked limits and disposes the ways in which any answer to it − right or wrong − may be given. . . . Therefore a philosophy is characterized more by the formulation of its problems than by its solution of them. Its answers establish an edifice of facts; but its question makes the frame in which

its picture of facts is plotted. They make more than the frame; they give an angle of perspective, the palette, the style in which the picture is drawn – everything except the subject. In our questions lie our principles of analysis, and our answers may express whatever those principles are able to yield.[9]

An analysis of Caribbean historiographical production in the last twenty years shows that Langer's note of caution is still pertinent. In many cases the questions asked and the methods used to answer them are within the parameters that male historians have used for a long time, in the Caribbean and elsewhere. These historical studies have excluded many of women's concerns and experiences.[10] They have adopted, without much questioning, some of the dichotomies typical of Western historiography – rational versus irrational, public versus private, collective versus individual action, linear versus multi-dimensional time schemes, objectivity versus subjectivity – as if life were made of such dichotomies. These studies have left out many of the ways in which women construct their world: their multiple identities, their many ways of understanding time, the parallel lives they lead in unison, the preference for connectedness and cooperation instead of competition as modes of being in the world. The basic kinds of sources traditionally used by historians exclude women. Many times women did not have access to the written word to portray their world in print; at other times women were transformed into mere statistical figures or historical facts in government, ecclesiastical and even private sources. Women's experiences were silenced from history by the very nature of the historical endeavour.[11]

Convinced that I also had to search for the woman's voice in my own work, I went back to some of the topics I had studied for years – work, labour organization, health and the family – and began looking again at the sources from a different perspective. The literally thousands of documents I had gathered throughout my life as a researcher did not provide the answers to my questions. Women's personal struggles were seldom recounted in those papers, even in those directly related to activities in which women played the central role. For example the documents on the needlework industry in Puerto Rico provided valuable data about the structure of the industry, economic conditions, and even workers' mobilization, but did not help me reconstruct the uncertainties that women like my grandmother faced. Thousands of papers on health did not touch on the ways women coped with the everyday realities of disease and death, nor how nurses, for example, promoted better sanitary conditions at the same time that they resisted the subordination implied in the American medical model imported after 1898. Church records, civil registers and censuses provided facts about people but gave me only the most superficial picture of the rigours of childbirth and child rearing, the pain of a hungry family, and the continuous discrimination that women workers faced in their daily journeys. Court records yielded rich information on the material conditions of marriage and divorce, but were mute on the strengths and resilience of the families involved and the demands of family life. How could I learn about the real lives behind the lifeless figures historians depict? I will share with you a fragment of a new and self-revisionist project. Rather than conclusions, I will unfold the experience of rediscovering a valuable treasure with an ancient technique – the study of lives and the use of storytelling in history.

Some time ago in a very provocative conversation with some women scholars at Stanford University, one of them asked me if I had done any autobiographical work. My mind flashed back to my grandmother. How could I have abandoned her in this way? She was my first project as a historian, but I had missed her story. I then decided to go back to the many stories that women had told me during my long hours of research on the needlework industry. It was a rewarding experience. I began asking new questions and getting new answers from my old sources. A different voice of women in Puerto Rican society was emerging. I now saw resistance where others had seen only subordination; subtle modes of empowerment where others had focused only on marginality. Let me illustrate this process with two stories.

Doña Adela's Story: Life in a Changing Society

Toward the end of her life Doña Adela, a needleworker from a small mountain town in Puerto Rico, observed:

> I have worked all my life. I guess I am working since I was 5, and now I am 79 and I am still working. When my daughters complain now of work, home, the family, children, husbands, I smile. They think I can't understand them, after all I didn't work like them. Since very young I used to get up at 5. I had to feed my brothers before they went to school and work. You know, two of them became teachers, the pride of the family. Being a teacher at the time was very important in our town. Everybody knew us. I always begged them to teach me to write. That was difficult . . . . I had no time from work. Later on, I helped my daughters to go through school. I always told them this was very important, especially for a woman; they should not depend on their husbands, the way I did.[12]

Doña Adela was sixteen when she married a widower with two daughters in 1914. He was a barber and had a small barbershop. They rented a small cottage where her mother, also a widow, joined them with two of her children. In some years they were fourteen altogether. Immediately after their marriage Doña Adela's husband began feeling the effects of the economic constraints prevalent in Puerto Rico at the time.[13] She began sewing for others. She had learned as a child – all girls had to know *costura* (how to sew). Doña Adela had to work very hard. Tensions increased as the husband's shop collapsed. They depended on the little that she could make. Two years and two children later, they moved to another town. Still he could not find work. He felt isolated from her family. For her the family meant the very extended network of relatives (and sometimes close friends) on whom a person could count. Her brothers, for example, were very important in the dynamics and economics of her home. They brought food, taught the children to read and write, and provided support in times of need.

In Lares, Doña Adela and her children became very active in church – a Presbyterian church, recently founded. Church provided a social network, a new sense of neighbourhood and community, and new activities and roles. She then bought her first sewing machine, a *plazos,* paid for in instalments with savings from her previous work. The needs of the family increased and they barely scraped by. Then disease struck. First Doña Adela lost her husband in 1923. A year later her oldest and only son died of typhus. Some years afterward her oldest daughter, who had married at fifteen, lost her first child to meningitis. "My life was a turmoil. I barely could make ends meet. My family became a family of women. I was 24 when I became the *jefa de familia.* My family depended on me in two ways: I was the provider, but even more important, I had to teach them *decencia.* My girls had to learn that they must be *mujeres decentes,* even if poor."

Becoming a widow, Doña Adela learned the hard lessons of life. In 1929 she decided that her daughters had to learn to work. She organized a *pequeño taller* (a very rudimentary needlework factory) at her home. The seven girls of the house learned sewing, embroidery and other related arts. Doña Adela contracted work in Mayaguez, the major western city, and her home became a small factory six days a week. Those children who went to school had to put in a full workday after school. In less than three years, Doña Adela became not only *jefa de la casa* (head of household), but *jefa del taller* as well. She established an order in which the youngest of her daughters took care of the smaller children, actually Doña Adela's first grandchildren, and was responsible for the house chores. All the others worked for long days to earn just a few cents, which almost invariably were invested in home expenses.

Four times their house was destroyed by fire in the neighbourhood. In each instance Doña Adela and her family had to build a nest all over again. Notwithstanding these trials, she continued devoting part of her energies to church activities. For her, church provided not only spiritual support but also a secure and healthy environment for her young daughters. In times of extreme need, the church community also provided moral and material support. "This was my mode of giving and receiving. After all, this is what Christianity is all about. You give support in times of need others will assist you. This was particularly true in times of sickness." Disease and death always lurked behind home stability:

> How many more family members do we have to lose? In a few years our family lost all its men. Disease scared me. The health of some of the girls was very fragile. I used to stay up all night when Mercedes got an asthma attack. It was frightening. It seemed as if she couldn't breathe. And we didn't have health care as today. Going to the hospital was worse than the illness itself. We couldn't count on it. The only help I had was from the spiritualist medium and the pastor. I always stayed close to them. Both helped me face and understand death and sickness. The midwives . . . they were really our only support. They knew not only about childbirth, but of all the *achaques* [maladies] that afflicted women. And they were part of the family.

In the 1930s Doña Adela's family experienced two important events – migration and labour mobilization. In 1931 the family moved to Mayaguez. Perhaps in sociological terms moving less than a hundred miles is not considered a migration, but for this family it meant a complete displacement, a change in the ways the family organized, and a transformation of their world views.

Mayaguez was the core of the needlework industry by 1930.[14] With the establishment of needlework factories, the population of the town had increased dramatically during the previous decade.[15] The incoming families went to live at the outskirts of the city, in houses with very few facilities. Many women left their homes to work in factories. The needlework factories meant new power relations – with the *talleristas* (owners), the *contratista* (management), co-workers, union leaders, and even Department of Labour bureaucrats. Industrial time, machines and division of labour substituted for the small family *taller* or factory. A new world emerged in which resistance expressions and assent to change intermingled in work patterns, family life, community action, beliefs, identities and self-definition.

For the first time Doña Adela, as a worker, considered joining a labour union:

> It wasn't that bad because we were all women. But still, it was difficult to come to terms with striking. As a *jefa de familia* I had more freedom; I didn't have to ask for permission from a man. Though deep in my heart, I wasn't sure if I was giving the right example to my children. We needed wages so badly, but the injustices were so big. The most important part was that we helped each other.

Strikes then became a self-formative activity for women in different terms than for men. They had an immediate impact on their daily family life. In one of those workers' groups, for example, Doña Adela met a family that later helped one of her daughters to try her luck in New York. At seventeen she left the island to search for work in New York, something quite rare for a single woman, *bien criada* (well brought-up). "But during the strike we became like family. I knew she was being taken care of as if at home."

While in Lares the family had faced intermittently the changes that new capitalist development in Puerto Rico had produced – unemployment for the father, piecework contracts for the mother, machines, reorganization of the family around industrial time, and so on. Even so, they viewed the changes as distant because many of the traditional ways of life and values were still prevalent. Mayaguez represented a new world. Different images of virtue and vice emerged in the new environment. A new sexuality confronted very traditional values, resulting in apparently contradictory models of behaviour. "I wanted my girls to learn to work, but I didn't want them to see what other women in the factory did. In this sense church was a blessing." As in other Third World societies, material relationships and cultural attitudes and practices were "both emerging and receding in the wake of . . . proletarianization".[16]

Doña Adela's life was at the same time passionate and tough. "I had to be the mother and father – love and discipline. That's why I never thought of marrying again, even when the children were already gone." Her life represented a making, remaking and unmaking of the multiple relations of domination and resistance in Puerto Rican society at the time.[17]

The lives of many Doña Adelas serve to reconstruct aspects of Puerto Rican history in the first half of the twentieth century in a different tune. Women faced the new forms of capitalist growth and multinational corporations in distinct ways from men. They moved into factory work before men. With factories came a different work discipline. Subordination was enforced in powerful ways by the capitalist organizations that moved to the island, the local intermediaries that facilitated their enterprises, and the bureaucratic apparatus at their service. Women looked inside themselves for strength to resist the many incongruities involved in the new changes. Their commitment to family, community and church was not necessarily an individualist reaction, as some studies have argued.[18] On the contrary, these were the ways to keep themselves together in times of adversity. They clung to traditional ways of understanding family and community relations, sexuality, language, education and health, among other things. At the same time, they dared to speak, to break their silence, looking to women's groups for support and action, and in many cases breaking into the ranks of political and labour organizations. Everyday transactions with their world were complex because they involved the cultural reconstructions of class, gender, family and morality within changing configurations of power relations.

Maria's Story: Resistance and Cultural Citizenship

María, a seventy-one year-old woman from Mayaguez, first a needleworker and later a teacher, explained:

> Ay, *mijita,* things then were much more difficult than you could possibly imagine. Six years after my marriage in 1921, my life was in trouble. Four children alive; the fifth died at birth. I was doing piecework, sewing pants, for very little. My husband got very angry when I stood to watch the protest that the *Unión de Damas* was making in front of the big *taller.* I couldn't participate. I was only a home-worker. When I came home he was waiting for me. Someone had told him that I was one of the striking women. I wasn't, but why not? In those days that was the only way to make them [the employers] understand. Then he screamed, shouted bad words and began hitting the children, as if they were responsible for what I did.
>
> I was the only one working at the house. Even he depended on what I made. But he wanted me to respect him. *"Por desconsiderada,"* he screamed when he left the house. He never came back.
>
> I knew that I had to care for my children from then on. Someone at the *taller* mentioned that I should divorce him. I didn't even know what that meant. But after asking a few friends from the *fábrica,* I thought of it seriously. I wanted to move to San Juan and perhaps that was the only way. In spite of the opposition

of all my family, who believed that *las mujeres decentes* never divorced their husbands, I divorced him in 1932. I tried to give the best example to my children. I went to live for a while in the interior. There, since I had eighth grade, I worked as a rural teacher. The conditions were very bad. To reach the school which was a one-room cottage, I had to travel for a long time. . . .

By that time my own children were in school, so you can imagine the things I had to do. Fortunately, my mother moved in with me and helped. . . .

Working at that rural school, I learned a lot about the people. The grinding poverty in which the children lived, no books, nothing, and . . . we were supposed to teach in English. That was the law, we were told; but I didn't know enough English myself, so how could I teach them to write their names in English?[19]

María's story was extraordinary. When she moved to San Juan with her family, she continued to work as a teacher. At the same time, she attended the *Escuela Normal* and slowly got her teacher's certificate. For twenty-five years she worked with dedication in the teachers' organization. Outspoken on labour issues for teachers, strong and well organized, María devoted part of her time in school to talking to her peer teachers. She insisted that they complete their degrees and assisted them in developing teaching materials; she helped the principal understand the teachers' needs for time. Twenty years later she still was defending the use of Spanish as the primary language in Puerto Rico. Otherwise María seemed a very traditional person – never remarried, active member of a Protestant church, attentive to her grandchildren's needs, a good home-maker. Both as a mother and as a teacher, she was fully engaged with her social environment and with herself as a woman and a person.

The world Puerto Rican women confronted in the first half of the twentieth century was qualitatively different from that of their predecessors. Increased dependence on cash and importation; the substitution of an industrial world for the traditional agricultural economy; growing urban development; new technological changes; radically different school, public health, legal, and mass communication systems, among other factors, tilted the lives of the people toward the American way of life.

Thanks to the work of social historians, today we understand better that Puerto Ricans, both men and women, did not sit quietly through the strains produced by these structural transformations. Historians have analysed some parts of the diverse spectrum of political and labour responses to these changes.[20] Although women's participation in social movements is less well known, the feminist struggles for political rights – the vote, elective positions and a role in the political parties – is beginning to be studied.[21]

Women's resistance in Puerto Rico in the first half of the twentieth century took multiple forms that we have yet to study carefully. Women struggled against the male-dominated culture that oppressed them, against the new capitalist economic order that subordinated them as workers, against the colonial power that attempted to Americanize them through schools, hospitals, churches and housing projects. Simultaneously, women became the agents of social change within their families, their communities and the larger society. Many of them went to school, and even got degrees in higher education in larger proportions than in other parts of the industrial world, while preserving some of their traditional values and transforming others to fit new realities. Women became active in the public health campaigns of the early twentieth century. At the same time they criticized the movement, and looked for alternative solutions to health problems that would be more attuned to their own beliefs and values.[22] Still, because women's political mobilization often focused on the needs of their families and immediate communities, it was disregarded as unimportant by their fellow male workers. Their stories were not incorporated into the mainstream historical discourse because they were told in unconventional ways, far from the kinds of sources searched by historians in archives.[23]

Resistance thus had many faces.[24] Taken together, María's story and the stories of many other Marías illustrate a variety of powerful forms of resistance. Subtle and intimate forms of resistance were rooted in women's lives, and often passed unnoticed. In many cases, these other forms of resistance served as the background and foundation for women's social action. In other cases resistance was related to everyday human struggles for morality, identity and self-definition.[25]

One of the difficulties faced in the study of women's resistance is the prevalence of the idea that there is a sharp rift between women's public and private lives.[26] But now we know that for women the public and personal are tightly related, and that beyond political and labour union activities, there are other forms of resistance that are more difficult to identify unless approached from the perspective of women's experience.

For the Puerto Rican women I have studied, the line between the private and the public was almost non-existent. Perhaps there is a public sphere – the bureaucratic, political relations with the dominant power – into which fewer men and women venture. But the public and private spheres intermingle when women work in their labour unions, churches, community centres, and civic and charitable organizations. The private is never totally private when the family includes not only parents and siblings but relatives and close friends. In criticizing the idea that public and private spheres are separate, black American novelist Toni Morrison has explained that Afro-American women do not have a choice between home-making and career; rather their lives are controlled by a constant "and" conjunction.[27] Similarly, Caribbean women are mothers, workers, wives, political activists, writers, neighbours and grand-mothers – all at the same time, without a choice and with many choices altogether. Their images, then, do not appear clear-cut for historians and other scholars who, in their efforts to understand structural relationships in emerging capitalist societies, sometimes do not hear the marginal voices in these societies.

Regaining the Voice: The Art of Storytelling Revisited

To tell women's story, to place them at the centre and make sense of their experiences, means that we have to reconceptualize Caribbean history "as if it were seen through the eyes of women and ordered by values they define".[28] For example, to reconstruct the meanings that industrial wage labour and urbanization have had on Puerto Rican women in the twentieth century, it is necessary to talk about women not only as the objects of historical analysis but as historical subjects, as creators of history. Positioning women as subjects rather than objects changes the perspective of our work as historians because we then study a person "capable of acting upon the world rather than one upon whom others act".[29] Placing Caribbean women at the centre is an invitation, a challenge to shift paradigms, to learn from women's voices as affirmative actors in history, rather than as underprivileged dependent others. "The struggle . . . to move from object to subject is expressed in the effort to establish the liberatory voice – that way of speaking that is no longer determined by one's status as object or oppressed being. That way of speaking characterized by opposition, by resistance. It demands that we learn to talk, to listen, and to hear in a new way."[30]

Traditional historical methods frequently constrain our search for this new understanding of women in history. "It becomes easy to . . . describe and define experience in a language compatible with existing images and ways of knowing, constructed within social frameworks that reinforce domination."[31] Historical research methodology has begun to change in an effort to accommodate new sources for the study of women's history. Literary works, the fine arts, wills, diaries and letters are shedding new light on some important experiences. However we are still far from accepting the voices of women telling us a different story as historical sources. To accomplish that we have to privilege women's voices (as we do with the testimonies produced by men and used constantly in our work as historians) and listen to their subjective experiences.

The question of how to evaluate women's experience becomes central. As Christine Littleton has argued in the legal context, we need "a dialectic between our own descriptions of our varying experience and the conditions under which such descriptions are made".[32] She has suggested that

> rather than viewing any woman's description as, on the one hand, potentially inaccurate, socially conditioned or merely the product of internalized oppression; or on the other, individualized, attributable solely to determinants other than gender, or exceptional, I suggest that we should use as a working hypothesis the assumption that women's descriptions of our experience are accurate, reasonable and potentially understandable *given the conditions under which we live*. Tensions and contradictions in women's descriptions give us a way to examine and criticize the conditions under which we live, rather than a reason to deny status to some descriptions or to consider other descriptions as relevant to some women but not others.[33]

Historians, especially those interested in recovering women's voices, must include narratives as one of their valuable sources of historical truth. Since for centuries women have been nameless and invisible in historical discourse, the only place where we could see ourselves, write about ourselves and define ourselves was in narratives. But, as Charles Lawrence III has cautioned,

> It is not enough for us to tell our stories. We must use them as text for research and interpretation. Giving narrative form to experience creates a rich evidentiary record for analysis and assessment of complex social processes. . . . What is also required is that narrative be valued as a source. . . . In embracing the use of narrative as cultural text, practitioners of "the word" must consider and employ methodologies of research and interpretation that draw upon the wealth of articulated experiences and feelings contained in stories, but these methodologies must also serve to give legitimacy and authority to this way of knowing.[34]

Most of our Caribbean women did not have access to the written word. For some publishing was beyond any reasonable expectation; they lacked the power both to make their stories thinkable in media controlled by men and to make them appear in print.[35] For others like my grandmother (a large proportion of women until very recently), the written word was inaccessible; they could not read or write. They were not given the gift of the written word. Does this mean then that the majority of women in the Caribbean were voiceless, thus ahistorical and without their own culture; or does it point to the need to revise our conceptions of what makes a voice a historical source?

Lives, as a manifestation of women's voices, become an indispensable part of our historical reality. In many cases they provide the only text on which we can depend to reconstruct the history of women. Oral historians have used living testimonies for much longer than we might think. But they often use oral testimonies in the same ways that we use written documents – that is to learn the facts about a topic. They maintain the dichotomy between themselves as subjects and the others as objects. As historians they have the truth; they use testimonies, oral or written, to corroborate it.

My proposal is different. What would happen if we gave the people, or in particular the women we study, a chance to talk back, to tell us that we are wrong in the ways we have been interpreting their reality; to tell us, for example, that subordination and marginality have another face, resistance?[36] Their voices would become active voices from which we could learn not only facts, but about real life in all its complexity and richness.[37] Historians would then have a different role . . . that of the positioned subject.[38] The "objective view" of the distant historical processes "that have definite locations in space with marked centers and outer edges"[39] would be continuously modified by the interaction of our experiences as historians with the experiences of the historical subjects we study. History would become, thus, a dialogue in which both historians and historical subjects would participate, creating a new paradigm for history – a paradigm that recognizes that we as historians are part of the history we reconstruct.

Carolyn Heilbrun has said that there are many ways to write a woman's life.[40] In our Caribbean cultures storytelling provides another way to write a woman's life. "Stories express depth and complexity. They allow for ambiguity, multiple interpretation, and refracted images. The reader or listener can be convinced and moved, by intellect and emotion. And stories are not exclusive property. One story invites another as people's words weave the tapestry of human connection."[41]

Isabel Allende, in her recent book *Eva Luna,* addresses this theme through the voice of her main character. Eva, a poor orphan girl, becomes a woman by telling stories. Storytelling is her only skill in life. When Eva finally learns to write and is able to write her stories, she announces:

> [A]s soon as I had begun dusting off memories and weaving destinies, I saw that I did not know where I was going, or what the resolution would be – if there was one. I suspected that I would reach the end only at my own death, and was fascinated by the idea that I was another character in the story, and that I had the power to determine my fate, or invent life for myself. The plot became more complicated, the characters more and more rebellious. I was working – if work is what that celebration can be called – many hours a day . . . even in my dreams I was still deep in my new universe, hand in hand with my characters to keep them from escaping their faint outlines and returning to the nebula of stories that remained to be told.[42]

We shall learn from the ancient art of storytelling as part of our effort to regain the voices of women in history. Telling stories was their way of being public from within their private sphere. When, twenty years ago, my grandmother spent hours telling me the ways employers tricked working women to keep them from voting in 1932 and 1936 (the first two elections in which women voted in Puerto Rico) and how she managed to vote, I disregarded her story as unimportant. Perhaps I already knew that this was a common practice in Puerto Rico, or probably I discarded it as difficult to corroborate with a document. But what was new in her story? By disregarding her story as historical testimony, I ignored her voice of resistance and the ways she placed herself in contemporary Puerto Rican society. In telling her story she was defining herself as a cultural being at the same time that she was talking back. In spite of all the economic, political and social pressures that challenged her life, she managed to succeed in constructing a space for herself.

On another occasion, a grieving woman told me how a group of mothers had to confront police in a public housing project to be allowed to mourn her drug addict son in what they considered the proper form – a long caravan of community members in trucks, playing salsa and drums. I should have viewed this as a valid account of a form of collective action to resist the depersonalized burial rituals identified with urban settings. It was their way of talking back, of becoming public, of resisting in the area of one of the most valued cultural symbols – the rituals of death. Another woman devoted long hours to telling me about the struggle of her community to claim the land on which their families had lived for years. Women were at the forefront, but their stories were subsumed under those of the "generic men" who also participated, as if for women and men home meant the same thing. At the time I put aside the emotional force of these stories because they lacked factual corroboration. I had also adopted the masculine voice of neutrality and detachment in history, in which knowledge and passion could not come together.[43]

Until very recently, the quest for objectivity has excluded from historical analysis feelings, emotions and the subjective experience.[44] Objectivity has been identified with the rational mode of understanding, with detachment between the subject and object of inquiry, and with epistemological neutrality. Subjective accounts have been equated with the irrational, the biased, the prejudiced voice. Without much thinking, we women historians have adopted the same voices that attempted to silence women. Believing that our endeavour is neutral we have rejected, or at least disregarded, the text that our experiences write and rewrite as we uncover and understand them.

Stories from biographies and autobiographies have often been conceived in the scholarly community as descriptions of individual, eccentric lives. By talking of a few, historians may silence the voice of the majority. And in using lives as a source, historians may also attempt to decompose groups into their individual constituents, adopting an approach already criticized in the histo-riographical literature as merely aggregationalist. Women's history is not exempt from these dangers. But perhaps, rather than drawing conclusions from the ways men have used narratives in the past, we should explore as part of our agenda the ways women historians can use lives and storytelling, two types of sources we know well from our own experience. We hope to be able to reconstruct women's lives in relation to their collectives, without transform-ing narratives into "a commodity, fashionable speech . . . or spectacle".[45]

Storytelling, poetry, the graphic arts and narratives may be perhaps the most important ways in which we women leave the marks of our lives in history. As Adrienne Rich has written:

> As we all do when young and searching for what we can't even name yet, I took what I could use where I could find it. When the ideas or forms we need are banished, we seek their residues wherever we can trace them. But there was one major problem with this. I had been born a woman, and I was trying to think and act as if poetry [in my case, history] – and the possibility of making poems – were a universal . . . a gender-neutral . . . realm. In the universe of the masculine paradigm, I naturally absorbed ideas about women, sexuality, power from the subjectivity of male poets. . . . The dissonance between these images and the daily events of my own life demanded a constant footwork of imagination, a kind of perpetual translation, and an unconscious fragmentation of identity: woman from

poet. Every group that lives under the naming and image-making power of a dominant culture is at risk from this mental fragmentation and needs an art which can resist it.[46]

Acknowledgements

Many people helped me in the process of conceptualizing and revising this chapter. In particular, I would like to thank Barbara Babcock for her thorough reading of the manuscript and her valuable suggestions; Nell Painter, Carol Stack, Charles Lawrence III, Gerald Lopez and Renato Rosaldo for their comments and their encouragement to look "at the other story"; and Franklin Knight for his continuous support and long discussions on "objectivity". The first draft of this paper was prepared while I was a fellow at the Center for Advanced Studies in the Behavioral Sciences in Stanford, California. The support of the Center is gratefully acknowledged.

Notes

1. B. Brereton, "General Problems and Issues in Studying the History of Women", in *Gender in Caribbean Development,* ed. P. Mohammed and C. Shepherd (St Augustine, Trinidad: Women and Development Studies Project, University of the West Indies, 1988), 123.
2. In this respect Brereton argues that "while the movement for history from the bottom up" can try to deal with the invisibility of the poor and oppressed, only a feminist perspective will see, and grapple with, the invisibility of women. In conventional history women are simply not there, except for the odd ruling woman when she cannot be ignored ("women at the top"). Ibid.
3. Gloria Anzaldúa, *Borderlands/La Frontera: The New Mestiza* (San Francisco: Spinsters/Aunt Lute, 1987), 23.
4. Bonnie S. Anderson and Judith P. Zinsser, *A History of Their Own* (New York: Harper and Row, 1988), 2: xiii.
5. Two numbers of the journal *Social and Economic Studies* 35, nos. 2 and 3 (June and September 1986) were devoted to presenting the findings of the project. The first article by Joycelin Massiah presents an overview of the project. Mohammed and Shepherd, eds., *Gender in Caribbean Development* reports part of the findings of the project.
6. Yamila Azize Vargas, ed., *La Mujer en Puerto Rico* (Río Piedras: Ediciones Huracán, 1987). The volume includes essays on work, religion, education, legal issues, communication media and literature.

7.   J. Massiah, "Women in the Caribbean Project: An Overview", *Social and Economic Studies* 35 (June 1986): 1.

8.   Most of the essays published in the volumes mentioned in notes 6 and 7 focus on the contemporary situation of Caribbean women. In general, they deal peripherally with the historical processes involved during the twentieth century. In the case of the volume on Puerto Rican women, there are two essays devoted to historical topics, one on the role of women in the Catholic Church and the other on the needlework industry.

9.   Susanne K. Langer, *Philosophy in a New Key*, 3d ed. (Cambridge: Harvard University Press, 1957), 3–5 *passim.*

10.   An analysis of the books on Caribbean history published between 1986 and 1989 did not show improvement in this respect. From thirteen books considered in the final round for the Elsa Goveia Award in Caribbean History, I noticed that only a few mention the word woman (or women) at all; much less do they incorporate the discussions of women's issues or women's perspective as part of their treatment of the topic.

11.   As Bridget Brereton has brilliantly stated: "At the risk of over-simplication, history was conventionally defined as the ideas and action of male members of the ruling classes of past societies. It was about government, state-building, war, formal institutions, founding official religions, mastering the environment – all activities in which male elites believed that women's roles were insignificant, or at best supportive only. Now this kind of history still lingers on in schools and textbooks and the popular mind" (Brereton, "General Problems", 123–24).

But even in the most recent historical production, linked to the new interpretations on the social and economic history of the Caribbean, women are mentioned only peripherally and their experiences are not incorporated into the mainstream historical discourse. Cf. Franklin W. Knight and Colin A. Palmer, eds., *The Modern Caribbean* (Chapel Hill: North Carolina University Press, 1989).

12.   Interviews on file, translated by the author.

13.   For a detailed analysis of the economic situation of those years, see James L. Dietz, *Economic History of Puerto Rico: Institutional Change and Capitalist Development* (Princeton: Princeton University Press, 1986)

14.   Blanca G. Silvestrini, "Women and Work in the Needlework Industry in Puerto Rico", in *A Selection of Papers Presented at the Twelfth Conference of the Association of Caribbean Historians,* ed. K.O. Lawrence (St Augustine, Trinidad: Department of History, University of the West Indies, 1980), 172–93.

15.   US Department of Commerce, Bureau of the Census, Fifteenth Census of the United States, 1930, Porto Rico (Washington, DC, 1932).

16. Aihwa Ong, *Spirits of Resistance and Capitalist Discipline, Factory Women in Malaysia* (Albany: State University of New York Press, 1987), 2.

17. In her study of Malaysian women workers, Ong found that "cultural change is not understood as unfolding according to some predetermined logic (of development, modernization, or capitalism) but as the disrupted, contradictory, and differential outcomes which involve changes in identity, relations of struggle and dependence, including the experience of reality itself" (Ong, *Spirits of Resistance*, 3).

18. Cf. Francisco Scarano, "Las huellas esquivas de la memoria: Antropología e historia en Taso, trabajador de la caña", in *Taso, trabajador de la caña,* ed. Sidney Mintz (Río Piedras: Ediciones Huracán, 1988).

19. Interviews on file, translated by the author.

20. Although I cannot include here a comprehensive bibliography on Puerto Rico in the twentieth century, I will just mention the work of the historians working on issues related to labour and social resistance. For example, see Gervasio I. García and Quintero Rivera, *Desafío y solidaridad: Breve historia del movimiento obrero puertorriqueño* (Río Piedras: Ediciones Huracán, 1982); A.G. Quintero Rivera, *Conflictos de clase y política en Puerto Rico* (Río Piedras: Ediciones Huracán, 1976); Fernando Picó, *Los gallos peleados* (Río Piedras: Ediciones Huracán, 1987).

21. See for example, Edna Acosta-Belén, ed., *La mujer en la sociedad puertorriqueña* (Río Piedras: Ediciones Huracán, 1980); Yamila Azize, *Luchas de la mujer en Puerto Rico, 1898–1919* (San Juan: Tipografía Metropolitana, 1979).

22. Examples of these movements are the midwives' organizations and education campaigns for public health. Cf. Blanca G. Silvestrini, "La política de salud pública de los Estados Unidos en Puerto Rico, 1898–1913: Consecuencias en el proceso de americanización", in *Politics, Society and Culture in the Caribbean,* ed., B.G. Silvestrini (Río Piedras: University of Puerto Rico, 1983), 67–83.

23. Most of the research on the history of women has used the prevalent historical methodologies, relying heavily on archival materials; therefore, they have not been able to incorporate some of the experiences of women that are not recorded in those records.

24. Barbara Harlow, *Resistance Literature* (New York: Methuen,1987); Amilcar Cabral, "The Role of Culture in the Battle for Independence", in *Cultural Resistance Art from Guinea-Bissau, Mozambique and Angola* (New York: African-American Institute, 1974), 8.

25. Similar findings have been reported by other scholars. See, for example, Ong, *Spirits of Resistance*.

26. Cf. Sandra Morgen and Ann Bookman, "Rethinking Women and Politics: An Introductory Essay", in *Women and the Politics of Empowerment,* ed. A.

Bookman and S. Morgen (Philadelphia: Temple University Press, 1988), 3–29.

27.   Carolyn G. Heilbrun, *Writing a Woman's Life* (New York: Norton, 1988), 61.

28.   Geida Lemer, *The Majority Finds Its Past: Placing Women in History* (New York: Oxford University Press, 1979), 168. As Catherine MacKinnon notes, the "methodological secret" of feminism is that it is built on "believing women's accounts", that is, on recognizing women's experience as central. Catherine MacKinnon, *Feminism Unmodified* (Cambridge: Harvard University Press, 1987), 5.

29.   Charles R. Lawrence, III, "The Word and the River: Pedagogy as Scholarship as Struggle" (paper presented at Yale Law School, March 1989), 25. Lawrence discusses three separate, although interconnected, meanings of the word "subjective" that are of particular importance in redefining our work to incorporate the perspective of those suffering from subordination. "These are: (1) subjective, as indicating the scholar's positioned perspective in viewing and recording social constructs; (2) subjective, as indicating non-neutrality of purpose, that the scholar embraces certain values . . . ; (3) subjectivity, as indicating that the scholar places herself in the linguistic position of subject rather than object."

30.   bell hooks, *Feminist Theory: From Margin to Center* (Boston: South End Press, 1984), 48.

31.   Ibid.

32.   Christine Littleton, "Women's Experience and the Problem of Transition: Perspectives on Male Battering of Women", *University of Chicago Legal Forum* 4 (1989): 27.

33.   Ibid.

34.   Lawrence, "The Word and the River", 12.

35.   Heilbrun, *Writing a Woman's Life*, 43.

36.   See Renato Rosaldo, "When Natives Talk Back", in *Renato Rosaldo Lectures* (Tucson: Mexican American Studies Center, 1986), 3–20.

37.   Sara Lawrence Lightfoot's *Balm in Gilead* (Reading, Mass.: Addison-Wesley, 1988) is an excellent example of the use of stories in this way. The author says: "I listen for how she feels about the family drama, not for bare facts. I listen for how she perceives community, prejudice, illness and healing, not for an objective rendering of the sociohistorical contexts" (p. 18).

38.   Renato Rosaldo develops this point in anthropological and ethnographic research in his book *Culture and Truth: The Remaking of Social Analysis* (Boston: Beacon Press, 1989), chapter 1.

39.   Ibid., 16.

40.   Carolyn Heilbrun has explained that "[t]here are four ways to write a woman's life: the woman herself may tell it, in what she chooses to call an

autobiography; she may tell it in what she chooses to call fiction; a biographer, woman or man, may write the woman's life in what is called a biography; or the woman may write her own life in advance of living it, unconsciously, and without recognizing or naming the process" (Heilbrun, *Writing a Woman's Life*, 1).

41. Sara Lawrence Lightfoot, "*Balm in Gilead:* On Justice, Love, and the Word" (paper presented at the annual luncheon of Equal Rights Advocates, San Francisco, 1988).

42. Isabel Allende, *Eva Luna,* trans. Margaret Sayers Peden (New York: Knopf, 1988), 255.

43. Cf. Michelle Z. Rosaldo, *Knowledge and Passion: Ilongot Notions of Self and Social Life* (Cambridge: Cambridge University Press, 1980).

44. Renato Rosaldo, "Subjectivity in Social Analysis", chapter 8, in *Culture and Truth,* 168–95.

45. bell hooks, "Coming to Voice", in *Talking Back: Thinking Feminist, Thinking Black,* by bell hooks (Boston: South End Press, 1988), 47.

46. Adrienne C. Rich, *Blood, Bread, and Poetry: Selected Prose, 1979–1985* (New York: Norton, 1986), 174–75.

CHAPTER 9

Women Field Workers in Jamaica during Slavery

LUCILLE MATHURIN MAIR

Any attempt to reconstruct the past of Jamaican female agricultural labour is bedevilled by the colonial/metropolitan orientation of much of Caribbean historiography. This is perhaps inevitable, given the primacy of European strategic and commercial interests in the establishment of New World plantations. As a result the enslaved African men and women who laboured in those plantations have been submerged in the archives, for centuries, barely making it to the footnotes. Women have suffered as well from the invisibility which has been the nearly universal fate of women's work, whether slave or free, in or out of the field, in the past or the present. When noticed it is usually seen as marginal to the national, not to mention the international, economy. This applies to that wide range of essential goods and services which women produce in the home: they are seldom if ever quantified, seldom if ever regarded as significant enough to be reflected in calculations of national income. It is equally true of women's enterprises in that sector of the economy which in Jamaica and the rest of the Caribbean is dominated by women, and is variously labelled the informal or parallel or underground sector, all of which imply activities that are imprecise, irregular and out of sight.

This syndrome of virtual non-existence constricts research. Economists who, for example, wish to compute female rural labour in regions of Africa, Latin America or Asia find their attempts to get hard sex-aggregated data frustrated by a widespread insistence on the part of men, but of women too, that women do not work. And this despite the clear evidence of the vital agricultural tasks in which women are engaged in so many areas of these continents, and have been engaged for centuries. For the Caribbean region, the new history of slavery, in which Elsa Goveia's work is a major landmark, now allows us to adjust that distortion of female reality.[1] In contrast to a generation ago, the greater body of knowledge at our disposal today about that formative period of Caribbean societies gives us the ammunition to reject the stereotype of a female labour force which is peripheral to the dominant sectors of the economy. Recent and current scholarship such as Orlando Patterson's work on the sociology of Jamaican slavery, Michael Craton's and James Walvin's study of Worthy Park estate, my own research findings, and Barry Higman's meticulous demographic analysis of the Jamaican slave population on the eve of emancipation, all testify to the extensive involvement of slave women in Jamaica's agricultural enterprises, and notably the prime productive processes of the sugar industry.[2]

It was sugar which placed Jamaica at a strategic point in the emerging international capitalist system of the eighteenth century, establishing it as Britain's most prized transatlantic colony. In 1805 Jamaica was the world's largest individual exporter of sugar. Sugar commanded the island's major resources of land, capital and labour. In 1832 sugar employed 49.5 per cent of the slave work force. The majority of those workers were women, the ratio being 920 males to 1,000 females.[3] It was the requirements of sugar that set the occupational norms for the bulk of the population, even for those workers not directly involved in sugar production. It was also those requirements, as identified by the captains of the sugar industry, that dictated a conscious policy of job allocation which concentrated black enslaved women in the fields in the most menial and least versatile areas of cultivation in excess of men, and in excess of all persons, male and female, who were not black.

Patterson examined the distribution of the slave labour force on Orange River and Green Park estates in the parish of Trelawny in 1832, as well as on Rose Hall estate in St James in the 1830s. He was struck by the large numbers of women who were engaged in field tasks, as contrasted with men who were spread over a wider range of skilled, non-praedial jobs. He concluded that the most distinctive occupational feature of Rose Hall estate was the preponderance of field women[4] – one to every two – as compared with one man in every eight. He attributed this partly to the fact that men had more job options available to them, and partly to the fact that women outnumbered men in the Rose Hall work force. This indeed was typical of the demographic situation throughout the island after the abolition of the slave trade in 1807, when the population structure was no longer manipulated by human importation, and moved by natural increase from a male to a female excess. However there is considerable evidence to indicate that women were tilling Jamaica's valleys for nearly a century before that period, and had been performing the most arduous tasks of agricultural cultivation in greater numbers than men, even at an earlier time in the island's development when men outnumbered women in the slave population.

The pattern of sex-differentiated labour deployment evolved out of colonial socioeconomic imperatives as well as out of traditional concepts about the sexual division of labour. In the seventeenth century, Jamaica was largely an island of small proprietors engaged in hunting and in subsistence planting, with some cash crops such as tobacco. During this stage of relative underdevelopment estate work was structured roughly along the following lines: a class of white indentured servants did some field work, but for the most part they supervised the slaves and carried out the skilled and technical functions of the estate. This servile white group numbered approximately 20 per cent to 30 per cent of the labour force. One of the rare censuses of the period, for example, listed 95 white servants and 527 slaves in the parish of St John in 1680.[5] Male slaves bore the brunt of the more physically demanding field labour. Female slaves, who at that period were present in approximately equal numbers to male slaves, supplemented male labour in the lighter tasks of the field and worked as domestics in the planters' houses.

White indentured servants had the advantages of race and of short-term bondage, and these factors enabled many to climb the creole socioeconomic ladder, eventually to become property owners or to migrate. As the whites moved up or out, taking their skills with them, male slaves were recruited into those areas of greater expertise which whites were vacating. The colonial establishment only grudgingly conceded this process and the local assembly, by a series of legislative measures up to the early eighteenth century, attempted to bar male slaves from supervisory positions, from trades, and from employing the more expert technologies of the plantations.[6] But the turn of the eighteenth century saw Jamaica's transition to a highly capitalized monocul-tural export economy operating in large plantations. This process accelerated the flight of small proprietors as well as that of the white indentured class. Male slaves continued to fill those work slots originally conceived for lesser whites. The occupational vacuum which they, in turn, left in the fields was filled by women.

Estate inventories of the 1720s and 1760s which have been examined make clear the wide range of specializations available to male slaves: they indicate also the limited choices that women had.[7] Particularly rich archival material exists in the estate papers of the absentee planter William Beckford, who was also the Lord Mayor of London in the 1780s. He owned a complex of twelve properties spread throughout the parishes of Clarendon, Westmoreland and St Ann. The majority produced sugar; the others were livestock and cattle pens. Together they provide revealing evidence of the conscious deployment of a labour force of 2,204 slaves containing a slight excess of men: 802 males and 778 females.[8] A minority of the men, namely 291 or 36 per cent of the male total, were field workers, compared with a majority of the women, 444 or 57 per cent of the female total. The men who were not field labourers were, among other things, stonemasons, blacksmiths, fishermen, farriers, wheel-wrights, wharfmen, coopers, sawyers, doctor's assistants, tailors, distillers and bricklayers. Many of these jobs involved the kind of special expertise which placed such men among the elite of the slave hierarchy. They sometimes combined praedial jobs with skilled occupations, so that a field man might also be a boiler. In contrast, women were confined within a much more restricted area, and field women were exclusively field women. Where they were listed in other categories of work apart from that of the field, a close look shows that they were often engaged in ancillary field tasks such as cutting grass.

Domestic work was the most significant work category next to agriculture and accounted for fifty-nine women or 13 per cent of the sample; within this group were washerwomen, house women and cooks. A significant number of house slaves, nine out of eighteen, were mulattos, consistent with the creole view of coloureds as being incapable of physically demanding labour such as field work. Elsa Goveia's observation on the occupational rating of domestics is relevant here: the female house slave on the plantation, she noted, was not so much a "skilled" as a "favoured" worker.[9]

Women with acknowledged "skills" numbered thirty-four or 8 per cent of the Beckford slaves, and included midwives, doctresses, field nurses and seamstresses. But even this group of non-praedial female workers overstates the black woman's access to special expertise. For mulattos dominated as seamstresses – eleven out of a total of fourteen – and the labels of doctress, midwife and nurse were often euphemisms for superannuated field workers, regarded as physically unable to continue in arduous agricultural work, but just about capable of providing services for younger workers.

The period of the 1780s to which these data relate was a period when the traffic in African slaves was at its peak, and planters had a clear policy of sex-selective importation of labour with a preference for men. As a consequence, African men constituted the majority of the workers on the plantation, outnumbering women right until the time when the slave trade ended. It was in the context of this sex ratio of male excess in the work-force that a pattern of job allocation evolved in which not only were the majority of the African women field labourers, but the majority of field labourers were African women. And this had profound implications for their working lives.

The routine of plantation agriculture, with its paramilitary regimentation, is widely documented. Youth and physical fitness were the main criteria by which manual tasks were distributed. The first or great gang of the work force, "the flower of all the field battalions", was comprised of both sexes, from ages fifteen to about fifty years, and was "employed in the most labourious work" on a sugar estate, which involved digging cane holes, planting, trashing, cutting, tying, loading and carting.

Female labourers used the same implements as men, the bill and the hoe. The most strenuous operation in the agro-industrial cycle of sugar production was the crop time, when continuous supplies of freshly cut stalks of ripe cane had to be processed without delay. Workers were then occupied from sunrise to sunset, averaging six days and three nights of work each week. In the words of one contemporary, "In the extraction of this labour, no distinction is made between men and women."[10]

A witness to the British Parliamentary Commission of Inquiry into the state of West Indian slavery in 1832 testified as follows:

Q.   Are the women employed for the same number of hours as the men?

A.   *Yes, except the women who have children at the breast.*

Q.   And at the same description of labour as the men?

A.   *Almost entirely, there are of course different branches of labour which they cannot undertake; they cannot undertake the management of cattle; they are excused from night work out of crop, in watching.*

Q.   Are they employed in digging cane holes?
A.   Yes.
Q.   In gangs with men?
A.   Yes.
Q.   And exposed to the same degree of labour?
A.   Yes.[11]

It is here worth noting that, as Higman's data reveal, women spent more of their working years in the field than did men.

It is interesting to consider what became of two prevalent gender assumptions regarding women's physical and intellectual capacities, assumptions which can be bluntly stated as follows: women are not strong enough to do tough manual work, nor are they clever enough to master things technical. Both assumptions were well proven to be without foundation, but both were also frequently invoked as strategies of female subordination. The Jamaican colonial establishment was, however, distinguished among other things for its pragmatism, which was unfailingly inspired by economic self-interest. This enabled planters, without reservation, to discard the image of woman as a frail creature and convert her into the mainstay of estate manual labour. At the core of that mental flip-flop was the racist ideology which supported African enslavement and which denied Africans normal criteria for judging human potential. Racism eased the process by which black women, and black women only, were massively drafted into the assembly line of the field.

The other gender assumption, concerning women's technical capabilities, proved to be of hardier stock. It was bad enough that planters had to overcome their aversion to the idea of a male slave with expertise, but to be female and skilled was unthinkable. And this had wider consequences for the political economy of the plantation system, functioning as the system did in a vicious circle of labour exploitation and retarded technology.

The Jamaican economist Norman Girvan has analysed this phenomenon with great insight, and in so doing has placed today's Caribbean technology policies in a relevant historical continuum. He writes, "If the artisan workshops of Europe were the basis of technological innovation, the mines and plantations of America were a prescription for technological stagnation. . . . The slave plantation system systematically underdeveloped the technical capacities of the population."[12]

Adding gender dimension to that analysis even further sharpens its relevance. Little scope existed in Jamaica's monocrop economy for the mixed farming enterprises, dairy production and cottage craft industries which rural people in other economies developed, and of all labourers on the plantation, it was the black female who was the least able to diversify or upgrade her economic potential. She could not, for instance, perpetuate the considerable range of skills and crafts characteristic of the African rural economy in which she had been a central productive figure before she crossed the middle passage.

Furthermore, female labour on the estate account book was expensive labour because of the inevitably high rates of absenteeism associated with child bearing and child rearing. So unless she was producing children and providing additional work units in numbers sufficient to compensate for her absences from the field gangs, the female slave offered relatively minimal returns on capital outlay. To offset the cost of her maintenance she had to be heavily utilized, and this need to extract maximum manual output from female labour was a factor in the plantation's reluctance to rationalize its operations. The planter-novelist Matthew 'Monk' Lewis tried to promote "the labour of oxen for that of negroes, whenever it can possibly be done".[13] The creole historian-proprietor Edward Long estimated that "one plough could do the work of a hundred slaves and should be encouraged . . . for no other work on a plantation is so severe and so detrimental as that of holing or turning up the ground in trenches with hoes".[14]

But both the economics and the politics of slavery mitigated against the introduction of oxen and ploughs. Estate managers and overseers, for example, had vested interests in their own slave property, whom they hired profitably to the estates for miscellaneous jobs such as holing, hoeing and planting. They were a significant pressure group in the creole resistance to technological progress. Moreover the power relationship inherent in a coercive labour system obscured considerations of managerial efficiency. The plantation establishment saw the slave as a special kind of multipurpose work equipment, a flexible capital asset which, unlike animals or machinery, could be deployed for almost any use at any time. Women were even more multifunctional for, of course, they could also replenish the labour supply. So as long as the most technically backward but versatile section of the labour force, slave women, serviced the plantation in large and growing numbers, little incentive to technological progress existed. And as long as Jamaican agriculture remained technologically retarded, women continued to be used in the field in overwhelming numbers as substitutes for animals and machines.

What did this mean for women's status? Elsa Goveia wrote of the ordinary field slave that no other group of slaves was so completely subject to the harsh necessities of slavery as an industrial system. They lived and worked under the discipline of the whip. They had fewer opportunities for earning a cash income than most other slaves. They were maintained on the bare margin of subsistence although they did the most laborious work, their standard of living was severely lower than that of any other group of slaves.[15]

An important index of status was the monetary value of the slave. The highest figure attached to a female slave was normally that of "a strong, able field worker". For a man, that tended to be his lowest price, for his market value rose as he acquired a skill. An official valuation of 1789 showed the most expensive women, field women, averaging between £75 and £85, with the exception of one midwife who was worth between £150 and £200. Male praedial workers were slightly more costly than their female equivalents, being priced at between £80 and £100. Eleven different categories of skilled male workers were also listed: their prices started at £120 and rose to £300.[16] The market's low assessment of field labour was also reflected in the regular use of such labour as punishment. No greater disgrace could fall to the lot of an artisan or a house slave than to be demoted to the field for some misdemeanour. This more often than not implied not only an instant decline in status, but physical indignities imposed "under the discipline of the whip".

Not surprisingly, field women's health was generally poor: 188 women or 13 per cent of the 604 women and girls found on the Beckford estates, were in various stages of physical disability; of 199 who were over the age of forty, 68 per cent suffered from impaired health. The condition of the young female adults was particularly revealing because they, presumably, were in the fittest condition to perform the demanding field tasks allocated to them. In fact 22 per cent of that prime group were listed as in poor shape. Few diseases or illnesses were diagnosed, but these young women were variously described as "weakly", "infirm", "distempered", and so on, suggesting a general debility associated with inadequate diet, inadequate care, excessive exertion and physical abuse. This had grave consequences for, among other things, women's child-bearing functions. Beckford's Clarendon estate, with a population of 274 women of child-bearing age, produced nineteen live infants in 1780, a year in which slave deaths numbered thirty-four.

The decrease of the slave population was in fact an islandwide phenomenon; the rate of decrease was estimated to be approximately 2 per cent per annum in the 1770s and 1780s. It was within this depressing demographic context that the abolitionist-humanitarian movement gained momentum and generated pronatalist measures, starting with the Consolidated Slave Acts of 1792 which gave official cognizance for the first time to the role of the female in population growth. Clause XXXVI of that legislation, for example, provided that every woman with six children living should be "exempted from hard labour in the field or otherwise".[17] The abolition of the slave trade in 1807 saw such policies intensified. The legislation of the period, while containing some elements of concern for the well-being of slaves, was primarily motivated by the need to sustain labour supplies: various rewards were devised for mothers, adopted mothers and midwives who produced healthy children. An example of the favoured status which prolific women received during the last decades of slavery is found on Matthew Lewis's estate at Canaan in the parish of Westmoreland. He instituted an order of honour for mothers, which gave them the privilege of wearing a "scarlet girdle with a silver medal in the centre" and entitled them to "marks of peculiar respect and attention". He even declared a "play day" for the whole estate, at which the mothers were special guests. He made sure that all the slaves knew they owed their good fortune of a holiday to the "piccaninny mothers; that is, for the women who had children living". At about the same time (between 1816 and 1817) that Lewis was celebrating motherhood on Canaan estate, however, the slave population had reached its numerical peak of 346,150 and thereafter moved steadily into a decline which only ended with emancipation.[18]

One may be observing here an example of that well-known propensity of colonial designs to self-destruct. The Jamaican establishment, while ostensibly assuming social responsibility for reproducing the labour force, was simultaneously pursuing economic policies virtually guaranteed to diminish that labour force. For official urgings and incentives to women to be fruitful and multiply went hand in hand with the oppressive work-loads of the field, and with punitive practices which had profound impact on women's ability and desire to bear and rear children. The highest mortality and the lowest fertility rates were found on the sugar estates, establishing a strong correlation between the labour requirements of the island's main industry and the decrease of the slave population. Slave women also themselves exercised effective control over their reproduction. They practised abortion, they prolonged lactation, they drew extensively on the midwives' knowledge of birth processes in order to depress their fertility deliberately. Both voluntarily and involuntarily they frustrated the establishment's hopes for a self-reproducing labour force. They could not escape the backlash of that frustration.

Creole attitudes towards slave women noticeably hardened in the latter years of slavery, almost in direct proportion to the plantocracy's dependence on women as a key source of their labour power. The most highly publicized cases of planter brutality are recorded in the 1830s: in most instances the victims were female slaves.[19] A telling example of the heightened antagonism towards women is the Jamaica Assembly's refusal to regulate or abolish the flogging of women, despite repeated recommendations for reform from the colonial administration in Westminister. Not even for aged or pregnant women would the plantocracy consider exemption from corporal punishment. Jamaica exactly reflected the view of the Barbadian council which debated the issue at the time, and which declared that to abolish the flogging of female slaves "would mean adieu to all peace and comfort on plantations".[20]

Women became even more conspicuous targets of planter hostility during the apprenticeship period which was mandated under the Abolition Bill of 1834 to phase out slavery in gradual stages. Ex-slaves, now apprentices, were required to give forty and one-half hours of work weekly on the estates to which they were attached. The rest of their time was theirs to place and barter on the wage market, if they chose. This stage of quasi-bondage was originally conceived as a six-year transition from a forced to a free labour system: it proved to be "an impossible compromise" and was terminated after four years. For the period that it lasted, planters used apprenticeship as a last stand to retain maximum control over what they saw as a dwindling labour force.[21] The increasing withdrawal of the female apprentice from the cane field was a critical factor in that perception. One contemporary analysed it aptly as women's rejection of that type of labour "which is inseparably associated in their minds with the idea of torture, oppression and degradation".[22]

Thomas McNeil, attorney for the estate of Lord Holland in western Jamaica, expressed the plantocracy's obsessive fear of a labour shortage and the need for an adequate supply of female workers to avert such a disaster. He calculated that even if the men gave sustained labour it would still be "quite impossible to continue sugar cultivation to give any remuneration to the proprietors unless the females also be induced to labour regularly".[23] "Inducement" of women took many forms, and was facilitated by the Abolition Act itself, which entrusted to the planter-dominated local legislature the detailed subordinate arrangements necessary for the implementation of the law.

Important aspects of the apprentices' welfare fell to the local legislature's discretion; and despite the appointment of special stipendiary magistrates to mediate between masters and apprentices, abuses and injustices were rampant and bore heavily on women. The Select Committee of the House of Commons appointed to inquire into the workings of the apprenticeship system reported in 1837 that women were "the principal sufferers" from various measures devised to manipulate and coerce the labour force.[24]

The maternal allowances and privileges which had been customary before 1834 fell into a grey area of the law and frequently were either curtailed or abolished. Women were being called on to work in the field in advanced stages of pregnancy, whereas they had previously been entitled to exemption. One stipendiary magistrate maintained that on several occasions when he attempted to protect such women from excessive labour he was threatened with action for damages by the estate owners involved. Mothers with over six children found their pre-emancipation right of work exemption reversed, and they were frequently sent back to the field. The services for field workers which were provided by cooks, water carriers, midwives and nurses were often withdrawn, and the women providing such services were redeployed to the field gangs.

Planters feared that apprentices, given an opportunity, would seek and find other occupational options outside of their obligatory forty and one-half hours estate time. And they had good reason to fear. During slavery women, despite overwhelming odds, had been engaging in semi-independent economic activities which offered prospects for a viable peasantry in a free society. It was the plantation system itself which inadvertently gave them the main resource for such initiatives; for the priority which the macro-economic system placed on cash crops for export, to the exclusion of food crops for local consumption, resulted in slaves having to assume responsibility for feeding themselves. As a consequence both female and male slaves enjoyed customary, and after the 1792 slave legislation, legal entitlement to their provision grounds. And there they put to their own and their family's use the chief expertise which the economy allowed them: women laboured hard and profitably in their own fields. They thereby generated a historical process which was to give Jamaican women, as food producers and distributors, a pivotal role in the domestic economy.

The diary of a St Ann doctor-planter, James Archer, reveals how threatening such slave entrepreneurship appeared to estate owners. Archer imposed strict taboos on the type of crops which apprentices could plant on their ground allotments. He also ordered that no additional help should be used for cultivating these plots: "The person, male or female, who has any sanction to work such land must work the same himself, or herself, no brother, sister or any other person to assist."[25] This created special hardships for women accustomed, as they frequently were, to pooling land and labour in a family enterprise. Women provoked such spiteful measures from the establishment not only because they could divert their time and energy to their own purposes and could so undermine the estate's labour power; they could also withhold their children's labour. For according to the Abolition Act, children under six years of age were to be free: as they became of age to be apprenticed, they could be employed with their mother's consent. Planters never lost sight of young blacks as potential estate workers.

But women stood in the way of their designs. As a contemporary observer expressed it in 1835, "A greater insult could not be offered to a mother than by asking her free child to work." At Silver Hill in St Andrew, an overseer asked a woman to let her eight-year-old son do light work on the estate in return for his clothing and an allowance. She flatly refused.[26] The Select Committee of the House of Commons on the workings of the apprenticeship system reported the evidence of one witness: "Negro mothers have been known to say, pressing their child to their bosoms, 'we would rather see them die, than become apprentices'." Jamaica's fractious females became the subject of extensive official dispatches. They were singled out for their "lack of co-operation, their ingratitude, and their insulting conduct. They were on all occasions, the most clamorous, the most troublesome and insubordinate, and least respectful to all authority. None of their freed children have they in any instance apprenticed to their former masters."[27] Women unequivocally stood firm on this issue; and of the 39,013 slave children who were less than six years of age on 1 August 1834, only nine were released by their mothers for estate work during the four years of apprenticeship.[28]

Motherhood, with its biological and customary social implications. is frequently perceived as a conservative force which imposes constraints on female activism. However in this instance it became a catalyst for much of women's subversive and aggressive strategies directed against the might of the plantation. When they could, they withheld their labour and that of their children from the dominant socioeconomic system. By their actions during slavery and apprenticeship, they placed themselves in the very eye of the storm of Jamaica's post-emancipation crisis. It was the crisis of land and labour which reached a flash-point in the Morant Bay Rebellion of 1865, and which ultimately created the jobless, landless proletariat of today – a proletariat which is largely urban and largely female, and whose significance in the evolution of Jamaica's modern labour movement is only now beginning to be illuminated by feminist scholarship.[29]

Some measure of the agony of free labour in nineteenth-century Jamaica was manifested in the exodus of the black population in large numbers from estate labour, a partly voluntary and partly involuntary process. In 1844, the year of the first official census, 80 per cent of the island's work force was engaged in agriculture. A hundred years later the proportion was 47 per cent, and it continues to fall. Female participation in agriculture fell from 57 per cent in 1921 to 28 per cent in 1943. In the 1980s it averaged 15 per cent.[30] As women attempted to escape the assembly line of the field they moved into the peasant domestic food economy, and increasingly into the urban service economy, in search of new options for economic viability and dignity. They encountered forces in the free society which would deny them these options: and so their search continues.

Notes

1.   Elsa Goveia, *Slave Society in the British Leeward Islands at the End of the Eighteenth Century* (New Haven: Yale University Press, 1965).

2.   Orlando Patterson, *The Sociology of Slavery* (London: McGibbon and Kee, 1967); Michael Craton and James Walvin, *A Jamaican Plantation: The History of Worthy Park, 1670–1970* (London: W.H. Allen, 1970); Lucille Mathurin, "A Historical Study of Women in Jamaica, 1655–1844" (PhD thesis, University of the West Indies, 1974); Barry Higman, *Slave Population and Economy in Jamaica, 1807–1834* (Cambridge: Cambridge University Press, 1976).

3.   Higman, *Slave Population*, 71–74.

4.   Patterson, *Sociology of Slavery*, 61, 157.

5.   J.H. Bennett, "Cary Helyar, Merchant and Planter of Seventeenth Century Jamaica", *William and Mary Quarterly* (January 1964); Colonial Office (CO) 1/45.

6.   The Laws of Jamaica, passed by the Assembly in 1683; Calendar of State Papers (Colonial America and West Indies), 1716–1717.

7.   Inventories, Libers 14, 44, 46 (Jamaica Archives).

8.   CO 107/43: Plantation papers of William Beckford, 1773–1784.

9.   Goveia, *Slave Society*, 229.

10. Thomas Cooper, *Facts illustrative of the condition of the negro slaves in Jamaica* (London, 1824).

11. Parliamentary Papers (PP) 1832: I (127), Report of the Committee of the House of Lords on the Extinction of Slavery.

12. Norman Girvan, "White Magic: The Caribbean and Modern Technology" (paper presented at a seminar on Caribbean issues related to UNCTAD IV, University of the West Indies, Mona, 5–7 February 1976).

13. Matthew G. Lewis, *Journal of a West India proprietor, kept during a residence in the island of Jamaica* (London: John Murray, 1834).

14. Edward Long, *The History of Jamaica*, 3 vols. (London: T. Lowndes, 1774).

15. Goveia, *Slave Society*, 233–34.

16. PP 1789: XXVI (84), 646(a), Part III, Jamaica A No. 29.

17. Bryan Edwards, *The History, Civil and Commercial of the British Colonies in the West Indies*, 3 vols. (London, 1801).

18. George W. Roberts, *The Population of Jamaica* (Cambridge: Cambridge University Press, 1957).

19. PP 1832: II (127), Report of the Committee of the House of Lords on the Extinction of Slavery.

20. Eric Williams, *Documents on British West Indian History 1807–1833* (Port of Spain: Historical Society of Trinidad and Tobago, 1952).

21. Douglas Hall, "The Apprenticeship Period in Jamaica, 1834–1838", *Caribbean Quarterly* 3, no. 3 (December 1953), 164.

22. Add. Mss. 51818, 1839 (British Museum): Holland House Papers, Letters from Edward Dacres Baynes, Special Magistrate, 1835–1840.

23. Add. Mss. 51819, 1838 (British Museum): Holland House Papers, misc.

24. *Negro apprenticeship in the colonies: a review of the report of the Select Committee of the House of Commons* . . . (London: J. Hatchard [etc.], 1837).

25. Add. Mss. 27970 (British Museum): James Henry Archer, MD, Accounts, drafts of letters, business and private memoranda, 1822–1845.

26. J. Sturge and T. Harvey, *The West Indies in 1837* (London: Hamilton, Adams and Co., 1838).

27. CO 137/215, Stipendiary Magistrate Pryce to Lord Sligo, 29 March 1836.

28. Hall, "The Apprenticeship Period", 148.

29. Joan French and H. Ford-Smith, "Women's Work and Organisation in Jamaica, 1900–1944" (typescript, 1986).

30. *Statistical Yearbook of Jamaica, 1980* (Kingston, Jamaica: Department of Statistics, 1981).

CHAPTER

Freeing Slavery
Gender Paradigms in the Social History of Caribbean Slavery

HILARY McD. BECKLES

I

This text accommodates some opinions I have long held on the project of historicizing women and gender in the slavery experience of the Caribbean world. The invitation by the Department of History to deliver the thirteenth Elsa Goveia Memorial Lecture at the Mona campus in 1997 occasioned the opportunity for their systematic articulation. Their architecture, in addition, was influenced considerably by reactions to analytic positions created and held on the subject by several distinguished scholars of West Indian history. The decision to name them "Freeing Slavery" may seem somewhat paradoxical. I hope, however, that it sends a strong signal that chattel slavery as a criminally enforced sociolegal order was not ontologically totalizing, and that discussion on the African cosmology and existential being in the Caribbean should not depart from this Eurocentric platform.

I am concerned principally with the importance of gender in the slavery period – its representations, ideological relations and effects, as well as its unstable social construction and reconstructions. As an important element in the politics of everyday life, gender awareness among Africans preceded their Caribbean slavery experience. It was challenged and transformed by slavery in a way that continues to highlight the process of historical continuity and change. The historiography of Caribbean slavery before the mid-1980s, unlike that of the United States, reflected the stigmatized and repressed condition of writing about gender within the context of women's colonial history.[1] Outside of the region historians have had good reason to ponder this reluctance of Caribbean "insiders" to adopt gender as an instrument of historical investigation and analysis. The absurd question has also been asked whether Caribbean slavery was in effect gender blind or gender neutral.

Interpretative inertia among male Caribbean historians has resulted in the study of women's history, and more so its gender aspects, being defined or claimed as a sort of minority area – the special responsibility and reserve of institutionally marginalized feminist scholars. This condition, in turn, is still used by some historians, male and female, as part of an ongoing political effort to devalue feminist scholarship, and to promote dissonance in relation to the dominant male-centred historiography.[2]

With respect to the social history of women the primary focus of research (and this is reflected in the structure of the historiography) is the black woman, with the coloured woman running a competitive second and the white woman trailing behind at a distance. In 1989–90, for example, three major monographs on the subject of black women's enslavement were published, all of which addressed directly and in detail the experiences of coloured women, but paid much less attention to the lives of white creole or European women.[3]

By way of contrast, a major theme of postwar Caribbean historians has been the study of white males within the colonial enterprise. This work focused primarily upon the politics and entrepreneurship of white males in shaping the Caribbean world, but paid no attention to gender paradigms as informing theoretical instruments. Such research patterns and trends can be accounted for in three ways. First, they were endemic to an earlier imperialist scholarship that assumed the normalcy of white masculinity in defining and shaping agricultural and mercantile activities and their supportive colonial cultures. Second, the many studies on the "rise and fall of the planter class" in Caribbean societies, for instance, paid no systematic attention to gender discourses, and removed the so-called master class from this form of discursive interrogation.

Lucille Mathurin Mair was first to challenge this theoretical posture when she argued that the right and power to sanction a possible past constituted an important feature of masculinist hegemony. Furthermore, she challenged the younger generation of Caribbean historians to contest this intellectual relation of power, and to privilege gender discourses within all debates about history as the social record of living memory.[4] Empowered by this opening, I published in 1989 a monograph entitled *Natural Rebels: A Social History of Enslaved Black Women in Barbados*. Prompted and pushed by the female student majority in my West Indian history seminar at the Cave Hill campus of the University of the West Indies, the project effectively revolutionized the contours and contexts of my earlier training in how to think about the slavery experience of African peoples.

There were a few surprises along the research trail, none of which was of any historiographic importance. Beyond the Caribbean the book was well received, but locally its announcement met with a "kind of silence", particularly among women historians. The first "noises" were heard in 1993 when Verene Shepherd took the magnificent initiative and organized the very successful Engendering Slavery conference here at the Mona campus. In one session *Natural Rebels* received a critical evaluation, the significance of which offered me the opportunity to rethink and recast its fundamental assumptions and arguments.

This chapter, then, is in part the beginning of an auto-critique, and a partial departure from the interpretations represented in *Natural Rebels*. It is a call, in fact, for a temporary putting away of the social history microscope so effectively used in the past two decades, and for the taking up – once again – of the telescope. It is a recognition, furthermore, of the necessity to return to the "old country" of general theory and wide social vision. The charge is that so much was overlooked when we sidelined social process and ideological formation and privileged social history empiricism. In effect, the recently published social history has located dominant images of the discipline in conceptual cul-de-sacs, denying it the theoretical energy needed to travel the highways recently opened up by postmodern criticism. Questions that now need to be asked are whether within the brutal institution of radicalized slavery there were two systems – one for women and the other for men. Also, how did men and women experience the formulation and reformulation of gender identities, and how did these experiences differ? Have we tended to flatten out such differences within the historiography, and have social history narratives been deprived of a richer texture? If the experiences of men and women in slavery varied, how did these variations create differentiated consciousness and patterns of decision making?

Mapping the origins and itinerary of gender in Caribbean history should enable us to sharpen our focus specifically on slavery as a constantly changing system of sociosexual exploitation of women, and generally to penetrate its internal economic dynamism as a mode of surplus extraction. Gender as a social construction that determined and reflected the sexual division of labour within the slave mode of production constitutes a clear vista through which the cultural working of patriarchy, as well as challenges to it at diverse levels of everyday life, can be illuminated. In some ways "modern" slave societies in the Caribbean facilitated a revolutionary restructuring and magnification of traditional African, European and native gender representations while producing unique features of their own. The institutional design of Caribbean slavery significantly affected the (re)making of gender identities of all males and females. Individuals evolved new self-identities within the contexts of the gender order they encountered and contested. The constant reordering and redefinition of conditions and terms of social living – and dying – determined that new gender representations were often perceived as paradoxical and contradictory. This circumstance, in turn, indicates the considerable fluidity in the ideological nature of slavery, and offers a barometer to measure the turbulence internal to the construction of gender orders.[5]

My chosen methodological approach is to explore the evolution of gender identities and their ideological effects. I propose that visits be made to three historical sites where gender discourses determined social relations and perceptions of popular identities. First, the gender order of pre-colonial West Africa is examined within the context of pressures exerted upon it by forces endemic to the wider Atlantic political economy. Second, the constitution of gender identities within the Caribbean plantation complex is examined with a view to exploring how it determined the nature of work and social reproduction. Third, the instability of gender representations under increasingly adverse circumstances of sugar production is accounted for within the context of the global political challenge to the legitimacy of slavery in the early nineteenth century. These developments are presented as causes of reforms to women's relations to production and reproduction, and the creation of a new gender order in response to pending imperially legislated emancipation. A principal objective of this exercise is to attempt to make a contribution to feminist theorizing in the Caribbean by examining how gender relations were historically constituted and experienced, and ought therefore to be thought about.

II

Most persons identified and used as slaves in West Africa during the period 1500 to 1800 were female. This was also the case in the older sugar plantation colonies of the West Indies between 1800 and 1833. Prior to 1800, however, West Indian slavery was overwhelmingly male biased. The mid-eighteenth century witnessed the transition in demographic structure. There was nothing paradoxical about it; the specific focus on the female in the conception, design and reproduction of these slave systems was the result of discernible social and managerial imperatives.[6]

Sex distribution patterns within the Atlantic slave complex had as much to do with the working of gender in traditional West African societies as with modernist discourses of work, gender and social life in Europe. After the 1750s the established Caribbean custom of male preferencing in the purchase and retention of slaves gave way to a pro-female trend that fundamentally transformed the sex structure and modified gender discourses. Barbados had attained the unique status of having a female majority in the slave population since the end of the seventeenth century; it shared this characteristic at the end of the eighteenth century with the Leeward Islands. Sugar planters in these colonies gradually moved towards the privileging of females as part of a revised strategic plan to promote the natural reproduction of the labour force. The effects of this demographic shift on gender representations and identities were considerable.[7]

New World slavery represented something altogether unfamiliar to most African males and females. It confronted, rejected and restructured the gender attitudes and identities legitimized by their traditions. The working of labour ideologies in most West African societies gendered certain types of work and relations of power; these were exploded and reconfigured within the Caribbean context. It is therefore problematical to propose fundamental continuity in forms of slavery between traditional experiences and the New World encounter. The gender implications of West Indian plantation slavery for Africans, furthermore, were culturally transformative.[8]

Initially, the Caribbean gender order as it related to types of work was considered more problematic for African males than females. The explanation for this circumstance has to do with the functions performed by women within traditional West African patriarchal societies. There was a considerable internal slave market on which the demand was mostly for women and children. Women were also traded through the Sahara into the North African Muslim labour markets. One compelling explanation for this pattern is that West African societies did not easily absorb male slaves.[9] A general tendency was for males captured in internecine warfare to be executed by the state; another trend was to retain limited numbers of men for military rather than agricultural or industrial purposes. As a result of warfare and other forms of political conflict, however, the majority of captives retained and integrated into local socioeconomic systems were women and children.[10]

The development of this pattern of sex specificity has to do with the greater local demand for females as slaves. This is reflected in the prices paid for female slaves in coastal and interior societies. Philip Curtin has shown, for example, that whereas in Senegambia African traders supplied men and women to European buyers at the same price, in the interior agricultural belt women slaves sold for twice the price of male slaves. An often-stated explanation for this trend is that women slaves were preferred because of their biological reproductive functions. This is only a minor part of the explanation. African men with property did demand within their immediate social space wives and concubines who were kinless, and whose progeny had little or no property rights or status claim within the inheritance system. But such kinless women and their children were secured by patriarchal elites primarily as workers, and were socially marginalized mainly because of their alienability as marketable labour.[11]

The ability of the patriarchal system to absorb, assimilate and subjugate greater numbers of kinless women is the critical part of a more complex explanation. The more expansive the economic system, the civil society and the state apparatus, the greater was the demand for female slaves. The wide range of possible forms of absorption of kinless women magnified the numbers any society could carry. The principal result of this process was to generate servile female labour for productive functions. Slavery, concubinage and patriarchal dominance assured that the woman was centred as the principal productive agency within the gender order. Women worked, and the majority of their labour hours were dedicated to agriculture.

This was the case in the period of Atlantic slavery and remains so now. (A recent survey shows that in the sub-Saharan region women still contribute between 60 and 70 per cent of the labour within the agricultural sector.)[12] Women planted and harvested crops, looked after animals, and generally engaged in all labour-intensive work such as crafts and domestic service. Importantly, women were expected to perform agricultural labour, which was prescribed and understood within the dominant gendered division of labour as "woman work".[13] Hard labour of the intensive low status kind came to be considered by West Africans as "woman work", beneath men's social standing within the gender order. With respect to their alienation from agricultural labour, therefore, West African men had reason to consider themselves privileged, and female slaves were gendered the "lowest creatures on God's earth".[14]

Caribbean slavery launched a direct assault on traditional West African gender orders. To begin with, significantly fewer black women entered the Atlantic slave trade than black men. The available records of European slave traders demonstrate this point forcefully. Klein's comprehensive analysis of the records of Dutch slave traders, who in the seventeenth century also supplied French, Spanish and English colonies, shows that only 38 per cent of Africans shipped were female. The adult sex ratio for Dutch traders was 187 men for every 100 women, and the child ratio was 193 boys for every 100 girls. Danish records yield a similar 36 per cent female cargo with a sex ratio of 186 men to 100 women and 145 boys to 100 girls. Using a broader-based sample of British slave trade records, Klein found a similar pattern of discrimination against females.[15] The general pattern, was clear. About 65 per cent of all slaves shipped from West Africa were males, with only slight variations across the West African coast from Senegambia to Angola. This pattern indicates the tendency for West African economies and societies to retain traditional commitments to the dominant gender order, in which men were considered more dispensable to internal processes of social and economic activity.[16]

The Atlantic slave trade, however, carried to West Indian plantations not only measurable units of labour, but also gender identities and ideological ways of thinking about gender. On early West Indian plantations enslaved African men, the social majority, were pressed into labouring activities which were gendered as "woman work". The social implication of this development was that the Caribbean witnessed an early modern encounter and clash of two formally contradictory gender orders – one European and one West African. Managerial power was held decisively by the European male, and the potency of African gender ideologies was tested against the background of the productive needs of colonial capitalism.

The European male held views with respect to gender and the sexual division of labour that differed from those of the African male; Englishmen, in particular, sought to reflect in social reality their views of gender, sex, race and work. White women they described as "ladies" were not expected to labour in the field or perform any demeaning physical task. This was clearly a class position, since the thousands of female indentured servants imported from the British Isles between 1624 and 1670 worked on the cotton, tobacco and sugar plantations in gangs alongside their male counterparts and enslaved Africans. It was not until the late seventeenth century that English planters, thinking through gender in terms of race and class, finally implemented the policy that no white woman was to work in plantation labour gangs. This ideologically driven initiative which sought to isolate white womanhood from plantation field work, however, had much to do with the social need of patriarchy to idealize and promote the white woman as a symbol of white supremacy, moral authority and sex purity. The patriarchal ideology of white supremacy required the social isolation of all white women, irrespective of class, from intimacy with the black male, in order to minimize the threat of miscegenation.

The space vacated within the labour ranks had to be filled. White men believed that black men were best equipped to the physical task of frontier plantation construction, but suggested that black women were better prepared for the subsequent maintenance of efficient production. Critically, they did not share the black male's view that field work was "woman work". Colonial managers, therefore, recognizing conflict within the gender order, used the brutality of the death threat in order to enforce a regime of field work upon black males that ran counter to their traditional gender identity. Black men found the reversal of sex roles a major challenge to their masculine self-consciousness, and reacted with both outright violence and a persistent negotiation for entry into prestigious, non-agricultural occupations.

The gender origins of Caribbean slavery, therefore, should also be discussed in terms of the military defeat and subsequent violent subordination of black men by white men. While it is true that the slave trade flourished in part as a result of some voluntary commercial exchange between Europe and

African business elites, the fact of European military conquest and superiority in parts of West Africa provides a compelling explanatory context. In most West African societies during the period of the slave trade, states were constructed and defended by armies drawn mostly from among men. The enslavement in the Caribbean of defeated male warriors, now required to labour on estates, symbolized the achievement of white male triumphalism. While women also participated in the political and military governance of some West African societies, the dominance of patriarchal formations reinforced the significance of this development.

Black men embarked on a Caribbean experience within the context of institutional environments that reflected the conquistadorial ideological interests of white patriarchy. Empowered white men ideologically represented their masculinities by reference to the successes of the imperial project. Central to these representations was the quest for monopolistic control, ownership and possession within colonial spheres. The right to power, profits, glory and pleasure was specified as a core element in the articulation of masculine ideologies in which black men were negated and relegated to otherness. Outnumbered by black men in West Africa and the Caribbean, white men privileged the power apparatus of mind over body, appropriating for themselves an iconography of the former and projecting an association of black men with the latter. The conquest and control of the black male body, and its denial of a mind, resided at the core of the dichotomized ethnic masculine contest.

The managerial logic of empire, established as a function of white patriarchy, fuelled forces that produced a complex framework for the ideological representation of black men. The control of slaves required it. The survival of colonialism mandated it. Black men, as the male majority, had to be "kept", and kept down, in order to ensure the success of these socioeconomic operations. Africans and their creole progeny, however, understood and shared important tenets of white men's ideologies of masculinity as represented within the colonial encounter. Political authority, economic power and domestic dominance held together the values of a white elite masculinity that was culturally familiar to black men. Similarly, the denial of these states of consciousness and experience to disenfranchised and dispossessed white women within the colonial project set in place the conditions for the definition and subjugation of womanhood. Like the white woman, the black man was denied what was familiar, and his masculine identities were targeted by surveillance systems that sought to direct the nature of everyday life.

Black masculinities, in addition, were politicized within the context of white patriarchal ideological representations. In terms of social relations, the black male and his offspring were fed, clothed and sheltered by white men whose hegemonic ideology determined that being "kept" and kept down were symbolic of submissive inferiority, and gendered as feminization. He received as a concession, in addition to his subsistence rations, allocations of leisure time; he was denied consumer access to the night by strict regulatory systems; he could neither claim nor assert any right beyond or outside those of his owner, in public or private social spheres. According to Patterson he was natally alienated, his masculinity dishonoured and his existential being rendered "socially dead". The condition of being "kept" and kept down located black masculinities within white patriarchy as subforms starved of role nourishment and ideologically "feminized".

Chattel slavery, an institution built upon private property rights in persons, was thoroughly gendered in its design and functions. Throughout the colonial world European enslavers decreed, for example, that the status of an infant at birth should not be derived from that of its father. Slave holders had neither social nor economic interest in black fatherhood. Black children entered at birth into a social relation that was predetermined by the status of their mothers. Legally, it had absolutely nothing to do with the status of the father. Children fathered by black men or white men were born into slavery once their mothers were slaves. Since white women, by virtue of their race, were not enslaved, their children under all paternal circumstances were born into freedom. Throughout the West Indies white women produced free-born children with enslaved men, as well as free black and free coloured men. Slavery as a sociolegal status, completely marginalized and alienated fatherhood, and focused its attention upon motherhood. Estate managers generally had no policy interests in the identity of the fathers of children. The documents on families, for example, are rich and detailed on the maternal dimensions of kinship but silent on paternity. Fatherhood as an aspect of masculinity, therefore, was buried deeper within the archival literatures of the estates.

Such issues raise the question of men's "invisibility" within historical records, a matter that has been considerably underestimated. Describing the enslaved woman as essentially a "submerged mother", Edward Brathwaite locates her "invisibility" within the "archival material" and suggests that it is but an "aspect of that general invisibility which haunts [black history]". For him the slave woman, being black and female, suffered a "double invisibility" which in turn promoted a historiography of neglect. There is, however, a significant conceptual and empirical problem to be tackled with respect to the "invisibility thesis". It has to do with the fact that the sources historians have (over!) used for social history narratives – deeds, wills, manumission lists, diaries, plantation accounts, managers' reports, and so on – say considerably more about enslaved women than they do about enslaved men. The male slave, in fact, is the one who was rendered largely invisible.[17]

This characteristic of the evidence has to do with the female-centred nature of the slave system. Its principal concern was with maternity, fertility, the management of white households and the sociosexual expression of patriarchal power and ideology. More is recorded about slave mothers than slave fathers; more was said about female slave lovers of white men than about male slave lovers of white women. Certainly, in this latter regard, enslaved men have been rendered largely invisible, though partly, it should be said, for their own safety. The general intimacy of slave women with the empowered agents of the colonial world – white males and females – placed them at the top of the documentary queue. In these records women appear in diverse social actions other than those related to labour and crime.

This condition, in turn, raises the more important question of whether modern historians of slavery – mostly male – have misinformed historiographic discourse with gendered constructs about enslaved women's "invisibility". Slave owners' fictional literature, where these representations of black masculinities were constructed and ventilated, used a language which made reference to the term "infantilization" rather than "feminization". Infantilization, however, was also a central concept used in slave owners' representation and "imaging" of women. The black male, by virtue of being denied dominant masculine roles and access to recognized institutional support systems on which to construct counter-concepts, and kept in a dependent welfare subsistence economy, was conceived to have degenerated into a pre-gender consciousness – a condition of nothingness associated with innocence and femininity.

In this literature, furthermore, slave owners coined the term "Quashee" to represent their ideological characterization of black men. Quashee was "gay, happy-go-lucky, frivolous, cheerful".[18] In his 1808 account of Jamaican slave society, John Stewart described Quashee as "patient, cheerful, and commonly submissive, capable at times of grateful attachments where uniformly well treated". He was also "possessed of passions not only strong but ungovernable

... a temper extremely irascible; a disposition indolent, selfish, and deceitful; fond of joyous sociality; riotous mirth and extravagant show". Stewart, in addition, was keen on informing his reader that "creole" white women exhibited many of the personality traits of "Quasheba" – the feminine of Quashee.[19]

Quashee was ideologically constructed and fixed within texts as the typical black male in a state of enslavement. He was docile but irresponsible, loyal but lazy, humble but chronically given to lying and stealing; his behaviour was full of infantile silliness and his talk inflated by childish exaggeration. In addition, his relationship with his master was one of dependence and childlike attachment; it was indeed this childlike quality that was the very key to his being. Slave owners' archives assure us that black males as a group of atomized, childlike individuals had no means by which to relate themselves to others save the integrative framework provided by the owner's authority. The self-(slave) they related to was a direct function of the other (owner).[20]

Congruity in the concepts of infantilization and feminization as systems of representation of the black male indicates clearly the direct nature of slave owners' political and ideological intention. As distortions of the relations of everyday life, these representations operated as important weapons with measurable political effects, in that they shaped the encounter between whites and blacks. By fixing reality through language and fantasy, slave owners denied that black men were "men" in the sense of their ascribed normative characterization of manhood. This discourse, as an apparatus of power, provided slave owners with several privileges – particularly the psychic courage to manage the colonial enterprise.

The slave owning community, considerably outnumbered by subordinated groups, devised systems of governance by which it could reproduce its dominance. Military might was important but insufficient. The slave owner had to walk among the slaves, eat what they cooked and sleep within their reach. To function within this environment it was necessary to psychologically "read", "write" and imagine subordinate black masculinities as inversions, represented within popularized gender ideology as timid, passive and submissive.

The systems of violent terror used to suppress and punish insubordination – burning alive, dismemberment, castration, lynching and so on – were conceived to offer slave owners a functional degree of comfort in their assumption of success. When we enter the world of Thomas Thistlewood, for example, an English manager-planter in Jamaica from 1750 to 1786, the language and political effect of this violent power is encountered. Thistlewood records in his diary:

- Wednesday, 28th January, 1756 – Had Derby well whipped, and made Egypt shit in his mouth.
- Friday, 30th July, 1756: Punch catched at Salt River and brought home. Flogged him and Quacoo well, and then washed and rubbed in salt pickle, lime juice and bird pepper; also whipped Hector for losing his hoe; made New Negro Joe piss in his eyes and mouth.
- End of October 1766 – A Stout Negro man of Dr. Lock's is now gibbitted alive in the Square . . . a resolute rebel.[21]

Actions such as these highlight the contradictory and ambivalent nature of stereotyped representations as major discursive strategies. The physical violence directed persistently against black men by white men indicates the fact of their recognition of an irrepressible black masculinity, and their inability to fix behaviour to fantastic patterns of constructions. This disarticulation between social reality and imagination, however, provided the instability needed to constantly reconceive the constituent elements of representations in order to express changing forms of domination. In addition it contributed to the evolution of complex language forms and perceptions that tracked and targeted the multiple forms and expressions of black masculinities.

The thought-leader (sage, priest, obeah man), for example, was stripped of power conceptually within a representation of his role as indicative of a childlike ignorance of rational thought and scientific methods. The Ashanti-Mandingo warrior was stereotyped and represented as easily tamed and subdued by caring friendship and compassion from an owner. In all cases, power to possess and define was pursued monopolitically by the dominant white masculinity. Subordinate white males, whose dependent social existence openly subverted from within the ideological texts of hegemonic masculinity, were driven into colonial outbacks. Their condition of exclusion was accounted for in terms of the degenerative impact of tropical climates and intimate exposure to black culture.

With respect to Jamaican slave society more needs to be known about the role of kidnapping and sexual exploitation of slave women in the formation of Maroon communities. Maroon men did kidnap plantation women in order to secure wives and forced labour; this much figures prominently in the social history of all colonies that harboured Maroon communities. Little is known, however, of the life experiences of slave women who were integrated into the polygynous households of Maroon males. It is entirely possible that some Maroon women experienced at the hands of black men a continuation of the kinds of occupational and resource discrimination, and sexual domination, that typified enslavement on the plantations.

For example Esteban Montejo, the Cuban runaway slave, expressed views about women and sexual relations in his autobiography that corresponded to the ideological expression of his owner's masculinity, and that of other men within the slave owning community.[22] Slave owners, of course, knew this and developed an obsessive interest in the sexual masculinity of black men. Terrified by their fantasies about the power implicit in this representation, white men developed a range of social attitudes and policies concerning relations between white women and black men. Castration and lynching were placed before black men as an inevitable response by white men to sexual access to white women.

The hostility of colonial power and the fetishism of black male sexuality were but aspects of a wider discourse that involved the violent responses of black men in the projection of their own perceptions of masculine values. Violence was the principal social action by which enslaved black men could subvert the security and stability of the slave owner's project. Only violence by slaves, as an act of self-empowerment by the enslaved community, could effectively terminate the colonial mission. Black men knew that they could take white men's lives and property through violence, and this became endemic to the discourse. Violence was what black men needed to assert or secure their masculinities, but the right to take life, which white men held as a constitutional privilege, could also be grasped by black men – hence the function of the subaltern's violence as the ultimate equalizer.

Thus colonial masculinities took social form within the context of a culture of violence which embraced all relations of social living and consciousness. It was the principal instrument of all contending parties; it held them together and tore them apart. It assumed a quasi-religious character, as groups sought constantly to possess the balance of power and terror. Creole black males were socialized as infants within this crucible of death, blood and suffering. They learned to use it as it was used against them. This explains in part the enormous loss of life that this region experienced in nearly one hundred slave revolts, indicating how relations between black men and white men were characterized by ongoing psychological warfare and bloody battles.

These contests, however, do not interfere with our conception of the female-centric nature of the slave system. As the internal frontier receded in all colonies, the centring of the slave woman was intensified in new and determining ways. A subsequent stage witnessed the natural reproduction of slaves as an important labour supply strategy. The minority status of women within the slave trade, and the fact that many of these "had already used up some of their potential fecundity by the time they had arrived", meant that slave populations in the Caribbean "could only have experienced a negative growth rate".[23] This fact was not emphasized or understood by slave owners. Over time, however, they problematized the negative growth rates of blacks and produced an expansive discursive literature. As they debated demographic trends and patterns, and concluded from colony to colony that natural reproduction was cheaper and more politically consistent with "progressive" managerial policies, the slave woman was further targeted and bombarded in an ideological frenzy of new gender representations.

Plantation slavery, therefore, was not only about material production and human reproduction. Work and social relations on the estates were particularly relevant to the reproduction of significant social categories such as "male" and "female". Work constituted the context within which the normative expectations attached to labour were gendered. That is, the work regime had as much to do with the production of sugar and other agricultural commodities as it did with the reproduction of the gender order. Field work came to be viewed by black males as slave work, rather than "woman work"; which included all blacks and excluded white women. In addition field work and other forms of unskilled manual labour were promoted as consistent with the "essential nature" of blacks, an ideological construct that finally created an escape hatch for landless white males. This shifting of class, race and gender relations within the division of labour is indicative of West Indian planters' distinct capacity for conceptualizing the nature of their social world and formulating hegemonic ways to manage its paradoxical and contradictory tendencies.

African arrivants were subjected to a process of physical acclimatization as well as regenderization generally referred to as "seasoning". During this initial phase of two to three years they were inducted into a new gender culture and protected from the physical rigours of plantation life. The objective of this policy was to allow slaves time to recover their physical and psychological strength, build up functional immunity to the new disease environment, and learn the political economy of a new gender order. It was at once an ideological, biological and labour apprenticeship.

Many slave owners in the West Indies were familiar with the gender traditions of agriculture in West Africa. They understood at once that black women could be thrown into the deep end of the labour regime and be productive. This explains in large measure their refusal to shelter black women from the most arduous physical tasks, as well as the suggestion that productivity differentials did not exist between the sexes.

The equalitarian labour regimes women experienced provided the context within which gender ideologies were conceived as constructions designed to promote the political economy of the colonial enterprise. The gender representation of black women was formalized in ways that offered coherence to the relations between sex, labour productivity and capital accumulation. The colonial gender discourse not only confronted and assaulted traditional concepts of womanhood in both Europe and Africa, but sought to redefine notions of black feminine identity. The black woman was ideologically constructed as essentially "non-feminine", in so far as primacy was placed upon her alleged muscular capabilities, physical strength, aggressive carriage and sturdiness.

Pro-slavery writers, furthermore, presented the black woman as devoid of the feminine tenderness and graciousness in which the white woman was tightly wrapped. Her capacity for strenuous work was not discussed in relation to the high mortality rates and incidence of crippling injuries that characterized enslavement. When mention was made of such circumstances, it was done in order to portray the black woman as clumsy, brutish and insensitive to the scientific nature of bodily functions. As such she was represented as ideally suited to manual labour as part of a wider civilizing social experience. Edward Long, eighteenth-century pro-slavery ideologue of Jamaica, had no doubt that the black woman was the perfect brute upon which the plantation's future rested. Her low fertility, he believed, was an additional feature that indicated her essentially non-feminine identity.[24]

The ideological defeminization of the black woman, recast as the "Amazon", allowed slave owners to justify within the slavery discourse her subjugation to a destructive social and material environment. It was said that she could "drop" children at will, work without recuperation, manipulate with ease the physical environment of the sugar estate, and be more productive than men. These opinions constituted an ideological outlook that, when articulated by white males, seemed contradicted by the evidence of commonplace miscegenation. Long's text reveals evidence of the ideological subversion that resulted from white men's sexual attraction to black women. The "goatish embraces" invariably produced a "tawny breed", he said, who in turn tantalized like sirens all categories of gentlemen.[25] Long was aware that the sociosexual reality of Jamaica could readily produce a gender reading of ethnic relations that exposes the contradictory nature of the race discourse. The discursive mechanism he adopted as a protective cloak was the invention of white feminine degeneracy that threatened, if left unattended, the future of the white male colonizing project.

Long's pro-slavery text could be read as part of the discourse of feminine subversion to hegemonic representations. The sexual embrace of the black woman as metaphor speaks to the black community's claim to an irrepressible humanity that gave life to and nurtured a morally imploded conquistadorial elite. Miscegenation was a double-edged sword within the context of slavery – evidence of human sexuality recognizing itself as such and transcending crudely constructed ideological boundaries, as well as an indication of the fragility and private irrelevance of the race discourse. Enslaved black women's protection and publication of their feminine identities took many forms, from insistence on procuring fine clothing and decorative jewellery, love and care for their kith and kin, pursuit of market engagements through huckstering, leadership and involvement in revolutionary struggle, to "loving" white men into a kind of oblivion by producing coloured children with them that acquired their names and, more importantly, their properties. Gender was socially contested in several ways, but as a relation of power, its role in the reproduction of masculinist class and race rule was critical.

III

Let us examine the case of Thomas Thistlewood, a slave manager and owner.[26] Thistlewood arrived in Jamaica in 1750 at the age of twenty-nine, an ambitious young man in search of a West Indian fortune. He was the second son of a yeoman farmer from Lincolnshire who died when Thomas was just six years old. Thomas's elder brother John inherited his father's farm, and Thomas was left a mere £200. He was educated as an agriculturalist and travelled throughout Europe, to Brazil and India before landing at Jamaica with letters of recommendation on 24 April 1750. He had acquired a reasonable grasp of the English imperial culture into which he stepped, and to which he was required to subscribe before launching of his project. The degree to which he could adjust and redefine the space and dominant social practice would be determined by his character and personal values. He was not a member of the English elite, more the "lower" part of a middling sort, but he shared the West Indian dream of his social superiors to attain riches by agriculture and slavery.

Thistlewood "discovered" Jamaica as England's principal Caribbean colony. The largest of all the islands in the West India empire (4,400 square miles) it dominated sugar production, accounting for about 20,400 tons of the 45,775 tons output. This production relied upon the labour of over 170,000 enslaved Africans, most of whom worked and died on the over 460 plantations of more than one thousand acres. In order to manage it all, Jamaica's 18,000 whites needed the support of some 7,000 free non-whites, most of whom were also dependent upon slave owning in order to make a living and secure their liberty.

Thomas Thistlewood's Jamaican project, like West Indian plantation slavery in general, was a site of gender discourses that codified in diverse "images" the social relations between men and women, and between and within the black and white "races", and exposed fully the meaning of being "male" and "female" in contexts of uneven possession of deadly power. Slavery also produced a legal and social culture within which the interrelations between racism and sexism elevated the black woman to a heightened visibility at the head of the pecking order of human exploitation and oppression.

Enslaved women resided at the centre of Thistlewood's personal and public worlds. His extensive diary is in fact an extended essay on self-discovery through the vista of sexual contact with black women who, he suggests, were made offers by him that they could not refuse. But it was a kind of discovery that empowered his masculinity, a construct of power backed by the canons of empire, with a capacity to convert slave refusal into an arcane voluntarism that also demonstrates the folly of the concept of a slave having a say with respect to slave owners' use of power. The pattern of his social life among enslaved women also supports much of what is known about European patriarchy. He established a "home" within a "house", placed a woman slave within it as principal lover, mother of his child, confidant, servant –but always slave – while he violently extracted sexual pleasures – and pains – from as many other slave women as he was capable. The domestication of his sexuality followed the familiar gender course that led to several habitations where small sums of money were left behind, all as a matter of right with respect to the enjoyment of his human property. By way of explaining his fetish with black women, or more correctly enslaved women, Thistlewood sought to convey that he was not alone in this regard, that his experience was different in no meaningful way from other white men, and that enforced miscegenation was part of the popular culture among white males.

There is a level at which Thistlewood's diary can be read as one very violent, bloody and dangerous quarrel with black women. The quarrelling did not stop. The sex went on and on and everybody, it seemed, was being infected with venereal disease. Thistlewood seemed almost celebratory in his references to men, white and black, free and slave, contracting the "clap", while appearing occasionally pitiful in his remarks about women. The "clap", it seemed, held them all together in a pathogenic family, though the subtext of the experience, as it relates to the violent quarrels, is missing. His slave "wife" Phibbah was badly infected. On 1 January 1761, she "complains of a violent pain at the bottom of her belly. She also has a running which stains yellowish." He gave her mercury pills at night to help her with the pain.

It is the story of his relations with Sally that indicates the full parameter of the slavery discourse. Like many slave women under Thistlewood's power, Sally was a free spirit who resisted and rebelled in ways she knew best under the extremely brutal culture of policing available to the white community. Sally could not be contained. Thistlewood's record of her details a curious mixture of sex, floggings and flight, the combination of which represents, perhaps, evidence of the strongest contradiction to Thistlewood's claim of mutualism in his sexual relations with slaves. Sally was born in the Congo, and was purchased in 1762 when about ten years old. An attempt was made by Thistlewood to start her "breeding" when she was about seventeen years old. To this end she was put to live with Chub but the arrangement was not successful. From the beginning she showed herself to be a strong, survivalist character, taking every opportunity to promote her own interests above those of Thistlewood. She was frequently flogged for taking and eating estate poultry, resisting his sexual demands, and making unauthorized visits to the kitchen store-room.

Thistlewood paints a portrait of Sally as a thief and indicates that this was part of her roguish, insubordinate and rebellious nature. Nonetheless she was one of his sexual favourites. On 7 August 1770 he writes: "As Sally steals everything left in the cook room, and eats it if eatable, Phibbah had her tied with her hands behind her naked for the mosquitos to bite her tonight. She bawled out lustily, but before 9 o'clock in the evening broke loose and ran away." She was caught a few miles away, her hands still tied, and placed under "lock and key". The sex session continued through October and November, but during the following year she ran away several times. Each time she was caught, flogged and a collar and chain applied. On one occasion she was sent to the fields as part of the punishment.

In between Sally's marronage, sex with Thistlewood is recorded. From 1772 to 1774 a similar paradoxical narrative is recorded – flight, flogging and sex. On Sunday, 20 November 1774 we are told that "Sally has the clap very badly", but during 1775 the process of flight and sex started all over again. Thistlewood did all he could but did not prevent Sally from absconding. In April 1776 he decided to employ her on another property. She ran away and went underground in the town of Savanna-la-Mar. Solon found her and took her back, where she was flogged, collared for a week and put to hard labour in the field. In June a lock collar was placed again "upon Sally as she will not help herself, but attempts to run away".

It would be dangerously incorrect to assume that enslaved black men did not participate in the violent exploitation of enslaved black women. African men understood and shared important tenets of white men's ideologies of masculinity as represented in the colonial encounter. Like Europeans, African men conceived of empowered masculinity in terms of political authority, economic ownership and domestic dominance. Thistlewood documents his relations to Lincoln, a male slave, and describes Lincoln's relations to women on the estate. He is ambivalent in his views on Lincoln but keeps him in good office, though not sparing him the rod for neglecting his duties.

Lincoln was a little Ebo man described as being about 5 feet 2 inches. His teeth were not filed and he had yaws marks on his hands and feet. Thistlewood added to these decorations with stamping "T.T." (Thomas Thistlewood) on each check and each shoulder, in addition to "some weals on his back". He worked as a house servant, a driver, a fowler and a fisherman. He was bought by Thistlewood in 1756 at about the age of sixteen years. In March 1760 he "made a match" with a slave woman named Violet; Thistlewood approved, and they were allowed to share the same quarters. The relationship was not a loving one and Lincoln would beat Violet from time to time. Thistlewood was often called in to mediate. He writes on Monday, 2 June 1760: "Lincoln beat Violet again, and is very impudent and ill-minded." Thistlewood, not surprisingly, had already had sex with Violet, and recorded the event on 22 August 1759. The quarrels between Lincoln and Violet were frequent and his physical abuse of her intensified. In October 1760 he claimed that he "got the clap from Doll", but Violet received it from him.

Lincoln and Violet soon parted company, and within a few years he had taken up with Sukey. By 1767 it was Sukey's turn to receive beatings from him. On February 5, he beat her "terribly", and she was "very bad". Thistlewood found her "speechless" and in great pain. Anticipating that he would receive a flogging from Thistlewood, Lincoln went into hiding and could not be found. When he returned he was deranked, put into demeaning labour for a while, but later reinstated. Between 1767 and 1770 he also had relations with Susanah-Lucy, who produced a daughter (Mary) with him. While mating with Sukey he also had a "wife" at a neighbouring estate. He was Thistlewood's favourite male slave. Thistlewood beat him occasionally but punished him mostly with withdrawal of privileges and extra hard labour. But he was always restored to favour, and was close to Thistlewood. In many respects they were similar characters – one a superordinate masculinity, the other a subordinate and honourless masculinity. Both engaged in the project of dishonouring black women and promoting their respective notions of patriarchy. None of this, however, was peculiar to Thistlewood's estate. Evidence suggests, for example, that *courrir les filles* (girl-hunting) was a pastime among male slaves in Saint Dominigue, which sometimes resulted in rape and kidnapping of women on neighbouring and distant estates. In addition the kidnapping of women by Maroon men in order to find wives and labourers figured prominently in the social history of all colonies that harboured Maroon communities.[27]

It should be emphasized, argues Moitt, "that the structure of plantation society was sexist and that sexism was reflected in the organisation of labour". The slave women's plight, he suggests, "resulted largely from patriarchy and the sexist orientation of Caribbean slave plantation society which put them into structural slots that had no bearing on their abilities". "This meant," he concludes, "that women were not permitted to move into roles traditionally ascribed to [black] males." Slave owners consistently discriminated against slave women in the allocation of access to skilled professions, and never were they allowed to hold the principal offices of head driver and overseer.[28] Victor Schoelcher, the French antislavery campaigner of the early nineteenth

century, explained the entrapment of most women slaves in the field gangs of
Martinique as follows:

> It is often the case in the field gangs that there are more women than men. This
> is how it can be explained. A plantation is, in itself, a small village. As it is usually
> established a considerable distance from major centres, it must provide of all its
> needs, [such as] masons and blacksmiths [and] animal watchmen. All the appren-
> tices who are destined to replace them are now in the field gangs (the slave driver
> included), and this diminishes the male population available for field work.[29]

In the sugar factories women were not trained as boilers and distillers –
prestigious, high technology tasks. Slave women, then, experienced the male
slave labour elite as representing another level of male authority which was
not necessarily supportive of their own sense of social justice and material
betterment.

IV

Subversive resistance by women to the gender order normally incurred
punishments. Slave drivers, such as Lincoln, had the authority to use the whip
to enforce conformity to the social implications of the gender order. African-
born women, for example, did not expect to work during advanced pregnancy,
nor in the three months after childbirth. Those who resisted the new regime
were punished as part of the gender retraining. Punishments were invariably
imposed by male slave drivers, who understood this expectation. The unfa-
miliarity of this labour culture to Africans contributed to the low fertility levels
and high infant mortality rates that rendered the black population unable to
reproduce itself naturally.

Eighteenth-century records placed depletion rates (the excess of a population's crude death rate over its crude birth rate) as high as 50 to 65 per cent,
while modern historians using case-study analysis place it much lower. Estate
records for Jamaica in the third quarter of the eighteenth century suggest
depletion rates of about 20 per cent, while slave import and re-export records
suggest 30 per cent between 1700 and 1750, and 25 per cent between 1750
and 1775. The depletion rate for Barbados in the first half of the eighteenth
century seemed worse than that of Jamaica: 49 per cent between 1701 and
1725 and 36 per cent from 1726 to 1750, but falling to less than 12 per cent
between 1775 and 1800. The demographic experiences of the Leewards
approximated those of Barbados, with depletion rates of 40 to 50 per cent up

to the 1760s and less than 15 per cent in the last quarter of the century. By
the time of the general registration of slaves between 1814 and 1818, and the
collapse of slavery in the 1830s, depletion rates in Barbados and the Leewards
were between 3 and 4 per cent.[30]

It was commonplace for visitors to Jamaica in the eighteenth century, who
were unfamiliar with the gender order of plantation slavery, to express horror
on observing the physical brutalization of females and slave owners' disregard
for black motherhood and maternity. Accustomed to a gendered culture in
which women were perceived as being in need of social and moral protection
from male tyranny, some individuals who remained pro-slavery during the
debate on abolition were moved to support policies for radical amelioration
of slave women's condition. To such observers it was in relation to women
that slavery was most vile, unjust and corrupting of civilized values. Not
surprisingly, therefore, abolitionists after the 1780s used evidence of corporal
punishments inflicted on females, splitting up of black families, and disregard
for domesticity in order to make their principal moral charge against slavery.
In so doing they encouraged West Indian planters to address as a separate
issue the matter of slave women's social and domestic conditions. An important effect of this successful political campaign was the reformalization of
gender representations. For the first time in slave society the notion of the
black woman as a member of the "gentler sex" – hence physically inferior to
males – became the basis of policy initiatives in slave management.

The black woman had finally caught up with the white woman. But what
do we know of the white woman? Very little indeed. The argument, for
example, that Caribbean white women were of marginal historical importance
in fashioning the colonial complex is striking when placed alongside interpretations found within the historiography of slavery in the southern United
States. Here historians suggested that white women, particularly planters'
wives, represented a kinder, gentler authority within the totalitarian power
structure of the plantation. Some historians have gone further and argued that
the plantation mistress was the unifying element within the slavery patriarchy.

While Barbara Bush recognizes the privileges afforded white women within
the slave system, many of which were predicated upon the subjection and
brutalization of non-white women, she seeks nonetheless to highlight the
common ground where womanhood in general was the target and prey of
white male patriarchal authority.[31] Lucille Mair, outlining a framework for
detailed historical research, reinforces the parasitic view of the white woman

by stating that in Caribbean plantation society "the black woman produced, the brown woman served, and the white woman consumed".[32] Again the diverse productive roles played by white women in the development and maintenance of the slave mode of production were peripheralized within the projection of hegemonic, culturally moronic consumerism in which they were apparently imprisoned. Caribbean historiography lacks a clearly articulated and empirically sound conceptualization of white women in their roles as pro-slavery agents within the world slave holders made.

None of these approaches adequately addresses questions concerning white women as economic actors, managers of slave-based households, and conduits in the process of socio-ideological transmission. As a result the traditional conception of the slave owner as male remains unchallenged, and the socioeconomic limit of patriarchy not identified. Nowhere is there to be found within the historiography, for instance, a dedicated assessment of the history of white women's autonomous roles as economic agents and positive participators in the formulation of pro-slavery values and institutions. Yet there is no shortage of documentary evidence which shows white women as accumulators of property and profits through their own-account involvement in commercial and service activities, and as ideological enforcers within the social organization of slave society. The complex pattern of women's roles, in addition, should be understood in relation to the internal evolution of colonial society, particularly in terms of the patriarchal foundations on which it rested.

White women were generally the owners of small properties rather than large estates, but their small properties were more proportionately stocked with slaves than the large, male-owned properties. In 1815, they owned about 24 per cent of the slaves in St Lucia; 12 per cent of the slaves on properties of more than fifty slaves, and 48 per cent of the properties with fewer than ten slaves. In Barbados, 1817, less than five of the holdings of fifty slaves or more were owned by white women, but they owned 40 per cent of the properties with fewer than ten slaves. Their extensive ownership of slaves, though less significant in the rural areas, was immediately obvious in many Caribbean towns. In Barbados, 1817, 50 per cent of the slaves' owners in Bridgetown, the capital, on properties stocked with fewer than ten slaves, were white women. In general, 58 per cent of slave owners in the capital were female, mostly white, though some were also "coloured" and black. Overall women owned 54 per cent of the slaves in the town. The typology of slave owning in the West Indies, then, shows a male predominance in the rural areas and a female predominance in the urban areas where properties tended to be smaller.[33]

White women also owned more female slaves than male slaves. The extensive female ownership of slaves in the towns was matched by the unusually high proportion of females in the slave population; female slave owners owned more female slaves than male slave owners. The evidence shows, furthermore, that in Bridgetown in 1817, the sex ratio (males per 100 females) for slaves belonging to male slave owners was more than double that for female slave owners. The majority of male slaves in the town were owned by male slave owners. The sex ratio for slaves belonging to males was 111 and that for slaves belonging to females was 49. The sex ratio for slaves belonging to white females, when separated from non white females, was even higher at 53. For Berbice in 1819 slaves owned by males had a sex ratio of 132, while those owned by females had a ratio of only 81.[34]

From these data the image that emerges of the white female slave owner is that she was generally urban and in possession of fewer than ten slaves, the majority of whom were female. That female slave owners generally owned female slaves indicates the nature of enterprises, and hence labour regimes, managed and owned by white women. It is reasonable, then, to argue that any conceptualization of slavery, especially with reference to the experiences of enslaved black women, should proceed with an explicit articulation that locates white women as principal slave owners.

Eighteenth-century observers, such as William Dickson, argued that the presence of the white female majority in Barbados tempered the brutish frontier mentality and contributed at an early stage to the maturity of hegemonic paternalism. By "civilizing" the white community in many respects, he suggests, the "social graces" of white women also tended towards the gradual amelioration of slave relations. Conversely, he suggested, the shortage of white women in eighteenth-century Jamaica explained in part the rapid rise of the mulatto population, accounted for the undeveloped state of white households, and promoted the violence endemic to relations between white and black males who competed for black females.[35] There is no evidence, however, to support Dickson.

The caring of children, and the promotion of motherhood and domesticity in Barbados, were discussed as social and economic responses to the need to breed rather than buy new slaves. Gender representations were destabilized and reconstructed in order to offer coherence to new reproductive policy initiatives. By the late eighteenth century there was widespread commitment to pronatal policies in an attempt to encourage natural reproduction as an important method of ensuring an adequate labour supply in the long term. This development meant that a "woman policy" had to be conceived, formulated and implemented on the estates. Traditional managerial attitudes and actions towards slave women were reconsidered and reshaped in a manner conducive to higher fertility levels. It was the beginning of a broad-based initiative to celebrate and promote black motherhood that resulted in the representation of the black woman as a natural nurturer – everyone's nanny, granny and auntie.

It should be stated, however, that slave owners had no direct evidence to prove that female slaves had been consciously imposing restraints upon their fertility, or that hegemonic gender representations helped towards its suppression, even though most believed it to be the case. No one considered that the slave woman, constructed as Jezebel, could possibly practise sexual abstinence (gynaecological resistance), but some believed that she possessed deep-rooted hostility toward child rearing in slavery, especially within the context of hostility to motherhood. Slave owners proposed to minimize the degree of female indifference and resistance to child rearing by systematically offering socio-material incentives and reshaping the ideological aspects of the gender order.

This radical managerial departure centred the woman as mother and meant that new gender ideas had to be popularized, carefully tested and evaluated. As a consequence the pro-slavery cause found itself the recipient of an upsurge in literature which directly addressed aspects of slave-breeding policies. Most contributors, many of them posing as experienced authorities on slave management, sought to encourage this trend, conceiving it as representative of new progressive organizational thought. Also successful slave reproduction was considered a political strategy to take wind from the sails of abolitionists who argued that the endemic suppression of motherhood and family values among slaves sprang from conceptual sources deep within the gender order.

One influential work, a pamphlet published in London in 1786 entitled "The Following Instructions are Offered to the Consideration of Proprietors and Managers of Plantations", was written by prominent absentee Barbadian planters. Printed in bold, capitalized letters in the introduction is the central thesis: "THE INCREASE IS THE ONLY TEST OF THE CARE WITH WHICH THEY ARE TREATED."[36]

The Barbadians had already achieved natural growth and were now offering for emulation the key features of their success to less fortunate planters in other colonies. The pamphlet emphasized the need for planters to implement a series of prenatal policies to assist pregnant women to deliver healthy babies. Most importantly, it stressed the need to protect fertile women from the tyranny of overseers. In addition emphasis was placed on the importance of post-natal facilities in order to assist lactating mothers and midwives in lowering the rate of infant mortality.[37] These policies meant, in addition to marginal reduction of labour hours for pregnant and lactating field women and improved material care, the representation of black women as graduant members of the "gentler sex" whose fragility required specific policy protection. In effect the authors recommended a significant reconstruction of the gender order to facilitate marriage and domestic union among young slaves.

Tinkering with gender by way of finding methods to remove as many irritants as possible from women's sexual and domestic oppression was considered necessary. Slave owners were urged to encourage young slaves to form Christian-style marriages, as monogamous relations were considered more conducive to high fertility than African polygyny. The nuclear family structure, as an institutional arrangement, was encouraged by slave owners and considered suitable to attaining the objective of high levels of reproduction. On many estates, then, Christian-style married slaves were found living in single households. Also, the use of financial incentives as stimuli to reproduction was institutionalized by many slave owners. By the 1790s evidence from plantation account books shows that such financial payments were commonplace.

"Monk" Lewis of Jamaica could not be satisfied with crude systems of monetary and material rewards as stimulants for the creation of life. Money was important, but for him it was insufficient and brutally inadequate when offered as an incentive to motherhood. He needed something more philosophical, befitting the nature of the new gender order. Slave women, he believed, were entitled to "honour" as mothers in their heroic struggle against nature. Respect was due to them, and such values, he believed, were necessary to encourage fertile women who were altogether too few on his estate.[38]

Abolitionists also centred the slave woman with respect to their campaign strategies, propaganda and analytical critiques. The slave woman was placed at the core of a contradictory discourse that sought on one hand to protect and prolong slavery, and on the other to undermine and destroy it. The discourse was transatlantic in nature. On the estates in the West Indies the increase in the slave woman's fertility after 1800 was hailed by slave owners as evidence of slaves' "good treatment". In Europe the slave woman was depicted as the tragic and principal victim of the worst system of masculine tyranny known to the modern world. The debate was part of a wider gender discourse that sharpened opinion on both sides of the Atlantic, and focused attention on the nature of slavery as a particular kind of gendered power.

The promotion in European discourse of the paternalist idea of "woman" as the gentler sex placed tremendous ideological ammunition in the hands of the antislavery movement. Campaigners sought to portray the evil of West Indian slave society as resulting from this bias – both in terms of the sex structure of labour gangs and the emphasis upon natural reproduction in the wake of the abolition of the slave trade in 1807. Thus while some hard-line pro-slavery advocates continued to defend female corporal punishment in terms of "the Amazonian cast of character" of the black woman, antislavery forces believed that they had discovered in gender the soft, vulnerable under-belly of the slavery structure.[39]

Slave owners, therefore, found themselves placed in a difficult and para-doxical position with respect to the gender discourse. While they made claim to possession of an equalitarian ideology within which black women were not recognized as inferior or subordinate to black men – as demonstrated by their labour productivity – there was no intention on their part of weakening dominant patriarchal systems to which black males also subscribed and by which they were partially empowered and privileged. The subsequent con-ceptual imprisonment of the black woman, within a restructured gender representation that promoted notions of difference and inferiority, had the effect of supporting her claim to legal emancipation but at the same time deepening her victimization within the gender order. Slave owners while promoting gender equalitarianism under the whip, sought to defeminize black women in this way by inferring a sameness with males.

The abolitionist discourse, furthermore, needed to cross a few turbulent rivers before it reached a comfortable resting place with respect to the objectification of the black woman. Was she in fact a woman, and if so, what did her femininity look like? In what ways, and to what extent, was she different from the white woman? Should she be regarded as a "sister" by white women, or subsumed within the category of chattel and brute? Was she a victim not only of white tyranny but also of black masculine tyranny – a kind of malehood that saw all women as "less than" and "other"? The answers to these questions would have policy implications for the movement, particularly with respect to such issues as the separation of children from mothers, attitudes toward family life, corporal punishment, and the general nature of sex, gender and work.

By the mid-1820s both male and female English abolitionists were satisfied that the "woman card" was their strongest in the struggle to win the hearts and minds of a seemingly indifferent public. Throughout England middle-class white women formed antislavery organizations and campaigned against slavery by promoting the "feminine" characteristics of the black woman, who was their "sister" in the search for a new moral, Christian order.[40] In most cases white female abolitionists claimed a special understanding of the plight of black women, and slaves in general, derived in part from their "essential nature" as female. The author of *A Vindication of Female Anti-Slavery Association* argued that their movement was part of a general struggle against human misery, social oppression and moral injustice. Elizabeth Heyrick, a popular antislavery campaigner, stated in her *Appeal to the Hearts and Conscience of British Women* (1828) that "the peculiar texture of her mind, her strong feelings and quick sensibilities, especially qualify [woman], not only to sympathize with suffering, but also to plead for the oppressed".[41]

The strategy of the British female antislavery movement, furthermore, was to construct a gendered trinity comprised of the woman, child and family, that slavery had destroyed in and denied to the black race. Without the emotional, spiritual and institutional bonds to enforce the viability of this trinity, they argued, civilization was not possible in the West Indies, and those responsible for its absence were guilty of contributing to the pool of human misery and backwardness. Hell was depicted as a place where men enslave and brutalize women, alienate them from their children, place a market price upon infants at birth, and deny them the right to religion, education and moral guidance. It was portrayed as a place best represented by a West Indian slave plantation.

Thus gender resided at the core of concepts and discourses of slavery and freedom in modernity. Extracted from West Africa by the slave trade and deposited in the Americas in considerably fewer numbers than men, women initially constituted a minority in frontier Caribbean societies. Minority demographic status gave way to numerical majorities as socioeconomic formations matured and were rationalized. Significant gender implications resulted from the fact that the entire system of slavery was female focused, as enslaved black women constituted the conduit through which black infants acquired slavery status at birth. As a consequence successive gender representations of black women developed around the need to align changing sex compositions and demographic requirements with the political economy of efficient resource use.

These issues were illustrated by the empirical evidence and conceptual articulations of the late eighteenth century, when slave owners shifted their labour supply policy from "buying" to "breeding". As the slave woman featured centrally in changing methods of slave reproduction, gender representations reflected the rationalizations of labour choices. Likewise, the politics of the antislavery movement in Europe privileged the gender discourse in order to illustrate and emphasize the greater social exploitation and physical brutalization of slave women. Abolitionists also used gender representations of black women in order to highlight the extreme moral and social oppressiveness and backwardness of societies based on slavery, and the moral degeneracy of elites that maintained and defended it.

The considerable turbulence in the gender journey of slavery requires that events and processes be examined and historicized with the view to obtaining critical forms of feminist knowledge about male domination. Feminist theorizing is best served by readings of history which illustrate how evolving communities actually thought about gender and formed opinions within changing social, economic and philosophical circumstances. Slavery was characterized by considerable internal conceptual fluidity and turmoil, both of which enable us to map the contours of the complex interactions between gender and relations of race and class. An understanding of the "enterprise of the Indies", as a project of modernity, therefore requires the creation and organization of knowledge about gender as a network of socially constructed relations of domination. The liberating counter-praxis of gender, then, should begin with and be guided by an understanding of how and why we came, over time, to think about the things we do and do not think about.

Notes

1. See for example Barbara Bush, *Slave Women in Caribbean Society, 1650–1838* (Bloomington: Indiana University Press, 1990); Hilary Beckles, *Natural Rebels: A Social History of Enslaved Black Women in Barbados* (New

Brunswick, NJ: Rutgers University Press, 1989), and *Centering Woman: Gender Discourses in Caribbean Slave Societies* (Kingston, Jamaica: Ian Randle Publishers, 1999); Marietta Morrissey, *Slave Women in the New World: Gender Stratification in the Caribbean* (Lawrence: University Press of Kansas, 1989); Lucille Mair, *Women Field Workers in Jamaica during Slavery* (Kingston, Jamaica: Department of History, University of the West Indies, 1986); Blanca Silvestrini, *Women and Resistance: Herstory in Contemporary Caribbean History* (Kingston, Jamaica: Department of History, University of the West Indies, 1989).

2.   Rhoda Reddock, "Women and Slavery in the Caribbean: A Feminist Perspective", *Latin American Perspectives* 12, no. 1 (1985): 63–80; Arlette Gautier, "Les Esclaves femmes aux Antilles Francaises, 1635–1848", *Reflexions Historiques* 10, no. 3 (Fall 1983): 409–35; Lucille Mair, *The Rebel Woman in the British West Indies During Slavery* (Kingston, Jamaica: Institute of Jamaica, 1975).

3.   See for example Catherine Clinton, *The Plantation Mistress: Women's World in the Old South* (New York: Pantheon Books, 1982); C.L.R. James, *The Black Jacobins: Toussaint L'Ouverture and the San Domingo Revolution* (New York: Vantage Books, 1963), 30–31; Morrissey, *Slave Women in the New World*, 150; Barbara Bush, "White 'Ladies', Coloured 'Favourites' and Black 'Wenches': Some Considerations on Sex, Race and Class Factors in Social Relations in White Creole Society in the British Caribbean", *Slavery and Abolition* 2 (December 1981): 245–62; Joan Gunderson, "The Double Bonds of Race and Sex: Black and White Women in a Colonial Virginia Parish", *Journal of Southern History* 52 (1986): 351–72.

4.   Lucille Mair, "An Historical Study of Women in Jamaica from 1655–1844" (PhD thesis, University of the West Indies, Mona, 1974); *The Rebel Woman*; "The Arrival of Black Women", *Jamaica Journal* 9 (February 1975): 2–3; see also Jacqueline Jones, " 'My Mother Was Much of a Woman': Black Women, Work, and the Family Under Slavery", *Feminist Studies* 8 (1982): 235–69; Marietta Morrissey, "Women's Work, Family Formation and Reproduction Among Caribbean Slaves", *Review* 9 (1986): 339–67.

5.   See Hilary McD. Beckles, "Sex and Gender in the Historiography of Caribbean Slavery", in *Engendering History: Caribbean Women in Historical Perspective*, ed. V. Shepherd, B. Brereton and B. Bailey (Kingston, Jamaica: Ian Randle Publishers, 1995), 125–40; also in this volume, Bridget Brereton, "Text, Testimony, and Gender: An Examination of Some Texts by Women on the English-Speaking Caribbean, from the 1770s to the 1920s", 63–94; and Rosalyn Terborg-Penn, "Through an African Feminist Theoretical Lens: Viewing Caribbean Women's History Cross-Culturally", 3–19.

6.   For the wider relevance of this discussion see Hilary McD. Beckles, "Black
      Masculinity in Caribbean Slavery", *Occasional Paper 2/96* (Cave Hill,
      Barbados: Women and Development Unit, University of the West Indies,
      1996); Lindon Gordon, "What New in Women's History", in *Feminist
      Studies/Critical Studies,* ed. Teresa de Lauretis (Bloomington: Indiana
      University Press, 1986), 20–23; Louise M. Newman, "Critical Theory and
      the History of Women: What's at Stake in Deconstructing Women's History",
      Journal of Women's History 2, no. 3 (1991); Mary Poovey, "Feminism and
      Deconstruction", *Feminist Studies* 14 (1988): 51–65.

7.   See Beckles, *Natural Rebels*; Gautier, "Les Esclaves Femmes aux Antilles
      Francaises"; B.W. Higman, "Household Structure and Fertility on Jamaican
      Slave Plantations", *Population Studies* 27 (1973): 527–50; B.W. Higman,
      Slave Population and Economy in Jamaica, 1807–1834 (Cambridge:
      Cambridge University Press, 1976); H.S. Klein and S.L. Engerman, "Fertility
      Differentials between Slaves in the United States and the British West Indies",
      William and Mary Quarterly 35 (1978): 357–74; Michael Craton, "Changing
      Patterns of Slave Families in the British West Indies", *Journal of
      Interdisciplinary History* 10, no. 1 (1979): 1–35.

8.   The protracted violent war between Africans and Europeans on the sixteenth-
      and seventeenth-century Caribbean frontier has been well documented, but
      the contribution of changing gender identities and roles to social turbulence
      and instability has not been accounted for despite the considerable evidence
      found in slave owners' texts. See Hilary McD. Beckles, "Caribbean
      Anti-Slavery: The Self-Liberation Ethos of Enslaved Blacks", *Journal of
      Caribbean History* 22, nos. 1 and 2 (1988): 1–19; Bernard Moitt, "Women,
      Work and Resistance in the French Caribbean during Slavery, 1700–1848", in
      Engendering History: Caribbean Women in Historical Perspective, ed. V.
      Shepherd, B. Brereton and B. Bailey (Kingston, Jamaica: Ian Randle
      Publishers, 1995), 155–75; Bush, *Slave Women in Caribbean Society*;
      Morrissey, *Slave Women in the New World.*

9.   See David Brian Davis, *The Problem of Slavery in Western Culture* (Ithaca:
      Cornell University Press, 1966), also, *Slavery and Human Progress* (New York:
      Oxford University Press, 1984); David Eltis and James Walvin, eds., *The
      Abolition of the Atlantic Slave Trade: Origins and Effects in Europe, Africa and the
      Americas* (Madison: University of Wisconsin Press, 1981); Thomas Hodgkin,
      "Kingdoms of the Western Sudan", in *The Dawn of African History,* ed.
      Roland Oliver (London: Oxford University Press, 1961); Jan Vansina, *Paths
      in the Rainforest* (London: James Currey, 1990); Philip D. Curtin, "Africa and
      the Wider Monetary World, 1250–1850", in *Precious Metals in the Later
      Medieval and Early Modern Worlds,* ed. John F. Richards (Durham: North
      Carolina University Press, 1982), 231–68; John Fage, "The Effects of the

Export Trade on African Populations", in *The Population Factor in African Studies*, ed. R.P. Moss and R.J. Rathbone (London: University Press of London, 1975), 15–23; Joseph Inikori, ed., *Forced Migration: The Impact of the Export Trade on African Societies* (London: Hutchinson, 1981); Ray Kea, *Settlement, Trade and Politics in the Seventeenth Century Gold Coast* (Baltimore: Johns Hopkins University Press, 1982); Claire C. Robertson and Martin Klein, eds., *Women and Slavery in Africa* (Madison: University of Wisconsin Press, 1983); Claude Meillassoux, "Female Slavery", in *Women and Slavery in Africa*, ed. C. Robertson and M. Klein (Madison: University of Wisconsin Press, 1983), 49–66; Walter Rodney, "African Slavery and Other Forms of Social Oppression on the Upper Guinea Coast in the Context of the Atlantic Slave Trade", *Journal of African History* 7, no. 3 (1966): 431–43; Walter Rodney, "Gold and Slaves on the Gold Coast", *Transactions of the Historical Society of Ghana* 10 (1969): 13–28.

10. Claire C. Robertson and Martin A. Klein, "Women's Importance in African Slave Systems", in *Women and Slavery in Africa*, ed. C. Robertson and M. Klein (Madison: University of Wisconsin Press, 1983), 4–5.

11. Ibid. Also see Martin Klein, "Women in Slavery in the Western Sudan", in *Women and Slavery in Africa*, ed. C. Robertson and M. Klein (Madison: University of Wisconsin Press, 1983), 67–92.

12. See Robertson and Klein, "Women's Importance", 9.

13. Meillassoux, "Female Slavery", 49; Robertson and Klein, "Women's Importance", 10, 11.

14. Robertson and Klein, "Women's Importance", 18. See also J.D. Fage, "Slave and Society in Western Africa, *c.*1455–1700", *Journal of African History* 21 (1980): 289–310; M. Klein, "The Study of Slavery in Africa: A Review Article", *Journal of African History* 19 (1978): 599–609; I. Kopytoff, "Indigenous African Slavery: Commentary One", *Historical Reflections* 6 (1979): 62–77; I. Kopytoff and S. Miers, "African 'Slavery' as an Institution of Marginality", in *Slavery in Africa*, ed. S. Miers and I. Kopytoff (Madison: University of Wisconsin Press, 1977).

15. Herbert S. Klein, "African Women in the Atlantic Slave Trade", in *Women and Slavery in Africa*, ed. C. Robertson and M. Klein (Madison: University of Wisconsin Press, 1983), 29–32.

16. Ibid., 33 (Table 2.6).

17. Kamau Brathwaite, "Caribbean Woman during the Period of Slavery", *Caribbean Contact*, May–June 1984.

18. Orlando Patterson, *Sociology of Slavery* (London: MacGibbon and Kee, 1967), 177.

19. J. Stewart, *An Account of Jamaica and its Inhabitants* (London, 1808), 234; see also Patterson, *Sociology of Slavery*, 174–81.

20. Patterson, *Sociology of Slavery*, 174–81.
21. Thistlewood Diaries, Lincolnshire Records Office, England. These handwritten diaries contain about ten thousand pages of manuscript. See Douglas Hall's edition, *In Miserable Slavery: Thomas Thistlewood in Jamaica, 1750–1786* (London: Macmillan, 1989).
22. See Miguel Barnett and Alistair Hennessey, *The Autobiography of a Runaway Slave: Esteban Montejo* (London: Macmillan, 1993).
23. Klein, "African Women", 33 (Table 2.6).
24. Edward Long, *The History of Jamaica*, 3 vols. (London, 1774), 274–76, 327–28, 330–31.
25. Ibid., 328.
26. References in this section are from Thistlewood's Diary.
27. J.G. Stedman, *Narrative of a Five Year Expedition Against the Revolted Negroes of Surinam, 1806* (Amherst: University of Massachusetts Press, 1971), 177–78; Leslie Manigat, "The Relationship Between Marronage and Slave Revolts and Revolution in St Domingue – Haiti", in *Annals of the New York Academy of Sciences* (New York: Academy Press, 1977), 420–38.
28. Moitt, "Women, Work and Resistance", 162.
29. Victor Schoelcher, *Des Colonies Francaises: Abolition Immediate de L' Esclavage* (Basse-Terre: Société d'Histoire de la Guadeloupe, 1976), 23–24.
30. J.R. Ward, *British West Indian Slavery, 1750–1834: The Process of Amelioration* (Oxford: Clarendon Press, 1988), 121–22.
31. Bush, *Slave Woman*, 8, 134.
32. Ibid., xii.
33. B.W. Higman, *Slave Populations of the British Caribbean 1807–1834* (Baltimore: Johns Hopkins University Press, 1984), 107; also, Higman, *Slave Population and Economy*.
34. See Higman, *Slave Populations*.
35. For structure of the Barbados and Jamaica white population, see Beckles, *Natural Rebels*, 15. Also Hilary Beckles, *Black Rebellion in Barbados: The Struggle Against Slavery, 1727–1838* (Bridgetown, Barbados: Antilles Publications, 1985), 58–59; William Dickson, *Mitigation of Slavery: 1814* (Westport: Negro University Press, 1970), 439–41.
36. See Beckles, *Natural Rebels*.
37. See K.F. Kiple, *The Caribbean Slave: A Biological History* (Cambridge: Cambridge University Press, 1981); K.F. Kiple and V.H. Kiple, "Slave Child Mortality: Some Nutritional Answers to a Perennial Puzzle", *Journal of Social History* 10 (1979): 284–309, and "Deficiency Diseases in the Caribbean", *Journal of Interdisciplinary History* 11, no. 2 (1980): 197–205.
38. M.G. Lewis, *Journal of a West India Proprietor, Kept During a Residence in the Island of Jamaica* (London, 1929), 108–9.

39. *Report on the Debate in Council on a Dispatch from Lord Bathurst to Governor Warde of Barbados* (London, 1828), 21–23.

40. See Clare Midgley, *Women Against Slavery: The British Campaigns, 1780–1870* (London: Routledge, 1992), 93–117; Louis Billington and Rosamund Billington, " 'A Burning Zeal for Righteousness': Women in the British Anti-Slavery Movement, 1800–1820", in *Equal or Different: Women's Politics, 1800–1914,* ed. Jane Rendall (Basingstoke: Macmillan, 1985), 82–111; bell hooks, "Sisterhood: Political Solidarity between Women", *Feminist Review* 23 (1986): 125–38.

41. *A Vindication of Female Anti-Slavery Associations* (London: Female Anti-Slavery Society, n.d.), 3–4; [Elizabeth Heyrick], *Appeal to the Hearts and Conscience of British Women* (Leicester: Cockshaw, 1828), 3; also cited in Midgley, *Women Against Slavery,* 94.

CHAPTER 11

Gendered Testimony

Autobiographies, Diaries and Letters by Women as Sources for Caribbean History

BRIDGET BRERETON

Over the last quarter of a century, historians have been engaged in the effort to rescue women of the past from their invisibility in the traditional record. This work of recovery and retrieval has made possible the redefinition of "history" to include aspects of life previously seen as non-historical because they are "natural" and (therefore) timeless and unchanging. This is especially true of family relations, domesticity and sexuality. It has made it possible – indeed imperative – for us to insert gender and gender relations into our work as historians, to "engender history".

These achievements have depended on finding sources which speak to women's experiences in past societies. Historians are always prisoners of their sources, and by and large, women's voices have been silenced in the records of the past. Women have left far fewer traces than men in the historical records; most of what they created has vanished forever, and men have monopolized the written word as well as the public arena. Of course the main body of records which historians use may contain rich data about women and gender relations, and such records have been mined fruitfully by researchers asking different questions and bringing different perspectives. These records include autobiographies, diaries and private letters written by men, which often yield excellent data about gender relations; Thomas Thistlewood's extraordinary Jamaican diaries come immediately to mind. Yet the evidence is usually scattered and problematic, and the records often are silent about the real lives of women. This is why historians concerned to engender history have sought to capture the actual voices of real women, and to make women's testimony, whether written or oral, central to their reconstruction of the past.

Oral history allows for the retrieval of life stories of women (and men) as they themselves conceptualize and tell them: real people, real lives. Its importance for reconstructing women's history is clear enough; as a French scholar puts it, "women have spoken a great deal more than they have written".[1] This dictum is even more true for Caribbean women than for Europeans. In the 1989 Goveia lecture Blanca Silvestrini, the Puerto Rican historian, urged us to accept women's voices and their lives as they tell them (whether in oral or written testimonies) and to make them central to the writing of history.[2] Several scholars working in Caribbean history have taken up Silvestrini's challenge. Patricia Mohammed, for instance, made oral history central to her brilliant study of gender relations in the Indo-Trinidadian community in the first half of the twentieth century. She sees the method as critical, not only because most of her "subjects" were illiterate or without access to the written word, but because she was seeking evidence on how women and men redefined and reconstructed gender in their private and family lives.[3]

Women's voices may also be captured through fiction. Literary sources, generally discounted by social historians as being too unreliable because generated by the artistic imagination, may be rich in materials. The Goveia lecturer in 1992, Elizabeth Fox-Genovese, argued that Toni Morrison's great novel, *Beloved,* evokes the story of women's experience of slavery in two ways. It depicts the feelings of a woman who endured slavery and is thus a source for the "elusive psychological 'facts' ". It is also a "source for another history, namely the history of the elusiveness of women's experience of slavery until our own time": why and how the story was repressed.[4]

Although women have left far fewer traces in the written record than men, "personal documents" left by literate women are a key source for women's history, a channel for the transmission of their own voices. They include autobiographical writings and memoirs, diaries and journals, private and family correspondence. Family papers and letters, Joan Scott notes, "have

revealed information about the texture of women's lives and family relationships". Women are "the scribes of the family", and their letters are rich sources
for "commonplace events and private life" which are the core of most people's
lives. Diaries were often important outlets for self-expression for women
whose lives might be very circumscribed. Autobiographies and memoirs
contain the life histories of literate women. These "personal documents" have
been important sources in the engendering of European and American
history.[5] I wish to suggest that we explore similar materials as sources of
gendered testimony for Caribbean history; I shall limit my discussion to the
English-speaking Caribbean.

It almost goes without saying that there are few such documents. The great
majority of Caribbean women up to the twentieth century were outside the
documentary culture, as were most men. Most of the women who wrote
memoirs, journals or letters – those which have survived because eventually
published, or found in private or public archival collections – were either
outsiders – British for the most part – or belonged to the white creole elite.
Black and Indian women were largely silent, in literary terms, until well into
the twentieth century. Except for the celebrated autobiographies by Mary
Prince and Mary Seacole, writings by black Caribbean women of the nineteenth century – letters, diaries, memoirs, fiction – have not often been located
or used as sources.

Unlike oral history testimonies, written personal documents have an inherent bias towards the privileged: letters, diaries, memoirs were much less likely
to be generated by poorer women, and were less likely to survive or to be
published. This bias, of course, exists for European or American history too;
Anna Davin notes that few nineteenth-century British workers wrote memoirs,
and "of women there are almost none".[6] In the Caribbean case, some of the
authors of these documents were British women, such as Lady Nugent,
engaged in the imperialist enterprise even if in a subordinate role. Although
this fact does not negate their value as sources of gendered testimony about
Caribbean society, we need to note, with Evelyn O'Callaghan, that their
writings give us access to the voice of the colonizer's "other half", even if her
position in the essentially patriarchal colonial project was often marginal.[7]

I have examined some memoirs, diaries and letters by women who lived in
the Caribbean since the early 1800s; most, but not all, have been published.
They include five autobiographical writings. That by Mary Prince, a Ber-
muda-born enslaved African-Caribbean woman, occupies a unique position

in Caribbean historiography. It is the only extant work written by an enslaved woman from the British Caribbean, and the first autobiography by a Caribbean woman. Born around 1788, Prince worked in Bermuda, the Turks Islands and Antigua before going to London with her owners in 1828, where she walked out of slavery. Mary Seacole's autobiography, first published in 1857, is, I am sure, well known to most readers. Then we have three memoirs all written by Trinidadian women born between 1888 and 1902: Yseult Bridges, a member of an elite French creole family, wrote a memoir of her childhood in the late nineteenth century; Anna Mahase, Sr, described her life as a student, teacher, wife and mother in Trinidad's Christian Indian community; and Olga Comma Maynard, a prominent Afro-Trinidadian teacher and writer, has recently published an autobiography.[8]

I have looked at the diaries of three women. By far the best known is that of Maria Nugent, the British-American wife of a governor of Jamaica who lived there between 1801 and 1805. It was published after her death, although she certainly did not write with publication in mind. From Trinidad, I examined two unpublished diaries. Amelia Gomez, the Grenada-born wife of a prominent Venezuelan-Trinidadian lawyer, wrote a diary in the early 1840s, part of which has survived; and Adella Archibald, a Canadian missionary and teacher who lived and worked in Trinidad between 1889 and 1934, left a diary for 1930–36.[9] Finally I read the letters of three women, British or Canadian, who lived in the Caribbean during the nineteenth century. Elizabeth Fenwick was a well-educated English woman who ran a girls' school in Barbados between 1814 and 1821; her letters to a friend at home were published over one hundred years later. Many letters by Sarah Morton, who lived in Trinidad between 1867 and 1912, were published as part of her biography of her husband, John Morton, the pioneer Canadian Presbyterian missionary to the Indians of the island. And Susan Rawle, wife of the Anglican bishop of Trinidad in the 1870s and 1880s, wrote many letters to her relatives in England which have survived.[10]

How far can these memoirs, diaries and private letters by women help us to reconstruct the history of the region over the last two centuries? They all permit us to listen to women's voices and women's experiences (mediated, of course, by national origin, ethnicity and class), in contrast to the vast majority of written sources on the post-Columbian Caribbean which have been generated by men. Like oral testimonies, they often tell a life story as the subject herself saw it, emphasizing the activities and emotions important to her own lived experience; they are potentially rich in experiential material. Though less democratic than oral testimony, they take us further back. Of course, as with all personal testimony, the shift from specific and individual incidents, experiences and emotions to generalizations about society is often problematic for the historian. Diaries, private letters and memories (written or oral) are essentially individual as well as culturally and socially determined. What Mohammed says about oral testimonies could equally apply to the kinds of documents I examine: they are "the lived examples of reality, which may or may not typify the norm, but which bring alive the actual people who have lived through and made this moment in history". And Silvestrini reminds us that traditionally, historians have only "listened" to the few individuals whose testimony made up the great bulk of conventional sources.[11]

One of the central insights of women's history is that no sharp rift existed (or exists) between women's "public" and "private" lives, and that the "private sphere" has been much more central to the lives of women than of men in most human societies. Personal documents like diaries, memoirs and letters can illuminate this sphere, and help historians of the Caribbean to reconstruct it. Testimony by women (written or oral) often reveals the centrality of personal and familial relationships in their lives, and the whole world of experience and emotion generated by them. Historians have more or less accepted by now that such matters are legitimate (and necessary) subjects for their enquiry; those of us working on the Caribbean need to locate and use such sources as may make this feasible.

In examining my sample of personal documents by women, I shall be looking for testimony on their gendered life experiences, experiences probably different from those of men because of gender roles and expectations. I want to see how far these documents yield gendered perceptions of Caribbean society over the past two hundred years.

The centrality of the "private sphere" to women's lives is reflected in most of our texts; they are a rich source of data on motherhood and marriage, health and sexuality, domestic life and household management, and the rearing and education of girls.

Mary Prince gives us a glimpse of the childhood of a slave girl in Bermuda at the end of the eighteenth century. In the relatively benevolent household of her first owner, Mrs Williams, she grew up with her mother, also a domestic, and her siblings. Mrs Williams's daughter made her a pet; "she used to lead me about by the hand, and call me her little nigger. This was the happiest period of my life; for I was too young to understand rightly my condition as a slave, and too thoughtless and full of spirits to look forward to the days of toil and sorrow." Prince's education consisted of instruction in the full range of domestic tasks, as well as care of livestock, from her various owners and fellow domestics. In her late thirties she was taught to read by the wives of Moravian missionaries in Antigua; she records with pride, "I got on very fast." Mary Seacole, born around 1805 to a white father and a free black Jamaican mother, was trained in medical and nursing skills by her mother, Mrs Grant. Mrs Grant was a noted "doctress", a traditional healer, held in high esteem by Kingston's military men who frequented her lodging house as much for medical care as for accommodation. Seacole acted as her assistant from the age of twelve, and took over her lodging house (along with her sister Laura Grant) upon her mother's death. Mrs Grant exemplified the enterprising, independent free black woman, making her way in a racist and sexist society, and Seacole's remarkable career owed much to this Jamaican tradition. She is explicit in her pride that she always earned her own bread and succeeded in life on her own.[12]

Both Maria Nugent and Elizabeth Fenwick saw how slavery corrupted the rearing of white children in the Caribbean. Nugent knew how hard it would be to prevent her little son, surrounded by domestics obliged to gratify his every whim, from "thinking himself a little king at least, and then will come arrogance, and all the petty vices of little tyrants". Children were "injudiciously treated" in every respect and were made "truly unamiable, by being most absurdly indulged". Fenwick dreaded, for her grandchildren in Barbados, "the sensual indulgences and luxury that most Children here are allowed".[13]

Many elite girls attended schools for "young ladies" of the kind run by Fenwick and her daughter in Bridgetown between 1814 and 1821. No coloured girls were admitted. The pupils, who stayed until they were seventeen or so, studied writing, arithmetic, geography, history, music, dancing and French. Generally, though, elite parents tried to send their girls to England for a "polish". Nugent noted how Miss Israell of Clarendon, educated at a "fashionable" London school, was forever consumed with anxiety lest her rustic parents embarrass her. In the 1890s, Yseult Guppy went to a private girls' school in Port of Spain run by an English lady; the teachers were young Creole women, badly paid, undereducated, and lacking any notion of how to teach. All the pupils were white. When the family moved to the country, Yseult received desultory tuition at home from her scholarly father. Then, at fourteen, came the inevitable: she was shipped off to England to be "finished" before entering "Society", to eradicate "the insidious singsong Creole accent and acquire that poise and complexion . . . which would enhance her chance of making a 'good match' . . . the whole object of a woman's existence".[14]

Anna Chandisingh (later Mahase), second-generation Indo-Trinidadian born into a Christian home in 1899, received a more useful education from the Canadian Presbyterian mission. She attended the mission-run primary school of which her father was headmaster, then spent four years in the mission's home for girls in Tunapuna. In 1915 she went to the Girls' High School in San Fernando, studying for the teaching examinations; she and four other girls were the nucleus of the female section of the mission-run Naparima Training College. They studied along with the young men: "To me it was a novelty, young East Indian men and girls in their teens, sitting and studying in one common room. It was the first of its kind. . . . These were the days of the beginning of the emancipation of our East Indian girls and women." Anna eventually passed the third class teachers' examination, and could begin her career (at eighteen) as a certified teacher in mission schools. Her autobiographical account of her education is usefully supplemented by Sarah Morton's letters and Adella Archibald's diary; both women pioneered the Canadian mission's work with girls and women. Morton described the operation of the first home for girls, which she founded. The teenaged girls studied academic subjects, including Hindi and English, and religion; "all the housewifely arts" were taught, including "the mysteries of English dishes"; and the girls gardened, did all the housework and laundry, and cleaned the nearby mission church. Many entries in Archibald's diary covering 1930–35 concern the Indo-Trinidadian women who became "bible women" (catechists) and teachers after their education in the Mission's primary schools, Homes for Girls and Training College.[15]

Anna Mahase's contemporary, Olga Comma (Maynard), was the daughter of an African-Trinidadian headmaster. Olga grew up in Belmont, a middle-class suburb of Port of Spain. Here she was socialized into gender roles. "There were never any little girls on the roadway. There were many small boys, with torn trousers, rolling barrel hoops. . . . Little girls seemed to be kept inside to play with their dolls or to help clean the house." On Saturdays, while her brothers ran errands like buying the coals, she cobwebbed and swept, or fed the latest baby sibling. She attended her father's elementary school, then the Tranquillity Girls' Higher Class, a sort of quasi-secondary school attached to a primary and "model" school. She left this to become a pupil teacher at her father's school, receiving five dollars a month, and studying for the teacher's certificate on her own. She never went to Training College, but had a successful career as an elementary school teacher, with a fourteen year break (1932–46) when she was forced to resign upon her marriage.[16]

So much of women's lives was lived in the "private sphere"; and motherhood is often central to that sphere. Maria Nugent gave birth to two infants in Jamaica. She wrote a lively account of her first "Creole confinement" in 1802. As if a labour of two and a half days, oppressive heat, semi-darkness and mosquitoes were not misery enough,

> the old black nurse brought a cargo of herbs, and wished to try various charms, to expedite the birth of the child, and told me so many stories of pinching and tying women to the bed-post, to hasten matters, that sometimes, in spite of my agony, I could not help laughing, and, at others, I was really in a fright, for fear she would try some of her experiments upon me. But the (English) maids took all her herbs from her, and made her remove all the smoking apparatus she had prepared for my benefit.

On the morning after the birth of her son she was allowed a warm bath (she must have had an enlightened doctor); she spent three weeks in her bedroom, then resumed normal life. She engaged the wife of an Irish soldier as a wet-nurse, though she was upset that the heat and her public duties prevented her from nursing the baby herself ("Why should I not be a mother indeed?"). The inoculation of the baby against smallpox was a source of great anxiety; and Nugent tried to keep the baby away from the black domestics as much as possible, vowing that "none of the blackies" should ever give him "a morsel". Her second confinement, in 1803, was easy: "My illness was literally nothing, for I was actually speaking and walking towards the sofa, the instant before it was all over."[17]

Amelia Gomez, in Trinidad in the early 1840s, was less fortunate. In 1841, after a long illness, she "became worse and lost my hopes of giving my dear Husband a little son or daughter. . . . I have been very much debilitated and have suffered more in that respect than I ever did before having been twice bled, and kept on a low diet." She soon became pregnant again, and had a rough time "being very unwell and obliged to keep to my bed for some days and afterwards constantly to be in a recumbent position, the least effort disposing me to lose my second hope of being again a mother". She had "seven months close confinement on my sofa", an "imprisonment" spent working and reading, worried at the "fatigue and annoyance" her husband endured by being "obliged to attend to the menage". She gave birth to a "fine handsome boy" in September 1842: "I was much favoured by the Almighty in my hour of trial." Gomez was constantly worried about the health of Richard, her son by her first marriage, and for several weeks in 1843 her diary is filled with references to his imminent departure for school in England (he was about eleven). He was to travel alone, in the care of the ship captain and his wife, to his mother's great anxiety. "Every hour as it passed brought me nearer to the time of parting with my dear child," she wrote a few days before he left; "this has indeed been a sore trial to me."[18]

Mary Prince was childless; at least, there is no mention in her text of her ever giving birth. Was she made sterile by the repeated physical abuse to which she was subjected all through her child-bearing years, as her modern editor speculates? As a teenager she witnessed the murderous flogging of a pregnant fellow domestic, Hetty, followed by the birth of a dead infant and Hetty's own death. Motherhood, in Prince's text, is pure tragedy. She describes her mother's misery when she, along with two sisters, was sold away at the age of twelve:

> The black morning at length came; it came too soon for my poor mother and us. Whilst she was putting on us the new osnaburgs in which we were to be sold, she said, in a sorrowful voice, (I shall never forget it!) "See, I am shrouding my poor children; what a task for a mother! . . . I am going to carry my little chickens to market" (these were her exact words) "take your last look of them" .

Slave mothers, Prince knew, "could only weep and mourn over their children", testimony to the "implacable war against motherhood" waged by the slave system and against marriage of the morally responsible kind, too. At the age of thirty-eight Prince married a free black carpenter. He tried to buy his wife's freedom, but her owners refused, and Prince records: "I had not much happiness in my marriage, owing to my being a slave. It made my husband sad to see me so ill-treated." After only two years of marriage, she left him in Antigua when (still a slave) she accompanied her owners to Britain, and seems never to have been reunited with him.[19]

For elite girls marriage was, of course, the only acceptable destiny. Yseult Bridges's French creole mother, Alice Rostant Guppy, monitored likely white bachelors with meticulous care. She firmly believed that marriage, children and home were "the very foundations" of a woman's life, and that love would follow marriage and motherhood, not the reverse. Both Yseult and her sister

Ruth were married at eighteen to well-connected English men working in Trinidad, who were considerably older than the two girls. At the close of the nineteenth century, elite girls in Trinidad entered the marriage sweepstakes at the annual Debutantes' Ball at Government House, and Bridges gives an amusing description of the drama surrounding Ruth's preparation for this event, on which "her whole future" might depend. Not getting married meant failure, and relegation "to the background of the home, there to live parasiti-cally or to eke out a genteel existence in some ladylike way". Mary Seacole's deliberate choice for independence as a single woman and then a young widow ("and here I may take the opportunity of explaining that it was from a confidence in my own powers, and not at all from necessity, that I remained an unprotected female"), seems to have been unthinkable for elite white girls of the time, except for those who took the veil. And even the fiercely independent Seacole, whose whole life challenged nineteenth-century gender roles, represented herself as morally upright and ladylike; she carefully disas-sociated herself from the "low" women she met in Panama, a place which, she said, "was not agreeable for a woman with the least delicacy or refinement".[20]

In the writings of Anna Mahase, Sarah Morton and Adella Archibald, we can trace the changes in marriage patterns and life chances for girls of the Indo-Trinidadian community. Mahase's mother, Rookabai, was a Hindu child bride in India who ran away at the age of twelve from a traditional marriage to a much older man (she was especially upset about his moustache). Defying the whole social and gender structure of traditional India, she emigrated to Trinidad in the 1880s. There she came under the influence of the Canadian Presbyterian mission. Converted, she acquired a new name (Elizabeth Burns), and went through a second arranged marriage to a prom-ising young teacher, Anna's father. The missionaries actively sponsored (or vetoed) matches among their young converts. As Morton makes clear, the main purpose of the Homes for Girls run by the mission was to prepare suitable brides for its teachers and catechists, and the teenaged pupils were married off at fifteen or sixteen to approved young men. She wrote in 1891, "many masculine eyes are turned anxiously in the direction of our Home. . . . We wish to keep our present pupils a little longer, for their own sakes. We shall then intimate to the expectants that they may advance their suit and the result will be to make room for new ones." Morton was actively engaged in "persuading" the girls to make the right choice, and she wrote, "I recall only one marriage arranged in the Home that proved a really unhappy one."

Anna Mahase might well have entered into a similar arranged marriage, as did most of her fellow pupils at the Home for Girls in Tunapuna around 1914. A young teacher working in Princes Town "asked for" her, but the missionaries vetoed the match because their policy was not to permit "Tunapuna girls" to marry "in the Princes Town field". Then the missionary's wife arranged a match with a teacher. She had never spoken to the young man, but "I did not mind because he belonged to a Christian family . . . so I decided in my mind that all would be well." Nothing came of this, and Anna was still single at eighteen, in her first teaching job. She met Kenneth Mahase, a student teacher, and a discreet but clearly Western-type courtship began. The two young people studied together and passed the teachers' examinations together. Once Kenneth was appointed as a headteacher, they were married; Anna was twenty. The missionaries approved, but this was no arranged marriage. By then (1919), the work of the Mission in many villages throughout Trinidad had given some Indian girls an opportunity for education, for deferment of marriage, for mixing with boys during adolescence in schools and in the Training College. Ideas of choice in marriage, even if still limited, could begin to develop, first among the Christian Indian community. Ironically, this meant that the missionaries lost a degree of control over their young converts' options. Adella Archibald, in the early 1930s, records a few marriages of Presbyterian girls to men she disapproved of, and mentions a young woman, a trained teacher from a "nice Christian family", who went "off the track" and produced an illegitimate baby. Archibald tried to help her get a job "as it was not advisable for her to take up teaching" in a Mission school.[21]

The health of husbands, children and friends was a constant preoccupation for many of these women. The Caribbean was a dangerous place for European residents at least up to the end of the nineteenth century, and fear of disease and sudden death pervades the journal and letters of Nugent and Fenwick. The latter wrote frequently about her grandchildren's many illnesses and the swift deaths of young pupils and friends. Her daughter was in constant ill health, and her beloved son, only twenty, succumbed to yellow fever after an illness of just three days. "We who seek for gain in these climates," she wrote, "have terrible penalties awaiting us." Nugent, too, worried endlessly about her husband's and her infants' health, and many journal entries record the illnesses and deaths of white people personally known to her. The many doctors who attended at King's House in Spanish Town are familiar characters in her journal. She noted that white women in Jamaica were far more successful in keeping their health than the men; unlike the women, who were generally temperate in their habits, the men "really eat like cormorants and drink like porpoises". Fenwick found the same situation in Barbados: "nothing is so common here as old Ladies of from 80 to 100 years of age. The men shorten their period by intemperance and sensuality." She was terrified that her son might slip into the almost universal "habit of drinking", and her son-in-law was a drunkard.[22]

In the later decades of the nineteenth century, Sarah Morton and Susan Rawle both worried about the health hazards of residence in Trinidad. Morton, her husband and their four children (three born in the island) all suffered severely from malaria and "ague" in their first years. She had two dangerous bouts of malaria in her first three years in the mission house at Iere Village, and in 1877 she nearly died from a serious disease (she does not name it in her letters) which forced her to spend over a year in Canada. Her letters to her husband in Trinidad indicate that she expected to die. Though Rawle says little in her letters to her sister in England about her own health, she often worried about English clergymen and their families getting malaria or yellow fever, especially during the 1881 epidemic. She also wrote about the health problems of the local population, noting with surprise the prevalence of tuberculosis: "it is astonishing how tender the coloured people are especially & what little things give them colds". Like Nugent and Fenwick before her, Rawle noted that "drink is the great temptation out here & is very fatal", especially among young men. She applauded the work of the local temperance movement, though irritated by the "humbug and overstraining of things" by its leaders. As in Britain and America, the temperance movement appealed especially to women, who saw how drinking threatened their domestic world.[23]

Elite women were threatened, too, by sexual liaisons between white men and coloured and black women, enslaved and free. Fenwick, writing in 1815 and no doubt influenced by the humanitarianism (or perhaps her own uneasy conscience) which had spread widely in educated British circles since the 1780s, showed some sympathy for the women involved in these relationships and their children. "It is a horrid & disgraceful System," she wrote;

> the female slaves are really encouraged to prostitution because their children are the property of the owner of the mothers. . . . What is still more horrible, the Gentlemen are greatly addicted to their women slaves, & give the fruit of their licentiousness to their white children as slaves. I strongly suspect that a very fine Mulatto boy about 14 who comes here to help wait on two young Ladies, our

pupils, is their own brother. . . . It is a common case & not thought of as an enormity.[24]

Maria Nugent swiftly became aware of the sexual politics of Jamaica: the black "chere amie", the "mulatto ladies" who said they were "daughters of Members of the Assembly, officers, etc., etc.". She concluded that "white men of all descriptions, married or single, live in a state of licentiousness with their female slaves". Though she was sympathetic to the children of these unions, especially the daughters, most of her concern was directed to the young white men who risked "ruin" from their "horrid connections" and "improper lives". Many journal entries describe her unsuccessful attempts to keep the British officers in the governor's staff from these entanglements. Driving around Spanish Town, Nugent encountered "several of the unfortunate half-black progeny of some of our staff; all of fine muslin, lace etc. . . . What ruin for these worse than thoughtless young men!" On the evidence of her journal, she spared few thoughts for the young men's willing or coerced prey.[25]

Sexual abuse is a submerged subtext in Mary Prince's narrative; extreme reticence characterizes her treatment of the subject. She explicitly describes only one episode of sexual abuse, when she defied the advances of Mr D—, her third owner: "He had an ugly fashion of stripping himself quite naked and ordering me then to wash him in a tub of water. This was worse to me than all the licks." At last "I defended myself, for I thought it was high time to do so. I then told him I would not live longer with him, for he was a very indecent man . . . with no shame for his servants, no shame for his own flesh." After this act of defiance, she got herself sold to new owners: "the truth is, I did not wish to be any longer the slave of my indecent master". Prince presents herself as the active and courageous defender of her "virtue", not as a passive victim. Moreover, her account shows that female slaves were capable, despite their own sexual jeopardy, of empathizing with white women victimized by male power. Prince herself risked serious injury in order to defend Mr D—'s daughter from her father's brutal beatings.[26]

Household management was, of course, the task of women, and for elite women in the Caribbean control of the domestics, whether slave or free, was pivotal to their daily existence. It was one of the few forms of power they possessed, and defiance of their authority by the servants was seen as an assault on their status as women of the ruling caste. Yet they depended on the domestics, and they interacted with them on a level of daily intimacy. The domestics intruded constantly into the personal and domestic lives – the real lives – of the white women. These relations of intimate enmity are salient in several of our texts.[27]

Nugent found the vast establishment at King's House to be disorderly and chaotic; but the domestics responded well when she met with them and promised them "every kindness". An evangelically minded Christian, she devoted a great deal of effort to religious instruction of the domestics, preparing a "little Catechism" for them and seeing to their and their children's baptism. She delighted the King's House slaves by dancing with "an old negro man" at a fête for the servants, "exactly the same as I would have done at a servants hall birthday in England", to the horror (of course) of the creole ladies. A British aristocrat, secure in her caste status, she dealt with her slave domestics with a degree of tolerance and civility. But as she travelled around Jamaica, staying on plantations, she found many disorderly houses with crowds of dirty and badly clothed servants. The creole ladies were "perfect viragoes; they never speak but in the most imperious manner to their servants, and are constantly finding fault". "The continual scolding at the servants," Nugent wrote, "is to me the most distressing thing in the world."[28]

Elizabeth Fenwick found dealing with her domestics in Bridgetown an appalling task. The management of her household, she wrote, involved "annoyances & fatigue . . . that the mistress of an English family, with even the worst of English servants, can form no idea of". Her slave domestics, hired from their owners, were lazy, self-willed and dishonest: "pilfering seems habitual & instinctive among domestic slaves". Keeping house for her daughter, Fenwick told her English friend, "I was several times almost mad with the provocations their dirt, disobedience & dishonesty caused me. . . . You would be astonished to hear me scold, – I do so, I assure you, & that with a vehemence which on reflection surprises and pains me." With no sense of irony, Fenwick complained of "the slavery of managing a family in the West Indies with Negro Domestics". Just after the end of slavery, Amelia Gomez often complained to her diary about servant troubles; "this evil increases," she wrote, "quite wearing to the spirits, as well as the body, it leaves no leisure for any agreeable occupation or even for necessary duties".[29]

It is Mary Prince who provides a unique testimony from the other side of the barricades. She was employed mainly as a domestic for most of her working life in the Caribbean (*c*.1788–1828). Three of her four owners treated her, and her fellow domestics, with extreme brutality. Captain and Mrs I— of Bermuda, who bought her when she was about twelve, routinely tortured their domestics and murdered Hetty, a pregnant "French" slave, who died after an atrocious flogging ("the manner of it filled me with horror", Prince recorded). Mrs I— flogged and beat Prince with her own hands; "she was a fearful woman and a savage mistress to her slaves". Prince had to do cleaning and general housework, child minding, and milking and general care of the livestock; "there was no end to my toils –no end to my blows". Her last owners, the Woods of Antigua, constantly abused her both verbally and physically, yet she was their chief "confidential servant" who was left in sole charge of the household during their frequent absences from home, and they refused to sell her despite several offers. The ability to control Prince, a woman of manifest dignity and intelligence, was clearly critical to the Woods's sense of power and status. When she got married at the age of thirty-eight to a free black, both the Woods were furious; they could not tolerate her assertion of a right to a separate and autonomous personal and sexual life. Mr Wood flogged her, and Mrs Wood said "she would not have nigger men about the yards and premises, or allow a nigger man's clothes to be washed in the same tub where hers were washed".[30]

Growing up in a white creole household in Trinidad fifty years after the end of slavery, Yseult Bridges recalls the black domestics and retainers as idealized servants of the old world. Her mother was a domestic tyrant, obsessively critical of her many servants, directing their lives with the arrogant self-confidence of a slave owner's daughter. The servants (at least in Yseult's nostalgic memory) were utterly loyal; she shows no recognition of the degradation and self-contempt at the heart of these traditional relationships. Zabette, for instance, born a slave, had been wet-nurse to the Rostant babies (the Ronstants were Yseult's mother's family) and head domestic in the Rostant country house. She identified wholeheartedly with the white family, and liked to tell stories of the wonderful old days of slavery and high living on the patriarchal French creole estates. Only rarely does a darker note creep into Bridges' memories of the servants. When her mother's maid was seduced by the handyman's son, both were instantly dismissed, the girl evicted pregnant and penniless; so much for paternalism. Though Bridges recalls the servants as affectionate presences in her childhood, blacks outside the domestic setting were vaguely menacing; she recounts what was, perhaps, the classic nightmare of the white creole girl: as a child of nine or ten, she was walking alone in a rough part of Port of Spain when she was stopped by a black man who must have assumed she was lost.

To my horror a huge negro stepped in front of me, grinning, and barred my way. "Let me pass", I said, trying to assume an imperious air. . . . The negro grinned still more widely. . . . I was now getting frightened. He gave a loud guffaw, echoed from all sides from the crowd that was collecting now, hemming me in, from the ragged children prancing around me. They gaped and jabbered, and the smell of their unwashed skin and clothes was rank and nauseating. My knees went weak, my stomach seemed to cleave to my spine. . . . The big negro man took a step towards me with his hand outstretched, intending to grip me by the arm. . . . I think I must have been on the point of fainting . . .

At that moment when she was "rescued" by a kindly (and masterful) Englishman.[31]

The diaries and letters of Morton, Rawle and Archibald often mention the difficulties of managing their households, though these women (all connected to the Anglican or Presbyterian churches) are generally appreciative of their various domestics. Morton told her relatives at home in Canada about the novel aspects of housekeeping in the tropics (ants, snakes, flies, as well as problems with the helpers), and the loneliness and monotony of life for the young wife in an isolated mission house (in Iere Village). When they moved to a house in San Fernando the kitchen was an old mulestall; "no doubt the mule had been fairly comfortable there, but cook and I were not". She wrote home in 1876: "My cook has left me to nurse a sick child; Willie (her baby son) has the mumps and cries a great deal; a silver spoon is lost; I often wish I had some one to attend to the house and let me teach the Indians." Archibald, who lived in Trinidad for about forty-five years as a teacher and mission worker, seems (on the evidence of her diary) to have had warm relationships with her (mainly Indian) domestics, such as Thelma Bahadur, whose wedding she attended and whom she frequently visited after her marriage.[32]

In her autobiography Olga Maynard gives an interesting account of housekeeping in a black headteacher's family in Port of Spain at the opening of the twentieth century. The large household (Olga's mother had twelve children, four of whom died as infants) employed one helper. An essential feature of domestic life was the many vendors (mostly women) who sold food from door to door each day: a black woman sold sticks of chocolate for the breakfast tea each morning; a "veiled Indian woman" sold milk from a pail, by the dip; an elderly Indian woman had vegetables and fruits carried on a wooden tray on her head; the fishwife sang her wares in Créole. The "old-time kitchen", detached from the house, was the centre of the housewife's activities, and

Maynard gives a detailed description of such a kitchen, with its coal-pot fire, its coffee mill and cocoa stone (for grinding the coffee and cocoa beans), its three-foot wooden mortar and pestle for pounding plantain or breadfruit. Maynard lived in Tobago during World War II, and describes how difficult it was to feed a family in the face of constant shortages of imported food. Butter, cheese, tinned food, Cow and Gate milk (she had young children), and onions all disappeared, and flour came and went (she would line up for hours to get maybe two pounds of discoloured flour with weevils). Housewives tried hard to prepare decent meals; fried green bananas substituted for bread, plantains "threatened to grow out of our ears", honey took the place of sugar. When Maynard returned to teaching in Trinidad in 1946, she employed a "maid of all work" to help, but she spent most of her evenings after school preparing dinner and the next day's breakfast and lunch.[33]

For middle- and upper-class Caribbean women the idea (derived from European gender ideology) that they should be largely confined to the "private sphere" had considerable force (it was never of any real relevance to working-class women after the end of slavery, far less to female slaves). Mary Seacole stands out as the great nineteenth-century exception: her extraordinary life was lived almost entirely in the public arena, indeed in a largely masculine arena, though she presents herself in her autobiography as a feminine person of "delicacy and refinement". Maynard and Mahase, each born at the turn of the nineteenth century to headmaster fathers, had satisfying careers as teachers; Mahase was not forced to resign upon her marriage in 1919, thanks to the intervention of the Canadian Mission, and she combined teaching with raising a large family. Maynard had to resign in 1932 but returned to teaching in 1946 when the Trinidad government quietly reversed its policy. But for women of the white elite, working outside the home was usually unacceptable before the 1920s, except for a few unfortunate spinsters or widows, as Bridges noted of her family's social circles. Religious and charitable activities provided one of the few socially sanctioned opportunities for these women to enter the "public sphere", in the Caribbean as in Europe.

A good example is Amelia Gomez. Her social life consisted of an endless round of private visits, dinners and luncheons, but a large part of her diary describes her participation in the life of the Roman Catholic church (she was a convert from Anglicanism) and its charitable work. Susan Rawle organized Anglican ladies of Port of Spain into a "working party" to make objects to sell for charity; "the ladies seem to like it so far", she told her sister, "& it is a good thing to get them out & lead them to take some interest, if ever so little, in something outside themselves". Some of her ladies taught Sunday school, others were involved in the temperance movement or worked with her in the "Young Women's Help Society" which she founded to help girls "to keep the right course". Both Rawle and Morton, as the wives of senior clergymen working in Trinidad, functioned in effect as full-time assistant missionaries, with (of course) neither status nor salary from their churches. Morton, coming to the island as a young wife, raising her four children in mission houses often in fairly remote villages far from Port of Spain, struggled against chronic ill health, loneliness, social isolation and exhaustion. But she was always fully involved in the mission's work, especially in its attempts to reach Indo-Trinidadian girls and women. She mastered Hindi after a few years, and she spent most of her time visiting Indian women in their barracks and cottages, teaching classes for girls and women, and running the residential Home for Girls which she founded; her daughter Agnes also became fully involved in all these activities after she left school in Canada.

Unlike Morton, Adella Archibald was a salaried employee of the Canadian Women's Missionary Society (of the Presbyterian church), charged with teaching in mission schools and working with women. She first came to Trinidad in 1889 as a young woman of twenty; she retired in 1934. Since she was not an ordained minister, of course, both her salary and her status in the church were lower than the clergymen's, but she did have a recognized position, and her forty-five years of work in Trinidad clearly won her considerable respect. The missionary endeavour, like the colonial enterprise to which it was so closely linked, was definitely a male project (even patriarchal), but it provided some opportunities for women, albeit in subordinate roles.[34]

Through the writings of Morton, Archibald and Mahase we can trace the impact of the Canadian Mission on the lives of Indo-Trinidadian women, as schooling and western values gradually changed life chances for many of them. Archibald's diary gives a detailed account of the innumerable "women's meetings" she held, in Indian villages or homesteads or estate housing, all over southern Trinidad in the early 1930s. Most of the women attending were Hindus or Muslims. With the help of Indo-Trinidadian bible women, she ran Sunday schools and organized groups of girls and women. Literacy and schooling for the children were, of course, key incentives for Indian women to respond positively. At a meeting of twenty-two women in Penal, for example, they asked Archibald to organize them and to set up a reading class, "as a number, even of the young women, are not able to read" (this was 1930). By then the Mission had a network of coeducational primary schools in virtually every area where Indians lived, as well as a girls' secondary school (Naparima Girls' High School), a female training college, and a residential home for girls. By then, too, a number of Indian women, educated and trained in the Mission's institutions, had emerged as Bible women, trained teachers and professionals. Many entries in Archibald's diaries record her pride in these women's achievements.[35]

The influence of the Mission's work with women – largely carried out by women, Canadian and Indo-Trinidadian – gradually changed their lives, by providing western education for many, by allowing for postponement of marriage and mixing between adolescent boys and girls, and by spreading western notions of love and courtship and western ideologies of gender. Morton encountered (and sparred with) a Brahmin father who remonstrated with her, "If you teach a boy you will get some good of it, but a girl is not yours; she is some other man's; why should you trouble with her?" Gradually such attitudes became less acceptable in the Indo-Trinidadian community, and a life like that of Anna Mahase, born in 1899 – Western schooling, a career as a trained teacher, a Western-type marriage – became possible, if only for a few.[36]

These autobiographies, diaries and letters by women provide some rich testimony about women's historical experiences in the Caribbean. They often speak to the real quality and texture of women's lives, so much of them played out in the private and domestic spheres. Along with oral testimony, and the mainstream of historical records generated in the vast majority by men, they may help us to reconstruct and understand the Caribbean past in a more holistic, a more nuanced way – in short, they may help us to engender our region's history.

Notes

1.   M. Perrot, "Making History: Women in France", in *Retrieving Women's History,* ed. S.J. Kleinberg (Paris: UNESCO Press, 1992), 50. The essays by Perrot, A. Davin and J.W. Scott in this collection include useful discussions on sources for women's history.

2.   Blanca Silvestrini, *Women and Resistance: Herstory in Contemporary Caribbean History,* 1989 Elsa Goveia Memorial Lecture (Kingston, Jamaica: Department of History, University of the West Indies, 1990).

3.   P. Mohammed, "A Social History of Post-Migrant Indians in Trinidad from 1917 to 1947: A Gender Perspective" (PhD diss., Institute of Social Studies, The Hague, 1993), especially 52–68; see also Mohammed, "Structures of Experience: Gender, Ethnicity and Class in the Lives of Two East Indian Women", in *Trinidad Ethnicity,* ed. K. Yelvington (Knoxville: University of Tennessee Press, 1993), 208–34.

4.   E. Fox-Genovese, *Unspeakable Things Unspoken: Ghosts and Memories in the Narratives of Afro-American Women,* 1992 Elsa Goveia Memorial Lecture (Kingston, Jamaica: Department of History, University of the West Indies, 1993).

5.   J.W. Scott, "The Problem of Invisibility", in *Retrieving Women's History,* ed. S.J. Kleinberg (Paris: UNESCO Press, 1992), 47–49.

6.   A. Davin, "Redressing the Balance or Transforming the Art? The British Experience", in *Retrieving Women's History,* ed. S.J. Kleinberg (Paris: UNESCO Press, 1992), 70.

7.   See E. O'Callaghan, *Woman Version: Theoretical Approaches to West Indian Fiction by Women* (New York: St Martin's Press, 1993), 17–28.

8.   Mary Prince, *The History of Mary Prince a West Indian Slave: Related by Herself,* ed. Moira Ferguson (1831; reprint, London: Pandora Press, 1987); Mary Seacole, *The Wonderful Adventures of Mrs. Seacole in Many Lands,* ed. Z. Anderson and A. Dewjee (London: James Blackwood, 1857; reprint, London: Falling Wall Press, 1984); Y. Bridges, *Child of the Tropics: Victorian Memoirs,* ed. N. Guppy (London: Harvill Press, 1980); A. Mahase, *My Mother's Daughter: The Autobiography of Anna Mahase Snr. 1899–1978* (Claxton Bay, Trinidad: Royard Publishing, 1992); Olga Comma Maynard, *My Yesterdays* (Port of Spain, Trinidad: Granderson Bros., 1992). For comparison with Prince's text, see Harriet Jacobs, *Incidents in the Life of a Slave Girl, Written by Herself,* ed. Jean Fagan Yellin (1861; reprint, Cambridge: Harvard University Press, 1987). Jacobs was a former American slave.

9.   Maria Nugent, *Lady Nugent's Journal of Her Residence in Jamaica from 1801 to 1805,* ed. P. Wright (Kingston, Jamaica: Institute of Jamaica, 1966); unpublished diary of Amelia Gumbs Gomez 1841–43, typescript and notes by Michael Pocock; unpublished diary of Adella Archibald 1930–36, typescript by Gordon J. Archibald. I had intended to include Edna Manley's diaries, published in 1989. But they tell the life-story of such an extraordinary woman, who lived so much in the public sphere, that I found it difficult to incorporate them into this discussion.

10. A.F. Fenwick, ed., *The Fate of the Fenwicks: Letters to Mary Hays, 1798–1828* (London: Methuen, 1927), 161–217; S.E. Morton, *John Morton of Trinidad* (Toronto, 1916); unpublished letters by Susan Rawle, 1875–86, Rawle Mss. File 8, Correspondence, Trinidad, Rhodes House Library, University of Oxford.

11. Mohammed, "Social History", 66; Silvestrini, *Women and Resistance,* 16. For a perceptive discussion of this issue as it relates to oral history, see Mary Chamberlain, "Gender and Memory: Oral History and Women's History" (paper presented at Symposium on Engendering History, University of the West Indies, Mona, 1993).

12. Prince, *History of Mary Prince,* 47–48, 73; Seacole, *Wonderful Adventures of Mrs. Seacole,* 55–57. For the Jamaican tradition of brown and black women keeping hotels which doubled as nursing homes, see A. Josephs, "Mary Seacole: Jamaican Nurse and 'Doctress', 1805/10–1881", *Jamaican Historical Review* 17 (1991): 49–65.

13. Nugent, *Lady Nugent's Journal,* 146–47; Fenwick, *The Fate of the Fenwicks,* 200.

14. Fenwick, *The Fate of the Fenwicks,* 167–69, 191, 202; Nugent, *Lady Nugent's Journal,* 58; Bridges, *Child of the Tropics,* 97, 116–20, 157.

15. Mahase, *My Mother's Daughter,* 20–28, 32–34; Morton, *John Morton,* 343–49; Archibald, diary, for example, entries of 5 August 1930, 21 October 1930, 8 December 1930, 6 April 1931, 16 March 1932, 12 May 1932, 30 December 1933.

16. Maynard, *My Yesterdays,* 4, 43–48, 104, 108–11.

17. Nugent, *Lady Nugent's Journal,* 123–32,118–22, 174–79, 198–99.

18. Gomez, diary, entries of 14 September 1841, undated (probably October 1842), 8 January 1843, April 1843, 7 May 1843, 10 May 1843.

19. Prince, *History of Mary Prince,* 50–53, 74–75; Fox-Genovese, *Unspeakable Things,* 11.

20. Bridges, *Child of the Tropics,* 157–66; Seacole, *Wonderful Adventures of Mrs. Seacole,* 59–61, 100.

21. For this and the preceding paragraph, Mahase, *My Mother's Daughter,* 3–5, 11–20, 22–44; Morton, *John Morton,* 47–52; Archibald, diary, for example, entries of 4 July 1931, 17 March 1932; cf. Mohammed, "Social History", 152–53.

22. Nugent, *Lady Nugent's Journal,* 186, 59, 81; Fenwick, *The Fate of the Fenwicks,* 182–87, 196–97, 204, 171, 173–74, 193.

23. Morton, *John Morton,* 6–91, 138–40, 173–84; Rawle letters to her sister, 23 May 1882, 24 June 1882, 6 August 1882, 10 June 1886, 29 September 1886.

24. Fenwick, *The Fate of the Fenwicks,* 169–70. Fenwick's correspondent Mary Hays, a radical British writer, had published an antislavery novel, *The Memoirs of Emma Courtney,* in 1796. See Moira Ferguson, *Subject to Others: British Women Writers and Colonial Slavery, 1670–1834* (New York: Routledge, 1992), 194–96.

25. Nugent, *Lady Nugent's Journal,* 12, 29, 30, 68, 78, 86–87, 172–73, 214.

26. Prince, *History of Mary Prince,* 67–68, 71–74, 48.

27. Cf. O'Callaghan, *Woman Version,* 26–27.

28. Nugent, *Lady Nugent's Journal,* 11, 12, 243, 156, 80, 82, 59.

29. Fenwick, *The Fate of the Fenwicks,* 163–64, 167, 168, 175, 188–89; Gomez, diary, for example, entry of 16 April 1843.

30. Prince, *History of Mary Prince,* 52–60, 69–78.

31. Bridges, *Child of the Tropics,* 27, 32 ,46–64, 82, 181, 188–91, 112–13. A sensitive fictional portrayal of the madam-servant relationship in a French creole family very like that of Bridges can be found in *Witchbroom* (London: Heinemann 1992) by the Trinidadian writer Lawrence Scott.

32. Morton, *John Morton,* 42–49, 97, 157–58; Archibald, diary, for example, entries of 17 June 1931, 4 July 1931.

33. Maynard, *My Yesterdays,* 4–6, 79–80, 93–94, 100–104, 110, 115.

34. Gomez, diary, *passim;* Rawle to her sister, 6 April 1878, 23 May 1882, 5 September 1883; Morton, *John Morton,* 67, 83–84, 223–58, 340–54, 355.

35. Archibald, Diary, *passim;* quotation, entry of 10 September 1930.

36. Morton, *John Morton,* 257–58.

CHAPTER 12

Unspeakable Things Unspoken

Ghosts and Memories
in the Narratives of
African American Women

ELIZABETH FOX-GENOVESE

Everybody knew what she was called, but nobody anywhere knew her name. Disremembered and unaccounted for, she cannot be lost because no one is looking for her, and even if they were, how can they call her if they do not know her name? Although she has claim, she is not claimed. . . .

It was not a story to pass on. . . .

So they forgot her. Like an unpleasant dream during a troubling sleep. . . .

This was not a story to pass on.

The concluding pages of Toni Morrison's novel *Beloved*, from which the epigraph is taken, evoke the difficulty of telling the story of women's experience of slavery — of the cost of slavery for enslaved mothers and their children.[1] *Beloved*, the ghost of the murdered, "crawling already?" baby, remains not lost but disremembered and unaccounted for, because no one is even looking for her. The story of her murder by her own mother, which implicated slavery in its entirety, including the other members of the community of slaves, was not one that anyone – black or white, slave or free – chose to tell. So they forgot. And their forgetting, even more than the original event, becomes a story that cannot be passed on.

The woman's story of slavery has challenged historians no less than it has challenged novelists and autobiographers. Since the nineteenth century it has been common to assert that slavery was necessarily worse for women than for men, since they were subjected to special brutality and indignity on account of their sex. In general, however, historians have primarily focused upon the injustice and indignities of slavery for men. Those who defended the freedom of labour, soil and men readily identified the enslavement of men as a violation of the fundamental principles of individualism to which they were committed.[2] It is not that historians have lacked sympathy for the violation of women's sexuality, but that many have found it difficult to write of it from a subjective perspective – from the "inside".

Recent historians who have devoted most attention to understanding the history of African American slaves in the United States have written, in large measure, from a commitment to documenting and representing the strength and vitality of slave culture.[3] They have, accordingly, emphasized the slaves' commitment to marriage and family. At the extreme, Robert Fogel and Stanley Engerman have even argued that slaves developed and enforced a sense of family loyalty and sexual morality that remarkably resembled the values of their masters.[4] The recent debates among these and other historians have primarily concerned the respective elements of African and American culture that the slaves forged under adversity.

Yet more recently scholars such as Deborah White, who have focused explicitly on the experience of slave women, have more directly emphasized the sexual exploitation of slave women by white men, notably their masters. Yet even as White exposed and deplored the abuse of slave women's sexuality, she especially argued that the experience of slavery, combined with African traditions, led African American women to develop a greater sense of autonomy and independence than did their white contemporaries.[5] Thus even she did not explore the possible consequences of sexual exploitation for slave women's minds and hearts, much less their relations with the other members of the slave community.

While working on *Within the Plantation Household*, I came increasingly to believe that slavery had taken a higher toll upon the sexual relations of African American men and women than most of us were prepared to face. On this matter, even more than others, the evidence tended to be oblique, veiled, indirect. Through the disguises and reticences, it nonetheless seemed to me that there lurked a troubling story. Countless slave infants may indeed have died from Sudden Infant Death Syndrome, from disease, and from inadequate supplies of maternal milk, but some undetermined number also fell victim to infanticide. No less disturbing, it seemed clear that the sexual exploitation of black women by white men might poison those women's relations with the men of their own people who might, in all too human a fashion, turn their rage against the victim. As a result, in any given instance the most violent abusers of slave women's sexuality might be black rather than white men.

Given the paucity of direct evidence and my wish to respect the reticence of others, and perhaps even succumbing to a measure of cowardice, I decided to avoid extensive discussions of sexuality. African American slave women had not left extensive accounts of their objective lives, and I was loath to probe their silence. My decision was bolstered by the knowledge that even when those, like Harriet Jacobs, who had written of their personal experience, had written of extramarital sexual relations and of sexual exploitation, they had refrained from exposing what must have been the most painful aspect of their experience – their own dehumanization. For from a woman's perspective, the worst of sexual exploitation is never simply that "he" desired me and (perhaps violently) overpowered my resistance. The worst of sexual exploitation is that "he" treated me as a thing – not as a unique object of his desire, but as an indifferent object of his lust.

The appearance of Toni Morrison's novel *Beloved*, just as I was completing my own book, provided welcome assurance that I was not alone in what I thought I was discerning in the fragmentary sources. It further confirmed my deepest sense that if slavery had indeed been the oppressive system most of us believed it to have been, those who endured it could not have emerged unscathed. Notwithstanding my having had formal psychoanalytic training, and the high value I place upon the insights that psychoanalysis can contribute to the understanding of history and culture, I have always recoiled from – more properly resented – the mechanical use of psychoanalytic theory that treats other people as intellectual fodder for the analytic mind – that makes complex and sometimes troubled lives and motivations conform to someone else's rigid model. But my sense of the complexity of slave women's experience and of the extraordinary mixture of courage and frailty, anger and love their survival entailed continued to haunt me.

Recent years have brought thoughtful new attempts to map and circumscribe the activities of slave women and their central role within the community of slaves.[6] But even now, with more than a century of distance, it remains difficult, perhaps impossible, to recapture the subjective story of slave women's experience. In rare instances, as in the case of *Beloved*, fiction can powerfully supplement elusive psychological "facts". And so I turned to *Beloved* for a plausible, if imaginative, representation of the feelings of some women who endured slavery and, like Sethe, continued to bear its scars. Even more I turned to *Beloved* as itself a source for another history, namely the history of the elusiveness of women's experience of slavery until our own time. For *Beloved* is less the story that could not be passed on – the story that was impossible to tell – than it is the story of how the story that could not be passed on was forgotten and, to borrow from psychoanalytic language, the reasons for which it was repressed.

Although slave women, like slave men, suffered oppression as labourers, some of their coerced labour permitted them to develop skills and expertise in which they could take the pride of craft. Even hard monotonous labour, which did not permit such development, did not necessarily inflict lasting scars on the slaves' sense of themselves.[7] But as women – as sexual partners and mothers – they confronted a constant threat. The culture of domesticity and separate spheres that prevailed in the non-slave, and even in modified form in the slave, states during the mid-nineteenth century emphasized women's purity as sexual beings and their selfless devotion as mothers. No less important, it steadfastly repudiated women's sexual passion and, perhaps even more, their anger.[8]

African cultures were generally less obsessive about women's sexual purity, although they did favour marital fidelity, but they placed high value upon children and upon women's roles as mothers. So even if African American slave women were not normally predisposed to take the cult of sexual purity very seriously and even if their circumstances too frequently permitted their observing it, they *were* strongly predisposed to take their roles as mothers and their responsibilities to their children as seriously as their circumstances permitted. And the sources movingly attest that they took the separation of a mother from one or more of her children as a slave holder's ultimate violation both of the system's professed values and of his minimal responsibilities.

Before emancipation the majority of slave women, being illiterate, had virtually no opportunity to write of their outrage at the violation of their sexuality and, especially, their motherhood. In the measure that committed free white women wrote of it for them, they invariably wrote in their own idiom of domesticity.[9] We know, from occasional accounts in the narratives of former slaves, that they spoke of their outrage to each other. But the narratives collected during the 1930s from those who had been children during slavery times could only tell of the outrage at a generational remove. As the African American community reconstructed itself following the Civil War, it too tended to adopt the idiom of domesticity, perhaps less out of conviction than as a defence of respectability, and from a wish to hide their scars from the curiosity of outsiders.[10]

All of the stories we tell depend heavily upon the ways in which stories have previously been told. Not surprisingly, the story of baby killing has had limited possibilities. Most commonly it has taken the form of a cautionary tale, closely associated with the horrors of war. That evil men kill babies serves to underscore their malignant overreaching of the boundaries of civilized exist-ence. Think of King Herod. And if men who kill babies in the public arena evoke horror, how much more so do women who kill them under the veil of domestic privacy? And if women in general, what of mothers in particular?[11] Medea has not been easy to inscribe in conventional images of motherhood.

All cultures have valued motherhood, but nineteenth-century bourgeois culture raised it to unprecedented heights of sentimentality and thus made it especially difficult for women to tell stories about its dangers and conflicts. Bourgeois idealization of mothers' natural inclinations for nurture and self-sacrifice virtually prohibited women from writing realistically of motherhood from a subjective stance. Or to put it differently, the sanctity that shrouded the conventions of motherhood virtually dictated that women would have to embrace prescribed motherly feelings when writing of their own emotions and experience. Occasionally a female author would touch upon a woman's possible resentment of, or failure at, motherhood by including an explicitly bad mother, but this projection would not include an empathetic exploration of the unfortunate woman's feelings. More frequently, one might write of an orphaned girl whose situation would permit an indirect exploration of women's feelings about motherhood.[12]

As for motherhood, so for sexuality. It is difficult to find a proper nine-teenth-century woman who wrote forthrightly of desiring sexual relations. To be sure, bourgeois women's limited experience narrowed the topics of which they could write with authority. But even more than women's limited experience – since women did, felt and especially knew many more things than they were acknowledged as doing, feeling and knowing – the conventions of women's narratives hedged women in. Thus even the most daring women writers found it difficult, if not impossible, to explore those aspects of women's subjective experience that frontally challenged narrative conventions of womanhood.

That the experience of female slaves openly mocked the conventions was not lost on all white women. During the late antebellum period many American women, notably Harriet Beecher Stowe, and Harriet Jacobs, began to insist that slavery indeed extracted an especially heavy price from women – that the evils of slavery ran so deep as to threaten the most sacred domestic bonds and virtues. In *Incidents in the Life of a Slave Girl,* Harriet Jacobs unambiguously insisted that if slavery is terrible for men, "it is far more terrible for women. Superadded to the burden common to all, *they* have wrongs, and sufferings, and mortifications peculiarly their own."[13]

Jacobs has primarily, and deservedly, been appreciated for her brave and perhaps unique account of slavery from a woman's perspective.[14] Jacobs, possibly following Stowe's example, left her readers no doubt that she was indicting slavery as a social system. Not least, she insisted, the evil of slavery made it impossible to judge a slave woman by the standards to which free women were held – "the slave woman ought not to be judged by the same standard as others" (p. 56). Yet even Jacobs never unambiguously stated that slavery made it impossible for women to be good mothers. In her narrative she tried to expose the aspects of slavery that made it impossible for slave women to conform to prevailing standards, but she remained reticent about slave women's personal motivations. Attentive readers can easily recognize that the anger instilled by her personal experience frequently threatens to explode her narrative, but only indirectly and without ever fully disrupting the conventions within which she deemed it prudent to write.

Accepting the dominant discourse of womanhood and motherhood as normative, Jacobs, who candidly admitted to having had children by a man to whom she was not married, attempted to justify her actions as the product of her inescapable circumstances. Thus *Incidents,* which superficially accepts northeastern, middle-class female norms and simply asks forgiveness for her inability to conform to them, on another level suggests that the norms entirely miss the realities of slave women's experience. Jacobs's anger obviously derived from her outrage at a social system the logic of which was to reduce a woman to a thing – from her own refusal to be treated as a thing. But it may also have derived from her recognition that there was no way that she could candidly tell her story, for there was no way that she could publicly admit to having been treated like a thing.

In acknowledging the impossibility of telling her real story, Jacobs presumably made a calculated judgment about the expectations of her prospective readers, shrewdly determining that it was better to meet those expectations than not to be read at all. And she assuredly could not have expected a sympathetic reading – perhaps not any reading at all – had she not respected the most cherished myths of those she hoped to reach. By the time Jacobs published *Incidents*, antislavery women, like Stowe herself, were insisting that slavery's greatest evil lay in its violation of domestic relations. But by the same stroke, antislavery women had also ensconced their own standards of motherhood and womanly virtue as the ultimate justification for opposition to slavery.

Stowe had mapped the imaginative universe into which Jacobs apparently felt obliged to write her own story. The strength of Stowe's vision lay in her uncompromising insistence that, as the systematization of absolute power, slavery corrupted everyone it touched – made it impossible for anyone to be a good person. Jacobs unquestionably concurred in Stowe's indictment, but nonetheless found it impossible to press her understanding to its bitterest and most naked conclusions. It is not difficult, as I have argued elsewhere, to demonstrate that Jacobs's text may more profitably be read as the account of her direct contest with the power of her master than as the remorseful confession of her fall from virtue.[15] But even as she permits us to doubt that the protection of womanly virtue ranks as her primary concern, she attempts to strengthen free white women's identification with her feelings of motherhood.

The hard truth is that there are feelings that Jacobs could not share with her readers and maintain their identification and respect. Notwithstanding her evocation of the support and assistance that her protagonist, Linda Brent, received from other women, she tellingly distances Linda from the mass of slave women whose plight she purportedly embodied. Jacobs thus represents Linda Brent and the members of her immediate family as speaking in the purest English, while representing other slaves as speaking in dialect. For similar reasons, she relegates her harshest examples of slave holders' brutality, notably the sexual exploitation of slave women, to cases of which Linda Brent has heard but has not personally experienced. Jacobs never shows Linda as beaten or raped, as dirty or disfigured. She never describes her as scantily clad or even as calloused. The scratches she receives derive from the difficulties of her escape, not from the degradation of her everyday life. Above all, the persecution she endures never seriously compromises her membership in a recognizable narrative, never pushes her literally beyond the pale of civilized discourse.

For understandable reasons, Jacobs sought the identification of her readers, sought to convince them to accept her as a woman like themselves. No wonder, then, that she introduces the worst specific abuses of slavery as reports rather than as subjective experiences. How could she have been expected to do otherwise? If rather than representing Linda Brent – and by implication herself – as the object of corrupt male desire, she had represented her as the victim of indiscriminate lust, she would have reduced her to that status as thing to which the logic of chattel slavery pointed. And she would thereby have decisively undercut her own claims to empathy and respect. Worse, to do so would have forced her to acknowledge that, through the eyes of Dr Flint, Linda Brent was little more than an animal – one occasion among many for the casual satisfaction of his lust.

Accordingly Jacobs's protagonist, Linda Brent, experiences little that an unfortunate free white protagonist might not have experienced, and, in the measure that she does, the experience remains abstract.[16] Even when slavery exposes Linda Brent to the threat of separation from her children, loss of the power to determine their fates, and even the possibility of their being sold away from her, her role as mother remains intact. She conveys the assaults, which might easily have been taken to compromise her identity as mother, in the most conventional bourgeois idiom. Thus Jacobs, even as she harshly indicts slavery for its violation of the minimal norms of womanhood, especially motherhood, sustains the prevailing fictions about women's innate feelings of virtue and mother love. She cannot bring herself to represent the full corruption of slavery lest that attempted representation erase her entirely from an acceptable plot. Her goal remains to indict slavery for its violation of womanly virtue and motherhood, while leaving the identity of the virtuous woman and mother intact. In Jacobs's account slavery prohibits slave women from behaving as they would want to behave, but it does not penetrate, much less permanently scar, the inner reaches of their hearts and minds.

Tellingly, Jacobs represents Linda Brent as revering the memory of her own mother, whom she barely knew. "When I was six years old, my mother died; and then, by the talk around me, I learned that I was a slave" (p. 6). Everyone spoke warmly of her mother, "who had been a slave merely in name, but in nature was noble and womanly" (p. 7). When, years later, Linda Brent enters the church for the baptism of her children, "recollections of my mother came over me, and I felt subdued in spirit" (p. 78).[17] Subsequently, at the moment of her flight, Linda Brent visits her mother's grave. "I had," she remembers, "received my mother's blessing when she died; and in many an hour of tribulation I had seemed to hear her voice, sometimes chiding me, sometimes whispering loving words into my wounded heart" (p. 90). And it grieves her to think that "when I am gone from my children they cannot remember me with such entire satisfaction as I remembered my mother" (p. 90).

It seems likely that Jacobs has reshaped Linda Brent's memories of her mother for narrative purposes, although a child who loses her mother at six may well not remember much. More important, such comforting memories serve the important mission of sustaining the ideal of motherhood among a people whose circumstances frequently threatened the reality. The interviews with former slaves collected during the 1930s abound with recollections of mothers, which, for painfully obvious reasons, significantly outnumber those of fathers. Many of those who had been children during the final years of slavery fondly remembered their mothers' skills as cooks or weavers, specific acts of kindness, or their general devotion to their children. Many others allowed that they could not remember their mothers, who had died or run off when the children were young.[18] As best we can tell, most slaves had a strong bias in favour of emphasizing the strength of mothers' love for their children under what were too often dishearteningly difficult circumstances.

Thus from the midst of shattered families and in the absence of legal protection for the most basic family ties, slaves and former slaves fashioned a collective memory of the resilience and devotion of mothers. But whatever the accuracy of the memory in individual cases, its collective version coexisted with the unsettling knowledge that slavery could lead individual women to behave in ways that might indeed be considered unmotherly. The former slave Lou Smith recalled that her mother had told her of a woman whose master had sold her first three children before they were three years old. It broke her heart that she was not allowed to keep them and, after the birth of her fourth child, she determined to forestall its sale herself. "She just studied all the time about how she would have to give it up", and decided that she would not. So one day she "got up and give it something out of a bottle and pretty soon it was dead".[19] At what may be presumed to have been a devastating cost to herself, that slave mother had enforced her right to define herself as mother, not as breeder.

Orlando Patterson has argued that the essence of enslavement lies in condemning those who suffer it to social death. Slavery severs the ties that bind people into society, effectively leaving isolate individuals to fend for themselves. Slavery denies the enslaved the right to establish and enforce social identities, including family identities, and also minimizes their possibilities (which is not exactly the same thing) of doing so.[20] We know that in the Americas the latitude that slaves enjoyed or seized to sustain their own families and communities varied considerably from one slave society to another. As a rule, the greater the ratio of slaves to free people, and the greater the ratio of blacks to whites (again, not exactly the same thing), the stronger the elements of African culture remained and the greater the opportunities that slaves enjoyed to sustain *de facto* community relations, including marriages.[21] But even under the most favourable conditions, the absence of legally sanctioned marriage left the sexuality and motherhood of slave women vulnerable.

The inherent violence of slavery in this regard appears to have been most intense and most fraught with contradiction in the slave society of the southern United States. For there the ratio of blacks to whites was lowest, the rate of reproduction was highest, the survival of African culture was most precarious, and the influence of bourgeois culture was greatest. Consider the implications of this situation. By the first quarter of the nineteenth century, slave importations had virtually ceased, many slaves had embraced aspects of Protestant Christianity, and African American reproduction was steadily increasing. Increasingly for the slaves of the southern United States such marriage as was possible embodied bourgeois rather than African norms, which slave holders as well as slaves sought to promote. The self-respect and Christian concerns of southern slave holders as a class depended heavily on their promotion of the idea of slave marriage, even when economic fluctuations or simple convenience might lead any given slave holder to break up marriages by sale. Similarly, the self-respect of southern slave holders precluded a crass view of slave women as mere breeders, although we know that many valued the natural increase of their slaves for economic reasons.

Both slave holders and slaves had their own reasons to promote a version of the bourgeois ideal of domesticity and motherhood for African American slaves. Both also knew that the reality remained so fragile as frequently to look like a hypocritical fiction. The precise blend of black African and white bourgeois values in the slaves' minds and identities will always remain elusive. But the evidence is strong that throughout the first six decades of the nineteenth century the force of the bourgeois ideals of marriage and motherhood steadily grew. It is at least clear that following the Civil War innumerable former slaves struggled mightily to ensure those ideals for themselves, which suggests that they had, in important ways, claimed them as their own. Clearly, this commitment to the ideals informed the way in which Harriet Jacobs wrote of a woman's experience of slavery. No less clearly, the commitment deterred her from a forthright subjective description of the horrible costs of slavery for a woman whom the realities of slavery continuously exposed to being stripped of all the conventional attributes of domesticity and motherhood.

More than a century after the appearance of *Incidents in the Life of a Slave Girl,* Toni Morrison, in *Beloved,* explicitly reopened the discussion of how to tell the story of women's experience of slavery. Gone is the gentility that dominates the tone of *Incidents.* None of the former slaves whose stories make up the novel speak in the conventions of domestic fiction, or even in standard English. Drawing upon references, images and figures of speech that derive from southern black culture as Morrison envisions it, their words evoke a distinct social, cultural and material universe. In sharp contrast to *Incidents, Beloved* anchors the experience of the slave mother in the horrifying tangible indignities of slavery. It is as if the examples of abuse from which Jacobs had so carefully distanced Linda Brent had come to life. No longer things that happen to others, the atrocities that slavery can perpetrate have become things that happen to you or me.

As a novel rather than a confessional narrative, *Beloved* does not present the harrowing events that occurred at 124 Bluestone Road or the history of the house's inhabitants through a single consciousness, but rather successively shows various characters' perceptions of them.[22] In the end, *Beloved* figures less as the story of a former slave woman who killed her own child than as the story of a community's rememory (to borrow Morrison's word) of that killing and of the events that led up to it and, especially, of the ways of telling unspeakable things. *Beloved* is a novel about personal and collective history. Like *Incidents, Beloved* embodies an attempt to come to terms with the legacy of slavery or, to put it differently, the attempt of former slaves finally to break slavery's shackles. But where *Incidents* had preserved the mantle of bourgeois discretion, thus effectively neutralizing the very horrors it sought to mobilize opposition against, *Beloved* lays the horrors bare, inviting readers to confront the ways in which slavery ate into the consciousness of all of those it touched.

Although the narrative of *Beloved* is infinitely complex, the story is chillingly simple. It is the story of a group of slaves who had, in the 1850s, lived on the Sweet Home plantation in Kentucky. When the slave holder, Mr Garner, died, Sweet Home had been bought by Schoolteacher, who rapidly made life for the slaves intolerable. Eventually the main character, Sethe, young mother of three and expecting a fourth, escapes to join her mother-in-law, Baby Suggs, in Cincinnati. En route she gives birth to the child, a girl whom she names Denver. Some time after Sethe's arrival at Baby Suggs's house at 124 Bluestone Road, Schoolteacher appears with a small band of men (the four horsemen) to reclaim his property. Sethe, recognizing his hat, flees to the woodshed, kills her oldest daughter, and is about to kill the other children when Stamp Paid, another former slave, stops her.

Such is the prehistory of the events of the novel, which begin in the early 1870s when Paul D, another former Sweet Home slave, arrives at 124. Just as he and Sethe begin to build a free love, Beloved, who is apparently the ghost of Sethe's oldest daughter, arrives and turns all of their lives inside out. The novel concludes with Beloved's departure and Sethe's acceptance by her world – Denver, the women of the black community, and Paul D, who gently tells her, "me and you, we got more yesterday than anybody. We need some kind of tomorrow." He then insists, "You your best thing, Sethe. You are."[23]

The core of *Beloved* lies in Sethe's murder of her cherished, "crawling already?" baby – the still nursing, not-yet-two-year-old girl, for whom she had braved nearly inconceivable horrors in order to provide the milk of her own breasts, which the baby needed to survive. "Why I did it. How if I hadn't killed her she would have died and that is something I could not bear to happen to her" (p. 200). Throughout *Beloved,* Morrison returns time and again to slavery's implacable war against motherhood. Baby Suggs bore eight children and was stripped of them all – "four taken, four chased, and all, I expect, worrying somebody's house into evil" (p. 5). Approaching death, she can remember only that her first-born loved the burned bottom of bread. "Can you beat that? Eight children and that's all I remember" (p. 5).

Sethe reproaches her own mother for never having let her be a daughter. A daughter is what she wanted to be "and would have been if my ma'am had been able to get out of the rice long enough before they hanged her and let me be one" (p. 203). Sethe's ma'am had had the bit so many times that she always smiled, but Sethe "never saw her own smile" (p. 203). Eventually she was caught and hanged, but Sethe did not know why or what she was doing. She could not have been running, "because she was my ma'am and nobody's ma'am would run off and leave her daughter would she?" (p. 203). But then how would Sethe know about a ma'am who had only suckled her daughter for a week or two and then left her in the yard with a one-armed woman who had to nurse the white babies first and frequently did not have enough left over for Sethe? "There was no nursing milk to call my own" (p. 200). She would never allow that to happen to any daughter of hers. Beloved had to understand that Sethe had cut her own daughter's throat precisely to ensure that she could be a daughter – that Sethe could be a mother.

The figure of Sethe standing in the woodshed, dripping with the blood of the murdered baby girl whose body she will not relinquish, offering her blood-dripping nipple to the surviving infant, challenges any recognizable image of motherhood. Schoolteacher, the leader of the four white horsemen who have come to return her to slavery, sees only "a nigger woman holding a blood-soaked child to her chest with one hand and an infant by the heels in the other". Never turning to look at the invaders, "she simply swung the baby toward the wall planks, missed and tried to connect a second time", while two bleeding boys lay in the sawdust at her feet (p. 149). Schoolteacher, who was not looking for a mother, saw none. He saw nothing there to claim at all. He saw only a woman gone wild, "due to the mishandling of the nephew who'd overbeat her and made her cut and run". The same nephew, although Schoolteacher does not see the connection, who back at Sweet Home, had held her down and stolen the milk she was saving for her baby girl (p. 149). Schoolteacher had tried. He "had chastised the nephew, telling him to think – just think – what would his own horse do if you beat it past the point of education. Or Chipper, or Samson. Suppose you beat the hounds past that point thataway" (p. 149).

Small wonder that Schoolteacher, seeing Sethe as a breeder, a skilful ironer of shirts, a maker of excellent ink, cannot understand her motivations. For him she is a domesticated animal to be handled and, if mishandled, should be expected to go wild. It would not cross his mind that her excesses could result from the violation of her humanity and the denial of her mother's love. Paul D, who had his own knowledge of the worst that slavery had to offer, who had known Sethe at Sweet Home, and who had loved her there and at 124, is another matter. Confronted by Stamp Paid with the newspaper account of Sethe's action, Paul D refuses to believe that the woman who killed her baby could be Sethe. "That ain't her mouth" (p. 154). "You forgetting," Paul D told Stamp Paid, "I knew her before. . . . Back in Kentucky. When she was a girl . . . I been knowing her a long time. And I can tell you for sure: this ain't her mouth. May look like it, but it ain't" (p. 158). And Stamp Paid himself, looking at the "sweet conviction" in Paul D's eyes, almost wonders if it really happened, if eighteen years ago, "while he and Baby Suggs were looking the wrong way, a pretty little slave girl had recognized a hat, and split to the woodshed to kill her children" (p. 158).

Paul D never asks Sethe directly if she killed her baby; he merely confronts her with the newspaper clipping, implicitly asking her to tell him that the woman it describes is not her. Showing it to her he smiles, ready for her to "burst out laughing at the joke – the mix-up of her face put where some other colored woman's ought to be" (p. 161). It may have been his smile or "the ever-ready love she saw in his eyes" that made her try to explain. Her trying led her back to Sweet Home, about which she did not have to tell him, and to what he may not have known, "what it was like for me to get away from there" (p. 161). For the getting away was her own doing. "Me having to look out. Me using my own head" (p. 162). And it was also more: "It was a kind of selfishness I never knew nothing about before. It felt good. Good and right" (p. 162). It was a selfishness that allowed her to love her children more than she ever had before. "Or maybe I couldn't love em proper in Kentucky because they wasn't mine to love." When she got to Ohio, a free woman, "there wasn't nobody in the world I couldn't love if I wanted to" (p. 162).

That Paul D could understand all too well. For him, slavery had meant the necessity to protect yourself and love small. Under slavery you picked "the tiniest stars out of the sky to own" so that your love would not be competing with that of the men who owned the guns. "Brass blades, salamanders, spiders, woodpeckers, beetles, a kingdom of ants. Anything bigger wouldn't do. A woman, a child, a brother – a big love like that would split you wide open in Alfred, Georgia." Oh yes, Paul D "knew exactly what she meant: to get to a place where you could love anything you chose – not to need permission for desire – well, now, *that* was freedom" (p. 162). Threatened with the loss of that freedom, Sethe explained to Paul D, "I took and put my babies where they'd be safe" (p. 163). The "safe" shakes Paul D, who knows it is precisely what 124 had been lacking when he arrived, who thought he had made it safe, and who thought that if Sethe her own self had not it was because she could not.

Sethe's definition of her murder as assuring her baby's safety shows Paul D how wrong he has been. "This here Sethe was new. . . . This here Sethe talked about love like any other woman; talked about baby clothes like any other woman, but what she meant could cleave the bone. This here Sethe talked about safety with a handsaw. This here new Sethe didn't know where the world stopped and she began" (p. 164). All of a sudden, Paul D could see what Stamp Paid had wanted him to see: "More important than what Sethe had done was what she claimed. It scared him" (p. 164). Paul D tells Sethe that her love is too thick, that what she did did not work. It did work, Sethe counters. How, Paul D queries, can she calculate that? Both her boys have run off, one of her girls is dead, and the other will not leave the yard. "They ain't at Sweet Home. Schoolteacher ain't got em" (p. 165). Maybe, Paul D responds, there is worse. "It ain't my job to know what's worse. It's my job to know what is and to keep them away from what I know is terrible. I did that" (p. 165). But what she did, Paul D insists, is wrong, there could have been some other way. And when she asks what way, without stopping to think he rejoins, "You got two feet, Sethe, not four" (p. 165).

No more than Schoolteacher can Paul D understand Sethe's motivations and, to the extent that he can understand something, he ultimately shares Schoolteacher's view of Sethe's deed as the deed of an animal. In his eyes Sethe's desperate act of claiming her motherhood, her children and her love for them shatters the boundaries between self and other, between self and the world. What Sethe sees as her ultimate act of self-definition, Paul D can only see as an act of madness. Frightened like her sons Howard and Buglar, who survived her murderous attack but ran away from home as soon as they were old enough, he leaves, leaving 124 to Sethe, Denver and Beloved, and the three women to each other. Stamp Paid, having suffered the pain of knocking and not gaining entrance, left 124 to its own devices and the women inside it "free at last to be what they liked, see whatever they saw and say whatever was on their minds". But behind the freedom of their words, which Stamp Paid could recognize if not decipher, lurked their thoughts, "unspeakable thoughts, unspoken" (p. 199).

From the start of the novel, we know that 124 is inhabited by the ghost of a murdered baby. No sooner than Paul D reappears after eighteen years, bathes Sethe's scarred back and moves into her bed, takes Sethe and Denver to the carnival and begins to rebuild a family at 124, does Beloved herself reappear as a material presence. Entrancing, demanding, seductive, Beloved gradually wreaks her revenge by consuming Sethe's life – by confronting Sethe with a love as totally demanding as that which led Sethe to kill her baby. Beloved, the ghost-become-presence, defies any neat interpretation. But complexities notwithstanding, she must in part be understood as a narrative device that Morrison saw as necessary to telling the story she wanted to tell. Beloved embodies some essential residue of the experience of all the other characters, embodies the parts of the story that still cannot be told – the unspeakable thoughts unspoken.

For Sethe, Beloved is the daughter who has come back to her. "She mine. See. She come back to me of her own free will and I don't have to explain a thing" (p. 200). Beloved is the child whom she can tell of Sweet Home, to whom she can talk of the things that Denver does not want to hear. For Denver, Beloved "is my sister. I swallowed her blood right along with my mother's milk. . . . Ever since I was little she was my company and she helped me wait for my daddy." Denver loves her mother, but knows "she killed one of her own daughters, and tender as she is with me, I'm scared of her because of it" (p. 205). Denver knows that there is something in her mother "that makes it all right to kill her own". And she constantly fears that "the thing that happened that made it all right for my mother to kill my sister could happen again" (p. 205). Denver does not know and does not want to know what that thing might be. She only knows that it comes from outside 124, and so she never leaves the house, carefully watching over the years "so it can't happen again and my mother won't have to kill me too" (p. 165). More frightening yet, maybe "the thing that makes it all right to kill her children" is still in her mother (p. 206).

The ghost of the victim – the name on the tombstone of the victim – of an infanticide prompted by too-thick love, Beloved is the custodian of the story that was not to be passed on. Her arrival at 124 signals her refusal to lay it down and get on with things. Nothing can be laid down or got on with until the story is told. The story belongs to no one person but to them all – the folks from Sweet Home who made it to 124. Baby Suggs feared that the murder had occurred because of the Sweet Home escapees' too great arrogance about their freedom. Twenty days after Sethe's safe arrival, Baby Suggs had given a party for ninety people who "ate so well, and laughed so much, it made them angry" (p. 136). So when they awoke the next morning the odour of their disapproval at what they took to be Baby Suggs's overstepping hung in the air, masking the odour of the "dark and coming thing" that was the four horsemen in pursuit of Sethe (p. 138). Had it not been for the party, Baby Suggs worried, might they not have recognized the threat soon enough to take steps to avert it?

Baby Suggs's worries link Sethe's infanticide to the free black community. Sethe's and Paul D's memories link it to Sweet Home and, beyond Sweet Home, to slavery as a social system. For Paul D fully corroborates Sethe's fragmented account of life at Sweet Home, demonstrating that we should not mistrust her memories. It was that bad. In fact, under Schoolteacher it was so bad as to cast doubt upon their belief that it had really been any better under the Garners. The issue is not a good or a bad master. The issue is slavery. And a slavery that leaves the definition of men to the goodwill of a master, rather than to the identity of the men themselves, is also a slavery that destroys the definition of women – especially mothers. Sethe, having barely known her own mother and lacking the companion-ship of other women, knew nothing of the practices of mothering. But by the time she arrived at 124, she knew that her very identity depended upon her children's being absolutely hers.

There are strong reasons to accept Sethe's infanticide as a desperate act of self-definition: by claiming her child absolutely, she claimed her identity as a mother, not a breeder. But in grounding her defence of her identity as a mother in the murder of her own child, she opened up new possibilities of being viewed as an animal. The responses of Denver and Paul D, like the absence of Howard and Buglar, remind us that Sethe's self-definition was also the "crawling already?" baby's murder. Was it a thing outside or a thing inside that made Sethe do what she did? Was slavery an external force or an internal presence? By giving Beloved a consciousness, however briefly and elliptically, Morrison seems to suggest that we cannot entirely cast the murder of a baby as an act of heroic, if tormented, resistance. By peopling Beloved's consciousness with memories that evoke the slave ships of the middle passage, she seems to suggest that we cannot entirely divorce the murder of this baby from the slavery that shaped its murdering mother's life.

In her own way, Harriet Jacobs insisted that slavery corrupted everyone it touched. But in sternly repressing her most painful personal angers, she left the impression that it affected behaviour more than identity. Linda Brent's personal war with slavery, as embodied in her master, left her identity as mother largely intact, blemished only by a few understandable lapses. Significantly, her daughter seems almost bemused that her mother feels obliged to ask her forgiveness. Morrison, in contrast, shows slavery as cutting to the quick of Sethe's innermost being – as jeopardizing any possibility of even beginning to sort out rights and wrongs. And the anger that Jacobs cloaks with a veneer of respectable discourse emerges in *Beloved* as the unquietable rage of the murdered "crawling already?" baby girl, whose ghost also embodies the boundary-obliterating love that joins mother and child.

The parallels between the two narratives bridge the chilling and the reassuring, leaving us only with the certainty that each embodies a different way of telling an impossible story. Slavery's contempt for the humanity of motherhood corrupted everyone it touched – black and white, slave and free, female and male. Jacobs could only begin to hint at the elements of the story, steadfastly distancing her protagonist from personal experience of the most searing pain and humiliation. Morrison bravely attempted to capture the subjective perspective – to tell the story that was not fit for passing on and to explain the story of the forgetting. But to do so even she had to create a ghost, since memory alone demonstrably would not serve.

Throughout American slave societies mothers have enjoyed a special place in humanizing a too-frequently dehumanizing social system, in standing as the last bastion against the full horror of social death. Many have chosen to see the predominance of mothers in different African American communities as a sign of pathology or social breakdown. From another perspective, mothers constituted the last bastion against the evil that slavery could wreak. And the power to define and defend motherhood emerged as the battleground over the irreducible minimum of the slaves' social identities. In that struggle it understandably appeared threatening to expose the worst horrors, for fear that they would confirm the worst consequences of enslavement. From this perspective, slavery's power to define motherhood becomes the power to define the slaves' humanity, and the slaves' power to defy the definition becomes the cornerstone of collective resistance. What, then, to do with the ghosts – the "unspeakable thing unspoken"? For Harriet Jacobs the risks of speaking were too high. But in the hands of Toni Morrison the speaking of unspeakable thoughts has emerged as the necessary recovery of a buried history – the cornerstone of a new resistance.

Thus Morrison, in the frontispiece to *Beloved,* quotes Romans 9:25: "I will call them my people, which were not my people; and her beloved, which was not beloved." Beloved, the ghost, acquired her name at the moment of her burial when Sethe had to provide a name for the tombstone of the "crawling already?" baby girl who had had no name in life. Her choice resulted from her having loved the words of the minister at the funeral service, "Dearly beloved, we are gathered together . . . ". Had that baby been killed in the name of the too-thick love that sought to put her beyond the claims of slavery, or had she been sacrificed to her mother's fierce determination to define her own identity as a mother? In the end the choice is no choice at all, for the baby died, her ghost born as a result of the intertwining of both.

Sethe had grown up with the knowledge that a mother's love and behaviour did not always observe the conventions that enshrined it. Had she not insisted that her own mother could not have been running away when she was killed, for no little girl's mother would run away and leave her? And does not the reader, like some part of Sethe herself, know that running away was precisely what her mother was doing? If slavery did make it almost impossible for women to be mothers then, in the measure that they could not, the children and frequently the children's children suffered the consequences. The horror of slavery, Morrison seems to be saying, lies in the intractability of two opposing truths: mothers might murder their own babies out of love and in an act of resistance, but that expression of love and of resistance nonetheless resulted in the extinction of a baby they had suckled and loved. There is no easy way to construct a vision of humanity out of the murder of children – especially one's own children. Only by telling the real story – by refusing the superficially ennobling conventions and relinquishing the pretension that the inequities of slavery as a social system left the hearts and minds of the enslaved untouched – would it be possible to reclaim an impossible past as the foundation for a possible future. Only by exposing their scars could African Americans as a people expose the full costs of the oppression they had suffered.

Notes

1. Toni Morrison, *Beloved* (New York: Plume, 1987).
2. Eric Foner, *Free Soil, Free Labor, Free Men: The Ideology of the Republican Party before the Civil War* (New York: Oxford University Press, 1970); Frederick Douglass, *Life and Times of Frederick Douglass: Written by Himself* (1892; reprint, New York: Collier Books, 1962); Frederick Douglass, *My Bondage and My Freedom* (New York, 1866); Frederick Douglass, *Narrative of the Life of Frederick Douglass, an American Slave, Written by Himself* (1845; reprint, New York: New American Library, 1968); Robert W. Fogel, *Without Consent or Contract: The Rise and Fall of American Slavery* (New York: Norton, 1988).
3. Eugene D. Genovese, *Roll Jordan Roll: The World the Slaves Made* (New York: Pantheon Books, 1974); Herbert G. Gutman, *The Black Family in Slavery and Freedom, 1750–1925* (New York: Pantheon Books, 1976); Lawrence Levine, *Black Culture and Black Consciousness: Afro-American Folk Thought from Slavery to Freedom* (New York: Oxford University Press, 1977); John W. Blassingame, *The Slave Community: Plantation Life in the Antebellum South,* ed., rev. and enl. (New York: Oxford University Press, 1979); George P. Rawick, *From Sundown to Sunup: The Making of the Black Community* (Westport: Greenwood, 1972). For a critique of the tendency to romanticize the strength of slave families and communities, see Peter Kolchin, "Reevaluating the Antebellum Slave Community: A Comparative Perspective", *Journal of American History* 70, no. 3 (December 1983): 579–601; and Elizabeth Fox-Genovese, *Within the Plantation Household: Black and White Women of the Old South* (Chapel Hill: University of North Carolina Press, 1988), especially chapter 6.
4. Robert W. Fogel and Stanley L. Engerman, *Time on the Cross: The Economics of American Negro Slavery,* 2 vols. (Boston: Little, Brown, 1974).
5. Deborah G. White, *Ar'n't I a Woman? Female Slaves in the Plantation South* (New York: Norton, 1985).
6. Lucille Mathurin, *The Rebel Woman in the British West Indies during Slavery* (Kingston, Jamaica: Institute of Jamaica, 1975); Hilary McD. Beckles, *Natural Rebels: A Social History of Enslaved Black Women in Barbados* (New Brunswick: Rutgers University Press, 1989); Barbara Bush, *Slave Women in Caribbean Society 1650–1838* (Bloomington: Indiana University Press, 1990); Marietta Morrissey, *Slave Women in the New World: Gender Stratification in the Caribbean* (Lawrence: University Press of Kansas, 1989).
7. Fox-Genovese, *Within the Plantation Household,* especially chapter 3.
8. On the repudiation of passion, see Nancy Cott, "Passionlessness: An Interpretation of Victorian Sexual Ideology, 1790–1850", *Signs* 4, no. 2 (Winter 1978): 219–36. For recent evaluations of the extensive discussions of

separate spheres, see Linda Kerber, "Separate Spheres, Female Worlds, Women's Place: The Rhetoric of Women's History", *Journal of American History* 75, no. 1 (June 1988): 9–39; and Elizabeth Fox-Genovese, *Within the Plantation Household,* chapter 1, and *Feminism without Illusions, passim.* It has long seemed to me (again, on the basis of psychoanalytic theory) that the ideology's repudiation of women's anger was at least as important as its repression of women's sexuality. Close attention to the experience of slave women helps to illuminate the point.

9.   The most celebrated example is obviously Harriet Beecher Stowe, *Uncle Tom's Cabin, Or, Life Among the Lowly,* ed. Ann Douglass (1852; reprint, New York: Modern Library, 1996).

10.   Barbara McCaskill, " 'Eternity for Telling': Topological Traditions in Afro-American Women's Literature" (PhD diss., Emory University, 1988); George Rawick, ed., *The American Slave: A Composite Autobiography,* 19 vols. (Westport: Greenwood, 1972); and George Rawick, ed., *The American Slave: A Composite Autobiography. Supplement,* 12 vols. (Westport: Greenwood, 1977).

11.   Women's narratives of infanticide do exist. See, especially, Deborah A. Symonds, *Weep Not For Me: Women, Ballads, and Infanticide in Early Modern Scotland* (University Park: Pennsylvania State University Press, 1997).

12.   For examples of inadequate mothers, see Stowe, *Uncle Tom's Cabin*; Caroline Lee Hentz, *The Planter's Northern Bride* (1854; reprint, Chapel Hill: University of North Carolina Press, 1970); and for an orphan, Augusta Jane Evans, *Beulah,* ed. Elizabeth Fox-Genovese (1859; reprint, Baton Rouge: Louisiana State University Press, 1992).

13.   Harriet Jacobs, *Incidents in the Life of a Slave Girl: Written by Herself,* ed. Jean Fagan Yellin (Cambridge: Harvard University Press, 1987), 77. Subsequent references to *Incidents* appear in parenthetically in the text.

14.   See Yellin's introduction to Jacobs.

15.   Fox-Genovese, *Within the Plantation Household,* epilogue. See also William L. Andrews, *To Tell a Free Story: The First Century of Afro-American Autobiography, 1760–1865* (Urbana: University of Illinois Press, 1988), 252.

16.   See, for example, Susan Warner, *The Wide, Wide World* (1850; reprint, New York: Feminist Press, 1996); Maria Susanna Cummins, *The Lamplighter* (1854; reprint, New Brunswick, NJ: Rutgers University Press, 1988).

17.   Why, she wonders, has her lot been so different from that of her mother? "She had been married, and had such legal rights as slavery allows to a slave" (p. 78). More important, "She was never in the power of any master; and thus she escaped one class of the evils that generally fall upon slaves" (p. 78).

18.   For an elaboration and specific examples see Fox-Genovese, *Within the Plantation Household,* especially chapters 3 and 6.

19. Smith, *The American Slave,* vol. 7, *Oklahoma Narratives,* pt. 1, 302. See also Fox-Genovese, *Within the Plantation Household,* 323–24.

20. Orlando Patterson, *Slavery and Social Death: A Comparative Study* (Cambridge: Harvard University Press, 1982).

21. For a general analysis, see Eugene D. Genovese, *The World the Slaveholders Made: Two Essays in Interpretation* (New York: Pantheon Books, 1969), and his *From Rebellion to Revolution: Afro-American Slave Revolts in the Making of the Modern World* (Baton Rouge: Louisiana State University Press, 1979). See also, for example, Fox-Genovese, *Within the Plantation Household,* chapter 6; Elizabeth Fox-Genovese, "Strategies and Forms of Resistance: Focus on Slave Women in the United States", in *In Resistance: Studies in African, Caribbean, and Afro-American History,* ed. Gary Y. Okihiro (Amherst: University of Massachusetts Press, 1986), 143–65; Barbara Bush, " 'The Family Tree Is Not Cut': Women and Cultural Resistance in Slave Family Life in British Caribbean", in *In Resistance: Studies in African, Caribbean, and Afro-American History,* ed. Gary Y. Okihiro (Amherst: University of Massachusetts Press, 1986), 117–32; Mathurin, *Rebel Woman.*

22. See Lucie Fultz, "Toni Morrison's Narrative Method" (PhD diss., Emory University, 1990).

23. Morrison, *Beloved,* 273. Subsequent references to *Beloved* will appear parenthetically in the text.

Our Debt to History

REX NETTLEFORD

Anyone who was ever a student of the late Elsa Goveia and has been called upon to deliver the Goveia Memorial Lecture will understand the trepidation with which I approach this signal honour. For she brought an awesome authority to the nurturing of an entire generation, or two, around to a deep appreciation of the responsibility that West Indians have to themselves in finding form and purpose first in their own backyards and, by extension, in the wider world. She did it all through the rigorous pursuit of her discipline, History, in ways which artfully portrayed intellect with passion, reality with morality, method with meaning, truth with virtue, understanding with compassion, and deep knowledge with wisdom. This brilliant mind exposed her students to the dialectical reality of human experience, the multifaceted nature of historical and, for that matter, all social phenomena, the contradictory omens (as Kamau Brathwaite, the poet-historian, would say) both in our stars and in ourselves, the varying densities, spans and velocities of the flow of narrative that constitutes human history.

The History honours course which I pursued here at Mona under the guidance of Elsa Goveia et al.[1] constituted, for me and others who were their guinea pigs, an innovative programme of preparation for a kind of life that would enable us to situate ourselves purposefully in a world which was beginning to undergo serious fundamental change, as Geoffrey Barraclough in his *Introduction to Contemporary History* back in 1956 was beginning to discern.[2] It is no exaggeration to emphasize the enormous debt owed by people like myself to history as it was offered by the University College of the West Indies (UCWI) (later the University of the West Indies) Department of History.

Apart from laying the foundations for graduate work that followed – in my case the study of politics – that sense of history has helped to maintain cool, calm and collectedness in the chaos and turbulence of contemporary times, as well as to persist in exploration and experimentation in trying to make sense of the cacophony of events and their resonances.

The notion that people of the Caribbean have no history, not having created and therefore not having achieved anything to write (home) about, was furthest from the mind of Elsa Goveia, as it came to be from the minds of her many students. The notion was, however, not merely the indulgence of a talented disenchanted maroon of a creative writer hanging out in the metropole and given to castrated metaphors.[3] It was part of the apparatus of ignorance among many of the well educated, some of whom would have seen the establishment of the UCWI as a threat to the treasured intellectual standards inherited from the mother country, or as the radicalization of the young West Indian mind already given to insolent self-assertion and wild dreams about governing self and taking charge of one's destiny.[4]

Hegelian notions about "historic" and "non-historic" peoples had long informed Marxist logic, which was later to seduce an entire generation of West Indians who had grown impatient with the slow pace of change after independence and the seeming lack of daring on the part of West Indian decision makers following the call for them to fundamentally change the world even though they could interpret it.

Anthony Bogues, in a paper entitled "Shades of Black and Red: Freedom and Socialism",[5] reminds his audience of Marx and Engels at their Hegelian best in a passage culled from a letter written by Marx to Engels in 1852. He (Marx) was reviewing a book on the slave trade:

> The only thing of positive interest in the book is comparison between the former English Negro Slavery in Jamaica etc. and the Negro Slavery of the United States. The present generation of Negroes in America on the other hand, is a native product, more or less Yankee fled English-speaking etc. . . . and therefore fit for emancipation.[6]

Bogues rightly concludes from this that "obviously the further removed the African was from Western civilization . . . the less fit was he/she for human freedom. The underlying assumption was therefore that Africans were uncivilised and consequently a 'non-historic' people."[7]

This notion of the people of the region being "non-historic" has prompted responses that have ranged from the polemically strident through the poetically passionate to the intellectually rigorous. It has engaged the talents of a wide range of people from Marcus Mosiah Garvey, the visionary; C.L.R. James, the astute political thinker; Eric Williams, the historian-turned-politician; Derek Walcott, George Lamming, Kamau Brathwaite and Phillip Sherlock, leading literary artists; to Elsa Goveia, academician par excellence.[8]

It was another of her students who dedicated his short life to giving the lie to this notion of the non-historicity of Africans on the continent and in the diaspora (including his own Caribbean).[9] As scholar and activist, Walter Rodney tirelessly advocated the urgent need to reconstruct history so as to give to Africa its well-earned place in human development over time, and to put into perspective the process of the underdevelopment of that continent by Europe. He did this without ever indulging that infantile romanticism which would deny the connivance of Africans themselves in the successful triangular trade which brought profits to Europe, enslavement and degradation to millions of Africans in exile, and shame to the past half-a-millennium of human history.

A brilliant account of the life and thought of Walter Rodney has been written by yet another University of the West Indies scholar, who is not from the Department of History but from the social sciences[10] which gave us two other much cited "history books": *The Sociology of Slavery* and *Persistent Poverty*.[11] Rupert Lewis takes his readers through an odyssey of his protagonist's struggle with the distorted history served up in the academy, and the reinforcement of the destruction by persistent ideologies that up to this day underpin the policies, programmes and priorities of contemporary power structures throughout the Western world, which was itself shaped by the events of the last five hundred years.

It is that sense of history which the formal study of history facilitates when approached in the way that Goveia and her early peers in the UCWI did. And Walter Rodney was a direct beneficiary of that vision. His sense of history no doubt made him understand that argumentation by analogy may be a joy to the poetic imagination, and that metaphors are often a gift for literary enthusiasms. But analogies have a cut-off point in serious analysis, since the temporal-spatial variable not infrequently puts paid to the fit suggested by seeming correspondences between one era and the next. Indeed, if we owe the social sciences anything it is the discovery that "man is not a completely 'free intelligence', but in large part at least, a product of his environment, conditioned in his feelings, his thoughts, his actions, by the society in which he lives". But the person with a sense of history also knows that "the society in which [one] lives is itself a product of the historical process, not a pattern of life designed and constructed by rational minds".[12]

Here the social scientist and the historian share common turf and, when acting in tandem, can be a powerful agent in the search for knowledge. But they can part company on the very matter of analogy. So in the heady days of Black Power during the late 1960s the literal transfer of things past on to the contemporary landscape proved inadequate to understanding. Political leaders marinated in the sauce of Westminster politics were described as "household slaves" for "selling out" to the power structure as their historical counterparts presumably did. But those counterparts, the Black Power lobby chose to ignore, were also the vital and critical conduits from great house to cane field or slave village; they served as highly valuable operatives in the communication and intelligence network bearing news, admittedly sometimes garbled, of impending amelioration measures for their slave siblings and relations, and of other indicators of moral concerns among statesmen and abolitionists in the metropole. History teaches that such a phenomenon must be factored into the history of the abolition process, itself far more complex than Eric Williams's powerful economic determinist thesis in *Capitalism and Slavery* or the voluminous antislavery tracts of the humanitarian abolitionists, would suggest.[13]

Such reductionist strategies in the academic enterprise I remember to be anathema to Elsa Goveia as they were to Professor John Parry, who himself encouraged the students to take on board every bit of evidence that could enhance one's sense of history – from the bodies of ideas in the minds of men dating back to the Greeks, to the material culture of the subjugated in the Americas, the encounters with whom were made possible by the progress made in nautical technology from the end of the Middle Ages into modern times. In this light even fables in the deeper recesses of the collective unconscious can be of value, since fables are sometimes allegorical representation of real things! Yet great care is advisable.

I remember John Parry being politely dismissive of an essay I wrote on the English Revolution which cost a Stuart king his head. I remember using a Marxist framework quite anachronistically and inexpertly.[14] So taken was I with the drama of that neat and tightly structured paradigm that I plunged recklessly into the torrents. One learned after that to look for far more than one sees with the naked eye, and even more carefully when such things are placed under the microscope.

Further honing in such careful handling of historical phenomena, both at the UCWI and elsewhere, prepared one for the somewhat robust invasion in the1970s of the Caribbean consciousness by the second of two prevailing seductive simplicities which, if not wrong, have proven inadequate for the Caribbean. For many of the region's tenants have come to know that "we are, in fact, creatures of history, and the story of the human race has been the story of our struggle to become . . . the creators of history".[15] The specificity of a people's history becomes, then, the driving force in the process; and any effort at "becoming" on the basis of other people's experiences and their own perceptions of their reality often proves a recipe for disaster.

To Walter Rodney's undying credit, and indeed to that of C.L.R. James who remained a West Indian shaped and determined by his cultural realities throughout his Marxist and Trotskyite embrace,[16] the historical and existential particularity of the Caribbean person and kindred souls in the African diaspora in the West remained the source of energy for their thought and political activism. Again it is Rupert Lewis who affirms that "Rodney's intellectual legacy, as a historian and as an activist, forms a part of the unfolding Caribbean intellectual tradition", which he feels had been "shaped by C.L.R. James to whom Rodney and many of his generation owed a major intellectual debt".[17] Lewis's use of the word "unfolding" is instructive. For it does not come from a mind given to the arid scientism that would entrap our unruly Caribbean social phenomena in iron-clad laws and paradigms which more often than not exclude the very variables too easily dismissed as "imponderables" but which may be critical to the balancing of the equation. It comes from the mind of someone with a sense of history who, like the early Marx, realizes that the search for truth and excellence is a dynamic and ceaseless enterprise. And the very act of making the Caribbean into a laboratory for the social sciences brings to the disciplines of sociology, politics, economics and history an experimental dimension which makes them "impermanent, ruthless, alive", turbulent and creatively chaotic. A study of ancient history tempts many to find correspondences with Greek civilization, whether it is Derek Walcott with the myriad "classical" allusions in his great work *Omeros*[18] or C.L.R. James himself who drew on the "performance culture" that was the civilization of Plato and Aristophanes in his analysis of the game of cricket as an agent of decolonization in his magisterial epic *Beyond a Boundary*.[19]

That Greek civilization, long celebrated as source of Western culture, was itself a "cross-roads" cultural phenomenon drawing on the contributions from all sides of the Mediterranean, including Africa, is now the subject of a strand of scholarship which revives Frederick Douglass's nineteenth-century attacks on "the hellenomaniacal excision of Africa from the narrative of civilization's development".[20] Marcus Garvey himself had views on this but conventional history in these parts would not have taken notice. However, things have changed.

There has been "intensely contested debate on the whole issue of the relationship among Ancient Greece, the Levant and Egypt"; and Martin Bernal has obliged with two controversial and well-researched volumes entitled *Black Athena: The Afro-Asiatic Roots of Classical Civilization*.[21] Correspondences with the later history of the past half a millennium have no doubt prompted the publication of *The Black Atlantic: Modernity and Double Consciousness* by University of London lecturer Paul Gilroy, who is in no doubt that black people have shaped a nationalism, if not a nation, within the shared culture of the black Atlantic.[22] Gilroy cannot but acknowledge his debt to history. And history, for its sins, must claim some responsibility for the now fashionable and, to some, faddish cultural studies agenda that has sprung up in the groves of academe.

Walter Rodney remains contemporary in his intellectual vision, and Lewis places the central feature of Rodney's contribution to the intellectual tradition in his "positive awareness of himself as a *person of African descent in the Caribbean,* the link he forged with Africa and the intellectual agenda that emerged in relation to the major challenges of decolonisation" (my emphasis).[23]

This makes Rodney's work an important juncture in the continuing discourse about self and society – the Caribbean self and Caribbean society – in its deep concerns about origins and relations, race and racism, identity and the access to power by the marginalized in societies which transform numerical majorities into cultural minorities and in a world which glibly describes two thirds of the world as the Third World on the basis of consumption patterns, productivity levels and command over and control of the products of science and technology.

On this last point the triumphalist posturing of a First World (so-called) following on the disintegration of the old Soviet Empire is dangerously poised to mislead yet again those of us who would rather let go of our history and cling to passing pieces of fancy, forgetting what history should have long taught us, viz., that the Caribbean is a welcoming graveyard for imported creeds and rotund rhetoric. Yet the temptation persists: there are those of us who may well wish to march for Jeffersonian democracy and the market even while the market-driven democracies, our proffered models, find that bothersome social services like health-care, education and housing are infrastructural imperatives that can neither be divested willy-nilly to something called the private sector nor monopolized successfully by the state.

Paradoxes and contradictions which are the stuff of Caribbean reality are here implied. A history that reminds us that the only time West Indian society enjoyed full employment was under slavery threatens to make a confusion of sequence and consequence. A knowledge of the historical fact that there is a correlation between being players in the game of fair competition in international trade and having control over the rules of that game, is critical to an understanding of just where people like us are, and have long been, in this spectator sport called the global economy. In that game, it is certainly not cricket to run onto the field in inflammable excitement.

So for us history persists, dynamic and ceaseless in the ongoing search for the kind of politics that will bring liberty and equality, freedom and equity into balance with a growing economy, and for civil society that will guarantee to its citizenry civilized living even before one's per capita gross national product reaches US$4,000. Such a hope is a far cry, indeed, from the view held by some that all the really big questions have been settled with the end of the Cold War, which was a war waged largely between civilizations deemed to be "historic".

This is the meat of a book entitled *The End of History and the Last Man* by Francis Fukuyama,[24] who is aptly described as the denizen of US policy institutes. But his celebration of market liberalism's triumph over the world ignores the sturdy growth of Islamic fundamentalism, tribal nationalism (as in the former Yugoslavia and the disintegrated Soviet empire as well as in Russia itself), and Asian authoritarianism which may be long on material development but short on justice that entertains mercy.

Herein lies the suggestion of existing choice, even if the choice is between creative chaos and technology-driven programmed robotic involvement. The anguish still turns on the choice between liberty and the denial of it (whether by armies or bureaucracies), between equity and a lopsided prosperity favouring the few at the expense of the many. No one knows better than Caribbean people from below that there can be no end to History (with the upper-case H) as long as fundamental choices remain to be fought out in the environment of power.

The years 1492, 1838, 1938, 1962[25] have taught the Commonwealth Caribbean, if not the rest of the region, one great truth that counters Fukuyama's thesis, and that is that "history isn't over because its achievements are fragile. [In any case] human beings [do] specialize in throwing away their own achievements",[26] as many would cynically insist in reference to the follies of post-independence Caribbean politics.

Fukuyama should have known better, for the very Marx his thesis is supposed to be countering was among the first to declare an end to history with his elevation of the universal proletariat, that universal class which would put an end to bourgeois rule, create the classless society and enter a new Jerusalem. The switch to an apocalyptic destination is here deliberate since scientific socialism is passionately apocalyptic. Fukuyama's technocrats in turn correspond to Marx's proletariat. But the world is inhabited by other than consultants, and still consists of other sensibilities and other skills with minds and goals different to the homogenizing tendencies of the North Atlantic – a lesson long taught by history. And whatever the paradigm shift may be deemed to be in terms of the making of one single world, there is ample evidence of countervailing forces everywhere seeking firm rooting in the specificity of ethnicity, tribal allegiance, gender, religion and the like.

The millenarian indulgence at end of century by those who have enjoyed a concentration of power for five hundred years completely ignores the reality of alternative ontologies and cosmologies long in formation in the rest of the world. The North Atlantic is even now psychologically grappling, by way of the integration of western Europe and a consciously reinforced Anglo-American alliance, with the threat of a shift of the earth's centre to the Pacific. But in the meantime the germ of an Atlantic civilization which is the product of the past five hundred years of varied encounters between civilizations from both sides of the Atlantic is yet to be fully acknowledged and given the sort of historical pedigree it clearly deserves.

Here again the Atlantic History of that early History honours programme at the UCWI prepared many for an understanding of the dynamics of the making of a new and distinctive civilization which was to take on new sense and sensibility in the advancement of human existence over half a millennium. All of this is part of the history of the grand clash of civilizations, ideologies and religions involving different races and cultures cross-fertilizing in the context of imperialism, plantation slavery and peonage, racism and colonialism.

But it is as much part of a history of discovery – though not of the kind described with upper case "D" – as part of Europe's history of conquest involving so-called lesser peoples deemed to be beyond God's grace and therefore subject to Christian conversion and civilizing. It is, instead, that history of discovery about human possibilities, about the diversity of human endeavours and the unity that underpins that diversity, about the inevitability of change and the regulative principles that underlie all change.

It was that programme which introduced us "guinea pigs" to the formation of new societies in a new world of the Americas and to the symbiotic character of the encounters between Native American, European and African cultures. It also prepared us for the discourse which received sharp focus in 1992, the year of Fukuyama's declaration of the end of history, but also the year of the much-sabotaged plans for the commemoration of the landing of Columbus in these parts. It was the year when such plans sparked controversy, negativism and cynicism but also serious reflection on the "cultural, historical, and scientific implications of the pan-hemispheric encounters that will continue to be of global importance" for the next century at least.[27]

That History honours programme had us well informed in more ways than we probably thought it would or ever could. The mandatory requirement of two languages other than English, for the purpose of access to research documents as historical evidence, provided excellent training for advanced work in historical and related studies. Bartolomé de Las Casas could be read in the original to get a feel of the castigation by this colonist-turned-priest of his countrymen for failing to live up to Spain's "pious intentions",[28] even though as a man of his times he saw Columbus as "God's chosen instrument in the propagation of the gospel to the heathen".[29] The Latin texts of papal bulls giving juridico-theological legitimation to conquistadors connected me with Valentin Mudimbe's textual critique of "Romanus Pontifex" of 1454, which I had to co-edit for a volume entitled *Race, Discourse and the Origin of the Americas.*[30]

Moving from "Romanus Pontifex" of 1454 to Caribbean carnival, from the Moorish enlightenment to the role of race in the shaping of the modern Americas, the volume posits an emergent world civilization of the Americas. And it is to that civilization that the Caribbean belongs. The turn to history to grasp the full meaning of that world civilization of the Americas is a personal debt which I and scores of others owe to the discipline, especially for the opportunity it afforded one like myself to interface with literature, science and religion both as challenge and as means for intellectual liberation. For it brought within range a more serviceable worldview that sees the world not narrowly from the time of so-called discovery to contemporary times when globalization safeguards the status quo, but rather from a view that targets a record of exploration, encounter and civilization in a new and changed world. And it is the specifically Caribbean worldview that pulls together in the volume the triad of Europe, Africa and the indigenous peoples, focusing on creolization and the social formation of the Americas, the "polyrythmic paradigm" of the Caribbean and the postcolonial meaning of religion.

We know that that other approach to the writing of history, that is from the point of view of Europe's "discovery", has had little or no input from "the discovered" as to how that history was written. There has also been limited opportunity for them to tell it as they feel it is or ought to be. "The past was erased," as George Orwell reportedly once said, "the erasure was forgotten, the lie became truth."[31] Those who heard Elsa Goveia in her prime came to understand that that received truth was, in large part, the lie.

In *Race, Discourse and the Origin of the Americas,* all contributors seek to find definitive articulation for this emergent new-world civilization one speaks about. So Antonio Benítez-Rojo, a renowned Cuban novelist and social commentator, turns to the poetry of Nicolas Guillen (*Sensemaya*), the historical drama of Derek Walcott (*Drums and Colours*), and a novel by Alejo Carpentier (*Concierto Barocco*) to illustrate what he dubs the "polyrhythmic paradigm of the Caribbean" which operates in a mix of premodern, modern and postmodern modes.[32] Edouard Glissant, the Martiniquan man of letters, deals with the process of becoming which targets the myth of relations over the myth of origins; while Maurice Bazin, a well-known science educator, delves into the diversity of Third World scientific creativity, a gentle reminder that that branch of knowledge is not restricted to "historic peoples".[33] The new religions of the New World also demonstrate capacities denied to the anthropological "Other",[34] according to Charles Long who holds a chair in at Syracuse University; while John Thornton of Millseville University writes on the early beginnings of Christianity in Africa before 1492, reminding the reader of a history of contact between Africa and Europe long before Columbus left Spain for the East via the Americas.[35]

In the respective explications of the dynamic of cross-fertilization on both sides of the Atlantic in areas of science and religion and in the shaping of new and distinctive forms of cultural expression in the development of humankind, the wretched of the earth emerge as creative constructive contributors to human history. All of this will have taken place in defiance of the strident and stubborn claims by Europe to a predetermined, if not divinely ordained, superordinate ranking on the basis of ethnic pedigree or perhaps territorial conquest.

Nor could such criteria be used to invest that "first" voyage by Columbus with undue claims to prior discovery in what was, after all, a point (albeit a decisive one) in a long and sustained historical process of scientific exploration by man in his effort to expand his physical space and sense of purpose. There were indeed myths about a barely known planet, but there were also real voyages. There were recorded visits by the Vikings to the North American continent long before the southern Europeans made theirs. The early explorers had come to see the North Atlantic as a bridge between northern Europe and the Western Hemisphere rather than as a precipice from which to tumble into an unknown abyss then perceived by the Latin-speaking Mediterranean as the *mare tenebrosum*.[36] Should not such historical happenings go alongside the event of 12 October 1492 as part of that dynamic process of human exploration of the natural environment in search of development and empowerment?

So if European discovery meant exploration, the particular activity stretched back way before Columbus as Theophile Obenga, the scholar-director of the International Centre for Bantu Civilization in Gabon, insists.[37] He presented his chapter for the Smithsonian publication complete with evidence from ancient Mediterranean Greek texts, recording the fact that the African continent was circumnavigated and accurately mapped by African cartographers. He pointedly emphasizes the persistence of such a spirit of exploration as evidenced in the modern race for the conquest of outer space, thus providing an important link between contemporary world and that of ancient Africa.

To Ivan van Sertima, the Guyanese anthropologist and linguist, that link resides as well in his historically grounded conviction of the active presence of Africa in the Americas, where the different cultures coexisted in creative collision long before Iberian Europe landed at Guanahani and encountered a native population in an act of co-discovery.[38] Need I relate that van Sertima's position provoked counter-arguments[39] as testimony of the vigour and intensity of the scholarly debate at end of century. This is part of an ongoing discourse not just on the role of race in the founding and shaping of the Americas (of which the United States, it needs to be stated, is only one part) but on the "origin" of the Americas themselves, as they have come to be known and perceived today by Europe, and more importantly by the hemisphere itself.

The discourse also seeks to establish beyond doubt the presence, prior to the advent of Columbus, of fully developed civilizations comprising inhabitants who now prefer to be designated "Native Americans". Enemies of the Genoan Wanderer (a Walcottian designation)[40] accuse him of genocide and the slaughter of some ninety million native inhabitants. But Columbus is not without his defenders. And while some admit to many of the indigenous peoples falling prey to slavery, diseases and more recent suffering, by descendants, of second-class status, supporters insist that the genocidal motives attributed to the Genoan explorer are at best "far-fetched".[41]

Russell Thornton, who teaches at the University of California at Berkeley, tries to clear up the dispute by estimating the Native American population to have been about seventy-five million in the hemisphere at the time of Columbus's arrival. The decimation is, as they say, history. But the demographic history of Native America in terms of decline and survival fuels among the Native Americans alive today great hope for continued survival "both as physical populations and [as] people".[42] Thornton, himself a Native American, feels this is a tribute to "their great perseverance in confronting the demographic legacy of contact".[43]

There is, as well, a demographic history of the Africans who were brought forcibly into slavery, and the work of scholars like Barry Higman[44] and others in North America contributes immensely to an understanding of this phenomenon. The African presence is a force to reckon with throughout the culture sphere known to social scientists as Plantation America. If the Africans fared better in their survival as physical populations, they fared no better than Native Americans (and in some places arguably worse) with respect to race and class status attributed on the basis of ethnic origin.

The inherent racism in the cosmology of conquistadors, their descendants and other European successors serving as perpetrators of plantation slavery and of its handmaiden, the trans-Atlantic slave trade, is central to the ongoing discourse about the American self and the irreducible kernel of "American civilization". A.J.R. Russell-Wood,[45] of the Department of History at Johns Hopkins University, addresses with scholarly detachment this passionately enduring item which is to be found on the agenda of concern of millions of inhabitants in the Western Hemisphere and elsewhere in the African diaspora, as well as in the diasporas of India, Pakistan and China – especially in western Europe, which has been duly colonized in reverse. But the concerns exist as well in West Africa and down the Atlantic littoral to Cape Coast in South Africa. His contribution to the volume is aptly entitled "Before Columbus: The Portuguese Contribution to Discourse on Race and Slavery in the Fifteenth Century". And a companion piece by Jan Carew, the Guyanese novelist turned cultural studies professor, sharpens the reader's insights into the provenance and stubborn tenacity of this most complex and irritating phenomenon that has distorted, even while shaping, human history through-out the half a millennium since 1492.

Then there is the contribution by Sylvia Wynter, the Jamaican academic who now works at Stanford University and who is known for her passionate advocacy of the Caribbean, the Americas – in fact any people worth their salt – getting a hold of their history as prelude to being creators of their own destiny.[46] Her "1492: A New World View", as is stated in the editors' Introduction,

> unravels the variegated threads in the complexly woven tapestry that is the Columbus enterprise, including all that followed 1492. Whether one views Columbus as saint or sinner, as icon or iconoclast, as myth or as metaphor, the real challenge of his voyages and their aftermath for what is today a genuinely *new world*, is to demonstrate an expansiveness of thought in forcing new and appropriate ontologies, cosmologies and epistemologies as part of the natural, inescapable and unending quest by *Homo Sapiens* for new horizons in pursuit of human growth and development, and presumably for the enhancement of the quality of life for the Third Millennium.[47]

The implications for the teaching of history and the pursuit of historical studies here in our Americas and elsewhere are far-reaching. The role of history in all this is by no means a monopolistic one, since its deep and extensive impact on human knowledge when acting as yeast to the dough is impatient of debate. The culturing of the yeast must naturally go on and engage the pure or specialist historian who wishes to maintain the intrinsic integrity, inner vigour and logic of the discipline. But its centrality in the cross-disciplinary methods of investigation into our region's and the world's quixotic social phenomena is no less a fact. Social scientists without a sense of history are not likely to last beyond today's project. Historians who have expanded their disciplinary horizons to take in demography, artistic and material culture and the like are likely to be better historians than they dared imagine. The whole world of the humanities will depend on history for perspective and wisdom. The output from this university deserves no less and Elsa Goveia, were she with us today, would be the first to agree. That expansiveness of thought and vision to which I earlier referred, if allowed to flourish, would surely render as counterproductive and pointless not only what for some people are still the ancestral claims to racial and cultural superiority, but also the attendant obscenities of unrelieved self-indulgence in the relentless exercise of raw power.

I have before now suggested that such expansiveness of thought and vision at the end of the twentieth century can be no less in quality and substance than what may well have obtained at the end of the fifteenth. Despite the detractors who have pilloried Columbus as the bogeyman bearing the guilt of human exploitation, there are those who equally invoke history to declare him a "Renaissance genius, a pioneer who expanded the horizons of a narrow medieval world".[48] Such diametrically opposing points of view are the legacy of historical studies and frank, free intellectual discourse which have led to a view that twentieth-century man may have good reason to have Columbus personify all that we hate about ourselves, namely "avarice, cruelty, racism and moral despair".[49]

If this is so the Americas, in large measure founded in greed and cruelty may at end of century not wish to repeat history for being ignorant of it, and may thereby free ourselves of the capacity for genocide, ecocide and the wanton exploitation of man by man. We may even want to find, promote and foster the appropriate designs for social living that will guarantee to individual men and women freedom for a creative and resourceful existence within the framework of civil society. This may then be what must inform, if not actually become, the very kernel of that emergent world civilization of the Americas which our history indicates is quite possible.

It is possible because we, the so-called creatures of exploration, came soon enough to the exploration by ourselves of our circumstances, away from ancestral hearths and in new and hostile environments. An entire people, or sets of people, became heroes and explorers as a result. Maybe man has grown too biased about his scientific and technological mastery over nature, despite his periodic helplessness in the face of raging torrents, violent whirlwinds, ferocious earthquakes – all natural disasters.[50]

It is history to which one turns to remember that one is less than the angels, however unscientific such a formulation may appear to some of us. But non-believers have a way of calling for last rites on the way out. It is to history that one turns to remember that humility has a place in human interaction, however pious this threatens to sound to the hard-nosed cocksure intellectual fired with the fuel of Anglo-American empiricism. People like us could well prepare to say with T.S. Eliot, an American who chose to find place and purpose in the old country (a truly Atlantic man of his generation),

> We shall not cease from exploration
> And the end of all our exploring
> Will be to arrive where we started
> And know the place for the first time.[51]

Indeed, part of knowing is knowing one does not quite know. History has an uncanny way of taking us via that route. Therein, perhaps, lies our greatest debt to the discipline which Elsa Goveia embraced with such grace, determination and passion; the discipline to which she gave new life in her meticulous transmission of events and their underlying structures to her students; and which she used to take a couple of generations of us well on the difficult but inescapable journey of emancipating ourselves from mental slavery.

On the basis of our history she would have found us fit to rule and fit to govern and, more than that, fit to succeed her in giving leadership in that dynamic and ceaseless enterprise – the search for truth. As is said at the end of a spirited Jamaican debate, "Argument done!"

Notes

1. Elsa Goveia, the first professor of West Indian History, Dr F.R. Augier (later Professor Augier), lecturer in Political Thought, and Professor John Parry, head of the History Department at the University College of the West Indies were the major teachers in the department in the 1950s. Professor William MacMillan (*Warning from the West Indies: A Tract for Africa and the Empire*

[London: Faber and Faber, 1936]), who taught Professor Augier at St Andrews University, Scotland, served as visiting professor early in the programme and concentrated on the Atlantic history segment of the course.

2. See Geoffrey Barraclough, *An Introduction to Contemporary History* (Harmondsworth: Penguin Books, 1964); based on an original paper read to the Oxford Recent History Group in 1956. This was expanded to become the Charles Bead Lectures delivered at Ruskin College, Oxford in 1963 and in revised form at the University of California, Los Angeles in 1964. Then came the publication of the book in the same year.

3. The reference is to the much-quoted remark by the renowned West Indian writer Vidia Naipaul, about West Indian people not having a history, not having created anything. Sir Vidia has since revised his position on this but many still identify him with the comment. The term "castrated metaphor" is George Lamming's.

4. By 1948, the year when the University College of the West Indies was established, the self-government movement was well underway in the West Indies, with Norman Manley of Jamaica as the best-known advocate. The road to independence had begun with a new constitution giving semi-responsible government to Jamaica and introducing universal adult suffrage (1944).

5. Barrymore Anthony Bogues, "Shades of Black and Red: Freedom and Socialism" (paper delivered in September 1994 at the conference Theory of the Black World, sponsored by the Afro-American Institute, Columbia University, New York.)

6. Karl Marx and F. Engels, *Selected Correspondence* (Moscow: Progress Publishers, 1979), 79, quoted in Bogues, "Shades".

7. Bogues, "Shades".

8. See Marcus Garvey, *Philosophy and Opinions*, 2 vols. (New York: Atheneum, 1969); C.L.R. James, *The Black Jacobins: Toussaint L'Ouverture and the San Domingo Revolution*, 3d ed. (London: New Beacon, 1980); Eric Williams, *Capitalism and Slavery* (Chapel Hill: University of North Carolina Press, 1944) and *From Columbus to Castro 1492–1968* (London: André Deutsch, 1970); Derek Walcott, *Omeros* (New York: Farrar, Strauss and Giroux, 1990); Edward Kamau Brathwaite, *The Development of Creole Society in Jamaica 1770–1820* (Oxford: Clarendon Press, 1971); George Lamming, *In the Castle of My Skin* (London: Longman, 1979) and *The Pleasures of Exile* (London: Allison and Busby, 1984); P. Sherlock, J. Parry and A. Maingot, *A Short History of the West Indies* (London: Macmillan, 1987); and Elsa Goveia, *A Study on the Historiography of the British West Indies to the End of the Nineteenth Century* (Mexico City: Instituto Panamericano de Geografia e Historia, 1956).

9.   Walter Rodney (1942–1980) a brilliant Guyanese historian and political activist, read history at University of the West Indies, Mona (1960–63), and would have been a student of Elsa Goveia. For an excellent account of his intellectual formation and political thought see Rupert Lewis, "A Study of Walter Rodney's Intellectual and Political Thought" (PhD thesis, University of the West Indies, 1994). [*Editors' note:* This thesis has since been revised and published with the title *Walter Rodney's Intellectual and Political Thought* (Kingston, Jamaica: The Press, University of the West Indies, 1998).] Rodney described the History programme he pursued at the University of the West Indies thus: "The History courses of the University College of the West Indies (as it was until 1963) were based on the general pattern of the University of London. There were nine final papers, to be written after three years. Two of these were in English History between 1487 & 1945, and there was a similar arrangement for European History. The West Indies and the Americas accounted for two further courses of the usual kind. 'Reconstruction' after the Civil War in the USA was the special topic which introduced the use of source materials and this comprised two papers. Finally there was a translation paper, involving two languages" (Lewis, "A Study", 73).

Rodney goes on to state that "the courses in New World History occasioned a very marginal interest in West Africa, so that I have done most of my reading in that subject since my arrival at the School of Oriental and African Studies".

A decade before (1953), when this author pursued the programme, the same obtained, though the Atlantic History papers exposed one to a good deal of the history of contact between western Europe and the United States. The special topic was "The War of 1812". My study of African history and politics started with Professor MacMillan at UCWI and continued in depth with my work in politics at Oxford in the late 1950s, when African studies attracted scholars such as Marjorie Perham and a young Colin Leys, looking at the Central African Federation. At UCWI there was a course in West Indian History and another in political theory from Plato to Rousseau. The translation paper was mandatory. This author offered Latin and Spanish.

10.   Lewis, "A Study", 73.

11.   Orlando Patterson, *The Sociology of Slavery* (London: McGibbon and Kee, 1967); and George Beckford, *Persistent Poverty* (London: Oxford University Press, 1971).

12.   R.H.S. Crossman, *Plato Today* (London: George Allen and Unwin, 1959), 14.

13.   See Eric Williams, *Capitalism and Slavery* (Chapel Hill: University of North Carolina Press, 1944).

14. The essay was clearly influenced by Christopher Hill's analysis of the English Revolution. See Hill's *The English Revolution, 1640* (London: Lawrence and Wishart, 1955).

15. Crossman, *Plato Today,* 14.

16. See Barrymore Anthony Bogues, "Political Thought of C.L.R. James 1934–1950" (PhD thesis, University of the West Indies, 1993).

17. Lewis, "A Study", 375.

18. Walcott, *Omeros.*

19. C.L.R. James, *Beyond a Boundary* (London: Stanley Paul, 1963).

20. Paul Gilroy, *The Black Atlantic: Modernity and Double Consciousness* (London: Verso, 1993) 59.

21. Martin Bernal, *Black Athena: The Afro-Asiatic Roots of Classical Civilisation* (London: Free Association Books, 1987).

22. See Gilroy, *Black Atlantic.*

23. Lewis, "A Study", 378.

24. Francis Fukuyama, *The End of History and the Last Man* (London: H. Hamilton, 1992).

25. The dates refer to the Columbus landfall, the final abolition of slavery, the uprising leading to the social revolution and self-government movement, and the coming of political independence, starting with Jamaica and Trinidad and Tobago in 1962.

26. See Michael Ignatieff, "History Is Not Ready for the Dustbin", *Observer* (London), 1 March 1992.

27. See brochure announcing the conference Race, Discourse and the Origin of the Americas: A New World View of the Americas, held 31 October–1 November 1991 in the Carmichael Auditorium, National Museum of American History, Smithsonian Institution, Washington, DC.

28. Bartolomé de Las Casas, *In Defense of the Indians,* trans. Stafford Poole (Dekalb: Northern Illinois University Press, 1974).

29. See an article defending Columbus by Harvey Harris ("A Good Thing Even", *Independent on Sunday,* 11 October 1992, 23). In this Harris "berates those who lay all the ills of the West at one man's feet".

30. Vera Lawrence Hyatt and Rex Nettleford, eds., *Race, Discourse and the Origin of the Americas: A New World View* (Washington, DC: Smithsonian Institution, 1995). The chapter by Valentin Mudimbe is entitled "Romanus Pontifex (1454) and the Expansion of Europe", 58–65.

31. Attributed to George Orwell and quoted by one Eric N. Danielson of Washington in a letter to the editor of the *Washington Post* (28 May 1991) as part of the debate sparked by Senator Ted Steven's attack on the Smithsonian Institution for its "left-leaning political agenda" (*Washington Post, Style,* 16 May 1991), allegedly evident in the Smithsonian's display of

nineteenth-century American western expansion through the eyes of contemporary artists and in a then still unfinished television series entitled *The Buried Mirror: Reflections on Spain and the New World by Carlos Fuentes* as part of the Institution's 1992 commemoration of the five-hundredth anniversary of Columbus's arrival in the Americas.

32. Hyatt and Nettleford, *Race, Discourse and the Origin of the Americas,* chapter 12.
33. Ibid., chapter 10.
34. Ibid., chapter 7.
35. Ibid., chapter 7.
36. Ibid., vii–ix, being foreword by Robert McCormick Adams, secretary of the Smithsonian Institution.
37. Ibid., chapter 5.
38. Ibid., chapter 3.
39. A contribution by way of "rebuttal" to Sertima's claims is made by David H. Kelley, professor emeritus in the Department of Anthropology at the University of Calgary, Alberta. His chapter is entitled "An Essay on Pre-Columbian Contacts between the Americas and Other Areas, with Special Reference to the Work of Ivan van Sertima". See chapter 4 of Hyatt and Nettleford, *Race, Discourse and the Origin of the Americas.*
40. Walcott, *Omeros.*
41. See note 29 above.
42. Hyatt and Nettleford, *Race, Discourse and the Origin of the Americas,* 227.
43. Ibid.
44. See B.W. Higman, *Slave Population and Economy in Jamaica 1807–1834* (London: Cambridge University Press, 1976).
45. Hyatt and Nettleford, *Race, Discourse and the Origin of the Americas,* chapter 6.
46. Ibid., chapter 1. Wynter's essay is entitled "1492: A New World View", 1–57.
47. Hyatt and Nettleford, *Race, Discourse and the Origin of the Americas,* introduction.
48. See note 29 above.
49. Ibid.
50. The reference is to the flooding of the midwestern United States in the mid-1990s, when the Mississippi River overflowed its banks, the typhoons and tropical storms which ravage India and other parts of Southeast Asia, the Caribbean, and the Atlantic coast of the Southern United States, and the earthquakes experienced by California, Mexico and Japan.
51. "Little Gidding V", quoted by Harvey Harris in his spirited defence of Columbus. See note 29 above.

Contributors

Brian L. Moore is Senior Lecturer in History, University of the West Indies, Mona, Jamaica. He has published several articles and books, including *Race, Power and Social Segmentation in Colonial Society* (1987) and *Cultural Power, Resistance and Pluralism: Guyana 1838–1900* (1995).

B.W. Higman is Professor of History in the Research School of Social Sciences at the Australian National University. He is the author of *Slave Population and Economy in Jamaica, 1807–1834* (1976); *Slave Populations of the British Caribbean, 1807–1834* (1984); *Jamaica Surveyed* (1988); *Montpelier, Jamaica* (1998); and *Writing West Indian Histories* (1999).

Carl Campbell is Professor of History, University of the West Indies, Mona, Jamaica. Among his many publications are *The Young Colonials: A Social History of Education in Trinidad and Tobago, 1834–1919* (1996) and *Endless Education: Main Currents in the Educational System of Modern Trinidad and Tobago, 1939–1986* (1997).

Patrick Bryan is Douglas Hall Professor of History, University of the West Indies, Mona, Jamaica. His publications include *The Jamaican People, 1880–1902* (1991) and *Philanthropy and Social Welfare in Jamaica* (1990).

Hilary McD. Beckles is Professor of Economic and Social History and Pro Vice Chancellor (Undergraduate Studies) at the University of the West Indies, Mona, Jamaica. He is the author of several books and articles including *The History of Barbados* (1990); *Natural Rebels: A Social History of Enslaved Black Women in Barbados* (1989); *Centering Woman: Gender Discourses in Caribbean Slave Society* (1999); and *The Development of West Indies Cricket*, 2 vols. (1999).

Bridget Brereton is Professor of History and Deputy Principal at the University of the West Indies, St Augustine, Trinidad. She has authored several publications including *Race Relations in Colonial Trinidad 1870–1900*

(1979); *A History of Modern Trinidad 1783–1962* (1981); and *Law, Justice and Empire: The Colonial Career of John Gorrie, 1829–1892* (1997).

Elizabeth Fox-Genovese is Eléonore Raoul Professor of the Humanities at Emory University, Atlanta, Georgia. Her publications include *Within the Plantation Household: Black and White Women of the Old South* (1988); *Feminism Without Illusions: A Critique of Individualism* (1991); and *"Feminism Is Not the Story of My Life": How the Feminist Elite Has Lost Touch with the Real Concerns of Women* (1996). She now serves as editor for the *Journal of the Historical Society*.

Douglas Hall was Professor Emeritus at the University of the West Indies, Mona, Jamaica, where he had taught history from 1956 to 1980. Among his numerous publications are *Free Jamaica 1838–1865: An Economic History* (1959); *Five of the Leewards 1834–1870* (1971); *The Caribbean Experience: An Historical Survey, 1450–1960* (1982); *In Miserable Slavery: Thomas Thistlewood in Jamaica 1750–86* (1989), *A Man Divided: M.G. Smith, Jamaican Poet and Anthropologist* (1997); and *The University of the West Indies: A Quinquagenary Calendar, 1948–1998* (1998). He died in 1999.

Joseph E. Inikori is Professor of History at the University of Rochester, New York. Among his many publications on slavery and the slave trade are *Forced Migration: The Impact of the Export Slave Trade on African Societies* (1982); *The Chaining of a Continent: Export Demand for Captives and the History of Africa South of the Sahara 1450–1870* (1992); and *The Atlantic Slave Trade: Effects on Economies, Societies, and Peoples in Africa, the Americas, and Europe* (1992).

Franklin W. Knight is Leonard and Helen R. Stulman Professor of History at Johns Hopkins University in Baltimore, Maryland. He has published widely on Latin America and the Caribbean, including *Slave Society in Cuba During the Nineteenth Century* (1970); *The African Dimension in Latin American Societies* (1974); and *The Caribbean. The Genesis of a Fragmented Nationalism* (1978). He has also served as president of the Latin American Studies Association between 1998 and 2000.

Lucille Mathurin Mair is a former Permanent Representative of Jamaica to the United Nations. In a career that has straddled both diplomacy and academia, she has been a pioneer in women's studies in the Caribbean; among her publications in that field is *The Rebel Woman in the British West Indies during Slavery* (1975).

Woodville K. Marshall recently retired from the University of the West Indies, Cave Hill, Barbados, where he was Professor of History and Pro Vice Chancellor (Non-Campus Countries and Distance Education). He was editor of the *Journal of Caribbean History* (1981–90), and has published extensively on the Caribbean peasantry, including *The Colthurst Journal* (1977).

Rex Nettleford is Vice Chancellor of the University of the West Indies. He has published extensively on Caribbean culture, history and politics including *Mirror, Mirror: Identity, Race and Protest in Jamaica* (1970); *Manley and the Politics of Jamaica: Towards an Analysis of Political Change in Jamaica 1938– 1968* (1971); *Caribbean Cultural Identity: The Case of Jamaica: An Essay in Cultural Dynamics* (1978); *Dance Jamaica: Cultural Definition and Artistic Discovery: The National Dance Theatre Company of Jamaica, 1962–1983* (1985); and (with Philip Sherlock) *The University of the West Indies: A Caribbean Response to the Challenge of Change* (1990).

Colin A. Palmer is Dodge Professor of History at Princeton University, New Jersey. He is the author of several publications including *The First Passage: Africans in the Americas 1502–1617* (1995); *Slaves of the White God: Blacks in Mexico 1570–1650* (1976); *Human Cargoes: The British Slave Trade to Spanish America 1700–1739* (1981); *Passageways: An Interpretative History of Black America* (1994); and *The Chains that Bind: The Worlds of Human Exploitation* (1995).

Monica Schuler is Professor of History at Wayne State University, Michigan. She has published on Caribbean slave resistance, Jamaican religion, and post-emancipation African labourers in the Caribbean and Guyanas, including *"Alas, Alas, Kongo": A Social History of Indentured Africans in Nineteenth Century Jamaica* (1980). Currently, she is writing a biography of the Jamaican healer Alexander Bedward.

Blanca G. Silvestrini is Professor of Modern Latin American and Caribbean History at the University of Connecticut. Among her publications are *Los trabajadores puertorriqueños y el Partido Socialista 1932–1940* (c.1978); *Violencia y criminalidad en Puerto Rico 1898–1973: apuntes para un estudio de historia social* (1980); *Politics, Society and Culture in the Caribbean* (1984); and (with María Dolores Luque de Sánchez) *Historia de Puerto Rico: trayectoria de un pueblo* (1987).

Printed in the United States
201100BV00008B/31-63/A